MW01622933

ISBN: 978-0-9785531-7-3

Akoben House
P.O. Box 10786
Atlanta, Georgia 30310

www.AkobenHouse.com

Cover design by Mwalimu K. Bomani Baruti. The Adinkra symbols on the front cover have the following names and meaning: top left – *Akoben* meaning readiness; top right -- *Dwennimmen* meaning strength; bottom left -- *Nsaa* meaning excellence and bottom right -- *Akoma Ntoaso* meaning love/unity. Though virtually all of the Adinkra symbols reflect some critical aspect of warriorhood, these four were selected by the students of Akoben Institute as being those qualities of character that good warriors should most exhibit toward themselves, each other and the community.

for

Baba Larry Obadele Williams

&

Mama Iyaire Atiba

two incomparable, unassailable warriors, jenoch, elders
indefatigably, uncompromisingly, diligently, quietly
doing the rigorous, practical work
of liberating, empowering and making again sovereign
Afrikan minds, resources and spaces

Acknowledgements

Without Odumankoma, the Abosom and the Nananom Nsamanfo I would not be to do this work. Without them, there would be no warrior's lineage to produce me or the community of nationbuilders which nurtures and galvanizes me to say what must be said and do what needs to be done. And, without the selfless human love and motivation that is so easily created and given by this community this discussion of the warrior's character would not have materialized, at least not in this way, in this time, in this reality. To all, their respective order, I say Meda ase pii.

Yet, nothing I say is mine alone. Given that all though worthy of human consideration has already been uttered and mastered within our ancestral wisdom, Yaa Mawusi has been the greatest influence on my thinking for over a quarter century. There are no words I am capable of composing which can begin to adequately express the level of gratitude I feel for the sanity and vision she brings to my life and writing.

Because he first moved me toward addressing this question within the conscious community, and because he continues his work for us in the realm of the Ancestors, I offer a special warrior's Meda ase pii to Nana Kwame Ahmad Abdullah. His voice still resounds in my higher mind, offering guidance at every crossroads I bring into my path.

No matter how small they may feel their contribution may have been, there are a number of individuals who assisted in strengthening the structure and body of this writing and, therefore, its mood. Included among them are Asafo Akhu Yaw Kamau for his proverbs and social/cultural interpretations of our traditions, the Warriors Akua Ma'at, Kwadwo Gyasi Nkita-Mayala and Obadele Bakari Kambon for the consistent flow and relevance of their proverbs and, of course, Mama Ayeesha Abdullah for her knowledgeable reference work.

Without the generosity of Mama Pamela Kolade Wynn & Baba Elijah Kambon Mann, Baba Morro & Mama Virgestine Sanyang, Brother Danny Donaldson, Sister Amika King, Brother Haki Ammi and Brother Jon Overstreet, this project would have proven immeasurably more difficult to bring into existence. We are most grateful for your belief, trust and selfless investments.

Beyond this, it would be nigh impossible to list all of the individuals, families and organizations who and which have positively impacted on my growth and development as a warrior scholar simply because there are so many. And, being human, I am bound to mistakenly overlook more than one, and this, rightly, might cause them deep personal injury. This is something for which I do not want to be responsible. Nonetheless, this is not a simple case of you cannot please everyone. Pleasing and honoring can be two quite different things. So, I will say that those who should know, do know. And, hopefully, all who have positively impacted my thinking will see their influence, if not on then between this book's lines.

Table of Contents

Introduction

> ...it is not accidental that during every epic in ancient Kemet, especially when things had gone to ruin, we would rebuild our physical, material monuments by first taking a stone from the ruin and seed the new building. Seeding just like when we used to make bread, we would take some of the old dough and use it to start the process of the new. It is that seeding process that we do when making bread because we know that the taste of the old bread that we used to eat was so good that we can guarantee that the new bread will be just as palatable if we take some of the old as a starter for the new. There's a lesson to be learned there. The lesson to be learned is not that the discussion of history is important because we want to play the dozens and say my mother did something more than anybody else's mother, but rather because it is in the history that we can find the seeds to build into the future. History is not the past. History is about the future. It is about understanding the psyche of which we have to deal.
>
> *Nana Kwaku Berko I-Ifagbemi Sangodare (aka Wade W. Nobles)*

Every book is a mission statement. Each is necessarily political because every writing is a complete thought and every thought the direct expression of a particular interpretation of reality. Unlike other works, though, this particular statement is admittedly, intentionally, insistently political.

Being a statement of the Afrikan self, it is full of spiritual intent. "Our spirit is political." It is full of cultural intent. Our culture is political. And intent, by its very presence, distinguishes friend from foe.

For this reason, some will feel compelled to strongly agree with what is said here. They will see themselves, their irrefutable truths and unconquerable vision. For equal reason, others will vehemently oppose any claims of worth for these words. They will read their most cherished fears and reflective hatreds into it. In the end, the warrior[1] decides what is or is not worthy of his or her mind.

To be more precise politically, this book was written full of intent, *Afrikan* intent. Consciously created to be a wake-up call for *our* warriors, it is an in-depth examination and explanation of what *we* should build and be like as Afrikan people.

As a power, no nation stands without its traditions. Powerful collectives always have a deep and abiding appreciation of self. And no people can build, or rebuild itself, without a class of warriors whose strength of character has been handcrafted by them to clear its path and keep that way open.

Every warrior's character is a direct reflection of his or her spiritual, psychological and physical inheritance. No one is separable from the ethical and moral mind of his or her people. All true warriors think, speak and act out of the genocultural genius bestowed on them through the blood and spirit of their lineage. They are who they are because of who they have always been.

By warriors, we mean those Afrikans who have opened their eyes to the insane horror of european culture and society, of yurugu's very nature,[2] and closed their minds to any fear of it.[3] We are speaking of those of us who have consciously chosen to move as a functional, dynamic vanguard of workers against the armies waging eternal war against Afrikan people.

We have always been destined to come. All the

evidence in humanity confirms that warriors are as inevitable as enemies. And we have enemies, many enemies, both kindred and alien. Destroyers bring forth rectifiers.

Considering the mentacidal nature of this anti-Afrikan reality, warriors can be defined as those among us who are brave enough to study and practice the uncompromised[4] Way and will of our Ancestors.[5] It is to these men and women, those of us who have made life's choices that others would not dare, as well as those yet unable but who earnestly aspire to such heights, whom we speak of when invoking the power of this term throughout this work.

We are warriors because we are Afrikan. And we have neither the time, energy nor inclination to play with what it means to be Afrikan.[6] We leave that to unanchored, paper intellectuals who have nothing better to do with their time but loquaciously entertain each other and play with those validating them. We are not gamesmen, looking to construct a protective shield around extremely individualized and highly treasured mentacidal[7] peculiarities. We are our Ancestors, still at war with the invaders of our people's spiritual, mental and physical space.

We are under assault from every possible angle, in every strategic institution. Every Afrikan of committed, uncompromising consciousness must know and act on this. There are no civilians in war, only warriors, enemies, traitors and ignorant, shrapnel-impaled bystanders.

War, in our tradition, is not only for the purpose of defeating one's enemy. Though necessary, that is only an incidental outcome. Conflict serves to bring back order, the warrior's people's order.[8] It is waged in the effort to bring life back in line with a universally balanced reality.[9]

Therefore, the correct vision must be encoded into the spirit of the warrior's mission. We need to know both what to eradicate or subdue and what to rebuild. For this, warriors need to not only know our mission but also the ancestral eternal vision of our people. Both aspects of warriorship are addressed herein.

Warriors have work to do. In fact, because of the situation we find ourselves in, we must fulfill two warrior roles. We, individually, have the responsibility of not only doing our own work but also that of many would-be warriors. Many do not know that we are at war and even more do not want to. What these individuals could potentially contribute, we ourselves must accomplish.[10]

This, however, is not to say that warriors are perfect in executing their given responsibilities. Without doubt, even under what might be considered ideal conditions within the ranks of our army, the work to be done within each of us is far from complete. Of course, we, those of us who are already making our stand on the frontlines, know this.

Sometimes we forget or do not fully enforce the warrior's will on ourselves. From time to time, we, too. have to be reminded of our work's urgency and direction. We, too, tire. But never does that entice us to quit.

And, when we pay attention, this lethargy is where we can feel the Ancestors most forcefully reveal themselves to us. This is when they sound the Akoben horn.[11] They call us to arms in defense of all that is us. This is their prerogative. They have earned the right. And know, in the midst of the chaos and clamor, they are exercising it.

Those of us listening have heard them call time and time again. They warn us to stay abreast of the season[12] and every opportunity. Speaking in Afrikan tongues, they repeatedly ask "What's the hour of the night?"[13] Each of them, in his or her own unique way, warns us, and anyone who would dare interfere with their children's liberation, that "every once and awhile I will come out and tell you what time of night it is."[14] Every possible sign is given, alerting us to the urgency with which we must "seize the time."

Some signs come in the form of charismatic speakers and prolific writers. Some come in more subdued fashions, camouflaged in our everyday spaces and relations, without the notoriety or celebration of such talents.[15] These rise above the noise and confusion by just quietly, consistently doing the work.

We eventually come to recognize most of those whom the Ancestors dispatch to remind us of who we are. None of them, whether we have come to know them publicly and/or personally, can we risk overlooking, for our ancestral spirits have dispatched so many warriors to express their restorative will that they are everywhere. There is ample evidence of a strong line of chosen messengers, showing us the Way through their noncontradictory, unassailable presence.

The message between these pages has been garnered from them. It is an attempt to consolidate the psychological and behavioral definition of the traditional Afrikan warrior's character.

This is for all Afrikan warriors. But, for more than for any others, it is for those newly awakening warriors who are now experiencing the spiritual, mental and physical trials of learning how to stand and walk along the narrow path others before them have paved through this alien and alienating cultural chaos. They must be instructed into patience and uncompromising, diligent determination.[16] For, in our zeal to be, and be with other, righteously enraged Afrikans, we all must never forget that this is a war-torn frontline and that we are very far from home.

For the moment, though, we must make home where we stand until each stand joins to form a global nation unshakably rooted in the power of our motherland. No other place can be as much like home as Afrika. That is understood. As John Henrik Clarke reminded us, "Africa is our center of gravity, our cultural and spiritual mother and father, our beating heart, no matter where we live on the face of this earth."

Others know of the power of this spiritual connection. The well-crafted deceit of the insecure, power-hungry western mind is, by far, the best example of those whose awareness is revealed through an exaggerated, reactive pretense of not knowing. Their, and others', groundless arrogance would have us to believe that the tradition of our Ancestors has no value in our lives anymore. In so many ways, they want us to internalize to the point of no return the conviction that tradition itself is constraining, outmoded.[17]

Especially for us, remembrance is depicted as being detrimental to our progress as human beings evolving away from an imaginary barbarity they would have us believe that held us in a backward captivity before their civilizing conquest.[18] The bearers of the lie of white supremacy[19] who have never even slightly deviated from their most ancient, core, defining traditions would have us dismiss our Ancestors' Way as having no space in this place and time. And this demand that we deny our Afrikan essence has become the beloved habit of those willful patriots among us sworn to mentacidally serve and protect this insane order. Their recruitment is indispensable for yurugu's false humanization and elevation. For only through our assistance could those who least reflect what it means to be human be deemed normal, superior or even ideal.

So, even under the meticulous onslaught of a proven liar's political science, true warriors know that yurugu's fantasy is that of a child's. It is the dream of a severely emotionally malformed child's desperate need for adult recognition and praise. Any warriors worth their weight in melanin at least know that we are ancient beyond wisdom itself. We are of the Creator, our most ancient ancestor. We know that "that which one comes upon is nothing to compare to what one has always had."[20] And "to break the spirit of a man who fights for freedom is not easy when that man has the strength of tradition behind him."[21] For tradition knows no place or time. It finds sanctuary and expression wherever its people are.

> We should allow no one to turn our heads. If we continually try to shape our identity in the form of others, we surely will not find our destiny. Man's destiny is the

> reflection of himself. We must be about the task of fortifying our ancient beliefs and traditional customs. It is only through this effort that strength is given.[22]

No matter what else we may think we know, it is for certain that we are now, have always been and will forever be, our Ancestors. We must bring that afrism[23] in line with our self-created, Afrikan realities.

Bearing this in mind as Afrikan warriors, our vision can point us in the direction of doing nothing less than making a way for Afrikan people to be happy, peaceful and comfortable for as long as they live, by any means necessary. Nothing more is required of us. Nothing less is expected or acceptable.

We, the warriors of our people, have been blessed to have inherited a consciousness of self. This knowing has been painstakingly passed on to us through the unbreakable umbilical cord of spiritual lineage which inextricably ties us to a vivid awareness of our first alien violation. This gift of knowing self, this obligation and duty to regain and maintain an Afrikan order at any cost, is not to be taken lightly. And our justified vengeance definitely should not be confused with simple angry reactions. It is prerequisite for returning order and balance.

What we carry within is a *righteous* rage. And righteous rage is a state of mind far beyond anger. Some, emotionally crippled[24] and unable to prioritize knowing over forgetting, may misinterpret it as just a dysfunctional emotional letting or a stubborn unwillingness to just get over it. But righteous rage, physically, mentally, emotionally and spiritually, dwarfs simple anger in explaining the cumulative realization and release of conscious, directed thought and action against the continuation of others' systematic, historical attempt to genocidally [25] remove Afrikan people from existence. It is consequential progress, [26] for it moves warriors beyond an oversimplified anger in our thought and action. It moves us into the "focused rage" stage[27] of being

Afrikan. Here we respond productively.

For, at this stage, we have located and studied the origin of our unredressed anger. And it is only here where we can find constructive ways to excise it through a program of corrective thought and behavior within ourselves and against those who have brought and continue to bring immeasurable pain to our people.

Clearly, righteous rage is in no way limited to the release of a festered, frustrated emotional build-up or, for lack of rigorous analysis, aimless expression of anarchy against any and all order. Nor is it a childish attempt at vengeance against some tattered ghost of past atrocities. Righteous rage is the outcome of well-reasoned historical and ourstorical study. When awakened in action-oriented warriors, it results in the deliberate mobilization of physical, mental and spiritual resources designed to correct that which has gone horribly wrong at the hands of unfathomably evil minds.

Our rage is righteous because it is a determined, reciprocal movement toward the return of balance. And our righteousness must possess an enduring rage because the Maafa has gone far too far and the nommo required to return normalcy to Afrikan people is necessarily violent in thought word and deed. "In a violent world, violence is not a moral question but rather a life-sustaining dynamic."[28] It has no choice but to be spiritually, verbally and physically violent because the same utterances which brought this chaos into being must be used to speak it back to the hell it came from. All else within human reason has been tried and found wanting. Righteous rage has become the only reasonable answer.

Studied and sure in the righteousness of our rage, we know that the voices arrayed against us can only be either those who created the conditions under which it came into being or those firmly pacified by it. Neither can be allowed to interfere with or divert us from our calling.

It requires a special talent to express our righteous rage in this dedicated way. But that "special talent," and the courage that accompanies it, is available to all who recognize and honor their Afrikan center.[29] Its application begins inside, extends outward to envelope our complement and children with love and, then, radiates further in every direction that mindful, and potentially conscious, family and community exist.

> Building a community is costly in time, energy and resources. It is a task that does not provide direct returns, immediate tangible benefits, or privileges. *Building the community is our duty.* It is a duty we must undertake to fulfill without excessive concern for the additional inconvenience, time or resources it requires. It is a duty that involves attending early morning and late evening meetings. It is a duty that involves intellectual work and physical work, that demands personal accountability and adaptability in one's behavior, that demands substantive and real personal interactions, that demands substantial financial outlay, that demands time. It is a duty that must be fulfilled if our children are to live; if they are to blossom to their fullest potential; if they are to carry forth in this mission to build a new reality for our people.[30]

This is our calling, our only instruction, in this day and time. It can only be ignored at the expense of our final destruction. There is no alternative. There is no compromise. There is no defeat. We must win or we will cease to exist as a people.

The akoben has sounded warriors. And, "a man is seen when the war horn is blown."[31] There is no escape; no easy way out. Know that the steadfast among us are either on the battlefield or have victoriously made their ascension.[32] Where are you?

IWA

This is a discussion of character. Specifically, it is a

working description of the Afrikan warrior's character. Therefore, character must be defined in such a way so that, when we complete this thought, no doubt will remain about exactly what we mean by it. When we finish, we must be clear as to what kind of person we are speaking about when referring to one of our warriors. Further, no confusion should remain over how this particular manner of thought, word and deed must be developed and modeled in ourselves, from whatever point we awaken into our warriorship, as members of a vanguard priesthood of revolutionary healers.

According to E. Bóláji Ìdòwú, author of *Olódùmare: God in Yorùbá Belief*, *IWA* (pronounced E-wah) is the Yoruba term for character.[33] IWA is what determines the quality of one's life here and beyond.

> To the Yoruba, man's character is of supreme importance and it is this which Olódùmare judges. Thus the demands which Olódùmare lays upon man are purely ethical. Man's well-being here on earth depends upon his character; his place in the After-Life is determined by Olódùmare according to his deserts. Olódùmare is the "Searcher of Hearts" Who sees and knows everything and whose judgment is sure and absolutely inescapable. Therefore, morality is summed up in Yoruba by the word *Iwà* which can be translated by the English word "Character." *Iwà*, according to the Yoruba, is the stuff which makes life a joy because it is pleasing to God. It is therefore stressed that good character must be the dominant feature of a person's life. In fact, it is the one thing which distinguishes a person from a brute.[34]

IWA is conceptualized in terms of a *divine ethicality*, a universal, Spirit-based definition of what is right and wrong thought and behavior. It is not individually, idiosyncratically decided on the earthly plane. It follows the order of "as above, so below." Accordingly, the measure of a woman or man is based on her or his observance of the collection of ideal principles of what is good and right according to the conscience given each of us by the Creator, *Olódùmare*.

Many of us have become lost to this respectful approach to life and living. We have become so thoroughly subassimilated into the perverted, weakened state of this ugly, hateful, vacuous reality that our human possibility has been reduced to almost that of Yurugu's.[35] As a result, we have ignorantly but gratefully accepted a role that deviates so far from our natural spirit as to make us unknown to ourselves. It calls us to master and even surpass its originators in their degeneracy.

In an attempt to defend our moral and ethical decline, we have even made the mistake of passing that insanity on to our children. It has wrenched our minds so far from our Ancestors' interpretation of reality that even those among our children who have chosen, in the face of everything working to crush them into a vanquished, pacified oblivion, to develop a warrior's character are having to virtually start from scratch in building themselves in the image of our Ancestors.

This must stop. Having to begin re-instilling a righteous warrior's mentality into each warrior class as they come of age will not sustain an army in perpetual war on all fronts. In fact, it only helps expedite our cultural, social, psychological and physical genocide. It is an attrition, barely discernable. By now, we should have learned that "maintenance and survival are no longer adequate terminology to pass on to the next generation."[36] We have to build from the beginning.

From birth, all potential warriors must be nurtured and honed to see and feel their genocultural[37] responsibility to carry on this nurturance and honing in the progeny they produce who will instinctively know and act likewise. This must be built into their character.

Character is at the spiritual and mortal core of our salvation as a people. If it does not exist in us as a righteous power, we do not exist. If it is not good, we can do no more than serve others. If it is weak, we are weak. However, if it is formed in our traditions, designed to follow our Way and improve on what was given us at the beginning of our existence, our salvation as a people becomes no more than another simple task on the way to godliness.

Character is what makes us Afrikan. It is what makes Afrikans human. Without it we become even less than those so arrogantly proud of lacking a human spirit or the honor it bestows. Our Ancestors teach us that "pride and arrogance are the destruction of their owner. But those who are gentle in character create their own fate."[38] They have shown us that "a person of character is a person of wealth."[39] Pride and arrogance destroy the humanity in us because they turn us into something other and less than what we naturally are. No wonder "pride cometh before a fall."

As warriors and makers of warriors, we have to first understand that, in an Afrikan reality, character is inseparable from the flow of what one thinks, says and does. Each of these, in its true manifestation, complements the other and shows the quality of your character through its expression. As it is said that a person's eyes are the window to his or her soul, our thoughts, words and deeds allow others to see into the true spirit of our character, whether righteous, depraved or caught somewhere in between.

Some people call character personality. And, with respect to the intent of this definition, one's character is reflected through the display of one's personality. Unless deceit colors the impression we give to others, which is highly characteristic of individuals in european society, even among those relating at the most intimate of levels, then one's personality should be a true representation of one's character.

This presents a critical problem for our discussion because, as just stated, this

> Deceit is fundamental to the personality of westerners. We have to acknowledge that, in this cultural context, except in our safest and most sacred spaces, *impression management*, or social (defensive, manipulative) lying, is more the norm than not. Europeans are only real in

> pretense, i.e., when they are acting. They are only real when they are creating unreal characters of themselves to deceive the world into believing that they are the lie they project. Theirs is an arrogance cloaked in a deceitful rhetorical ethic and impression management that has found residence in a mental space far beyond the borders of psychosis.....no matter how deftly concealed it is, we can see that the arrogance that drives their deceit (one must in some way feel superior to the one spoken to in relations of systematic deceit) is necessary for their insanity. In this reality, manipulation is the primary approach individuals (both Europeans and those they hold culturally captive) take toward each other, no matter how minor the manipulation or theft. Such distrust (engendered by a psychotic self-hatred and xenophobia among this culture's makers) is passed on to all assimilated into western society. In this world, any who would dare wholly open themselves to friends or strangers are looked upon as weak, gullible prey. Knowing this, warriors must always be very careful of how much of our truth we allow aliens, negroes and lost souls to possess. The Ethiopian proverb "Confiding a secret to an unworthy person is like carrying grain in a bag with a hole" is an appropriate caution. At the same time, we must reestablish truth among ourselves because truth is the mother of trust and trust has been largely broken among us.[40]

You give negroes [41] negro answers, as you give Europeans empty ones. Why would you speak truth to someone who does not have the capacity to understand honest thought, except seeing it as the speech of a fool looking to be played?

By "capacity," I do not mean "ability," as in the physical presence of the brain. In speaking of its absence in an Afrikan, I mean that such an individual is so encumbered by eureason [42] (mentacidal thought processes) that she or he cannot even consider the possibility of an alternative (i.e., in this case, different and better) perspective. I mean that such an individual is not intellectually curious and intrepid enough to openly listen to, logically consider, recognize, seriously embrace and permanently internalize correct Afrikan thought.

In any case, warriors must be very careful of using the word "alternative" when describing Afrikan phenomena because for many it gives the impression that whatever it modifies is a lesser option and not the better option. Such adjectives clearly operate politically, subconsciously stimulating those socially embedded, self-defeating associations which peripheralize us and keep that which is European as primary and at our center.

That stated, just what is the essence of this thing we call character, this IWA? Where does it come from? How is it formed? And what are our choices?

2. Vision and Mission

> Endless our struggle must seem to those whose vision reaches only to the end of today.
>
> The present is where we get lost – if we forget our past and have no vision of the future.
>
> A healer needs to see beyond the present and tomorrow. He needs to see years and decades ahead. Because healers work for results so firm they may not be wholly visible till centuries have flowed into millennia. Those willing to do this necessary work, they are the healers of our people.
>
> *Ayi Kwei Armah*

Even given the breath of this analysis, the reader must remain cognizant of the fact that this is a book of both fact and theory. It speaks to that which, from our frame of reference, was, is and can be. Even though this is a practical book, meant to move Afrikan warriors toward acting in a nationbuilding fashion, readers cannot approach this single work as a cure-all. It has only brought together some of the fundamental social and cultural universals that must actively be in place in order for Afrikan society to exist.

There are no such things as panaceas. There are no absolute solutions to any problems. But, if we are to move toward operational stability, the solutions we devise must be grounded in a dynamic vision. They have to be designed and implemented by and for us with the understanding that this work toward "perfection" is eternal. A people, aware that cultural regeneration, and the social evolution based on that cultural rebirth and stabilization, involves continuous improvement, implement workable schemes. Any all-encompassing, "final" solution[1] for our people would have to involve a ceaseless, positive and corrective progression toward what our Ancestors have wisely defined as an ideal humane society. Any such society would have to be scientifically patterned after the Creator-given universal order.

Nonetheless, we cannot rush forward without considerations of family in our nationbuilding. Politically defining culture is a discussion *among Afrikan people* as to direction. And we must be careful of the framework within which this conversation occurs because we cannot speak of Afrikan sanity in a conference room ruled or peopled by nonAfrikans who naturally hold insane assumptions about what constitutes a sane reality. We must be clear that insanity is but insanity and that it undermines the possibility of having a real discussion.

This problem must be addressed because so many of us are entering this discussion as if the european creation of reality really makes sense, that it is a viable path for us to follow,[2] that it can be blended with whatever snippets of the Afrikan tradition we feel we can safely keep (without upsetting Yurugus), that it is a choice we can make and still live as Afrikans. We are allowing ourselves to continue participating in a debate riddled with invalid/illogical ground rules. In other words, some of us are trying to have/make reasonable arguments within the matrix of a reality that makes no logical sense, for us or any other human beings.

This is the nature of what makes having this discussion with many Afrikans so problematic in the first place. It is past the time when we can afford to get bogged down in the politics of precisely replicating how our Ancestors formed consensus.[3] We have to stop allowing others, even among us, to play the tradition card when they choose to derail us from pursuing Afrikan centered agendas. It should be obvious that we do not live in homogenous, uncompromised Afrikan communities and that most Afrikans have no real desire to do so. Therefore, every Afrikan voice is not worthy. Frontline inclusion must be a conscious consideration, early eliminating those who do not politically move to an Afrikan rhythm but will conveniently want to force us into the precise formality of its traditions to undermine Afrikan discussions.[4] "A fool does not talk in a council."[5]

The mentacidal among us firmly believe that american culture is not european culture (that this society is multicultural, a flawed concept in its own right) or that european culture is an even more valid, progressive and appropriate way for Afrikans to live than Afrikan culture. These Afrikans are completely oblivious to the heart of the european mind. So, before we even begin, their discussion is already couched in an unconditional confidence in the european way.

The mentacidal cannot see that Europeans can only be what they are within their culture. To change it is to change them, and they will not be changed.

While yurugu's immediate goal has been the physical domination of others, cultural domination has always been the ultimate desire. For only in making others into them can Europeans have and control a world where they are accepted and applauded for their insanity.

This confusion must be removed from the table before we can move forward, or it will continue to drag us back toward obsolescence. As long as it remains, our minds will be drawn backward into it until, by dent of attrition, it has overpowered all sense of what it may mean to be Afrikan.

There is another very important reason why this book was written. It is a study of the morals and ethics of warriors and those who wish to become the kind of warriors our people need. Although this aspect of warriorhood has been a personal concern of mine ever since I entered the serious, conscious, centered Afrikan community and saw that the ideal can often be quite different than the real, it only became an issue worth taking to pen and paper after being challenged to do so by a number of dedicated Elders[6] who quietly expressed their dismay and feelings of relative hopelessness over the public and private character of a number of the warriors claiming to be following in their footsteps.

To some degree, most of us are already aware of the contradictions that openly exist between the kind of character warriors are supposed to exhibit toward their peers, complements and others in the community and the actuality of that expression. Most would agree that our warriors' character could use a "little" work.

The good thing about these discussions is that those actual and developing Jenoch[7] who understand their role as guardians of our tradition clearly recognize that children do not raise themselves. They also humbly, and without offering excuses, completely accept their fair share of the fault for allowing the quality of our warriors' character to reach its current state of degradation.

However, in their defense, we have to recognize that a good many of our warriors were raised beyond the gaze of those parents, guardians and other significant others who were practicing and rearing their children in the Afrikan Way. The influence of a world in disorder, even on the most basic protection of Afrikan children, is a persistently pernicious factor pulling them away from the Afrikan Way.

The guilt of these elders should also be lessened by the obvious fact that many of our warriors, both youth and adult alike, have only fairly recently in their lives come under the care and guidance of the Afrikan centered community and the collection of those who now comprise our Elders.

Sadly, because of the current disorganized state of our community, one of our greatest warrior resources is ignored.[8] Some of our truest, most dedicated and courageous warriors are Elders without an ear among our youth.

In further defense of our youth, those who have traditionally comprised the warrior class,[9] their voice are equally heard, especially as it speaks to the contradictions evident in the thought, word and deed of those senior to them. They make the valid point that respect is something that must be earned. And they have convincingly argued and stand behind their demand that it should be reserved for those who have built proficient, dynamic, visionary institutions, whether large or small.

Frustration over the gap between those who expect them to look up to them and what they have actually done to deserve this honor has grown among those aspiring to stand and work on the frontlines of our Center. They have increasingly expressed their dismay over being repeatedly disheartened over finding that the spaces that they were trained to move into have not yet been prepared by those who instructed them in their training, or have only been poorly constructed. This is a legitimate expectation, and members of the new vanguard may indeed be correct to interpret its disappointment as a character deficit in those whose mission it was/is to build these intergenerational institutions.

However, serious consideration of the evidence would be in order. Warriors eager to do this work must bear in mind that this fault may not have been their elders intent. Therefore, it may not reflect character deficits at all. Often, with those who have spent their lives building for us, it is the result of being overwhelmed, others' laziness and/or systematic subterfuge, regardless of their best efforts.

Regardless of the complaint's source, whether from our

youth, our elders, or those in between for that matter, we have to address its overall glaring truth. It seems that good character is a quality that has come to be found less and less frequently among the warriors at all levels manning our frontlines. As we have come to more meticulously follow the tradition of our oppressors, there is a growing weakness of character. So many of us have fallen victim to the subsidization and glorification of compromised character because it is easier and more profitable. And, unless corrected, it will set the stage for failure even when we "succeed." I suspect that the majority of those of us with our eyes open, even including a good number of those warriors guilty of backsliding, would agree that much work needs to be done in this area.

Yet, the problems of disrespect and lack of discipline are not new among the warrior class. It goes back to the time when the first Afrikan became convinced that subintegration[10] into european society and culture was a viable and desirable ambition. In fact, this problem's spread and escalation follows the natural progression that all other mental illnesses found disproportionately among european people, which were forced upon us, have taken. Although nowhere nearly as reprehensible as the bulk of their peers in the general Afrikan community, the thought and behavior of many of those we recognize and honorably treat as defenders of the conscious Afrikan community are in no way as clear, strong and practiced as that of the ancestral vanguard they should use as the standard to assess their individual and collective character.

If we are not who we say we are, if we do not treat each other as we traditionally have, we should wonder what, as a people, we are really about. If we teach our children to speak respectfully, but do not ourselves act accordingly, the level of respect we deserve should come into question.

Reciprocity is universal law. What is given is returned. If we worship individualism, there can be no respect, except that based on the expectation of a larger return or enforcement.

This is the delusion of yurugu's boundariless world. If there are no rules, there is no definition for disrespect. Social insult becomes individually defined with power being the ultimate mitigator/arbitrator.

If the best of us are all talk, what more can we expect but less than what we are? If there is no evidence of "genuine" caring, concern and respect between us, except that which is exhibited when we are in predatorial pursuit of each other for praise, attention, possessions, labor, protection, information or sex, then any victory we achieve together will be hollow. And the contradictions we point out in others to mark what we should not be like will be even more evident in us.

Character is something that must be developed. It must intentionally, specifically be cultivated. We are not born with it.

History teaches us that good character is what ourstorically separates Afrikans from others. It is the marrow of our genocultural inheritance. Whether we accept or suppress it, we are born with a greater ability and propensity to easily and without forethought respect and be respectful to those who are family, to those who have always loved us and kept us sane. This is evident throughout ourstory.

However, it is not something that, in this cultural context, automatically comes to us. Sankofa must be enacted. We must go back and fetch it. It must be tapped into.

As we noted earlier, genocultural inheritance refers to those cultural traits that are genetically encoded in a people. We accept that a people's asili, or foundational/core culture, is genetically encoded in them throughout time. In terms of those areas where people do have choices, genetics, beyond basic instincts, is culturally bound. Although they have had no problem in misusing the concept of genetics to inferiorize,[13] dehumanize[14] and destroy other people,[15] it has yet to be accepted by the European scientific community that most thought and action they claim to have a biological origin were molded within a cultural genetic structure. And culture is molded within an asilic genetic structure.

Therefore, based on this understanding, there is no reason to believe that the human personality, any less than any other living thing, lacks a significant genetic makeup. It is equally plausible that this genetic makeup predisposes particular genocultural types to distinctive collections of preferences in thought, word and behavior.

Beyond the elemental drives which compel us to seek out and secure water, food, warmth and shelter, the human genetic structure evolves out of a people's adaptation to their social and physical environment. This occurs over many hundreds, even thousands, of generations through their common lineage. Habitual behavior comes from the refinement of adaptive strategies which, in turn, become biologically locked into the genes. When a people has done something in a particular way for uncounted generations, it becomes natural, it becomes genetic. And, as culture evolves, human biology (genetics) adapts accordingly.[16]

We often speak of *being* an Afrikan warrior, of warrior class members having good speech and a good Afrikan character. But, for those who are just coming into an awareness of their Afrikan selves, this concept, character, can be quite vague and is often confusing when not adequately defined in practical, ancestral terms. This book attempts to make what Afrikans have ourstorically considered good character, regardless of a person's station or mission in life, or at what point he or she is in their life's journey, as clear and simple as possible.

Aspiring warriors should not have to go through undue struggle to find their true selves and way home. Our Way as Afrikan people belongs to them.

And, once victorious in this war against the imposition

of others' oppression and insanity, they should not have to ask where to go from there. The difficulty should lie in the elemental work of nationbuilding. There should be no questions about the concept of community or nation, which in the Afrikan mind are one in the same.

Nationbuilding is fundamental to the empowerment of Afrikan people everywhere. It is the process of creating reality in one's own image. And authentic nationbuilding requires a culturally grounded spiritual, philosophical and ideological knowledge of direction.

For Afrikans who recognize that we are at war for our very survival and sanity, it also requires knowing how misdirected we have become. It calls for us to understand what we have come to know we must move away from and go toward. A working knowledge of the nation we are building must be guided by the true heading which will return us to the traditions that nurtured and elevated us as respected, self-loving people. Whether their traditions are real or imagined, no nation rises to power, or remains so, without this.

The measurement of our success as an Afrikan people must be based on an honest comparison of where we are now with where we were prior to our physical violation, psychological misorientation, cultural contamination and spiritual disruption by others. Measurement from any other point would render estimates of our "progress" which lessen the potential and quality of our character.[17] The belief that the only progress that Afrikans can realistically make is that which brings us directly back in line with our original traditions must be kept as sacred.

So, just going around claiming warriorhood without knowing what to build is counterproductive and counterrevolutionary. This is why identifying what we must build is so critical to this analysis. The fundamental forms and expression of the social structures and institutions that we must rebuild must be in the Afrikan Way. Without an understanding of where we must go, warriors are aimlessly spinning their wheels and lending support to our enemies' rampage of destruction against us. They become so easily distracted with faulty, limited, sugar-coated utopian visions of existence while others continue to walk all over us with impunity.

Even though there is absolutely no question in my mind that the role of warrior is intrinsic to both Afrikan women and men (and girls and boys), I began this task with the intent of writing specifically to Afrikan men and boys. To do so would be to follow Afrikan tradition, at least one dominant stream within that tradition which says building men is men's work and building women women's. And no stream can successfully be ignored if we are to practice and be the whole of our tradition, knowing that tradition is the accumulated practice (the collection of those studied, tested, specialized streams of thought and behavior) of what works for a people, given their asilic imperatives and geopolitical environment.[18]

As I have stated in introductory statements elsewhere,[19] my focus has primarily remained on Afrikan men. This I did, even though I fully recognized and admitted that any discussion of Afrikan men could not be held outside the Afrikan woman's domain, which is wherever Afrikan men spiritually, mentally, emotionally and physically reside. Up to this point, tradition and the desperate state of Afrikan manhood have dictated that I specifically address the Brothers because, in a civil, egalitarian, functional society, it is primarily the role of men to constructively critique and build men and together rear boys into them.

Men transform males and boys into men. Women do the same for females and girls. "A man trains a man and a woman a woman."[20] Otherwise, "confusion has a warm place to grow."[21]

Like women know themselves, their domains and what they want and need as women, men most intimately know about the secrets and requirements of manhood. This Afrikan reality is easily recognizable when the chain of tradition remains unbroken.

Furthermore, generally speaking, it is in Afrikan men's interaction with Afrikan women where we can identify the greatest evidence of problems with our character. Afrikan men can never forget that the greatest testament to our manhood lies in the honor we accord Afrikan women. For how we treat this most precious resource is indicative of how we view life. And Afrikan women have always been recognized as the source and cement of life in our community. As has been said, "The man may be the head of the throne, but the woman is the heart."[22]

Uncountable Afrikan proverbs and sayings speak to women's divine, enviable essence. The Akan believe that "a good wife is more precious than money" and, in fact, "a good wife is wealth." While, at the same time, "a beautiful wife owes her beauty to her husband."[23] Complementarity is at the heart of mature, adult, intimate, nationbuilding relationships between Afrikan women and men.

In reference to another, proverbially expressed, inextricably interrelated role of Sisters, the Mongo say that "a mother is not to be compared with another person – she is incomparable." We are aware of the ourstorical pride we Afrikans take in our mothers, biological and otherwise.

A variety of other Afrikan proverbs speak to the man's honorable role of protecting and nourishing women. They tell us that "the woman is the flourishing garden, the man her protective fence," "a woman is a flower in a garden; her husband is the fence around it," "when a woman makes a shield it is stored in a man's room," "no people goes down until their women are weak and dishonored," "if they come and get your men at night, they will be back in the morning for your women," "if the men are not slain, the women are not carried off" and, of course, "real love knows not danger."[24]

As Brothers consider what these *nyansasem*[25] mean, we have to go outside the sexist conceptualization of this male-dominated, misogynistic, materialistic society in order to gain the Afrikan understandings of them. Only this will allow us to truly feel what these and other proverbs and sayings should mean for us. And while doing so, we should remember that even proverbs tell us that proverbs do not have to be explained to the wise. "The wise individual is spoken to in proverbs but not in plain language"[26] and "We speak to a wise person in proverbs and not in stories."[27] Though we tend to think of this truth in terms of adults, the Akan also tell us that "a wise child is spoken to in proverbs, not in plain words."

As found in proverbs, our ancestral wisdom must be contemplated for its deepest meaning. Only in this way can the Afrikan proverb "thinking is wealth" be fully apprehended. Our understanding of proverbs' most profound meanings grows as we mature from merely bearers of information to wielders of knowledge to repositories of wisdom. But even without hearing the wisdom of our Ancestors, ourstorical evidence demonstrates Afrikan women's pivotal role in the spiritual, psychological, emotional and physical stability of our families, lineages and nation.

Nonetheless, for reasons already given, I was initially uncomfortable with the prospect of offering guidance to both males and females in the area of warriorhood.[28] However, some elder, and not so elder, Sisters took me to the side and explained in no uncertain terms that the problem of character in girls and women is just as bad and, in some ways, worse than that of the boys and men. Like Centered Brothers, Centered Sisters want the problem of character associated with Afrikans trying to force european ways and ways of relating into the community to be made known to all responsible Afrikans. In no uncertain terms they have explained that they want any warrior who wants the rights and privileges of warriorhood, but not the duties and responsibilities, whether a son or daughter, father or mother, grandfather or grandmother, husband or wife, to be corrected.

Although it should not really be a question, some may ask why so much time is being spent addressing the issue of women in the introduction to a book addressing the character of both Afrikan men and women warriors. Again, the answer would be that the greatest problem negatively affecting us as Afrikan people from the outside and inside is the artificial divisions that have been engendered, ripened and now fester between our men and women.

In our individualistic reactions to a common oppression, we forget that we are the social inheritors of an exceptionally sexist culture, the product of a people who are veterans at "taming shrews."[29] We cannot ignore the fact that, globally, patriarchy has come to rule.[30] Neither can we forget that patriarchy, in its disfigured form of systematic, sexist oppression, is largely the invention of western man. Although some of us make the mistake of using what we see around us today as the template for measuring humanity for all times, patriarchy is not some preordained developmental stage. It is not the natural universal byproduct of an evolutionary transition from hunting and gathering society to an agrarian or industrial one where the methods of acquiring resources favored the mobility and skills of vain, covetous, power hungry, sexually insecure, egotistical, aggressive adult males. It is an example of euroversalism[31] at its finest.

Because patriarchy must be spread under the delusive cloak of historical universalism, we know that every people do not naturally follow the european pattern. In fact, most do not, until blinded and caught in the cultural tractor beam of their eureason. Obviously, though, with time, globally, the way of a dominant minority can become the way of a dominated majority.

As with everything else we have adopted as a result of the imposition of european cultural imperatives on us, we have moved from our natural order to an unnatural state in the balance of male-female power. We have moved from a benevolent matriarchal system grounded in a "twinlinearity" or "harmonious dualism" justly honoring women for their divine procreative abilities and an unqualified appreciation of their political, economic, educational and familial brilliance by the men they love and respect to one relegating them to the dregs of labor, to economic insecurity and physical and emotional vulnerability, with seemingly only each other (or the european male) to save them. The disrespect leveled at our Sisters in this sick sexually caste, racist society is beyond reason.

We know that, in the western cultural context, whatever troubles Europeans damages us exponentially more. In this system, Europeans are the greatest recipients of its benefits and Afrikans the greatest recipients of its misery. As has already been undeniably proven time and time again in public and private records, where oppression is concerned, we are the common denominator. In a system of merciless, unrelenting racist domination, this is only reasonable.

Yet, as manifold as they may be, all of our other problems are ancillary to those which antagonize our men and women. And, because of the pivotal nature of the divide, those problems ancillary to it can only truly be effectively dealt with once we have cushioned and balanced this most intimate, interpersonal situation.

The family is the heart and soul of the Afrikan nation. That it is the primary institution of Afrikan society is evident in the disproportionate amount of anger theoretically and institutionally applied, and the destructiveness of the assault with which Europeans and Arabs have leveled, against it.

Therefore, if we are to rebuild, we must start here. In our search for worthy complements, we must first and foremost weigh their hearts, the true intent of a warrior's character, against that feather representing the commitment and expression an Afrikan man or woman should ideally have toward each other and every other participant and ritual within the boundaries of this most sacred of institutions.

Women are the first carriers, first teachers, first nurturers and primary defenders of the sacred, innermost circles behind the frontlines Afrikan men are supposed to establish and defend. Here, under their watchful eye, our young are free to be their Afrikan selves.

It takes nothing away from one's manhood, the prestige that comes from being a real man, to assume these difficult boundary maintaining responsibilities. We must defend our community's perimeter as if our lives depend on it, because they do.

An Afrikan's life is not limited to self. It rises out of the past through our Ancestors and extends into the future through our children. And, if we cannot see ourselves in those we birth and whose essence we protect by giving them every opportunity to be the Afrikan we aspire to be, then we are not living.

Truly, nothing said about the men who battle for us takes away from the woman's share in the responsibilities of warriorhood. There is no doubt that the stability and protection of the family institution are no less hers than his. In this, ourstorically, she has proven more than worthy, resolute and resilient time and time again. In fact,

> the singular role of males as warriors is unAfrikan and ahistorical. Lest we forget, Queen Nzinga, Queen Judith of the Falashas, Nefertari Aahmes, Queen Hatshepsut, [the Kandaces, Yaa Asantewa, Queen Nehanda, Acheompong Nanny, Queen Tetisheri, Queen Kahia-al Kahina, Queen Tiye] and Queen Makeda of Sheba were some of our best Afrikan warriors. Black women on the Continent and throughout the diaspora remain part and parcel of the Afrikan fighting tradition. I dare you to dismiss Assata Shakur, Winnie Mandela, Ida B. Wells, Harriet Tubman, Fannie Lou Hamer or Sojourner Truth...[32]

The list goes on for uncountable volumes with millions of like names, known and unknown, but never forgotten.

Also, as an extension of *Complementarity: Thoughts for Afrikan Warrior Couples*,[33] it is hoped that this book will also assist warriors in choosing those of the complementary sex whom they can trust to stand by their side on the frontlines of this war. We can least afford weakness within our complementary couples.

> The couple is the bedrock of the nation. Without it there is no family, no people. Without couples there can be no family to procreate and rear confident, untroubled, anchored children. No viable, community-respecting generation can be born to continue the process of life, living, building and defending. Afrikan couples must be whole, individually and as one. They must be able to trust themselves and each other implicitly. And that is what makes it imperative that we carefully choose our mates for Afrikan reasons. We must choose with vision. For we are the vanguard.[34]

Bearing that and the lingering effects of western patriarchy's arrogance in mind, it only seems appropriate to take a moment to specifically speak to the Brothers on one final point with respect to Sisters. Just in case some of us are thinking outside of our Afrikan mind and from within a european-induced coma which has left us deeply confused about the correct "place" for Afrikan women, we should ask a Sister, like Laini Mataka, who declares that

> every inch of space i occupy is a woman's place.
> everywhere i dare to stride is a woman's place.
> everywhere i lay my head, everywhere i wrap my legs,
> everywhere i spread my dreads, is a woman's place.
>
> anywhere i shake my butt, anywhere i leave a thought,
> anywhere i leave a drop of blood, anywhere i conceive or
> delete is a woman's place.
>
> anywhere i leave a footprint, a fingerprint, a body print,
> an image, or a scent is a woman's place...and I'm talkin'
> history here.

> except for where penises bloom, sho me a space that's
> not a woman's place and i'll show u where u lost yr mind.[35]

Just as Afrikan women are defined and measured by their grandfathers, fathers, husbands and brothers, Afrikan men are defined and measured by our grandmothers, mothers, wives and sisters. We know who we are and recognize our worth through them, humbly, gratefully and with great pride and honor. They are the critical, uncluttered, loving mirror through which we see how well we stand. Sisters are our barometer, the gauge of our manhood. Let no bad encounter confuse us on this fact.

Regardless of how male-centered this book's discussion may appear at times in its use of the term warrior, every point made is directed toward both Afrikan women and men of this class. There is no sex distinction among Afrikans for warriors. Each and every act committed by any warrior toward the war effort is critical.

The division of labor in the activities of war is essential to victory in any war within which the entire community is involved. And there is no victory in war if the entire community is not involved. To act as if only one segment or sex are the "true" warriors would be a grave mistake.

The war is against us, as a people. Therefore, there should be no question that the points made here apply equally to the men and women in our community in regard to the appreciation and respect we should hold and express toward ourselves and each other.

Family is innately extended in Afrikan society. All, who do not work to compromise our traditions or make a practice of acting inhumanely, are included. Therefore, the character of all respectable Afrikans who fight on our behalf are of concern. The definition of who is and is not family is found in lineage and evidence of one's sense of obligation and duty to others. The true measure of love and happiness is to be found in one developing one's own talents to the best of his or her ability and in assisting others to do the same in order to benefit the whole of the community. Many on planet Earth do not think in this way.

Europeans are a perfect example of the oppositional ideal. They are intrinsically anti-family, except in a utilitarian sense. Regardless of public pretense, they are familialphobic and familialcidal.[36] Though recognizing the need to procreate for survival, their imperative of extreme individualism dictates that they search for ways to replenish their numbers without taking away from their members' selfish individualism. As a people, they instinctively recognize that selfish individualism among adults who are able to reproduce and the bearing and raising of children are incompatible. For this core reason, they search for ways to have birth without a human presence, bring babies into adulthood without burdening their biological donors and make marriage an insignificant choice, easily voidable and with little value outside of the consumption associated with its limited romantic periods.[37] This has already been outlined in *The Sex Imperative*.[38]

Ultimately, individualism, as defined and refined within the european mind, is self-serving and antagonistic to any institution that makes others equally or more important than the self – a quality central to the Afrikan personality. No wonder Yurugu covertly (in an effort to conceal their peculiar imperative) seeks to destroy family by any and every means necessary. In being its natural self, the mind of Europe has no choice but to reduce this sacred social institution to the point where there is nothing but disconnected, emotionless (emotionally sterile), purely predatory individuals. Only in this way can individuals, who believe they are acting of their own conscious/intelligent volition, easily be directly controlled by whatever european powers that be. By catering to the unnatural appetites of those who are innately Yurugu, as well as savagely manipulating those among others they have socialized into thinking and acting they are anything other than themselves, they control all comers.

Individuality and Communalism[39]

Here, in speaking of individuals, family and community, we must consider the assumptions of free will and individual choice, as well as personal freedoms, as a self-interested forces within the context of culture. Culture exerts an enormous influence over both a people and its individual members. Therefore, all decisions are made within the realm of the cultural imperatives of the cultural personality within which one exists.

Though only a delusional reflection of the psychopathic, racist personality, white supremacy is the prime european cultural imperative. And, as such, it is unaccepting of criticism. It cannot tolerate blame or condemnation from others, or even its own if their goal is to change its supremacist aspirations.[40] Recognizing this makes it easier to understand why and how western society trains people, especially its victims, to see themselves as wholly responsible for their plight.

In terms of success and failure, it is unwilling to concede that any significant external influences meaningfully impact on individual choice. Individuals who experience failure must see the errors that led up to, actualized and continue to insure it as their fault, and their fault alone. European society knows that otherwise they will rebel against those external forces that created the conditions that systematically produce failure.

> The individual who accepts the ideology of *individualism*, and sees his failure to achieve as the result of some deficiency in his personality, and thinks that opportunities exist and that if he merely had the right personality he could make the best of these opportunities, when the achievement does not occur, is faced with a major contradiction....Dissonance, contradictions and conflicts are painful and are hard to bear. They make life discomforting, and hence motivate the individual to seek to resolve the contradictions – to try and remove these

contradictions and to put them out of existence.[41]

This is not to say that individuals have no personal decision-making power. However, their choices are never without external influences. In fact, in many cases individuals make decisions that otherwise they would not necessarily make given different circumstances or balances in power. We do not operate within a vacuum.

Our enslaved ancestors had choices. And they did, for the most part, come to individually make decisions based on the best interest of their children and the understanding that Europeans will kill for nothing. The concept of individualism they were forced to engage in and pass on has had a devastating effect on our sense of trust, community and genocultural identity. This disempowered, self-negating version of individualism has become one of the most damaging values that we have adopted and accepted as normal for ourselves in this land and culture. Within it, individuals make selfish choices that have no allegiance or connection to their people or heritage. And, by default, their decisions are often unwittingly loyal to the European way.

The acceptance and internalization of such extreme individualism creates disadvantage in everyone, except members of the group who perfected it and whom it, regardless of collateral benefits to outsiders, exclusively serves. It leads to crisis after crisis for individuals who exist beyond the pale of that privileged family. And, for individual Afrikans, these crises can only be resolved through our re-creation of and reintegration into the global Afrikan community (empowerment/life), or our continued submission to a self-hating inferiority (powerlessness/genocide). It can only end with life or death.

In western thinking, not being an individual (i.e., being part of a communal group) implies not having a mind of your own. You are like the "Borg" of *Star Trek* fame who have absolutely no identity outside of the group which thinks with one mind. You are a drone in a hive with a specific repetitive task (like being on a social assembly line) designed to insure the survival of the queen. Beyond that, you have no life or thought.

In the same way that we have been led to inevitably conclude that it required the European women's feminist movement to make Afrikan women recognize their "exploitation," we have come to believe that it required the divine intelligence of European individualism to correct/improve the "suffocating" communal nature of the majority of humanity. The logic is that everybody on the planet except for Europeans, was locked up in an atrophic, individuality-stifling, group-domineering mentality. In other words, we, as individuals, were controlled and owned by overbearing, creativity-suppressing societies and had no independent thoughts of our own.

As the tale goes, Europeans saw our pain. They diagnosed us as repressed individual personalities who must be liberated from our group confinement. Following this line of reasoning, it took an enlightened european intervention to unleash our constrained, natural individual abilities. Therefore, western culture with its highly focused individualism has freed Afrikans from our communal shackles and has, therefore, liberated and improved us. And, of course, for this divine blessing, we should overlook their destroying us and be grateful for the intervention which brought the destruction.

When you have usurped the power to force your way, you can claim that every aspect of your individual character is correct. And this power, in the hands of a people disrespecting of any and all other cultural realities, has facilitated European individualism's deadly assault on Afrikan communalism. Clarity on this issue comes in the words of a most wise ancestor.

> No amount of individual achievement or the gaining of personal acceptance by Whites on the part of Black individuals, will remove from them the stigma of their

> membership in a powerless race. It will not truly enhance their personal power or freedom. The fact that they have to deny an intrinsic part of their being and identity to achieve "success" and White approval means that a crucially important part of their full humanity has to be negated, that their authentic sense of power and efficacy, their need to be loved unconditionally remains ache-ingly unfulfilled. It connotes that they are isolated and defenseless because they must reject the ability of their group to protect and shelter them in times of social and personal upheavals; that their power is a counterfeited, delegated power, conditionally, tenuously and arbitrarily based on their willingness to ally themselves with Whites in their genocidal assault against the interests and lives of their Afrikan brethren whose fellowship they disdain. The racially isolated Afrikan individual will learn too late that he cannot aid and abet the destruction of his "former" race without ultimately aiding and abetting his own personal destruction.[42]

Simply put, western culture is a vast nexus of closed individuals who operate within the boundaries of a social contract made to protect them as a group from others while they practiced their individual insanities without constraint or boundaries. This is in contradistinction to Afrikan culture where individuals find their greatest expression in doing for others within the group which brings their talents to heights they could never individually imagine.

> The community was the main characteristic of the African Society. It was the group which determined the life which must be followed. Every individual had to render certain duties for the community and in return the community gave him protection. Private property existed but it was not selfish individual ownership, because it might at any time be utilized for the benefit of another member. Each individual felt the community in which he lived, as the coherent embodiment of something higher than himself, something which he and his fellowmen had been inspired to create together. It was the general community, the co-ordination of its life as an integral whole, which was of permanent value, rather than

> the particular individual who wa already implicit in the community....African society was built on the spirit of helpfulness.[43]

The idea that the group/communal nature of Afrikan society submerged the individual into insignificance is totally flawed. As a progressive communal people, Afrikans have always thoroughly believed in individuality.[44]

Our communalism is not the communism or socialism that Europeans misguidedly fabricated to try to soften their capitalistic exploitation of themselves and others. Exploitation of family is anathema to Afrikan communalism. Afrikan is first person plural. There is no "I" without "we." To say Afrikan is to say "we"/"us." "I am because we are."

Communalism is a state of mind. It is the understood relationship between a much extended family that welcomes everyone with clean hands to eat out of the same pot. It is the expectation of love and fairness from all relations, and receiving it as if it were expected but unnecessary. "A cousin does not ask and is not refused anything."[45]

Reason and Meaning

Inevitably, when books are written much is overlooked or intentionally omitted because of space, time and/or the relevance of the material at hand. Since writing *Asafo: A Warrior's Guide to Manhood*,[46] I have come to see that there is a greater need to elaborate on the attitude of warriors, both men and women. And that is what this book is about – the character, the thought and behavior of Afrikan warriors, of our Asafo[47] and Jenoch, toward each other and other family members.

And as a relatively unimportant aside, because others should never dominate our center except when we are deliberating their deconstruction and removal from our presence, it also touches on what should be our approach and level of interaction with traitors and aliens, particularly Yurugu. *IWA: A Warrior's Character* is an attempt to make the contradictions in the relationships between us and others known and offer an Afrikan logic to the mode of interaction that should always be exhibited by warriors toward themselves and others.

Before going on, though, we should take a moment to seriously question the insistence, so many of us feel morally compelled to do, of including european people in family discussions. Unfortunately, we find this in the writing of so many Continental and Diasporic Afrikan writers whose works on our traditions must first be validated by the european press in order, in most cases, for them to be published and distributed anywhere. This is telling, not of the writers so much as the naivete with which we unquestioningly accept this assumption of white inclusionism.

The idea that Europeans should be included as having a natural awareness of and/or being active, equal participants in this universal consciousness which distinguishes (and consciously rewards and punishes) what is good and bad in all humans must be questioned. Their thought and behavior from the beginning of their existence to date indicate otherwise.

In the wise words of our Ancestors, "Every man teaches as he acts"[48] and "When deeds speak, words are meaningless."[49] So, possibly the most pressing question here, is if it is true that this divine moral consciousness is spiritually encoded to the same degree in all of us, how is it that Europeans have been able to successfully block its regulation or influence?

It is more than obvious that their common, moral and ethical sense, when compared to most of the rest of the world, is next to nonexistent. And, it is equally obvious that this dysfunctional "conscientiousness" fits and makes absolute sense to them. If not, they would not try to defend it so and doggedly endeavor to contaminate others with it.

Therefore, we must be very careful when inferring from humanity to them. At a fundamentally mentacidal level, drawing erroneous similarities between our nature and theirs speaks to our burning desire to declare them a normal part of the human race. It leads the truly vanquished[50] to dredge up that misrepresentation of historical fact, even when the subject matter has nothing to do with them and all evidence is to the contrary.

Ìdòwú describes IWA as being an "armor" the individual wears to protect her or himself from the evil in this world.[51] Righteousness, especially that which is inherently corrective, must be protected when it is forced, by its mission and vision, to exist within an inherently confusing and corruptive, evil reality. Good character, that is, in such a reality, righteously enraged character which actively refuses to submit to lies and physical and mental tyranny, is the best protection for warriors.

Not only does it serve as a shield against the evil onslaught from without the community for the knowledgeable, determined warrior,[52] but it also provides a substantial defense for the less ambitious in the community. IWA shores up those who, though day in and day out badgered and battered into private rebellion, patiently await reasonably secure opportunities to strike out against a psychopathically racist tyranny and restore a benign Afrikan world order.

In a community where members believe in the concept of *Ubuntu*, i.e., "I am because we are, and since we are therefore I am,"[53] a person's reputation determines how openly others receive and trust him or her. In fact, to our Ancestors, "the purity of your name is worth more than the purity of your body."[54] One's reputation is a function of one's character. It is through the development or maldevelopment of character that one's reputation becomes good or bad. And, "the outcome of good character is, of course, good reputation."[55] Likewise, the opposite applies to bad character.

Under ideal, communal conditions, your reputation accompanies, if not precedes, you. Your name is determined by the expression of the character you have developed as an individual. "A person takes her name with her wherever she goes."[56]

This same communal logic applies to families, clans, lineages, ethnic groups and nations. Only here, it is the combined character of all included individuals that has created a reputation that bestows praise or shame upon them.

According to Ìdòwú, for those of Yoruba ethnicity, there are rules which must be followed by individuals in order to gain Olódùmare's favor. Persons of good character:

1) practice chastity toward all except their complement
2) are hospitable toward others, especially deserving strangers[57]
3) act selflessly toward others
4) are driven to express kindness toward others, especially those in need
5) eschew wickedness, meanness, cruelty and retaliation
6) speak truthfully and follow a path of righteousness
7) do not steal
8) are trustworthy
9) are not hypocritical
10) unhesitatingly protect the innocent and those physically weaker than their attackers
11) honor and respect their elders.

All of these accurately describe what should be the thought and behavior of the Afrikan warrior. However, considering this cultural context and the context of war that Afrikans find themselves in with relation to the creators and maintainers of this culture, a couple of qualifications are in order. Conditions dictate the relevance of rules and the degree to which they can and should be applied. Rules which normally hold sway in a respectful society only conditionally apply when that society is made imbalanced.

First, we *always* have to bear in mind that this is not traditional Afrikan society. We do not live in a place where the cultural or social climate our Ancestors created prevails. There is nothing about this society, as an unnatural naturally occurring phenomenon, that prizes or nurtures the Afrikan Way. In relation to this, like any other form of wisdom discovered and spoken by our Ancestors, neither can our proverbs, sayings, riddles, kwk. be carelessly spoken and acted out or upon in the context of this evil world we abide in. This is not traditional Afrikan society.

Secondly, these rules for molding good character were determined long, long before our first encounter with Europeans or other aliens.[58] Therefore, the relentless face of evil that they brought to the table of "human" character was not encountered during the thousands of generations of learned human interaction that molded the Afrikan perspective of interpersonal relations and character. In the words of Nana Jedi Shemsu Jehewty (aka Jacob H. Carruthers),

> The one flaw in the ancient worldview which may have persisted seems to be the inability of African wisdom to account for the nature of the Eurasian....Does not history deny the possibility of really civilizing and humanizing those who by nature are barbarian?[59]

To have hindsight and still not learn, to make this same mistake again, would be an indictment of incredible stupidity. As is commonly expressed in our community, "Fool me once shame on you. Fool me twice, shame on me."

Certainly, every day was not the greatest day for Afrikans and there were those who strayed away from the Way. However, in our case, it actually was a case of the few bad apples[60] and not the norm. But, for Yurugu, bad character is the norm. And they arrogantly carried this defining feature with them as they blindly charged down the Caucasus Mountains against the world. The momentum of their desperate, insatiable rage carried them ever deeper and deeper into others' physical, mental and spiritual space as they swarmed outward in all directions off of the Eurasian Plains in search of a civilized world to raze and recast in their own barbaric image.

Obviously, these Yoruba guidelines to good character are neither selfish nor self-centered dictates. While we know that you cannot love others if you do not first love yourself, each guideline for living a righteous life instructs one's thoughts, words and actions outward, toward others.

Still, these rules definitely imply the presence of a secure self-esteem and love of self. Although each one, by default, speaks to relations within families, the first, tenth and eleventh particularly do so. However, we must be careful in how far we take these as special rules about treating family members. This is because all of the other rules also apply to family members and the definition of family in traditional Afrika extends far beyond its primary, limited description in the West of the parent(s) and child(ren) nucleus.

The first rule, which has the weakest support in western relationships, is to "practice chastity toward all except their complement." This is fundamentally an issue of respect and self-control or discipline. Fidelity is dismissed as the habit of fools (or those incapable of exploitation and deceit due to their fortune, position, assertiveness, incompetence, kwk), in a world (1) ruled by extreme individualism and insatiable greed; (2) where adults and the media alike model both primary and secondary relationships[61] as if they are essentially games of power, pleasure and pain; (3) in which your prestige, whether male or female, comes from a tally of your conquests and (4) where lying, deceit and the ability to masterfully manipulate others is the mark of intelligent assertiveness.

There is almost nothing in yurugu's reality, besides an occasional feigned call for abstinence, to make one take being chaste seriously. The temptations are too great. And, daily, discipline reaches an all-time low.

Loyalty has become a word reserved for those who unconditionally serve you, not something you desire to freely give. As stated, to reveal any degree of serious fidelity to another, in what in a human reality should be a reciprocal relationship, is to set oneself up to be used. In such a world, machines and animals become human substitutes in the campaign for loyalty.

How is any Afrikan to find and practice chastity in this reality? Is it even fair to ask an Afrikan to voluntarily expose his or her emotional self to another, to take the chance of being loyal to someone who, in all probability as an emotionally dysfunctional product of western culture, may not reciprocate. And, for the warrior, emotional vulnerability is the least desired predicament.

We can only answer this as Afrikans who have a rich tradition of reasoned chastity, parenthood, family and emotional respect between males and females. Subsisting in this material, commodity-based reality, it is hard to imagine a vision taken from a time when men and women respected each other as equals. It is even more difficult to imagine such a higher reality, if you are without the inner strength to constructively visualize a world or aspiration that goes beyond this minute, day, week, month, not to speak of this year, decade or even centuries or millennia. If there is no visionary expectation grounded in the practical application of our skills toward a just, honorable and empowered future for Afrikan people, then what is the purpose in lying to ourselves about being warriors, about living?

Warriors must know the heart of what they have decided to build. They must know what interpersonal choices are involved in the decision to be Afrikan. Their study of those warriors who have survived the test of time show that they have taken seriously the fact that to be Afrikan is to be paired with a complement.[62]

And complementarity, if it is to work, must operate on the Afrikan principle of fidelity and not the european game of serial monogamy[63] or, rather, playgamy. Most importantly, in your choice of a complement for life, you should not be with someone whom you do not literally trust with your life. Why would Afrikans want to share their spirit with someone they do not trust?

The other two rules specifically speaking to family relationships have to do with the role of protection and the honor accorded elders. Here we will briefly address the warrior's protective responsibilities. Honoring our elders will be discussed later in this work.

Giving protection is not a sex specific role or responsibility. Still, both the man and woman have specific responsibilities in protecting the other family members, with more physical strength and skills/training associated with the larger, more exterior, defensive functions. This we will speak more to later. But, for the moment, let it suffice to say that the men have the responsibility of defending the periphery and the women the core of the compound, however defined or laid out.

Without strength of mind, discipline, awareness and preparedness for any possible exigency, especially those injurious crises which have repeatedly occurred historically, this cannot be done. Each of these requisites is embedded in the makeup of a true warrior's character. Each requires a constant testing of one's abilities and study of what has happened and what the current conditions open up as possibilities for or against the family.

Change must be managed. And the management of drastic change and/or violent upheavals requires a strength of mind that has encountered and handled increasingly more trying situations and, from them, grown.

Seeing problems as sources for learning is part and parcel of a warrior's character. Without it, every formidable difficulty becomes insurmountable. And true to its universal utility, adversity continues to serve as one of the most consistent means of ascertaining the true character of those claiming warriorship.

The other warrior's characteristics of being hospitable, selfless, kind (especially toward others), trustworthy, truthful, honest and noncontradictory should be applied to everyone in the community. They are basic to building and sustaining good wholesome relations within a community.

However, we must remain ever vigilant of how "community" must be qualified. It must be defined within the context of the destabilizing, degenerative sabotage that has historically accompanied our fight to liberate ourselves from a progressively evolving and intensifying western invasion. For us, this reconceptualization[64] must take into account the frontlines of communities where vanquished individuals are bountiful, covertly active and entrenched. It demands that we see through the many disguises of pseudo-revolutionaries who see their war not as against those who would deny our people their spatial and cultural sovereignty. They focus their energies on attacking easy targets such as those particularly visible individuals, selected as scapegoats for the entire enemy, who most adamantly refuse to reform and unqualifiedly include more of us in the distribution of the spoils of their rampant destruction and, especially, those within the community, whose voices are most dreaded by a community bent on subintegration, who refuse to surrender their essence – the warriors.

Warriors of good character can least afford to treat those who have a proven record of doing everything in their power to undermine and destroy us as if they are part of our community. We should know that innocence is not a european trait. It is only strategically staged by them in an effort to further confuse their victims. What they have consistently done tells us of the sincerity of their deception. Deception is but the truth of chronic, consistent, calculating liars. They know exactly what they do.

Nonetheless, the reader should note that a number of the qualities listed by Ìdòwú above are said to become even more praiseworthy when they are applied to total strangers. That, of course, is the true test of altruism. Just as we know that actually being willing to die for someone, some cause or your people is the ultimate indication of love, so, too, is acting as if a stranger were your most precious and deserving family member the ultimate indication of your heart's kindness.

Of course, considering the history of our relationship with Europeans and other anti-Afrikan aliens and our truly involuntary presence in this cultural context, "total stranger" must also be qualified. What this constitutes must be tempered by our knowledge of the enemy. Too often in the past our benevolent response to total strangers has resulted in allowing them to gain a foothold in our space so that they could begin or intensify the process of destroying us. Xenophilia, what in an Afrikan world is an asset, has, in a European world, become one of our worst liabilities.

The Context of War

Some Afrikans remain completely oblivious to our traditions before their violation and fragmentation during our enslavement and colonization. These naysayers of an optimum past, present or future Afrikan reality unashamedly wallow in their ignorance of our genocidal relationship with Europeans and other people. In their doubt and denial, they would sarcastically ask for proof that we are at war. Most of them, hiding behind a steadfast refusal to admit the past is the present, or the constancy of our destruction at the hands of their "friends," "allies" or, at minimum, those they consider to be "human," would brazenly deny that the European is truly our enemy. They cringe and scoff at the idea, asking for evidence that they neither dare nor have the capacity to conceive, less known believe.

In return, we would be wise to expend no more energy on them than is required to spark the possibility of conscious thought. And this would be to simply send them to our primary sources, to the sesh[65] who have studiously given voice to our righteous rage. At most, they should only be asked to open their Afrikan eyes and ears, so they can see and hear ourstory as told to us by our most dedicated and sagacious master teachers. They should be directed toward the works of those like Chancellor Williams who uncompromisingly spoke our truth against seemingly insurmountable odds. For it is they who have dedicated their lives and every resource at their disposal to deliver to us the wisdom and ignorance, the triumph and tragedy, the correctness and flaws[66] of our Ancestors. And, from this intense, selfless study, it is they who have tirelessly issued the warnings to those with the will to survive to ever beware the psychopathically racist malevolence that will always be waiting behind the destroyers' smiling faces.

> The necessary re-education of Blacks and a possible solution of racial crisis can begin, strangely enough, only when Blacks fully realize this central fact in their lives: the white man is their bitter enemy. This is not the ranting of wild-eyed militancy, but the calm and unmistakable verdict of several thousand years of documented history.[67]

Such thoughts can only flow from the minds of lions who refuse to glorify the hunter.

For members of us in the western hemisphere, one intimate example of this war against Afrikans is the *Ntoreasee Otuko*,[68] a horrific ourstorical event many mistakenly, euphemistically call the "Middle Passage." Along with the deceit, corruption and treason that informed and accompanied the battles to capture us, we were intensely and unremittingly assaulted every step and stop of the coffles we formed[69] in marching from these battlegrounds to the dungeon deathtraps we were imprisoned in until those who survived passed on through the doors of no return to embark on the slavers which carried us across the Kemetic Ocean under unimaginably inhumane conditions.[70] All of this took a toll of, minimally, 280 million Afrikan people,[71] to include those who would have been born to those who were brutally murdered in this racist crusade to destroy the Afrikan so fully that we would give up our spirit and just die off in peace.

Although the slavers have stopped their routine sailing to this land, Afrikans are still being trafficked into Europe and the "Middle East" under the most brutal and horrific conditions to slave for others in their fields, homes and beds. Dazed by a desperate confusion that mistakes whiteness (or, in fact, any unAfrikan people, thought or technology) for ultimate power, many of us on the Continent and dispersed throughout the Diaspora even volunteer to serve as slaves. These sad shells of their Afrikans selves allow Europeans and others to abuse them and our children in whatever sadistic way they see fit. Others, particularly in Afrika, existing under unbearable conditions of abject poverty, find themselves left with little choice other than starvation and death, or to sell the only resource they have, their bodies, to the lowest bidder for whatever use any gutless exploiter would sadistically desire.

This murderous rampage has never stopped. Those questioning this only need open their Afrikan mind to know this. Some things cannot be studied or understood, except through the voices of our Ancestors and those who today speak through them. And these voices are not willing to forgive or forget the unforgivable and unforgettable.[72]

Our collective rape is another ongoing example of this war. In the european mind, rape is a justifiable tactic and perk of war, just as is the murder of innocents. How can we deny this range of complexion spanning tens of millions of us? It is a still evolving, systematic, "whitening" process that has taken hundreds of years of constant, day in and day out, rape.

Nothing about it was or is voluntary (except among the mentacidal and, among them, their "free will" to identity Europeans as the enemy and the intelligence to decide whether it was in the best interest of Afrikan people to sleep with the enemy was lost along with their minds).

The mentacide of those who do not wish to see turn it into something less than the hateful human violation it is. Embracing, and even celebrating, rape (completely misdefined as sexual intercourse resulting from "love") voids the mind of the ability to distinguish destroyers from family and especially works to turn foe into friend and vice versa, to turn enemy into lover and vice versa. "One love" in the hands of the mentacidal is an ideology without historical or political awareness. "One does not bless one's ill-wisher."[73] When we seek a psychological plateau of unqualifiedly loving everyone in a space where we are systematically being destroyed, we become less and less able to distinguish genuine friends from proven foes.[74] We leave ourselves emotionally naked and open to the spiritual, mental and physical violation of others who see us as prey. Who in their right mind would seek to turn insistent destroyers into lovers to experience but a moment's artificial peace?

For many of these "doubting Thomases,"[75] though, it is not a question of whether or not we are at war. They simply want to distract us from our mission with meaningless, time-consuming debate. It makes no difference how much evidence we give of this fact or the quality and profoundness of our analyses. Truth is not the answer sought.[76]

The truth about Yurugu for these self-hating sycophants is not susceptible to reason. For these willful individuals, the quantity or quality of the evidence is irrelevant when the answers might call them to question their eurosupremacist loyalties. They cannot see themselves beyond the mind of Yurugu.

Such individuals tend to follow the path of least resistance. Hence, whoever controls the gateways to resources, power and personal validation controls the directions these people see as viable cultural and political paths to follow and, therefore, how and what they should think and must defend.

So, no matter how many answers are given, or what their particulars are, they would never declare themselves at war with the European. Things like freedom from others' thinking, culture and imperatives, truly self-conceived (out of self-awareness) self-determination and Afrikan power are, at this point in their sub-existence, beyond the possibilities of their vision. Their thoughts follow a simpler, weaker, more docile, treasonous line of reasoning:

> If we help the whites get this control, we stand to profit from the changes. Those foolish enough to go against them will of course be wiped out. I'm among those who'd rather profit than be wiped out....Nothing will ever make me stand against those guns....[in other words] in this world there are those who thrive, and there are those who don't. Those who thrive, thrive because they respect power. They see where it comes from, and they take care to place themselves beside it, never against it.[77]

This is the negroes' creed.

Now, we can couch this war in whatever polite terms we want. But, anyone even remotely aware of the act of war, openly declared or otherwise, *and* ourstory,[78] knows that we have been engaged in a life and death struggle with our "mortal enemy" for over two thousand years now. We are fighting against eurosupremacy and an attendant destruction of all that is purely Afrikan.

It is Afrikans, and only Afrikans, who are fighting for our survival as a people. Everyone else, even those pretending to fight on our behalf, have ulterior motives that involve their survival and elevated self-esteem, accompanied by the maintenance and ascension of their power.

Europeans, in particular, but also Arabs, Asians and any other people who can place themselves in a position to do so, are doing all in their power to destroy Afrikan people, Afrikan solvency, Afrikan traditions, the Afrikan Way. The reasoning is not complicated. They see reality as a battle for power, for global domination. There is nothing sophisticated about their worldview. It does nothing more or less than render relations between peoples as attempts to get to or remain at the top of this planet's natural resource (including human minds and bodies) chain.

Technically, their only problem with us is that we are the inheritors of a homeland where most of the world's natural resources are found. And this problem they have chosen to resolve by disconnecting or removing us from her. In the meantime, their strategy is simply to continue finding ways to continue stealing as much of these resources as they want, while convincing us to proclaim that this rape, which will eventually leave us with nothing, is welcome. As evidenced many times before in our dealings with others, their rise to power necessitates a concomitant reduction of others' power relative to theirs. They rise because, and only because, we fall.

Choices

We must understand the magnitude of what Europeans are doing and have done and how it touches every fiber of every culture outside of itself negatively, except those who asilically mirror it. Their midas touch turns all they come into contact with from beauty into beast, from that which it is into something that it would never naturally or sanely become.

We have to meditate long and hard on what Europeans have set in motion in order to understand what is to come. It is an incredibly aberrant, monstrous, global transformation that they have put into motion and upheld through the coerced deculturalization and self-hating, mentacidal socialization of all others into an alien and alienating way. This arrogant sacrilege of universal order has caused a manifestation of hatred for life and peace in every institution that holds the possibility of initiating and supporting these generally desired goals. In order to make themselves fit in and reign supreme without the guilt that would normally torture the conscience of humans who have consciously committed act after act of mass destruction, they have turned this world upside down.

There is nothing surprising here. Naturally, they have created a reality out of the only consciousness they know and can possibly know. What they have created reflects their possibilities.

> [T]hese people are dead. There's death around them somewhere, which is the reason they are deadly as a people, why every advance of knowledge for them is an advancement in the knowledge of destruction. Every advancement in knowledge is an advancement in the ability to kill and destroy the earth, kill and destroy nature, kill and destroy others, rape and rob the earth of its wealth, people and life forms, so much so that now they are having great difficulty even reproducing themselves. At the very center of their lives is death and destruction.[79]

Dead things lose life, color. As the glorification of paleness expands, this world deadens (to emotion, to love, to humanness, to grief, to memory or self, to virtues, to life itself). They are the resident evil on this planet.

And, because we have some insight into the progression and life of socially created evil, we must know that it will not just painlessly whittle away or easily transform itself into something it cannot possibly become. We have to know in our hearts and spirits that this parasitic death which has infected everything must run its course. It is too virulent, pandemic and adaptive a plague to be stopped in mid-stride. The world has been contaminated with the blight of a severely diseased, spiritually, morally and ethically destitute, desperately psychotic people's personality traits.

The Afrikan Way, because of the antithetical, starkly

irreconcilably different reality it presents in contrast to Yurugu's, has been most targeted for destruction. If all of us cannot be made to disavow our Afrikanity and internalize the european way as normal and natural for us, then we must be removed from this world's memory. For, if we remain in our tradition, we will reveal Europeans for what they are just by our very presence. Just as adult males work to destroy men because their presence naturally shows that these adult males are not men, the Afrikan's presence negates the possibility of the european's humanity.

In this world's story, nothing about our being invaded, destroyed and genocidally removed is seen as undeserved. It cannot. For if it were, Europeans would be seen for the immoral, inhuman invaders, destroyers and genocidists that they are. This perception of Afrika and Afrikan people as expendable liabilities has never changed. All that has changed is our perception of this removal. More and more Afrikans have come to also see (whether it be conscious or subconscious is irrelevant because the outcome is the same) this invasion, destruction and genocidal removal as our manifest destiny. Consequently, the mentacidal among us see Europeans as our rightful master destroyers/saviors.

According to this rapidly growing number of converts to the contract with Yurugu against Afrikan existence, we need and deserve this transformation.[80] When they look at the Continent, they conclude that it is the "backwardness" of our indigenous religions which failed us. Quite obviously, these vanquished individuals see our spiritual systems as useless against the vindictive fury of european gods. Therefore, it only makes sense to be onward soldiers for somebody else's god. The war has long been over for them and they have fought long and hard to have their defection to the enemy's side sanctioned by the enemy.

These europeanized, arabized and asianized zealots, frustrated and angered over their limited inclusion in and absorption into others' sterile, pale lairs, have also reached the tactical conclusion that our most ancient and traditional political orders have failed us because they have only badly followed the european model they were forced into during colonization. They have convinced themselves of the necessity of dismissing our traditional fair, human, efficient orders as being nonexistent ourstorically or having no value in a world of individuals. They do this in order to gain an escapist's peace and the favor of wealthy warlords. Now, their crumbling fiefdoms, thoroughly corrupted though quite ably aping various forms of primitive european democracy, are studied only as sorry attempts to master the dominate european political form.

Our traditional family structure is also targeted as useless, before and now. Marked as oppressive to individual needs, far too extended and overburdened and abnormally diffuse in its distribution of power, the Afrikan family has been the most demonized by european cultural politics. This derisive interpretation of our foundational institution is a must for negroes and lost souls[81] dying to become honorary citizens of the West.

No wonder most Afrikans see themselves as deserving of whatever our past gullibility and inferiority, as interpreted by others and the europhiliacs among us, brings. Those possessing but a smidgen of historical knowledge believe that we had our chance to rule in the international jockeying of nations for supremacy. Seen in this light, obviously we failed. Now it is European's turn to rule and mold humanity in their superior image. We have been deemed the lowest who can only rise to respectable levels of servitude in european society on their terms. In other words, we should justly feel ourselves their inferiors and extend a profound gratitude for having been honored with being made into their eternal slaves, regardless of the size trinkets with which we have been blessed.

There is ample evidence, on the Afrikan continent and throughout the Diaspora, of our acquiescence to this sense of inferiority. Everywhere, we are fighting to get as far away from our origins and selves as is humanly possible. "I hate fucking Africa!....Slavery was a good thing. Anything you gotta do to get the fuck out of Africa is o.k. with me."[82] Self-defensively, we laugh at all that is characteristically Afrikan, that is, until Europeans show an interest in and approval of it. And, even then, we affirm it guardedly, ready to trash it at their first signal.

There is little doubt that the vast majority of us rely on Europeans to master and name the world and any other "untamed" frontier they "discover." Our single most important social function is to celebrate their namings and reduplicate their discoverings. As in so many other blatant contradictions, this is revealed in our self-congratulatory pride in "Black Firsts."[83] So sad how genius has been reduced to pridefully parroting disingenuity.[84]

However, if we believe that this insanity about us must run its course, we have to assess our knowledge, power and free will as Afrikan warriors. Although evil may be destined[85] to follow its course, we do not have to follow suit. We always have choices. To the point here, we know what is fueling this reality. So why would we choose to follow a death which feeds off life? Except for mindless, mentacidal fools, "nobody walks with another man's gait."[86]

Nonetheless, we must not be sidetracked by individuals who want to show the exception to the rule or want to debate whether or not Europeans are "literally" evil or not. We define certain characteristics as embodied in Europeans not always because Europeans are the only people evincing them. We do this because Europeans have historically and are now much more disproportionately doing these things. This understanding is in the same vein as Elijah Muhammad defining Europeans as "devils." Evil is as evil does. It is a matter of practice and record.

The Coveters

What we see happening on the Continent now is not a fluke, it is not some historical aberration without precedence. Now, as before, like carnivorous predators trying to cut the youngest and/or weakest from a frantic herd, Europeans seek out and befriend those Afrikans among us who are weak and appetite driven enough to look elsewhere for validation, then decorate and arm them as champions of their genocidal cause. They attack our cultural nervous system like a pedophile let loose in an orphanage. Today's invasion has been long in coming.

The negotiations over resource access in exchange for financial aid (aid amassed through our exploitation) to fill the coffers of corrupted negro misleadership, the invasion of urban centers and rural areas by Afrikan figureheads and missionaries of the europeanized Christian church with sights on pacifying more Afrikans, the establishment of foreign military bases and command centers strategically located to compensate for those places in central Afrika which Israel and Azania (S. Africa) military arms cannot so easily reach or justify openly attacking and the demonization of revolutionaries and leaders who refuse to allow Europeans to freely steal their resources and claim land that inherently is not theirs are indicators of the present invasion.

But these only speak to the tail end of a process that has been in the works for two thousand years. The material, human and cultural resources they have historically worked to wrest from the Motherland and horde in their spaces continues. Only now, with a machine technology that allows them to more comfortably live on the Continent and a people beaten into loving submission and adoration, do they want to call the fertile landscape of our Ancestors their home also. Unquestionably, their covetous eyes have never left Afrika. The "Scramble" never ended.

Only now, their covetousness has been made to appear

as the benevolent, amazing grace of emotionally grounded, caring, selfless humans who want nothing less than to help heal a gaping, growing, chronically infected wound in Asase Yaa's[87] skin that is given all the appearance of being unable to heal through the efforts of its indigenous people. Some even want to say that they, too, are Afrikans, by human origin or settler rights, and that all in Afrika belongs equally, if not more because we have had our turn and fair share, to them as us.[88]

The current invasion of Afrika is only a propagandic pretense at re-invasion because they have never stopped invading it. Annexation,[89] colonization,[90] neocolonization[91] and, now, a massive and growing, concerted, permanent immigrant occupation designed to canvass the Continent with heavily capitalized settlers coming from every european (as well as asian and arab) country have successively continued this process. This has been ongoing for over two thousand years and constitutes a never ending invasion and occupation, assuaged from time to time by the momentary distraction and developmental needs of the european nation and its wars against the rest of the world, including the righteous revolutionary rebellion of Afrikan people against their dogged destroyers.

The strategy against Afrika has not changed. The tactics also remain constant and effective. In fact, they are no different here than what they were when used elsewhere.

The pattern is familiar. First, they come in to study, explore, trade and proselytize. Next, they settle on land, trying to make the indigenous population accept their "right" to argue their private property rights, refusing to leave as they spread themselves outward into others' space. It is here that they begin the process of befriending those most vulnerable to their propaganda and begin to nurture divisions between whatever individuals and groups they can influence. Once they are found out or provoke a reactionary response from their unsuspecting hosts, they have all the excuse they need to initiate an armed offensive which will eventually justify a military invasion because any people will rise up against unwelcome encroachments into their space. This is the beginning of an annexation which leads to colonization. It is the same everywhere they go – "death, destruction and domination."[92]

Ironically, this process is extended even further as, after an extended colonial period, the indigenous people are able to successfully revolt. However, having lost sight of their traditional political, economic, familial, educational and spiritual order, and having operated within the colonizer's mind for many generations, they are caught in a dependency relationship with absentee owners. These former official colonizers control the economy through the culture (technology and aspirations) and administrative structure they have left in their wake.

In addition to the antagonistic divides already firmly established by their initial carving up of the Continent, the erstwhile invaders, misnamed colonizers, agitate differences between every group that will fall for their ethnicity,[93] clan, country first game. These differences, fueled by the ex-colonist military resources and intelligence/information, eventually bring the country into a state of convulsive, regressive turmoil. With time, this externally controlled chaos reaches the point where bloodshed persuades all concerned to beg for the military occupation of their space by "peacekeepers," armies under the sponsorship and direction of their former colonizers, to come in and save them from themselves.

Once this occurs, Europeans are free, and encouraged, to settle and occupy these places in mass. Now that the indigenous people have been used to clear the land, build the infrastructure and Europeans have developed the technology (such as refrigeration and vaccinations) that will allow them to safely and comfortably survive in others' environments, they can come and finally, fully turn these spaces into their personal fiefdoms.[94]

While we are having this discussion, we must come to the stark, historical realization that, for Europeans, there are no civilians in war (except, their own, through propaganda). Therefore, we are all at war, whether we recognize ourselves as being so or not, whether we have any ambitions for warrioring or not. Even when we decide to do nothing or act as complicit pacifists, we are actively participating on the frontlines. We are just facing in the wrong direction.

Through inaction and negative reaction, we assist the enemy in their campaigns against us. "Inertia...is entrapment in confusion..."[95] Regardless of how we personally feel about the reality of or desire for violent, whether overt or surreptitious, confrontations with Europeans and others who assist in their genocidal assault against us, we are all engaged in battle with those who seek to destroy us. In the scheme of things, our recognition or ignorance of this fact is irrelevant.

Therefore, it is up to those of us who know to make ourselves and other thinking, willing Afrikans into the warriors we need to be. We must be willing to fight to the death for the right to peacefully commune with our Ancestors forever in our secure, autonomous, sacred, uncontaminated spaces. That is the only way we can access the essence of what it means to be Afrikan - through the direct connection with our eternal, spiritual self.

In doing so, we automatically recognize that those who have been waging war against us know of the potential of our unified power and consciously, systematically, seek to do everything possible to disarm us and turn our power against itself. If for no other reason, it is imperative that we recognize the enemy without and within who would seek to turn us against ourselves.

The only way to permanently defeat these enemies, the external one(s) and the one(s) others have carefully injected and led us to cultivate in ourselves, is to go to our source. Only in knowing and following the traditions of our Ancestors will we be able to know how to treat each other as being, becoming and seasoned warriors in this effort toward building an empowered, independent, self-defining and fully conscious ReAfrikanized nation.

> Even as we stand here we move from the past to the future. The task on which we have embarked, the making of Afrika, will not wait. We must act to shape and mold the future and leave our imprints on events as they pass into history. We seek...to determine whither we are going, and to chart the course of our destiny. It is no less important that we know whence we came. An awareness of our past is essential to the establishment of our personality and our identity as Afrikans.[96]

The reader will see that fairly extensive detail is given to specific aspects of both Afrikan and european culture and society as they relate to the issue of character. There is good reason. If we are to identify and understand the good and bad qualities of character, we have to understand the power of culture (and the asilic origin and regulator of that culture). If we are to truly grasp who we are and what we must again become and what they are and will remain, we must understand why cultural context is so critical to our understanding of nonAfrikans and us and the meaning that Afrikans, as well as irreconcilably different others, give to the different qualities individuals choose to exhibit.

Individual behavior, at minimum, is a social phenomenon. And, while personalities are indeed personal, they are significantly influenced in perspective and temperament by the societies in which they are socialized and live. Credible examples of this are xenophilic and xenophobic societies, as well as veracogenic and crimogenic societies.

A xenophilic society, i.e., one which can be characterized as having a hospitable and receptive disposition toward others/strangers, encourages its members to care for others, especially strangers. It sees this disposition as the greatest expression of its humanity. The same can be said of a veracogenic one, which we recognize as naturally producing individuals who respond honestly and respectfully toward each other and their possessions. Such societies lead their participants to be honest in their dealings with each other as the basis of their social glue. In such societies, one's word is bond.

This type of society is quite different from a xenophobic one, appropriately defined as being irrationally fearful of and/or hating others/strangers. Accordingly, it is crimogenic in that its normative lack of respect for human worth naturally facilitates the production of inordinate levels of criminal (immoral, unethical and harmful) thought and behavior in a population.[97] Xenophobic, crimogenic societies operate on principles of domination, control, fear, distrust and hatred of others, even fellow citizens.[98] However publicly disguised and/or propagated, treachery and deceit are the modus operandi of interpersonal relations. There is no basis for respect of self and/or between individuals, except power and violence, however kinder and gentler an impression is managed toward others.

It is said that "people in power have long range fears."[99] This is true for all individuals in a xenophobic, crimogenic society when compared to members of xenophilic, veracogenic society, regardless of where they sit on the range of actual, effective participation. The social contract[100] is based on their excessive level of infighting controlled through outward expressions of even greater, more inhumane aggression against outsiders (other people).[101] Like politicians who use incriminating information on each other to keep each other in check,[102] such people are bound to each other by fear of exposure of their true selves to others and the feeling of being united in a common war cause against all aliens.

In general, Afrikan culture and societies have been

ourstorically characterized as xenophilic and veracogenic while history has shown those of the European nation to be xenophobic and crimogenic. Politicized anomalies and the transformation of Afrikan society by alien invasion and destruction do nothing to change the fact of this irreconcilable difference.

We are social creatures, by birth and need.[103] And, because of our frailty as living beings, we require a protracted period of socialization in order to learn the thought and behavior which is appropriate for the people of whom we are a part. However, as already noted, we must bear in mind cultural context and our group's relative position of power in western society in making assessments of individual and group outcomes.

We are in an alien cultural context which cannot be used as a guide to our thought and behavior. To do so automatically compromises our core Afrikan thought and behavior. When we lie to ourselves about who we are relative to who we know we truly are, we allow that alien dynamic to enter, changing us from who we are naturally. And, the more we lose ourselves through self-deception, the more we become like them. When our personal and collective cultural container, held within a vat of chaotically ordered, consciously invasive, purely anti-Afrikan insanity, is punctured and seeps out, that which we are least like finds its way through the cracks and fills that void. As our culture empties out, their interpretation of reality, as it defines us and them for us, replaces it.

Therefore, through extensive, politically guided examination, we must look to the culture of our Ancestors and contemporary traditionalists for our lead. We must be knowledgeable of self in order to remain intact. At the same time, we must study the cultural context (especially the contemporary social setting as evidence that the European's traditions have in no meaningful way been altered by others' influence) we have long been forced into and currently subsist in to understand what we are up against inside and outside of us. With this in mind, an authentically Afrikan representation of social order based on a scientific understanding of true human beings, fully cognizant of our power and what influences what in this world, needs to be reconceptualized and put into motion.

3. The Rules of IWA

Speak right and do right.

Khun-Anup

Character cannot be disentangled from culture because it is within the cultural framework that character is defined. It is the culture that defines those qualities and values to which all individuals within its purview should aspire. It is the culture which logically brings the right amount of every possible thought and behavior together in such a way as they form a coherent whole in order that its members may see in themselves the kind of people they want to be. Within the realm of all possible human thought and behavior, it is the culture that shows, through the way of its people, those character traits which should be selected and emphasized by individuals who wish to be seen as worthy and contributing members of that society.

In fact, it is the culture, much more so than the society, which distinguishes a people from others. It is the culture which gives any given, genoculturally sovereign, people their characteristic flair. It is what determines their image, positively or negatively, in relation to others. And, it is the culture which ourstorically or historically identifies its people by their worldview and way as insiders and others as outsiders.

Therefore, it is mainly through the study of the culture that we can distinctly identify Afrikans as Afrikan and Europeans as European and understand that we are quite different people.[1] In this way, we can clearly understand that these differences are meaningful in terms of our aspirations, self-esteem and humanity.

For Afrikans ignorantly caught up in the planned confusion over what culture is and who rules this reality, thinking, speaking and acting as an Afrikan or as a European has erroneously come to be seen as a real choice. We forget that culture has roots, and different cultures have cultivated root systems or families much more similar to themselves than those of others. Yet, to be or not be Afrikan has come to be a choice we believe ourselves capable, entitled and free to individually and independently make every second of every day of our westernized lives.

It is no accident that we remain oblivious to the fact that all choices have consequences, some good and, of course, some bad. The degree to which choices beneficial to oneself or one's group/people are perceived as difficult or reasonable is a factor of one's or one's group's/people's power relative to others with whom such choices impact.

From this reasoning we understand that the more constrained and oppressed a people are in terms of the options they accept as being available to them, whether of their own mentacidal fears or the direct suppression of these options by those who control their space, or both, the more difficult it is to know, make and consciously pursue self-defining, self-empowering decisions. In other words, the more historically and contemporaneously constrained and oppressed a people are, the harder become choices of or, more accurately, decisions about being their natural selves.

Unnatural environments produce unnatural thought and behavior. And we have found ourselves in a wickedly unnatural environment over the last two thousand years. The confusion and pain have never ceased, except in the minds of those who have made a full transition into something other than themselves. Yet, even for them, there is intense confusion and pain. They have just lost the ability to recognize it for what it is.

Because we operate in an unnatural environment, we have developed a whole collection of unhealthy responses to personal and interpersonal issues that work to our detriment. We have come to embrace and display self-loathing personalities without shame. Seemingly known to everyone except ourselves, the defense mechanisms we have developed to mask our mentacide and protect what remains of our fragile, fragmented egos are legendary.

In general, the character of Afrikan individuals in this day and place is weak, deceitful, back-biting, vanquished, domineering, selfish, short-sighted, kwk. When most of us look in the psychological reflections of ourselves and other Afrikans, we do not experience an undying appreciation for our individual selves or the us we see in them. We see just what our personalities express – monstrous hatred. Even if only to ourselves, we must be honest enough to admit the emptiness of Afrikan "love" in this insane reality if we are going to begin to heal.

And, as painful as the prospect of going through what it will take to heal is, we must know that peace will only truly come when we embrace and become our Ancestors, for they are the ultimate expression of who we are and must become if we are to fully recover. We must look back in order to build a wholesome, sane world of our own. We must build the Ancestor within. We need our "Ol' Soul For a New Day."[2] Sankofa is our only option for sanity and sovereignty.

Right now, only a few of us are capable of assisting us

attain such remarkable heights. Many warriors know how to fight well. But only a few have learned how to struggle without end. Only a few will be able to reach beyond this entrenched state of vanquishment to see a victorious, healing Afrikan vision. And it is they who must do the incredible work of providing hardworking, uncompromising models for those who are not completely lost, as well as the unborn who have yet to follow.

Amilcar Cabral taught us that "the best way to fight an alien culture is to live your own."[3] No aspiration could be more appropriate or difficult for Afrikans to realize. In searching for the truths that have always characterized our humanity so that we can live again as *human* beings, we should look at the guidelines our Ancestors have left us. Let us take a few points from each to examine their practical application for a warrior's character, his or her IWA, today.

In this effort, we will survey several ancient and traditional sources from which we can derive the essence of a warrior's good character. They include lists from the ancient texts, such as The Oracles of Ma'at, the rules to which the neophytes in the Kemetic Mystery System had to adhere, and the Akan concept of who is human. Additionally, we will look at quotes from traditions spanning the Continent, the rules given by Kwame Nkrumah to fighters engaged in guerrilla warfare, Civil Rightist James Forman's code of conduct for revolutionary organizations' membership, the guidelines put forth by Zak A. Kondo for Afrikan students in the West's institutions of higher formal miseducation (now diseducation)[4] and a few other relevant sources and listings. We start with the Oracles of Ma'at.

The Oracles of Ma'at

We will begin our discussion of the rules of good character with one of the oldest collections of spoken and codified rules[5] designed to guide well-meaning Afrikans down the path of righteousness – the 42 Oracles of Maat.[6] However, because we are reconstructing ourselves within a eurocentric cultural context, many of these oracles call for clarification from an Afrikan center before their application in self and toward others.

Before going on, though, it is important to make a quick note on origins. The wisdom of Greece, Rome and the motherless child they birthed called Europe is not of indigenous origin. It was stolen from Afrikans.[7] One of the best examples of this is the Ten Commandments which were directly, plagaristically derived from the Oracles or Principles of Ma'at.[8]

Beyond questions of origin is the question of emphasis. When contrasted with similar principles for Europeans, what is most interesting about the moral and ethical guidelines Afrikans established for human thought and behavior is how they are stated.

The Oracles are stated as personal affirmations, whereas the Commandments are instructions to individuals.[9] Here we can see a clear distinction between assumptions of individuals being internally (self) versus externally (other) controlled or directed. The Oracles are stated in terms of "I have not..." while the Commandments are given as "Thou shall not..."[10] Even the word "commandments" speaks to this distinction.

Oracles, as Metu Netcher, as divine words of wisdom, are understood as accessible to all. The choice of embracing them is based on personal choice. The different spiritual, cultural, social and political assumptions about the nature of individuals who are personally committed to a set of rules seen as universally divine which provide the parameters of righteous living are different from those of individuals whose thought and behavior must be directed/controlled externally.

The ever expansive and coercive/punitive nature of european laws (created and enforced by the state from above, though the creators and enforcers remain, more or less, above the laws they have created) implies the necessity of an enforcement external to the individual. Extreme individualism and the genocultural drive to have power over others in order to have worth insures this necessity. The continuous need for this external enforcement of spiritual law in european society is quite evident and clearly speaks to the blatant personal disregard for any spiritual law that interferes with personal gain through exploiting others and/or requires the individual to practice some form of self-control. There can be no higher moral authority for extreme individualists than self.

The "social contract" that eurocentric social scientists so proudly speak of has little to do with individuals agreeing to act civilly toward each other for the sake of operating on a higher spiritual plane. It is a contract where the individuals agree to be regulated by the state in order for them to relatively calmly coexist while they, as one, exploit others. Beyond that, in general, europeans and westernized individuals consistently break each and every one of the few spiritual laws that they have purposively selected from the Oracles of Ma'at.

Even though we generally think of the Oracles of Ma'at as Declarations of Innocence (misnamed Negative Confessions) individuals affirm after they have made their transition from this life into the purely spiritual realm where they stand in judgement before the goddess Ma'at, we should intuitively know that these Ma'atian declarations formed a core part of the daily contemplation of the Kemites. We know this because the purpose in life for them was to become as godlike as possible and these rules served as guides to their every thought and behavior. Therefore, the Oracles of Ma'at were guides as to what they should not do, not what they should feel free to do as long as they were forgiven for them.

Nationbuilders should be clear on the point of present or future orientation. In a reality where personal accountability is measured more by one's racial standing, material assets, relations and proficiency at deceiving others and self than one's moral or ethical bearings, warriors must constantly remain cognizant of the kind of person they have been and who they desire to become. For this reason, in that many of our warriors were raised to internalize and outwardly express a Northern "Womb"[11] mentality and have involuntarily and pre-consciously probably already committed numerous of these negatives, it makes better sense to use the introductory phrase "I will not" in our discussion of the Oracles.

We do this as an affirmation of change until enough time has passed where we can look back and see a clear Afrikan path in our wake. We do this with an eye on the future, a time when we have returned our people to their correct cultural disposition and the social environment is again an Afrikan place where it will be more appropriate to say "I have not." "I have not" would seem to be the aspiration we would have for our children once we have created a reality in which obeying such moral instructions makes common sense.

The Oracles of Ma'at are as follows:

1) I will do no wrong.
2) I will not steal.
3) I will not act in violence.
4) I will not kill.
5) I will not be unjust.
6) I will not cause pain.
7) I will not desecrate holy places.
8) I will not lie.
9) I will not waste food.
10) I will not speak evil.
11) I will not commit sodomy.
12) I will not cause the shedding of tears.
13) I will not sow seeds of regret.
14) I will not be an aggressor.
15) I will not act guilefully.
16) I will not lay waste the plowed land.

17) I will not enter into a conspiracy.
18) I will not bear false witness.
19) I will not be wrathful and angry, except for a just cause.
20) I will not commit adultery.
21) I will not commit adultery.
22) I will not pollute myself.
23) I will not cause terror.
24) I will not pollute the earth.
25) I will not speak in hot anger.
26) I will not turn from words of right and truth.
27) I will not utter curses, except against evil.
28) I will not initiate a quarrel.
29) I will not be excitable or contentious.
30) I will not prejudge.
31) I will not be an eavesdropper.
32) I will not speak overmuch.
33) I will not commit treason against my ancestors.
34) I will not waste water.
35) I will not do evil.
36) I will not be arrogant.
37) I will not blaspheme the one most high.
38) I will not commit fraud.
39) I will not defraud temple offerings.
40) I will not plunder the dead.
41) I will not mistreat children.
42) I will not mistreat animals.

To this list we are adding a small collection of other very worthy oracles not listed above.[12] And we are making the same qualification as before in changing the introductory phrase "I have not" to "I will not." These additional declarations include (numbers have been given only to convey a sense of continuity with the above listing):

43) I will not mistreat my family and associates
44) I will not associate with evil or worthless persons

45) I will not begin a day by demanding more than I was due
46) I will not do what is hateful to God
47) I will not be blind to injustice
48) I will not misrepresent my nature
49) I will not covet others' property

We will now qualify a number of these instructions for those Afrikans of the mind to refine or reconceptualize their character in terms of our ancestral Way. Of course, such warriors would have to be of those who fully intend to move themselves along that righteous path of their own volition. And they would have to be serious and conscious enough to stay on guard against falling victim to compromises of their actual meaning, compromises which are necessarily instigated by this intentionally deceptive, immoral, eurocentric, anti-Afrikan social context.

While it seems reasonable to assume that most of these Oracles are generally understood, it is important that we be clear about what they always should mean for the proper development of a warrior's character. This clarity should especially be a given in the here and now. Therefore, we will only give special attention to a portion of these instructions.

To begin with, all three of the oracles, *I will not cause pain*, *I will not cause the shedding of tears* and *I will not cause terror*, bring our attention to how we should act toward others. These specifically direct us to control those acts or words we generate which can bring unnecessary harm to those we should unconditionally love. Yurugu's model has taught us well that "cruelty is the strength of the wicked."[13] Why would any warrior choose to be them?

Afrikans should not bring difficulty into the life of other Afrikans, *unless* that Afrikan must be stopped from bringing unnecessary difficulty into the lives of other Afrikans. We are family. We should act accordingly.

These three oracles should cause warriors to ask themselves questions about how we can possibly develop trust, which we most need to cultivate between Afrikan people, if we use each other as convenient targets for the anger and frustration we should direct toward others, its original source. While, yes, one often must destroy, dismantle or alter something to rebuild it, or something, better, we should not expect any undisciplined tearing down to facilitate productive [re]construction.

Positive self-confidence and an abiding sense of nationhood are largely determined by how people are treated by those who look like them. How much of a sense of community with other Afrikans does the chubby, dark skinned, bespectacled girl with striking Afrikan facial features and naturally short, kinky hair feel when Afrikans around her deprecate her appearance. In her desperate effort to be released from the pain inflicted by her own people, and fulfill the demands of the insatiable neediness instilled by western socialization, she gives her complete, unquestioned, undying loyalty when she is befriended by european classmates, coworkers and/or neighbors who can smell her despair and asilically understand the tactical advantage of keeping enemies as pets.

How can we hurt those whom our Ancestors have charged us with protecting? How can a Brother take out his frustrations at a world trying to emasculate him on his complement and/or their offspring? How can a Sister use her children or the european state as a weapon against their father? We must either learn to do more than walk around in frustration, or our thwarted aspirations and wounded egos will actively assist those who so determinedly work to remove us from existence.

The warrior's primary role is to protect the nation. There is nothing in that charge that instructs her or him to bring pain to anyone in the community who does not deserve correction. This is pointed out by the oracle *I will not mistreat my family and associates.* Except in the case of those members of the community who are treasonous (and even though we know that a europeanized mind will continue to betray its Afrikan spirit until that mind is *forced* to return to its disciplined, Afrikan way, correction there still does not mean mistreatment), there is no reason for any warrior to bring harm to another warrior or anyone else in the community.

Still, this oracle cannot be read as supporting a pacifist's posture. Neither does it lend support to those who misguidedly claim and advocate nonviolence as a personal life's philosophy, adhered to no matter the circumstances or nature of the enemy. It is a more than reasonable approach to take when dealing with Afrikans who comprise the dedicated community though. Suffice it to say that only a fool approaches an enemy the same way as a friend.[14]

The bulk of Kwame Nkrumah's "Rules of Discipline,"[15] which we will come to momentarily, addresses this point – the commonsensical instruction that warriors should not cause needless pain. He is clear in his admonition that warriors take personal responsibility for not adding to the chaos of war by abusing their assigned privilege of wielding power in the name of the people. He also states that guerrillas should never take from the masses what does not belong to them, always return what was borrowed and never physically or mentally assault anyone, especially women. These actions would do nothing but create additional pain and hardship among a people already under vicious assault from the outside. And the people are those to whom warriors have ultimate responsibility to shield from harm.

The next oracle we need to discuss involves being wasteful: *I will not waste food.* Of course, it is inseparable from the 34th oracle which tells us to not waste water and the conserving nature of Afrikans which abhors waste. Nothing in the Universe is here just for us to throw away. Such a notion would be ludicrous to any selfless being.

Waste, like spoilage and decadence, in any form, is the

brainchild of lineal thinking.[16] Lineal thinking is the product of the mind of one who intimately knows long-term, extreme scarcity and want, who comes to desperately consume and hoard above and beyond what he or she needs, believing that life is the end of all so you have the God-given imperative to get all that you can now. It drives these individuals to take more than they can possibly use, which generates waste.

This must be contrasted with circular thinking,[17] for Afrikan reason based on a philosophy of continuous restoration is derived from a deeply rooted relationship with a resource-rich environment where things are taken only to be replenished so that a plentiful life extends itself indefinitely. Here, consumption is not frantic because life and its fulfillment are understood to never end. Afrikans know that when we physically "die," it is just a transition from one state to another.

Lineal thinking, or having a jaded, envious view of the world (and Universe) that necessarily sees its resources as exploitable and expendable, with no care for others' needs or the future state of these resources,[18] is an arrogant mentality, full of blatant, callous disrespect. It requires a self-centeredness that sees no one else as important, except those that either serve your ego for the moment or who can harm you. Breaking this oracle seriously goes against Afrikan order.

As stated, Afrikans are conserving by nature. In knowing that we are the Universe, we understand that waste is inherently harmful to our being. We know that the environment sustains our very existence. Ours is not a way of excess or unnecessary waste. It is not a way in which using only what is needed is a reaction forced on undisciplined minds by failing economies or the symptoms of global warming.[19] Conservation of resources has always been one of our most endearing characteristics. We do not have to "go green." That is our natural state of being.

So, the selfish panic[20] we see going on now in western society and its privileged satellites over global warming and the outcome of the systematic stripping, poisoning, cloning into sterility and general destruction of Asase Yaa speaks volumes about the fundamentally wasteful character of european culture. This rash carelessness, with respect to being wasteful, is not characteristic of our Ancestors, culture or asili. Therefore, it is not a model we should follow with respect to this planet, Spirit, our individual selves or each other.

I will not speak evil is another oracle warriors must focus on in a world where "noise and confusion" (our Kemetic Ancestors' description of the Greek language) have been elevated to an art form. There are two main problems which make it difficult for warriors to adhere to this declaration. One is that cursing and hateful, disrespectful language is the normal speech through which Europeans communicate. As the story goes, their grunts evolved into words equally unfriendly, aggressive and violent.

Now, under their tutelage, we have come to accept that vulgarity and obscenities are a normal part of human language. Most of us are oblivious to the fact that it is historically common only to the warped, hateful mind that is euroversalizing itself by grafting its abnormal peculiarities onto the thought processes of other people. And this effort to normalize this aberrant, violent speech among Afrikan people has met with significant success.

When asked, most of our children, not only do not know anyone who does not curse, but also do not believe such a person does or has ever existed. And, because of this, their children will know of no other way of communicating, except through cursing at each other, whether in jest or sheer self-hatred.

Regardless of others' efforts, we should know that this is not a normal part of human communication. All we need do is visit the "other" Afrika, the rural uncontaminated one, where our traditions are still largely intact. These Afrikans do not use profane language.

Another problem making it difficult for warriors to submit to this oracle is the practice of gossiping. And, make no mistake, this is something which applies to male and female warriors alike.

Gossiping is the intentional spreading of unknowns and lies as truths. Yes, sometimes we can find truth folded into these lies. And, yes, sometimes it is fused into them to the point where they are inseparable and, as a result, those lies, logically, become truth also. But this distortion changes neither the lie's overwhelming presence nor the negative impact gossip has on the health and psychological well-being of its target. For, almost always, gossip is meant to harm someone, whether by causing others to bring physical harm to someone or to ruin a reputation or relationship. Those who gossip forget that "if you damage the character of another, you damage your own."[21]

Gossiping is an irresponsible act committed by emotionally insecure and immature individuals who want to lessen the importance of others in the community. And it is a very dangerous practice because it destroys a person's reputation, the one thing that precedes all interpretations of an individual's character in our tradition.

Jealousy is a natural accompaniment of gossip. Jealousy is a living, reactive, thieving emotion. Like a vile instigator, it eagerly feeds gossip and gives it license to manufacture untruths to remove the honor or position of whoever is the source of the jealousy.

Gossiping is in the innate character of western society for, at heart, it is and produces insecure, hateful individuals who take delight in destroying the names and lives of other individuals who are seen as perpetual competition. Warriors often gossip because it is a habit born of being socialized in this emotionally crippling reality.

However, warriors should be knowledgeable of the divide and conquer tactic historically employed by european forces to keep us disunited and disempowered. Therefore, regardless of its source, warriors must think hard about what we are up against and doing before spreading unfounded rumor, no matter how questionable and/or repulsive its target or appealing its possibility. We should know that it is a weapon from the enemy's arsenal in our minds. Regardless of why, gossip inevitably brings harm.

If we think back to many of the efforts by enemies to undermine our movement, COINTELPRO not being the least of these,[22] we see that others recognize the value of gossiping as a tool of disruption. Around us today, we have ample examples of how misinformation was brought in to misdirect us and our children over the nature of our movements and leadership. One of the worst to date is the crusade by homosexualized and promo[23] Afrikans to emasculate and europeanize Malcolm by attempting to homosexualize him.[24]

Under normal conditions, perversity would be considered unthinkable warriors (and all others in society for that matter). *I will not commit sodomy* is one such challenge for both young and old socialized into a sexually perverse society founded on a culture of male and female homosexuality, pedophilia and their anal and oral manifestations.

We have to remember that sodomy covers any and all forms of sexual deviance. Warriors must bear this in mind as we reconsider what perversions this reality proclaims and champions as the human norm.[25] There is no gray area here unless we are so weak that we would redefine that which is European as Afrikan.

I will not sow seeds of regret is the promise one makes to not do things which will later cause sorrow. Some things can never be retracted, corrected for or forgiven. Everything does not, and some things should never, have a statute of limitations. Having committed such acts or made such statements is not a place where warriors want to find themselves. Regret is usually the outcome of inconsiderate, misplaced disrespect and/or the release of uncontrolled, blind rage. For those of us with an operative conscience, it inevitably causes us to feel remorse about wrongly speaking or acting.

This insightful oracle advocates prudence in thought, word and deed. As the Senegalese say, "To spend the night in anger is better than to spend it in repentance." And it directly warns against anger that stunts critical, responsible, caring thinking. When directed at the wrong person for the wrong reason, by someone with a heart, inappropriately expressed anger usually ends in regret.

I will not be an aggressor is surely the most fitting attitude warriors should take toward family. By extension, this also applies to those who act like family at the ethnic and national levels. Again, at whatever measure of intimacy, warriors must be able to distinguish between friend and foe.

Of course, we know that aggressing against other conscious Afrikans is patently wrong. However, aggressively defending oneself, one's family, one's community, one's nation against confused Afrikans is not. This unacceptable behavior is no different than that of Europeans and others who act against Afrikan interests. On the other hand, by now, we should know that there are those Afrikans who, lost in love with Europeans, will work even harder than Europeans to harm us. Therefore, as Malcolm said without qualification, it is not aggressing when dealing with those who seek to destroy or assist in destroying us. That is, as he said, not blind violence. It is intelligence.

No matter how distorted its presentation, ourstory tells us that conscious Afrikans have never launched the first offensive (unless to correct disorder which, in itself, is an offensive). It is always we who act against others in response to their offensives. We simply do what Afrikans do, nothing more, nothing less. We act against only those who work against us being ourselves. Our in-kind, aggressive responses to these offensives are only what they naturally should be.

Sadly, mentacide has increasingly deadened our defensive nervous system. Mostly, these actions have come to reflect a reactionary incredulity about our ongoing destruction and the systematically conditioned lack of preparedness that fosters skepticism about anything that threatens to weaken or disable the blind belief we have in our enemy's love and benevolence. And others, even those who look like us, but who are fanatically ashamed of their Afrikan selves and in love with anyone who will toss even a diseased crumb in their direction, diligently work to keep us from doing even that.

History makes the context of our relations with Europeans abundantly clear. Although knowing more of the details of the magnitude of their assault might prove useful to some, there really is nothing more warriors need to know. Toward Europeans, and other nonAfrikans who have proven that they consider assaulting and exploiting us an inalienable part of their constitutional human rights, we cannot possibly be aggressors. Such people have already committed uncountable offenses against innocent, warmhearted, loving Afrikans without cause or justification. As warriors bearing this oracle in mind, our duty is simply to stop this onslaught and prevent its recurrence.

I will not act guilefully is also a critical personal warning issued by the Oracles of Ma'at. In *Centered: Building Afrikan Realities*, I spoke of the negative impact self-deceit and lying to others within the community have on warriors and our nationbuilding efforts. [26]

> It should go without saying that warriors should not consciously deceive other Afrikan people of good character and intent. How can people who call themselves revolutionaries be successful in their work if

> they make a practice of deceiving themselves, each other and those for whom they say they would lay down their lives? Regardless of the level of deceit religiously practiced among the creators of and adherents to the aberrant reality many of us choose to remain hostage to, that way of thinking, speaking and doing is unAfrikan. It works to intensify our fragmentation....Lying to others within the community is bad enough. But lying to oneself about oneself is about the most damning thing that a person can do. This is delusional. Still, lying to those one is sworn to protect and whose shoulders brace yours on the frontline is tantamount to treason. And, if you will deceive yourself, you will deceive them. Know that not speaking truth, i.e., being silent and/or letting lies circulate unchecked, is still lying.[27]

"If you sow falsehood you reap deceit."[28]

Intuitively, we know deceit is wrong, regardless of how deeply the practice has become entrenched and how expected, acceptable and functional for survival it is socially and psychologically in this distorted, retarded, immoral reality. Our Ancestors recognized the deleterious effect lying has on the community and self long ago. Through the example and rules they established for everyone, they warned us against this divisive vice.

There can be no trust with it. There can be no love with it. Nothing of worth is real with it. Everything and everyone become manipulable commodities and reality a facade ruled by the most accomplished liars. A reasoned awareness of this explains why our Ancestors did not hesitate to include guile as a vice to be consciously avoided.

For most of us, at first thought, *I will not lay waste the plowed land* makes little sense in the "modern" world (except as a fad or a transitory survival reaction). As we mentioned earlier, some of these oracles must be updated. They must be reconceptualized (given an appropriate meaning in the contemporary cultural context) within the mental framework of a ReAfrikanizing nationbuilder.

Even though we all should, most of us do not garden or farm and are totally unfamiliar with the concept or sight of tilled land, not to mention actually turning earth over to loosen the soil, remove rocks and debris and more evenly distribute minerals and nutrients in preparation for planting. Many of us have not actually delved in dirt in any capacity whatsoever (seeing it as something dirty and alien versus being quite clean[29] and the closest natural substance to us). Although land as actual, physical matter and an indispensable resource will always be of ultimate significance to nationbuilders, how might this oracle prove even more relevant for us today?

If nothing else, plowed land would be symbolic of the resources we, as sentient beings, possess, have unearthed and begun the process of cultivating. One invaluable, nonmaterial example of such a resource is our ancestral wisdom. Taken in this way, symbolically, the ground represents whatever nutrient rich "soil" we use to grow whatever we need to survive as a thinking, self-defining people. There is no richer soil for Afrikan people than that of our Ancestors.

A parallel thought, using this approach and example, would tell us to follow the Sankofan process to its logical end when moving "backward forward." It leads us to go back and get the wisdom of our Ancestors, to plant our own seeds in its rich, fertile soil and tend them in its healing properties until they can be harvested and used to fortify this wisdom under our current conditions.

We can see the utility of this example in an often repeated Guinean proverb: "Knowledge is like a garden, if it is not cultivated, it cannot be harvested." If we do not use the fertile wisdom our Ancestors left planted for us, it will not be available for us as we need it. It will be as useless to us as the nutrients in unused plowed land are to unplanted seeds. The land grows fallow. The seeds rot or are consumed by the worms, rats or other more nefarious creatures.

This oracle should be seen as a warning against wasting

talents and skills. It exhorts us to turn over the hidden ancient wisdom so that it can be seen and used again by those for whom it has lain dormant.

Of course, no matter the symbolism, the cornerstone of nationbuilding is the return and protection of our original land from aliens. As we re-acquire the intellectual tools to build our nation, we must also look toward re-acquiring the land to do so.

I will not be wrathful and angry, except for a just cause is a most interesting oracle. It speaks to the connectedness of common sense to an Afrikan's character. The word "except" is the door our Ancestors left open for us to understand that there is a qualification to this commandment, a valuable condition which we will turn to momentarily.

We have every right to be "wrathful and angry" or, rather, given the negroes' and lost souls' confusion of this with "hate,"[30] righteously enraged. We have every right to define our enemies as enemies and pursue a nationbuilding path of absolute sovereignty using rules established by our Ancestors in their entirety.

Except for those among us pacifistically mentacidal enough to willfully follow an enemy's imbalanced rules of engagement which functionally disarm us, logically, a different, more balanced set of rules for interaction must be applied. Again, in terms of how enemies should be treated, there is a stark contrast between friend and foe.

By any reasonable measure, self-preservation is positively self-serving. And we should be intelligent enough to know that there is absolutely nothing wrong with this. It is an immutable law of nature, both for individuals and societies, which are simply larger, more complex organisms or life forms.

Nationalism, the political term used to identify a love of self and people, is normal and functional for a people. Was it not Marcus Mosiah Garvey who so lucidly articulated this truth for us?

> No race is free until is has a strong nation of its own – its own system of government and its own order of society. Never give up this idea, let no one persuade you against it. It is the only protection of your generation and your race. Hold on to the idea, of an independent government and nation so long as other men have them. Never be satisfied to always live under the government of other people because you shall ever be at their mercy.[31]

And was it not Amos N. Wilson who extended the revolutionary force of this truth into the contemporary reality?

> The power of the group amplifies and extends the power of its individual members. Nationalism has been used by nation-states to facilitate the consolidation of a distinct people(s) and territory as well as to create colonies and empires. Conversely, it has been, and can be utilized to overthrow colonial and imperial domination. Nationalism creates a collective, focused power which enables a people to achieve ends which, as separate individuals pursuing their own unrelated self-interested ends, they could never achieve. The power generated by nationalism is the bane and harbinger of destruction to those who wish to establish or maintain imperial control over other peoples. This is the main reason it is defamed vociferously by imperialistic peoples and nations despite the fact that it is the main instrument of their own domination of other peoples and nations. Nationalism is often catalytically brought into active existence by oppression. As an instrument of power it is often logically chosen as a means of overcoming oppressive and repressive conditions by a people who perceive themselves to be oppressed by another. Such is the case in regard to Black peoples and in regard to Black Nationalism.[32]

Nationalism, like any other social phenomenon, becomes abnormally bloated and dysfunctional when formed in the interests and image of oppressors. Its negativity is exacerbated even further when those they dominate define and implement it as given them and accept it as the only way in which it can be defined.[33]

Almost without question, what you would willingly do for a friend is the exact opposite of how you would respond to a foe. What you do to benefit a friend benefits you. And, for warriors, the enemy of my friend is my enemy.[34] Quite naturally, when friends work in each other's interests, such doings are acts of *adiama.*[35] The only thing shared between foes is distance and/or an appreciation for dispensing each other's pain.

In an Afrikan setting, what you do to benefit other individuals in the community who are family benefits the entire community. If it were not for our confusion over whether we are Afrikan or European, this would be self-explanatory.

The enemy presents a threat. And, for people conscious of exactly who their enemy is, the threat is always perceived as a clear and present danger. It matters not how reserved or nonconfrontational the threat may be at any given moment. In peacetime or during war, the nature of our enemies and the definition of enemy do not change.

Most often in war's theater, this threat is a mortal one. No matter whether it is immediate or not, whether it is physical, psychological (conscious or otherwise), spiritual or all three, warriors take it as a threat against their people's lives. Threats, even and especially those accompanied by disarming smiles, must be taken seriously. If not, there is a price to pay.

Those Afrikans who do not recognize that we are at war with Europeans, or worse, who are incapable of recognizing the possibility of there being one, are in the greatest mortal danger because they are least aware of their impending destruction. Remember, mentacide and deicide, or spiricide,[36] are most serious forms of mortality at the individual and group levels. Above all, in their ignorance or willful stupidity in the face of sworn enemies, such Afrikans are more subject to capture and psychological torture by the greatest threat to everything Afrikan.

Those who recognize both the enemy and war and

attempt to warn the blind are most likely to be targeted for character or bodily assassination. Still, we are compelled to issue the warning. There is profound satisfaction in knowing conscious warriorhood's immeasurable value for those with a need to know, in contrast to many a coward's silent foolhardiness or weak-minded belligerence. Dying for nothing and living to die for everything are quite different.

Interestingly, and again noting that the ten commandments were taken from the Oracles, the "except" clause is curiously absent in the professed beliefs of those embracing a religion which cannot allow Afrikans to recognize Europeans as their enemy. In terms of power and its racist exercise in a society controlled by people dreaming of supremacy, those who have it keep it while, those who don't weep.

We need not belabor this obvious point when it comes to religious etiquette. The practiced faiths of the oppressed are the religious systems defensively tailored to suit their masters, regardless of origins. As has been proven by so many of our revolutionary minds, Christianity, as practiced by the majority of Afrikan adherents, is european nationalism and Islam Arab nationalism.[37]

The point is that we must enter this study of the Oracles relative to the IWA of Afrikan warriorhood with an active consciousness. This means that we have to consider the contemporary relevance of this ancestral wisdom in the entirety of each principle as *originally* given.

We must actively consider those rules our Ancestors decided would guide their lives, and should guide those of their ascendants. However, we must go farther. For, while we must consider this with a clear understanding of the genoculturally homogeneous context in which they were written, there must be an equally knowledgeable comprehension of the alien, anti-Afrikan context within which we are now forced to apply them. We must study these principles as warriors, and not as stupefied, politically pacified eunuchs.

I will not commit adultery is another immediately understandable Ma'atian oracle. To adultery, though, being on the "downlow" (a euphemism for homosexuality) and at least equal to these two, sleeping with the enemy, should specifically be added, given the deteriorating moral and ethical state of the Afrikan community. All of these are ultimately destructive toward our families.

This instruction speaks to a weakness in a warrior's discipline and a character flaw that allows one to easily submit to baser desires. In respect to the inability of some westernized Afrikan men (and increasingly their female counterparts) to restrain themselves from wayward sexual behavior, ancestral wisdom should consistently serve as our guide. The sage Ptahhotep warns us that "he who is ruled by his appetite belongs to the enemy." He further makes the point that

> If you want friendship to endure in the house that you enter, the house of a master, of a brother or of a friend, then in whatever place you enter beware of approaching the women there. Unhappy is the place where this is done. Unwelcome is he who intrudes on them. A thousand men are turned away from their good because of a short moment that is like a dream, and then that moment is followed by death that comes from having known that dream. Anyone who encourages you to take advantage of the situation gives you poor advice. When you go to do it, your heart says no. If you are one who fails through the lust of women, then no affair of yours can prosper.[38]

Again, this is not limited to Brothers. In the western cultural context, Afrikan women and our daughters are being led to defile their sacred womb.[39] Our Sisters, who once set the standard of sexual morality in our community, have increasingly become willfully caught up in the rapture of the western sexual playground. Their wombs, once understood as directly linking us with divinity because of their procreative power and connection with this overriding universal principle, have become tainted by excess and perversion.

Truly, individually, our Sisters are not at fault. Like the Brothers, they have become entrapped in the pale vortex of euroversalism or, what has been more deceptively called, globalization. It is the nature of this desacralized, misogynistic, anti-Afrikan, hedonistic, pleasure-driven, physically and sexually-obsessed cultural context to drive us deeper and deeper into yurugu's vulgar interpretation of reality. It is the pressure from this all-encompassing sea of insanity which has systematically forced Afrikan women into the psychotic trap of insatiable, never-ending predatory-prey sex. Within this imperative, there can be no boundaries.[40]

Specifically, in terms of adultery, it makes no difference if the one committing the transgression who claims warriorhood is the spouse going outside his or her marital relationship or the one outside the marital relationship who is violating its sanctity. Once you know such acts are wrong, you are fully accountable.

In relating this oracle directly to the intimate compromise of racial loyalties, we have to conclude that interracial coupling is absolutely counterrevolutionary. We have got to stop picking up their trash. It should go without saying that the insanity of "locks chasing strings," for whatever reason, is completely unacceptable.

The oracle *I will not pollute myself* tells us to be aware of what we mentally, physically and spiritually ingest. Abusing drugs and alcohol, eating genetically modified, chemically contaminated food, breathing polluted air, watching corruptive imagery and engaging in materialistic practices are all negative ingestions that harm the spirit, mind and body of Afrikan warriors. The saying that you are what you eat equally applies to what you drink, breathe, see, study, mediate on and call forth for assistance. Pollution can enter the self in a multiplicity of ways. Just as noise and distraction (the absence of silence/stillness) keep one from accessing Spirit, drugs in all forms, be it food, media,[41] sex, kwk, do exactly the same.

We must be careful not to follow eurocentric "scientific" qualifications that give us excuses to use any drug (especially chemical, recreational substances). This especially applies to their propaganda of pointing at priests and shamans who use natural drugs in order to access and/or heighten a spiritual experience. We are not these traditionally trained experts and this is not the time that anthropologists write about. This is not traditional Afrikan society and we cannot use the manipulations of it by others as an excuse to continue engaging in eurocentric habits. Selective mentacide is no less mentacide.

I will not pollute the earth is one of the most telling guidelines for living that reveals just how far we have fallen from being human.[42] Any violation of it shows that we have moved outside the unqualified reverence traditional Afrikans held toward Asase Yaa. Our Ancestors acknowledged the Earth, like life, as a great gift to be cherished and treated with the utmost respect and care.[43] Otherwise, they would lose it (it would turn against us). And, in losing it, they would lose themselves. For, without it, there would be nothing to sustain them and no place to live.

> The ecological implications of collective moral responsibility lie in African notions of the Earth and of the human community consisting of the living, the dead and the unborn. This logically implies an ethics which is Earth conscious in so far as the living, as custodians of the land, have a moral responsibility towards providing a means of survival for future generations. This collective moral responsibility basically means that whatever a person does has consequences which extend beyond him or herself to affect his or her community and environment. The ancestors as the owners of the Earth provide a

> supernatural level of moral authority. They are the ones to whom the living are accountable; whilst the future well being of the unborn represents the upmost moral responsibility of the living. In many traditional African societies, the ecological system and human community are of necessity in harmony. This is because the law of the land is also the law of the Earth and the ancestors that lie buried within it. The ancestors have the special role of being official guardians of the social and moral order, and concern themselves with the social and moral responsibilities of their descendants. Most African traditions show them to have some influence over the natural and social order. Should they let their vigilance slip, it could result in harm for their living descendants of whom they are guardians.[44]

There are so many proverbs which testify to the honor and respect with which Asase Yaa is held by Afrikan people. All are encapsulated in the proverbial Akan observations that "All power is from the land" and "The earth is heavier than the sea." Of course, thinking as Afrikans, the love with which we, as a people, hold for Mother Earth should be obvious.[45]

Common sense would tell us that disrespecting and intellectually separating ourselves from what feeds, clothes, houses and educates us, from what we stand on, from what sustains our lives, is absolutely absurd. "If the Earth does not give birth to grass and grain we die."[46]

Although, from time to time, this oracle concerns all Afrikan warriors, *I will not speak in hot anger* is especially relevant to our newest and most frustrated class of warriors. Hot anger is not just angry words, for angry words can be spoken without the force of a directing emotion. It is the word "hot" which sets this instruction apart from telling us to not use words meant to convey anger.

People in the West often jokingly curse in casual conversation using harsh, angry words. Here we are being instructed not to be angry in our speech. This is because hot anger takes us away from our ability to think rationally, to communicate cooly.

Notice that this instruction does not tell us not to be or speak when angry. Unemotional Afrikans, Afrikans unable to express their emotionality, are deprived of their humanity because, in the western cultural context, it does two negative things. One, it changes us into pacified, overrun creatures who are emotionally crippled and unable to functionally operate constructively in our own behalf, something that is wholly unAfrikan. The other is a suppression of the overt expression of feelings. Outside of an occasional, unplanned belligerence, the absence of emotionality in speech is a european trait.

Righteous rage cannot be constructively and effectively expressed without anger. Anger is coalesced, concentrated energy. Energy must be directed or it becomes misaligned and misguided.

This oracle simply relays that a warrior's words should not be expressed in "hot" anger. Hot anger is beyond control. A warrior's mind and, therefore, a warrior's anger should never be uncontrollably violent or belligerent.

When we speak of what has happened, is happening and will continue to happen to our children, naturally, we become emotional. Afrikans have always been a highly emotional people and completely accepting of that emotionality, that is, until Europeans came along and convinced us that it was evidence of a primitive, immature mind. Since then, we have come to seriously question its appropriateness and earnestly worked to suppress our emotional being. Only now, with aliens attempting to vicariously experience emotional joy through us, are we embracing that aspect of what we naturally are and easily were in our genius before them. However, under conditions of subtle subservience, we all too often animate our emotional essence in severely distorted and exaggerated forms of entertainment for them. In doing so, we allow these emotionally impoverished beings to indirectly feel what it means to be human.

Therefore, unpretentious emotionality is only natural to Afrikan people. It is not something that needs to be concealed or forced. Therefore, righteous rage should be expressed as it comes, in a clear, concise, instructive, corrective form. But it should not be loosed to the extent that the speaker loses the ability to logically think.

The lifeless, stoic persona is not more indicative of greater intelligence than an inspirited one. This is as much a myth as the objectivity it is said to prove. It is only what we have been led to believe because we have taken their emotional immaturity and sterility and spiritual detachment as the ideal human model. Many of us have accepted emotion as being synonymous with childishness, play and lack of seriousness intellectually. We have come to associate unemotionality with intelligence.

Because surliness is their way,[47] they must have all conform to their definition of personality in order for them to be seen as normal. They must have everyone believe that gesticulating while speaking, interacting with the audience and letting one's feelings be known is somehow a less intelligent way of having a conversation or making a presentation than an emotionless, motionless being. The exceptions to this, their norm, always involve deceit, as when riling people up for war or now (since their incursions against others' minds has progressed to the point that direct, physical oppression can begin to be replaced with a more indirect, psychological one) that they want to change their appearance into that of a more humane, emotional people. They have learned the art of imitation well.

A Twi proverb tells us that "if you allow your emotions to rule you, you are lost." And this is true, considering that one can be emotional without being ruled by it. At the same time, however, if you have no emotional context, beyond pleasure-seeking, for all intents and purposes, you are disconnected from your higher warrior self. You would be without connection to life or a living, humane, Ma'atian vision of what life is and your purpose.

Most Europeans, and those Afrikans who feel it is now safe and expected for them to release some of their Afrikan emotional self, have altered their presentation so as to give the appearance of being more emotionally charged and physically enlivened. This conscious attempt at impression management[48] is done as a tactic, a well-rehearsed exercise designed to convince others of their authenticity as living, breathing, feeling human beings.

For the most part, though, it is not real. Europeans are what they are. We know this if only because the wisdom of our Ancestors tells us that "a snake will shed its skin, its poison never."[49] The show is only intended for the benefit of culturally captive observers already softened up by the disarming programming of eureason.

In this pretense is further evidence of the european's insecurity. They rely on the approval of the emotionally charged to affirm and boost their emotionless egos. They know they are without. Only we can truly convince them otherwise. Only we can make them emotionally human. And so the greatest compliments to Europeans come from Afrikans.

I will not turn from words of right and truth is truly a warrior's promise. It is said that "truth is the first casualty of war." This applies to the unrighteous aggressor as well as their subdued prey. The difference is that, for the former, it dies so much earlier.

Among a sane people, fear is a social/socialized quality. In terms of its source and sustaining power, it is a group phenomenon, not an individual one. It occurs when a self-empowered people have been held captive in a disordered (outside their norm) state within which they are terroristically assaulted for so long that living in fear of the inevitable seems a normal part of their disposition. Such a people, long lost and huddled together in fear for protection, blindly moving through a dense, endless fog of monstrous, abusive insanity, tend to gravitate toward any peace, even if the clearings it hides in do not keep the relentlessly encroaching insanity at bay.[50]

negroes and lost souls are naturally engendered under such conditions. These people suffer from mentacide, an often malignant condition brought on and fueled by a loathing self-hatred.[51] Fear is the driving force behind the negro imperative and the panic driven stampede of lost souls.

Mentacide is made acceptable among the vanquished because they have developed a slave's mentality. A slave is one who accepts his or her subordinateness as preordained. A slave's mentality is one in which a person is individualized to the point that surviving at any cost, even if that cost be the freedom of family members, the life of one's complement, the minds of one's children or their people's future. The state of psychological terror to which they have submitted completely retards their ability to recognize and embrace truth and righteousness, them being the way of last resort in western society. Such a state could only possibly be understood by them as an escapism from the only reality they want to know, not an effort at determined liberation.

The positioning of the children is one of the most telling indicators of the state of consciousness of a people. A living people, aware of being assaulted, corral their offspring within the inner circle of their defensive wall. They do all in their power to make them invisible to the enemy. Those people who are unaware (or welcoming) of their destruction allow the most vulnerable among them to play beyond their protection in the killing fields. Often, as bearers of the individualist, survivalist slave mentality, they use their own children as a sacrificial shield against others' vicious onslaught.

Because slaves know that their masters will kill them for no reason they are consumed by a fear of giving them any possible reason. That fear makes them submit to, and rationalize that submission as being in their best interests. Their oppressors' unspoken desire is obeyed as if divine.

When this happens, when this is fully internalized and these persons truly become the ultimate slaves, there is no right or truth other than that of the master. Any right or truth that falls outside the will of their owner automatically becomes wrong and false. It is made invisible and, therefore, impossible to consider and act upon. We can begin to grasp the enormity of their fears in the depths of their denial.

Character wise, Asafo and Jenoch stand in diametrical opposition to slaves. They cannot walk in fear. It is an impossibility inherent in their definitions. Fear stifles unfettered, conscious action, giving way to a life of progressive compromise. Asafo and Jenoch do not compromise. They would never give their power to another so it could be exercised against themselves. Men and women of this caliber know that they cannot become slaves to others without becoming less than them.

"Words of truth and right" are their guideposts to their every thought, word and deed. And these words live in our Ancestors.[52]

As stated when discussing the 19th oracle (*I will not be wrathful and angry, except for a just cause*), the instruction *I will not utter curses, except against evil* focuses our attention on the common sense side of a warrior's character. Curses can be called for. There are conditions, situations and times in which they are appropriate. In those conditions, situations and times, anything less would be cowardly. Then, not uttering curses would evince a weakness and willful passivity in an individual, community or nation. "One swears when it is time to swear"[53] and, certainly, "One does not bless the enemy."[54]

Again, a very different set of rules apply when engaging friends in contrast with foes. Almost without exception, what you would willingly do for a friend is the opposite of how you would treat a foe. A deliberate, active, unremorseful enemy should be cursed, repeatedly, until they no longer exist or, if based on the historical record, can be made to no longer exist as a threat.

> Oppression should be shouted down / life a bully on a playground / or beat down like a rapist.[55]

Afrikan people know of and believe in the power of the spoken word. Speech is power. They know that what goes around comes around, that what you give the Universe it returns in kind. Time is not accountable to us. We do not decide when. To know we are right is enough.

There is a word we have given this power of thought and word. We call it "nommo." In our oral tradition, nommo is power.[56] Thoughts manifested in language create reality. Words give ideas form and power.

Yet nommo is not just "creative visualization." Nommo is spoken reality, thought spoken into existence. It is more than just "the magic force of the spoken word,"[57] for utterance is not always directed by positive intent.

> Nommo seeks to conceptualize the ability to activate....It is more, even, than the spoken word. Nommo often takes these forms, but its essence resides in the activating energy that *makes use of* the forms. Nommo can be thought. Nommo can be played on an instrument. Nommo can be sung. It is prayer. It is curse. It is incantation! Nommo is a praise song. Nommo is our use of the spiritually activating principle. Nommo is will and intent. Nommo is consciousness.[58]

So, Afrikans have ourstorically been very careful of what they think and say. We know that words have effect. And this controlled verbalization of thought requires the kind of personal discipline most Afrikans in western cultural strongholds are unfamiliar with.

It is easy to imagine this transformation from absolute belief in the power of the spoken word to its compromised, unconscious retention. The probable origin (if not expanded, practical application) of "knock on wood"[59] would be a good example of this concern for what we say and how it is said. When "good" speech (language and personality) is forced into a situation which demands increasing levels of cursing (i.e., when Afrikans are forced into subordinate interactions with vulgar europeans using a language we neither own nor control), coping strategies designed to protect one's spirit, mind and body are adopted. Such mechanisms allow contradictions between how one knows the Universe operates and the new corrupted reality to be lessened. "Knock on wood" must have been devised to keep bad things spoken about self (and others) from happening.[60]

"If a problem remains long enough, it becomes clever."[61] So, with time, such strategies lose their spiritual significance as the vulgarities of the european mind and tongue are more thoroughly assimilated into Afrikan minds. In other words, the steady subintegration of Afrikans into yurugian thinking, the attendant downgrading of the seriousness of cursing, as well as the dismissal of cursing as problematic because of a lack of clear, immediate, physical evidence that curses come true, facilitated by our vision becoming more limited to the physical plane, caused many of us to question and deny the spiritual power of nommo. With time, the internalization of ugly, hurtful language and its normalization in our minds have removed us from the cause and effect foundations of afreason.

Most of us have yet to fully realize the innate evil nature of european society.[62] And, because of this, we have been unable to see that what worked in our traditional society does not immediately work in their world where evil rewards evil. Once we were psychologically and spiritually trapped within it, cursing it was to little avail.

Furthermore, in a material culture, spoken words are thought to have limited physical value. They definitely are not seen as having the same type of power as they had with our Ancestors. In a spiritual culture, the power of speech is clearly understood. But, because we live in a reality where Afrikan beliefs about power can be ignored, both cursing and counterbalances like "knock on wood," are seen as nothing more than superstitious nonsense.

This radical psychological transition from our reality to Yurugu's has left many Afrikans scarred with an almost total disbelief in the power of the spoken word (except as a blind hope that it can affirm them success/peace in chaos). Europeans, who have always recognized its power (the very reason they convinced us that there was no power there), have used it to their ends. They are now bringing it back to us, but only because we have been subintegrated enough to see them as ourselves and therefore can only imagine our using it to their benefit.

For warriors, the oracle *I will not speak overmuch* is an issue of both time and security. In terms of security, it tells us that we should keep those things we are told in confidence and which we can see are of strategic importance for the survival of Afrikan people to ourselves and other Afrikans who have a vested need to know. It should go without saying that what is important for the survival of an Afrikan family and/or Afrikan community should also be important for the survival of the Afrikan nation, i.e., Afrikan people.

Secrecy is a vital component of security. For only through the control of indispensable information, through keeping secrets within a closed circle of loyal warriors, can security be guaranteed. "Absolute secrecy, a total absence of information in the enemy's hands, should be the primary base of the movement."[63]

Secrecy maintains integrity. Through not revealing what should not be known to outsiders and traitors, a people keep destruction from getting a foothold in their reality. It keeps fissures from becoming fractures by keeping those without a direct, functional need to know from being privy to the intimate formulas to our social glue and the khemists who mix the khemicals and lock the vaults in which they are safely held. The gravity of confidentiality is one of those lessons our Ancestors have gone to great sacrifice to leave with us.

Obviously, because of our studied access to the Afrikan mind and special nationbuilding role, secrecy is a priority among warriors not found among other callings and social relations. We keep secrets because we know the consequences of revealing them to enemies and the gullible.

negroes, on the other hand, have no real secrets from Europeans or anyone else they see as powerful validators of their existence. For them, secrets are the domain of masters, the favor of whom one gains by offering up the secrets of those who look like them but they consider to be the masters' inferiors.[64] What secrets Europeans have decided to toss down to them, under the guise of identifying them as most trusted slaves, are protected with their very lives.

This oracle warning us against speaking overmuch is also, in its spirit, intended to draw our attention to amount. Talking for the sake of hearing one's own mouth is a selfish, highly egotistical act.[65] Individuals infected by this form of verbal diarrhea conceive of themselves not only, as we used to say, as being at the center of the world but, in this time of extreme arrogance, also of being the world. Everything feeds and listens to that ego as if it knows all and every word it spews forth is golden. Knowing all, these individuals cannot listen.[66] And competent Afrikan warriors, whether positioned primarily as leaders or workers, must have mastered the art of earnestly listening to be successful.

Talking simply to be heard also introduces the problem of speaking so much that no work gets done.[67] In thinking of a similar saying, we might even say that those who can, do, and those who can't, talk. Speaking overmuch creates distractions which take warriors away from their work, mission and vision. As simply stated by Hannibal Tirus Afrik, "The only way you can convince me you are Afrikan centered is by your work." Besides, it is common ancestral knowledge that "one has great respect for the silent person."[68] The wise know why.

An old, anti-teaching european saying[69] can be altered to say that "Those who can do. Those who can't talk." Only sometimes, if ever, do those who incessantly talk do.[70]

Carefully consider the words of these sages.

> Speak only when you know you can assist in the solution of a difficulty. For silence is better than useless chatter. There is an art to giving sound advice in council. Surely it is more difficult than all other duties. Those who grasp this can make it serve them.[71]

> Conversation was never begun at once, nor in a hurried manner. No one was quick with a question, no matter how important, and no one was pressed for an answer. A pause giving time for thought was the truly courteous way of beginning and conducting a conversation. Silence was meaningful with the Lakota, and his granting a space of silence to the speech-maker and his own moment of silence before talking was done in the practice of true politeness and regard for the rule that, "thought comes before speech.[72]

> The liberator is he who from a necessary silence, from a necessary secrecy strikes the destroyer. That, not loudness, is the necessary beginning.[73]

Definitely, this is not to imply that there should not be conversation between warriors or warriors and those with whom we need to communicate issues. "When you see it but you do not speak against it, it affects you."[74] Important things require verbal expression. And real needs should not be held back. "An infant that does not cry out dies on its mother's back."[75] Neither is the above to imply that some ideals (which, really, all warriors should be talking about) do not require lengthy explanations. But lies and circumlocution (which is a form of lying) have taught us that "truth is short."[76]

We understand the need for voices, for articulate

agitators, relentless instigators, eloquent awakeners, astute articulators, articulate, poignant orators. But that is the job for a few who brought those talents with them and have found themselves compelled to use them to teach/correct what is wrong. Everyone does not have the gift of gab, the lion's heart or roar or the martyr's selfless intrepidity.

We are merely saying that there should be no inquiry, no conversation, no declarations, without concomitant concrete action that begins the process of realizing those words. As Hannibal Tirus Afrik often declared, "Our deeds will be the defining issue."

I will not commit treason against my ancestors is the most profound and all-encompassing of the Ma'atian oracles. It covers every possible transgression. Most actions of Afrikans loyal to the european way is treason against their Ancestors.

What exactly is treason for Afrikans? To act as if we do not know what has been done to Afrikan people is treason. To act as if we cannot see the genocidal plans others have in store for Afrikan people is treason. To allow our children to be spiritually, mentally and physically enslaved and subjected to a racism based on white, or any other, supremacy is treason. To forgive the unforgivable and forget the unforgettable is treason. To embrace those who have always been our enemies in hopes of gaining their love at our expense is treason. To act as if Afrikans are just another people and pretend that being European is being human is treason. To selectively honor only the names of those who protected and served european ideals and society and compromised an empowering Afrikan vision as our true heroes and sheroes is treason.[77] To despise those courageous enough to challenge us to be the divinity and genius within, and not only conspicuously the material without, is treason. To care for the monuments, words and images of the ancestors of those who worked so diligently to destroy our Ancestors or whose pain was/is incomparable is treason. To hate our essence and appearance is treason. To not be our Ancestors, to not be Afrikan, is treason. To know all of these things and do nothing to liberate, empower and make sovereign Afrikan people is treason.[78]

Unlike when individuals are forced to betray their people under extreme duress (such as when the enemy has a loaded gun pointed at one's spouse or child[79]), treason, as defined here, is an intentional act. And this definition applies to all such cases where intentionality is directed against one's people. There is no excuse for this. "In a revolutionary situation it is a crime against the people to forgive those who have betrayed them."[80] "When a brother opens the door to the murderer of his brother, then is the deed unspeakable."[81] And, throughout time, in every self-empowered, autonomous, sovereign nation "the wage for the traitor is death."[82]

Degrees of awareness of self do not change the nature or effect of the act. In itself, hatred of Afrikans by an Afrikan amounts to treason.

Technically, though largely overlooked, the subtle acts of suicide Afrikans commit against themselves are acts of treason. Self-destruction, in whatever form, lessens our power. And to assist in this is no less than "subtle homicide."[83]

Remember Afrikans believe "I am because we are" and vice versa. So, to destroy oneself is not a victimless crime. It is a crime against self which, by default, is a crime against Afrikan people.

However conceptualized, treason is an intentional act. This holds no matter how mentacidal the individual involved. Unless completely oblivious to one's contribution, i.e., completely ignorant and innocent of one's involvement, a choice is being made against Afrikan people and interests. Treasonous Afrikans willfully and without provocation choose to betray their people.[84]

To some, this may seem an insensitive definition because it permits little room for naivete. However, I would remind the reader that we are at war. And, in war, intent is much less important than the actual act. It is the individual warrior's responsibility to rigidly control all actions to the degree that intent becomes a non-issue. Europeans know that they are at war. And that is why one of their fundamental judicial principles is that "ignorance of the law is no excuse."[85] Punishment occurs based on the act, not necessarily on the intent. This stand keeps them ahead of those they oppress.

Warriors must weigh this question of "insensitivity" against the reality of the battlefield because that charge will repeatedly be defensively leveled against us by those among the vanquished seeking asylum in both worlds. As a distinct minority among such a people, indefatigable warriors of their people's liberation will always be accused of "not understanding" or "overreacting" to the treason committed by others within the community. Yet, at best, the charge of insensitivity should only be considered plausible in cases of proven ignorance and/or when the resultant act does not contribute to an already unmanageable chaos.

When a family, community and/or people are already in the throes of destruction and one of their own, aware of their condition and the politics involved, knowingly contributes to that destruction, there is no room for sensitivity toward that person. Understanding has no place. This applies regardless of the level of consciousness or degree of viciousness. And this is especially the case if this treason is the outcome of an arrogant, repeated refusal to listen to the reason that keeps the family, community and/or people from falling deeper into chaos. It, therefore, becomes not a question of guilt. Instead, it is a question of what form the corrective should take.

We know that our Ancestors took great care not to attribute a bad act to the actor's nature. They always took individuality and circumstance into consideration. But we also know that this is not then and most of us do not know (or care to know) that we are still them. The relevance of this discrepancy relative to treasonous acts will be brought out in greater detail later.

Another point which cannot be overlooked here is that Black-on-Black acts of treason, by default, whether at a conscious or subconscious level, require an arrogant attitude.[86] And, "If you are arrogant, you get lost,"[87] you lose sight of who you are. Haughtiness, or the feeling of being above, or in some delusional way separate from, one's people, even if not quite equal to the enemy, is one of the defining characteristics of so many treasonous Afrikans. "A haughty person dislikes people."[88]

And we can readily detect a rise in the arrogance among Afrikans. Therefore, we can expect nothing less than the level of thought and action against other Afrikans, especially those well-grounded in their Afrikanity, to escalate accordingly. Often, however, this is a subtle arrogance, much like that characteristic of Afrikans who "pass" for white or would claim any race (or combination thereof) except Afrikan.[89]

Arrogance is a highly offensive vice, a defamation of the caring self and a devastating affront to one's spirit. So, not being arrogant should be an integral part of the Afrikan warrior's character. Humility, expressed first toward one's own people and, then to others (if they have dis-earned this level of respect, to the degree that they re-earn it), is the warrior's way. Again, this is not traditional Afrikan society and the tenets of that time and place do not unqualifiedly apply within yurugu's cultural context. We must always remain cognizant of this fact.

The measure of the quality of an Afrikan's character can no longer primarily be of how altruistically one treats a stranger. It must now be based on how well one treats those among his or her own people who deserve this heightened level of respect. In this anti-Afrikan, highly disrespectful, predatory-prey cultural context, humility for strangers must come only as they earn it.

Arrogance is a quality found in those who have deluded themselves into believing that they are naturally superior to others. In the mind of the arrogant, they have no true equal among those they consider their lessers (but with whom they have been forced to be classified and/or coexist). They can accept that there may be individuals who can better them, but only when they happen to not be at their best. Their paranoia and egotism lead them to the erroneous conclusion that they have no true equals.

Some of the most arrogant Afrikans are some of the most self-loathing Afrikans.[90] And these Afrikans see themselves as apart from and above other Afrikans. Their intense self-hatred has led them to believe they are different from those most like them and most like those they are least like. So, naturally, when they are able to project this anguish over being everything they despise, venting it in a destructive fashion outward, they work to destroy that which they are really like (and allowed to act against) in an effort to ease the constant reminder of that in them which they so desperately desire to obliterate. Analytical works such as Nathan Hare's *Black Anglo-Saxons*,[91] Franz Fanon's *Black Skins, White Masks*,[92] George S. Schuyler's *Black No More*[93] speak to the ignorance of arrogance among the treasonous.

Arrogance is an attitude taken by individuals and people who "rise" as the result of belittling and destroying others. In such small minds, the greatest evidence of their superiority is shown through the effect of this successful lessening and negative treatment of others. Pure and simple, it is a bully mentality given the appearance of civility.

Particularly looking at Europeans in this respect, their greater arrogance is reflected in their absence of any sense of humanity in consciously flaunting the one intellectual and mechanical technology they have mastered to a greater degree than any other people – the sadistic infliction of pain. No other people can match their skill at corrupting, maiming, killing and otherwise bringing pain to others for no reason other than a psychotic, mindless greed evolved through centuries of insatiable jealousy.[94] It is through this destruction of others that they gain worth.

Their haughtiness is best expressed in their unwillingness or, rather, genocultural inability to distinguish warriors from those the warriors are protecting. Despite lies to the contrary (e.g., the United Nations, Red Cross, Geneva Convention and relief, refuge and "peace"-keeping efforts), there are no, and never have been any, civilians, no innocents, no unkillables, in european wars against the world.

We find the same haughty glee encrusting the minds of Afrikans trained to suppress the true character of their spirit. Most act even more barbaric toward themselves and each other than their deranged mentors because of the amount of energy that must be expended to confuse and negate self.

Warriors are not this way. Our character is a manifest meditation, a quiet, consistent contemplation and reflection of the best of our Ancestors' thought, word and deed. We know that

> The ideal man is, thus, supposed to be the epitome of Maat. That is, he will demonstrate balance. He will be modest and reserved and yet firm and straight forth. He will not be arrogant. He will show respect for his elders, his superiors in status. He will love and honor his mother and his wife and children. He will be sober and moderate in all things. He will also enjoy life and be a gracious host to his friends, rather than a miser and spendthrift. He will work hard and seek comfort, but not become obsessed with material possessions. Above all, he will speak and do Right.[95]

Yes, we know that Europeans bring pain to each other. Aggressors fight amongst themselves as practice. This is a normal, needy expression. So, fanatical competition among themselves is to be expected. If nothing else, we must understand this white-on-white violence as training. It is real life preparation for venting their never-ending anguish and frustrations on others. These aggressions against their own are in no way comparable to what they do to others.

Truth be told, for these "harbingers of death," the delusion of superiority lies in their willful determination to defy reasonable boundaries, disrupt established tradition and flaunt this flagrant disregard for established universal/human order with the greatest possible disrespect. Doing so allows them to forge our global reality in their lawless image. It allows them to childishly claim, as an uncontested honor, a badge of ruthless courage for having gone where others would normally never wish to dare. And they do this as if the rules and order others respect are without scientific reason or somehow limiting their possibilities.

In the europeanized Afrikan community, it is so sad to see the brash, vainglorious, infantile baiting and other unsportsmanlike conduct[96] so many of our youth have been socialized to arrogantly exhibit by humiliating and demeaning their peers.[97] And people ask why bullies, people who have always been an intimate part of european society, thrive in the various spaces where our children interact. In an immoral, insensitive, crimogenic culture where esteem is defined in terms of exploiting and dominating others, what else should one expect? They better us at insanities. This show of arrogance is even sadder when exhibited by those trying to pass themselves off as adults simply because of their age. This retarded play is so unlike our Ancestors.

Following this model of individualistic children without shame or empathy better than anyone else is the reason why many homosexualized Afrikans are some of the most arrogant, self-centered and hedonistic slaves on this planet. Their egotism surpasses even that of well-heeled negroes.

For us to follow a child's lead and take pride in aping yurugu's arrogant nature is to go against the solemn humility embedded in our spirit. It is to openly defy this oracle against committing treason against our Ancestors and flaunt an enemy's contempt for their wisdom. For they well knew that no one is greater, better, superior than anyone else. And those who pretend so have serious psychological issues revolving around deformed, fragmented, insecure egos.

A final, critical point here, with reference to treason, is that it has never been possible for Europeans, or any other aliens, to militarily overcome Afrikans without the assistance of Afrikans who have allowed themselves to become confused as to their identity and loyalty.[98] There is no greater sin one can commit against one's people, one's Ancestors, one's spirit, than treason. This is a universally accepted truth among humans (as well as all other self-interested beings).

It is interesting, though, to contrast humans and others claiming to be so, with so-called "lower life forms." Among the latter, treason is literally unknown. In the animal kingdom, for example, except for those animals which have been domesticated by humans, or otherwise tainted by our touch, it is unheard of. And, even when these "treasonous" (domesticated) animals escape or are released back into the "wild" for whatever reason, they are spurned (and physically attacked and/or killed) by their species until they have proven that they are no longer some human's pet/agent.

How can a human knowingly form his or her thoughts and lips to debase the source of their existence? *I will not blaspheme the one most high* is a warning against committing the ultimate disrespect against the Universe and self. Marcus Mosiah Garvey wisely cautioned us to "never forget your god." To blaspheme the Creator is tantamount to cursing existence.

Atheism is a highly evolved and organized form of cursing Divinity.[99] It is the ultimate statement of spiritual self-hatred and a deep and abiding anger against the Creator. As a belief system, it custom fits the european personality, an ego-ridden, incomplete self which places itself above all else. And, make no mistake, atheism is a religious philosophy for it is a comprehensive, reality-defining and creating godless reason.[100]

> Atheists do have belief. No matter what one professes, there is always belief. Belief just may not be defined as such because it is not couched or perceived in spiritual/religious terms or fit the conventional ideas we have been publicly led to believe are their dominant religious affiliations. Everyone has belief. It is reflected in what you do. Your fixations, your addictions, your appetites, your most attended interests, reflect your god(s).[101]

No people exist without belief. Every nation of people has a conception of reality and the cosmos whether they have taken the time to fully intellectualize it or not. Western society diligently works to confuse individuals into believing that they can live without having a belief in any power higher than self. (This is the same nonsensical logic some use to convince themselves that they are participants in no particular culture.) At minimum, the belief of those so confused is hidden only from them, designed and manipulated by others at the subconscious level.

While this irreverent attitude among Europeans would be correctly interpreted as normal for them, it makes no sense for thinking Afrikans. We recognize that, while we are an inextricable part of the whole, we do not run this Universe, we did not create it and we do not regulate its order. We abide within it, knowing our beautiful, anointed place in Creation. We are not a god-vying people.

Atheism, the worst form of religious insanity (including Satanism), is clear evidence of yurugu's self-worship. There is no surprise that blasphemy of the Creator is common daily conversation in european society.

I will not plunder the dead warns us against one of the most morally reprehensible acts. This dastardly, sacrilegious act has already been committed uncountable times by

Europeans, as well as the Arabs and others who have joined in this necrophiliac carnage of the resting places of our Ancestors (and those of every other people they have encountered as they continue to expand their violation of human society). They have stolen the bulk of what little archeological evidence of our traditions has been found. In the process, they have systematically misconstrued what we wrote to their advantage, thereby making it extremely difficult for us to practice or re-acquire the skills necessary to decipher our Ancestors' wisdom.

The historical evidence of their avid participation in this nefarious practice is found throughout their literature, both fictional and nonfictional alike.[102] Fictional characters such as Dr. Frankenstein and, if not all, then the vast majority of their university trained anthropologists/archaeologists (as well as those who take up these studies as pastimes), epitomize this socially acceptable, glorified practice. Yet, this would not be so if they were not among those who see the dead and their possessions as little more than another thing to violate. Beyond the archaeology, the "scientific" discipline used to elevate this violation above the desecration that it is, we see evidence of this ongoing plunder of the dead particularly in the very profitable businesses of undertaking and medicine. Here, the possessions, both organic (such as organs and other body parts) and inorganic (such as precious stones and metals[103]), of the dead and dying are stolen for personal and corporate profit. There is telling evidence strewn across the continents and time.

This thought and behavior establishes a clear distinction between us and them. We are not plunderers of our, or anyone else's, deceased. As evidenced from ourstory, that is not in the character of honorable Afrikan people. We respect the possessions and resting places of those who have gone before us. Unlike Yurugu and others who follow their desecrating way, we have a rich tradition in this respectful practice. We honor our Ancestors with daily libations. Whenever/wherever possible, we bury them where we live, not in some forbidden, out of the way place to be visited on some date set aside to remember those who died to expand or strengthen european or some other supremacist patriotic designs, an occasional three-day weekend or an annual visit home.[104] We do this so we can be with them constantly. This is our tradition.

If anything, because others have desecrated our dead in the name of their insatiable avarice and despiritualized science, it is our responsibility to return them to their rightful burial grounds, for the time being places found only in our and our children's hearts and minds. Even so, we must gather all that we can from what we can find of them and continue the process of completing the puzzle and circle of what it is to be Afrikan. We must make all that we know of what our uncompromised Ancestors were into what we are and need to become. We must return them to a peaceful rest by earning their forgiveness for our forgetfulness and by becoming what they need us to become – warriors of character exercising the righteous rage of hundreds of millions.

I will not mistreat children is an oracle that would naturally be valued in a child/family-centered society. Our prime directive must be to protect and educate the children we have produced as a community. They are returning spirit, replenishing us with a greater sense of our Afrikan vision of reality. They are our most important obligation and duty, our most valuable resource.[105] They should never be mistreated. This, too, is our tradition.

Discipline, both exhibited by the adults[106] and applied to the children, sits at the center of this obligation and duty. It enforces order and structure. This discipline is distinct from physical abuse that results in hospitalization and/or death.

Specifically, in terms of the children (but equally relevant to the adults), discipline is not, as western society would wrongly have us believe, mistreatment, as long as there is balance. In fact, a lack of conscious discipline is mistreatment, for a child cannot grow into the true power of his or her potential and self without it.

Such an enormous responsibility helps remove play as a overriding priority in an adult warrior's life. Being able to visualize oneself as a committed, farsighted educator,[107] a jegna (in training) and elder (in training) to this living, evolving Afrikan future, gives greater strength and direction to the mission of warriorhood. This requires discipline.

The question is not whether or not "He who teaches speaks to the future."[108] That is a given. It is a question of what is taught by example. It is a question about the quality of the character the educator brings to the students. Children are not contradictions.[109] They operate within the character and contradictions of what they see.

For those who follow eurocentric guidelines defining adult male or female roles in this society, there is no character to consider. Within such minds, character is defined by the ability to successfully deceive and exploit extremes. Such minds seek out the most vulnerable among their people because of the cowardice that western society engenders in them.

These misguided individuals' foremost priority is the psychological and physical violation of Afrikan children. They measure their success according to how well they better the unnatural practices of Europeans. And european culture, being homosexual by nature, makes this an appropriate mission for mentacidally broken, confused Afrikans and parents who trust their children with them, having willfully forgotten the ancestral wisdom, "A goat is not a wise choice as the guard over yams."[110]

It is in the nature of homosexuality, especially its classical expression, to violate children. Pedophilia is at its heart, as evident in classic european (or proto-european if you prefer) society.

As the western empire expands its hold on others' cultures, in parasitic fashion imitating and invading its host until it is able to overtake and consume it,[111] we find ourselves ensnared in the morass of an open return of european "civilization"[112] in its classic Greek and Roman form. This is a natural regression. As we know, in this society, and those formed which are grounded in its asilic foundation, cultural imperatives and social philosophy, the dominate form of "sexual" relationships was between adults and children.

It is a reality of super individualism, bereft of self-accountability. Here children are socialized to smile at the pain, until they are old enough to sadistically laugh as they do what has been done to them to children now vulnerable to them.

It is no wonder this oracle is the flagrantly transgressed. Understandably, it was one of those which did not survive their theft from Kemet. It could not possibly make sense within any yurugian social construct, except in imperialistic pretense.

It should go without saying that "two 'things' of diametrically opposite natures cannot graft."[113] We cannot be Afrikan and European at the same time. These two irreconcilably different cultural orientations carry mutually exclusive imperatives and, therefore, definitions of "good" character. Society cannot both honor children, holding them up as the preeminent social priority and, at the same time, see them as sexual prey.

Only in a world where chaos reigns supreme and only those who have mastered it to their advantage would the affirmation *I will not associate with evil or worthless persons* not be sensible. Not associating with evil persons is self-explanatory for good, intelligent people. It makes obvious sense to Afrikans, except those who religiously and/or masochistically believe that their life's mission is accepting punishment from evil persons in order to somehow awaken them to their inhumanity. Usually, such sycophantic philosophies are based on the belief in being rewarded for such self-sacrifice and the hope of being able to peacefully sleep with them in some utopianized material hereafter.

In terms of associating with evil, warriors' guidelines are simple. Our mission is to remove it/them from our community. We want to restore an Afrikan order for Afrikan people, not take up the european way against ourselves.

Worthless, as a descriptive, is equally self-explanatory. Individuals exhibiting this quality can be defined as "lacking worth: valueless...useless...contemptible, despicable."[114] Synonyms for "worthless" include incompetent, incapable, sorry, ineffectual, weak, unqualified, purposeless, inutile, good-for-nothing, no account, flawed, meaningless, useless, defective and valueless. The spirit of worthless individuals is characterized by the most negative of these words.

Of what value is such a person to us? How can someone who consciously embraces these qualities fit in with any successful tactic or strategy of war? What can a person who does not value him or herself, let alone his or her nation, do for a warrior on a ReAfrikanizing nationbuilding mission? Worthless individuals are a waste of our precious time. And we have no time to waste because we know that "association breeds assimilation."

I will not begin a day by demanding more than I was due speaks to controlling the vice of greed, which precipitates and is wedded to cheating and lying. It is no secret that "greed for money brings about evil."[115] Ptahhotep instructed us:

> If you want to have perfect conduct, to be free from every evil, then above all guard against the vice of greed. Greed is a grievous sickness that has no cure. There is no treatment for it. It embroils fathers, mothers and the brothers of the mother. It parts the wife from the husband. Greed is a compound of all the evils. It is a bundle of all hateful things. That person endures whose rule is rightness, who walks a straight line, for that person will leave a legacy by such behavior. On the other hand,

the greedy has no tomb.[116]

He further warns us to "not be greedy in the division of things. Do not covet more than your share. Don't be greedy towards your relatives."[117]

This oracle speaks to the virtues of being worthy and expecting returns based on one's demonstrated worth. It is an oracle about adiama, about a natural, selfless reciprocity. The amount of work one puts into something is the amount of return one should expect from one's work. Therefore, doing one's best at all times is emphasized in warriors of good character. Excellence in effort should be rewarded with excellent returns.

For many experienced, conscious Afrikans, reciprocity, as an intrinsic expression of adiama between the individual and Spirit, is understood as operating on a schedule beyond their understanding and control. We have learned that what is reciprocally received, i.e., received in kind for what one has given (what you put out into the Universe you get back), comes when it is time. We realize that this return is often not when or what we may think it should be.

Returns come as they are truly needed and only when the recipient is physically, psychologically and spiritually ready to receive, i.e., correctly use, them. We are daily reminded that our Ancestors afford us all that we ask for *and* are ready to receive. The maturity and integrity of our thoughts and actions, as assessed by them, not us, is the determining factor of when.

This oracle, therefore, speaks of one's worth. It directs our attention toward assessing how much time, energy and truth individuals put into their efforts to maintain or increase their spiritual, mental and physical possessions.

Vices such as greed, cheating and lying diminish people's capacity to receive what is deserved in good faith. Using these vices as a means to acquire possessions corrupts the individual and lessens her or his value as a human being. Obviously, wrongly or ill-gotten gains are not the warrior's way.

However, the things seized through guerrilla operations fall into another ethical category. They are not unjustly obtained. Just as the "the slave that kills his master practices an act of legitimate self-defense,"[119] to take the implements of war necessary to gain one's people's freedom from a murderous enemy only shows intelligence.

This oracle goes hand in hand with *I will not increase or diminish the measure of grain*. Fairness is one quality warriors definitely want to be remembered for. To do otherwise is to lie and cheat in an effort of greed. The outcomes of the decisions made in situations involving choices related to reciprocity and/or fairness speak volumes about one's worth.

I will not do what is hateful to God requires that we believe in the Creator and Creation and to intuit from that knowing what is good and right. Traditionally, for Afrikans, that which is harmful is evil and that which is helpful is good.

To know what is hateful to the Creator calls for us to constantly consult with our Ancestors (who considered wrong anything which unnecessarily brought harm and pain), the Deities and the Creator, with Spirit, *tiboa* (intuition).[120] For those with common ancestral sense, there are obvious rules about what is morally and ethically right and wrong in the Universe.

The question for us now, in this day and age, in this theophobic,[121] deicidal, despiritualized, anti-Nature, anti-natural, anti-Afrikan cultural context, is what would drive Afrikans, a most spiritual people, to do what is hateful in the eyes of the Creator, which is itself being hateful to the Creator? What would cause a people who are "notoriously religious"[122] to be the opposite of how we are born? What type of circumstances would lead individual Afrikans to question the Creator's presence, to embrace agnosticism, atheism and even satanism[123] (inherently death-affirming religions), so that they could be comfortable with being anti-Afrikan? In truth and reality, to do what is hateful to the Creator requires one to disbelieve in the Creator's omnipotence, omniscience and omnipresence. There is no other justification.

I will not be blind to injustice is a core directive of the warrior. Consciousness, gained intuitively and through rigorous study, of the unrelenting, unprovoked injustice against our own people should be enough to make us act. This, combined with our adamant refusal to accept the condition imposed on us by this reality as being "just the way it is," "the way of the world," as a natural stage in "human" evolution or the Creator's will, makes the injustice heaped upon Afrikans by Europeans and the european way crystal-clear to warriors. "Is it not wrong when a balance tilts, a plummet strays, and the straight becomes crooked?"[124]

Neither Asafo nor Jegna can ignore the forces which are crushing Afrikan people and our spirit. No conscious Afrikan of good character would ignore this assault while playing dress up in the trinkets trickling down to us and/or studiously aping the thought and behavior of our enemies in the desperate hope that they will accidentally mistake us as them.

Traditionally, the politics and honing of warriors have never been accidental for us. We have always systematically searched for those with the innate talents we need. So, it is important for us to be able to identify them early so that their thought and energy do not become misdirected away from and against us. An intimate aspect of this oracle can be found very early among those children who have a great potential to be serious worker/leaders among their generation. Anger over others' dishonesty and the conditions imposed on our people, as well as a natural drive to create a just world regardless of personal cost, is an observable quality we must look for in our children.

Being committed to our cause in the face of seemingly overwhelming odds requires this type of personality. So, looking for and nurturing this quality in our children where it is most apparent makes sense to a community of people who are working to intergenerationally create a better class of warriors to carry on the higher struggle for independence.[125] It is in the honorable tradition of progressive nationbuilding that we work to establish and continuously replenish a priesthood of warrior healers who see it as their personal duty to serve Afrikan people first.

Warriors do not just happen. Social circumstances alone do not produce the best of them. It is fateful conditions, or an ominous, awakening confrontation with reality, *acting in conjunction with* a personality (no matter how well disguised/suppressed) that despises inequality, unfairness and deceit that produce just warriors.

I will not misrepresent my nature should deter warriors from being anything except Afrikan because that is what we are. By nature, we are not European. We are not Asian. We are not Arab. Therefore, we should not think and act as any of them.

This is not meant to suggest that we should not be fully aware of alien minds and personalities. In fact, it means just that. We must be fully aware of them in order to know how to correctly navigate, counteract and check their madness.

But, above all, it means that, being Afrikan, we should act, internally and externally, as Afrikan people. We should not act as if we are something that we are not. To do so is to demean and dismiss the reasoning of our traditions and Way. To do this would be to commit treason against our Ancestors.

One particular concern that immediately surfaces in many reAfrikanized minds when thinking about this oracle is the growing presence of gender confusion in the Afrikan community. Of course, it would be easy to also identify other, lesser, forms of self-negation[126] spawned under the pressure of self-denial. Black-on-Black violence, negroitis, extreme individualism and conspicuous consumption are a few. But none come close individually in taking us away from ourselves.[127]

I will not covet others' property addresses a vice which erodes trust and respect between individuals. Just as wanting what is not ours that we have not worked for, or that we should not have works against good character so, too, does creating an atmosphere where want generates covetousness.

> Be generous as long as you live. What goes into the storehouse should come out. For bread is made to be shared. Those whose bellies are empty turn into accusers and those who are deprived become opponents. See that none such as these are your neighbors. Generosity is a memorial for those who show it, long after they have departed.[128]

We must develop a mind that distinguishes needs from wants and weighs each according to its consequences for our liberation struggles. That which does not serve to promote and/or works against our liberation must be "discarded."

At the same time, we must also value what we already have, searching for a liberating purpose in each thing, throwing away only that which serves our enemies. We must thoroughly count each blessing, carefully judging its contribution to our liberation, empowerment and sovereignty. If, then, we discover we need more than what we already have, we should be willing to independently work harder to acquire it.[129] This desire and will to do the work necessary to achieve what we need for self, by self, or in conjunction with other warriors having a shared need, is a mark of a warrior's maturity.

Of the above oracles, there are none which european people have not systematically and flagrantly disobeyed. Not one have they not been perfect in its opposite. And it is the spread of their mastery of every abnormal, evil and disruptive thing into our communities with which we are now having to contend.

Again, we are not perfect. However, as ourstorically measured along the continuum of virtues and vices, we have diligently worked to concentrate our lives at the virtuous end of the spectrum of all possible values. More than ample evidence of this can be found throughout our literature, spoken and written. Even our fall from grace reflects this virtuous personality.

There was a fall, several in fact. The laws of social physics tell us that any fall requires a previous height. And ours was from a great height. In its historical depravity, european culture and society exhibit no such heightened moral state, before, during or after their multiple implosive convulsions, from which to descend.

Neophyte Rules

According to George G.M. James' study of the Kemetic Mystery System,[130] there was a basic set of rules that neophytes must learn and become if they are to mature into living embodiments of the god force within. Nothing short of the mastery of these rules would elevate their minds to a level where they could begin to comprehend and fully immerse themselves in the wholistic, multi-disciplinary understanding required for great thinking.[131]

This cultivation of the mind, body and soul required decades of quietly, attentively, inquisitively sitting at the feet of those who had long mastered the subject matter and were infinitely wise in the Way of Afrikan people. This psychic elevation demanded minds capable of intensely studying the materials and Universe from which this knowledge was systematically gleaned over protracted periods of precious time. It called for minds with a vast capacity and the patience to meticulously devote thought, over and over again, to what had been learned but had yet to be refined and adapted to novel situations, conditions and circumstances. And this divine cultivation required the extraordinary meditative ability that is indispensable in stilling the body and quieting the mind so that creative thought could freely flow and appease the spirit within. Only such an intense and prolonged disciplining of self could have facilitated the natural manifestation of a priestly character.

In the end, a master stood, in all ways inseparable from his people. He religiously practiced the art of good speech. And, always, he exhibited good character in all facets of life.

There is no question that the Kemetic Mystery System was a way of learning that fit the sacred, higher planes of the Afrikan mind. It required the kind of unselfish, enthusiastic devotion to learning of self, on behalf of community and nation, that remains unsurpassed by any people to date.

The following is the collection of rules every neophyte to the Kemetic Mystery System was given in order to begin the priest's journey of learning which, for the most determined, extended over an intense forty years and, then, continued throughout life. In keeping with the purpose of this book, we will address these rules within the contemporary context of Afrikan warriorhood. The neophyte must:

I. Control his thoughts

Sometimes, warriors intent on being Afrikan, feel that we are in a battle for our sanity against ourselves. That voice and video projector softwired[132] into our heads seem to be on auto pilot, determined to force us to embrace nonAfrikan thoughts and images. At times, it can be most distracting and demoralizing, having to spend so much time and energy fighting against an insanity-driven rogue lower mind. Even worse, as we progressively become more Afrikan centered, this "mind," socially forced on Afrikans through an anti-Afrikan interpretation of reality and self, which in Sigmund Freud's terms might be called the id,[133] becomes more determined and disrespectful. It becomes like a disgruntled bad habit clinging desperately to its formerly compliant host.

Knowing the evolution of lost souls into warriors,

however, gives us good reason to take this desperation as a sign of impending doom for this wayward ego and victory for our ReAfrikanizing spirits. Its escalating reaction to our fight for psychological liberation signal's the ego's recognition that it is under assault by an awakening Afrikan consciousness. And it is determined to maintain its parasitic hold over us.

It may be comforting to know that these irritating disturbances in our steady movement toward Afrikan peace will dramatically decrease with every focused effort we make to wean ourselves of european insanity. Affirmations of who we are, repeated with each violation of our sensibilities by our lower mind, are effective defenses against depression or relapse. Bear in mind Nana Garvey's instruction to "let no voice but your own speak to you from the depths." His wisdom must be made operational in the deepest recesses of our consciousnesses if we are to be free warriors.

We should not fault ourselves for the difficulty of gaining release from the quicksand of insanity. It comes with the territory of "deyuruguization." Recognize that, to some degree, all warriors are recovering addicts whose minds were held captive by the drug of european insanity. In the whole of this wretched world, very few remain unscathed. And with dealers all around, it is an addiction hard to fully break. But, with a curing knowledge of self, sufficient doses of a warrior's awareness and a loving, caring patience, in time, the distractions will stop. We will again be free within ourselves.

II. Control his actions

In a world of sugar and other chemical additives, many of us have become unable to focus our bodies or minds. And the removal of self-discipline through spoilage, supported by a media which has taken erratic imagery (rapidly changing television and movie scenes purposely shot with cameras held unsteadily at bizarre angles) to mind-boggling levels, does everything to ensure the normalization of a virtual total absence of self-control.

This neophyte instruction, however, goes deeper in meaning than just being able to control one's physical body (e.g., tapping of fingers, sitting still, staying in one's seat, holding in one's waste until an appropriate time to release it, kwk). It connects one's actions directly to the self-control of one's subconscious as it relates to physical actions. This instruction is mandatory for warriors in this contemporary setting who must co-exist with the aggressively violent and over-sexualized nature of western society.

The warrior must know when to fight and when sex is appropriate. Since sex is discussed elsewhere,[134] we will limit our discussion here to fighting. The warrior must know which battles to choose, not only in terms of those which will be won but also as to the relative productivity of their outcome. This requires thought, not uncontrolled, directionless rage.

There is a reason for the order in which these rules are given. Though the neophyte is expected to begin learning them all at pretty much the same time, they are epigenetic[135] in their acquisition and development. They build on each other, with each requiring at least the beginning of the development of the preceding one. Therefore, controlling one's thoughts precedes controlling one's behavior.

III. Have devotion of purpose

Warriors must remain intensely focused on their mission. They must dedicate their lives to the fulfillment of their obligation to attain and sustain Afrikan liberation. There can be no question in the warrior's mind as to its importance and necessity. The warrior must know that if we are to be Afrikan, she or he must do their part or all of us will suffer as a result.

Individually, warriors are already doing the work of thousands. We are working against those falling outside the circle of humanity (as proven by their historical record, if nothing else) as well as doing the work of the lazy, fearful, incompetent and completely confused with whom we share a common lineage, heritage and legacy. Even though there is much room for joy and comradery, there is little room for play. War is work, dedicated, focused work.

IV. Have faith in the ability of his master to teach him the truth

Having been victimized by a brutal, dehumanizing enslavement, there are many terms which Afrikans naturally find offensive. "Master," of course, is one of them.[136] It invokes a righteous rage toward those who did the unbelievable to convince us of their right to treat us as their property, things, children, toys and targets with impunity.

However, as Afrikan warriors, we must always look to the heights of our civilization for real meaning in words and the truth. For our Ancestors, who knew the source and value of wisdom accumulated through experience, master, as a title given to those whom we honored for their knowledge and wisdom, was not an insult. Like jegna, it was a great honor, not only to be one but also to sit at one's feet. Masters were those who were adept in the knowledge bases of their areas of study, a knowledge they were guided toward by the masters who had preceded them and at whose feet they sat.

A master was also a most humble individual who had advanced their intellect responsibly, selflessly using it to expand and make the knowledge base of our people more useful. Humility necessarily made masters "sharers."[137] In the Afrikan mind, a master is someone diametrically opposed in every meaningful way to the european's concept of master, before, during and after our enslavement.[138]

According to the Afrikan tradition, masters are those with whom you can trust your mind. Their reputations precede them. Their wisdom verifies the strength of their genius. Easily, they expose your untapped genius to you through you.

Warriors should only allow the voice of Afrikan wisdom to instruct them. If we do not trust the wisdom, politics or intent of the one instructing us in the Afrikan Way, then we should not allow him or her to inform us.

Another qualification here, because of where we are now, is that too many warriors (as neophytes) will have to do most of the footwork (research and study) of acquiring wisdom on their own. Significant numbers of us will even be forced to do it without the assistance of peers or an age group or rites programs. Worst of all is that most will be without able masters whose wisdom they respect and at whose feet they can sit. For many, the only master they may ever become acquainted with will be between the pages of our classics.[139]

But, for the conscious, eager and willing among this group of warriors, these issues are not deterrents. They know that "those who know what to do with the knowledge will know how to get it."[140] Moreover, they know that struggle strengthens and striving to succeed against seemingly insurmountable odds at the deepest of personal levels hones one the most because "iron is passed through fire to be hardened,"[141] and "smooth seas do not make skillful mariners."[142]

V. Have faith in himself to assimilate the truth

Warriors must believe in the unlimited capacity and power of their intellect. They must know that they can learn and master whatever information and knowledge is placed before them. Our higher minds will not allow us to make mistakes, except to teach us more profound lessons. However, the inevitable occurrence of these deliberate, purposeful mistakes must not be misconstrued as giving us a license to willingly make mistakes because, then, mistakes become excuses, and excuses have no place in a warrior's creed.

VI. Have faith in himself to wield the truth

Likewise, warriors must believe they have the balance and vision to bring truth into reality, for themselves and their people. They have to believe that they can effectively apply what they know for their people's good. Both rule V and VI relate to self-esteem issues.

VII. Be free from resentment under the experience of persecution and VIII. Be free from resentment under the experience of wrong

Of all the rules, VII and VIII require the greatest qualification because resentment (even though it may be preceded by bewilderment from ignorance) is a natural response to insult. These are also the two rules which most speak to the admirable qualities of mentally and physically self-disciplined warriors fully aware that this reality considers them its eternal enemy.

On the one hand, these rules require that warriors interpret persecution and wrong as acts of ignorance, defiance and/or fear of truth. On the other, warriors must understand that persecution goes with the territory of being Afrikan uncompromisingly. To speak truth in the reality of anti-Afrikan liars determined to keep their ill-gotten social hegemony and material privilege at any cost is to invite trouble. So, given this, warriors should expect to be persecuted for just being themselves. In fact, unless operating in total secrecy, if the warrior is not being persecuted in some way, in all probability, he or she is not effectively fighting.

Nonetheless, the intelligent, revolutionary qualification for both of these rules, is that they do not instruct warriors not to act when being persecuted or wronged. If nothing else, just like panic, resentment clouds our thinking and prevents us from calmly and rationally devising constructive (and, if necessary, devastating), permanent ways to stop the persecution and wrong.

Equally important, once resentment sets in, many find themselves so caught up in its vacuous blindness that they are unable to go beyond it to correct its source. Therefore, the stress created by the emotion of resentment only builds internally to the point where the person consumed by resentment, spiritually, psychologically and physically collapses and/or blindly vents on loved ones and other innocents.

Both rules VII and VIII relate to humility. In the face of an enemy or mentacidal Afrikan, needing to show your lack of control proves to others that they are right in dismissing you. Not only "if you argue with a fool you become a fool" but, for those who may be listening to the argument, "if you argue with a fool, no one will know who the fool is."[143]

Warriors must expend that anger and frustration productively.[144] It must be used to figure out how to relieve such individuals of their power or influence. Frustration must be returned to its source. Wrongful confrontation must empower us, not further exacerbate problems. "Don't let your enemies get in the way of your work."[145]

IX. Cultivate the ability to distinguish between right and wrong

Both rules IX and X concern developing the warrior's ability to think independently. Rule IX challenges warriors to cultivate the ability to distinguish between what should and should not be as a reflection of universal order. There is no *human* society without this, only a prearranged, predatory chaos. There are no men or women without this, only immature children. There is no true recognition of the presence of war without this, only limited shelter under despots.

Only through knowing the difference between right and wrong can warriors do right and know that they are right in doing so. Without the ability to distinguish the two, warriors would not know which side to be on or what to do once victorious.

X. Cultivate the ability to distinguish between the real and the unreal

The same challenge requiring warriors to think independently applies when neophytes are instructed that spiritual and intellectual elevation requires them to consciously gauge the worth of the reality in which they exist. For reality is objectivity defined subjectively.[146] What we know is a subjective decision. Knowledge and wisdom are culturally relative and socially reinforced within that cultural context.

Because of this we know that the reality concocted by the european mind is insane. It is a reality anathema to any real form of life – an enlivening masochistic world for itself (where self-inflicted pain attests to life/emotional existence) and an insufferably sadistic one for all others (where power over noneuropeans gives substance to their delusion of supremacy). Clearly, as so many have said before, for us, the european way is one of death. It does not give life. Therefore, it is not real.

According to these ten commandments, there are six primary issues that the neophyte must deal with in order to improve self: self-control, focus, respect, self-esteem, humility and independence of thought. These issues are basically presented in sets of two, except for the ones of focus and respect.

Succinctly, controlling your thoughts and actions are a function of self-discipline. Having faith in your ability to assimilate and wield truth speaks to one's sense of self-esteem. Being free from resentment under the experience of persecution and wrong relates to the quality of an individual's humility. Cultivating the ability to distinguish between right and wrong and the real and the unreal is indicative of a person's ability to independently think from his or her ancestral consciousness. And, having devotion of purpose and faith in the ability of the Master Teacher to deliver truth speaks to the issues of focus and respect.

Because of the deceitful and false nature of the reality we find ourselves in, the question of just who are these masters in whom the neophyte is to have faith should immediately come to mind. Just who are these individuals who, day in and day out, uncompromisingly live these disciplined qualities we associate with warriorhood? The best answer is that they are our Ancestors, those we have selected and hold in highest honor because they have not wavered in being Afrikan in their thought, word and deed.

And, even now, in this primitive social reality, we know of Afrikans who have consciously internalized and epitomize these qualities. There are masters in the here and now. But, whenever and wherever they exist, masters, in order to become masters, have first studied our uncompromised traditions as if our very sanity depended on it and, then, meticulously applied their meanings and intent in their lives.

In closing our discussion of these rules, it must be said that all of us who aspire to become our Ancestors are neophytes to our traditions. Each of us has to hold these rules as the fundamental guidelines in our approach to acquiring the wisdom of the Ancestors from those who have studied and have the capacity to teach through example what they know.

As aspiring Afrikans, we must adopt a sincerely humble mentality in this respect. Humility, *practiced* in earnest among those who are genuinely selfless, is not a demeaning quality in our tradition.[147] In fact, according to our Ancestors, "The strong arm is not weakened by being uncovered. And the back is not broken by bending it *in respect*."[148]

In spite of what this alien reality we subsist in tells us, we must always remember that the characteristics we are speaking of here are universal virtues. And at the heart of all virtues is a bed of humility. There must be a substantial presence of humility in all Afrikan warriors, lest arrogance confound us. There must be a deep and abiding love for that inner sense of self that honors Afrikan people.

If we are to be Afrikan, we must follow the Afrikan path of righteousness while being able to discern who is worthy of our studied devotion. We must be unconditionally critical, based on who we know we are as Afrikan people, of who qualifies as a Master Teacher. At the same time, we must take time to determine who should be ignored and dismissed based on this criteria as measured by their obedience to these rules in our community.

Those who literally are our Ancestors, in the wisdom of their thoughts, words and deeds should be, in all ways, honored accordingly. Those who know and may be able to well articulate our Ancestors' thoughts, but who act counter to them, should be responded to accordingly. Our respect for them must be moderated based on the extent of their compromise. We can embrace the knowledge they have brought, but not sit at their feet. Without question, those who twist our nyansasem (wise words) to fit their willful submission to eureason must be outrightly dismissed.

As in our study of all things ancient and Afrikan, we must always remain cognizant of the fact that our Ancestors came into their realization of universal truth in the absence of a nation of despiritualized beings dedicated to bringing chaos. It is not possible for these rules to have evolved as a natural way of being in the presence of an immoral, unethical people. Our Ancestors would never have ignored the nature of a spiritless people who recognized no truth or authority above their own individual, limited self and whose ignorant arrogance, selfishness, self-hatred, xenophobia and unbounded avarice could tolerate no boundaries beyond those which allowed them to vent their hatred without moral sanction, especially if these people's existence was known and felt by them.

Reverence

In *The Heartbeat of Indigenous Africa*, R. Sambuli Mosha lists six "fundamental virtues" which are highly valued by the Chagga Afrikan ethnic group.[149] They include *reverence* (a deep and abiding respect, love and appreciation for the Creator, our Ancestors and elders), *self-control* (which is a measure of maturity in controlling one's body, thought, emotions and words), *silence and thoughtfulness* (having the sapience to think before speaking and acting), *courage* (our ability to stand in the face of uncertainty and danger), *diligence in work* (willingness to engage and persist in productive activities, regardless of the probability of immediate return) and *communality* (putting others' needs over those of the individual and interacting with all in the community as family – exercising a "we are one" mentality). He indicates, however, that, while there are more of these virtues (or "subvirtues" as he calls them) held sacred by Afrikans generally, these six comprise the core that is found throughout Afrikan society.

Warriors must seriously meditate on each of these if they are to work toward the perfection of their own good character. We, claiming to be uncompromised examples of Afrikanity, must reflect the best of this spirit. And that spirit is invested here, in these virtues.

Of these, though, we will only focus here on reverence because it is the most misunderstood by warriors. There is good reason. It has been mainly used as a pacifying instrument against us by our enemies. It has become equated with subservience to Europeans and their god, a god which mirrors and profits from their inhumanity against our humanity. As such, it engenders a personal philosophical posture specifically designed to break the Afrikan spirit, not build it. Warriors bowed in this way are already destroyed.

For this reason, across the PanAfrikan world, we can make sense of the significant number of Afrikan men and boys who equate spirituality and spiritual submission with passivism. We are not surprised to discover that many have resigned from the possibility of a definitive manhood, fully accountable to The Creator, Spirit and Universal Law. They reject Spirit because they believe it takes away from their manhood. (Unfortunately, some broken males embrace what they misconceive of Spirit to be for the same reason.)

For those whose higher consciousness is strong and connected enough to keep them from becoming fully caught up in the rapture of the thought-deadening requisites of man-created religions, the contradiction of being a warrior without spirit remains a persistent, penetrating frustration. Being acutely aware (even if only subconsciously) of one's incomplete stature in this reality creates a disturbing imbalanced state of eternal entrapment. Nonetheless, ascribing to "religious" teachings that lead to an earthly salvation of an endless carefree childhood, a mirthful, willfully powerless stupor, a sleepwalking[150] amnesia or an otherworldly punkdom is not within the ambitions of our warriors.

However, as we look around, we see that this is not a phenomenon affecting our males only. It is coming to increasingly be felt among our younger sisters, also.

Afrikans subintegrated into european culture have been psychologically traumatized into a split personality that goes far beyond any interracialist confusion making us question whether we are Black or white. In fact, we have been cursed by a tearing away of our spirit from our being. And, under the unrelenting assault of an anti-Afrikan reality, this has created havoc in Afrikan minds that are totally disconnected from the truth of our Ancestors and the justice they demand for their ascendants.[151] This schizophrenia will not end until warrior and Spirit are aligned.

Spirit and mind are one for Afrikans. Spirit not only

brings Afrikan people into an awareness of their origins and humanity. It also connects them with their personal responsibility to the rebuilding of an Afrikan world. Disconnected from Spirit, Afrikans become frightened, "other-directed"[152] individuals, fraught with the same psychopathic apprehensions as their destroyers, only from a more impotent, subassimilated position. We find ourselves being drawn deeper and deeper into a downwardly spiraling abyss of spiritless eureason.

There are many questions we need to have answered about this mind-spirit disconnect and the process of reconnection that warriors must experience if we are ever going to be able to bring our Creator-given talents back in line with our true power. Warriors have to learn that an intimate awareness of our true abilities and the source of our suprahuman power is only accessible through a deep, honest, unconditional, uncompromising spiritual union with The Creator, the Deities, our Ancestors and Elders.

This is what our Ancestors mean by reverence. And, this reverence is a state of being which can only be reached by searching inwardly.

Possibly of more immediate importance because of the unrelenting, malicious assault against our Afrikan being, an unconquerable Afrikan warriorhood can only be realized when we come to intuitively know that, while spirit is the essence of our lives, european religion murders it.[153] Eurocentric institutions, religious and otherwise, completely separate the individual from spirit. They place his or her personal power and self (i.e., communally)-regulated moral sensibilities under the government and mercy of an externally dedicated, supremacist/nationalist vested, staunchly bureaucratic, capitalistic/materialistic church.

A spiritual connection for Afrikans only fully manifests itself when we realize that this lesser, alienating (from ourselves, each other and the Creator) way of relating to a divinity outside us begets nothing more than a growing personal frustration. And this frustration has already too long festered in the mire of the institutionalized pacification of subject peoples.

Only with a spiritual connection grounded in our traditions and ways of knowing can we discover the value of, and give meaningful direction to, the righteous rage we have legitimately inherited from our Ancestors. But along with a conscious awakening of this righteous rage comes the awareness that there is a need to attain and maintain an inner calm and comfortable security within it. Rage, incorrectly directed or left to fester in an internal furnace becomes extremely destructive to its possessor as well as anyone living with, or coming in and out of, his or her space.

It has been said that if only a fraction of our priests were clear on the fact that we are at war and the primacy of Spirit's role in our victory, we would not find ourselves increasingly lulled into this despiritualized, religiously emasculating reality. Though, obviously, there are those who know and intrepidly act on this knowing, they are not the norm among those initiated into traditional Afrikan spiritual systems. And even a significant number of those who erroneously consider themselves to be in the same league with our true warrior priests have not relinquished their european selves in their quest for Afrikan spirituality. Their initiation did not alter the impotence of their politics.

The dilemma inherent in grafting european politics onto Afrikan spiritual systems, however, points even more directly to an obvious solution to the spiritual disconnect which keeps us spinning our wheels while being at war. We cannot be both one and the other. Therefore, to characteristically be an Afrikan warrior, everything european must be stripped of its barnacle-like hold on our spirit.

Righteous models of Afrikan priesthood do not try to redefine the frontlines along non-genocultural lines.[154] They never remain behind counting their beads as the warriors go out to risk their lives challenging an enemy's right to enter sacred space. Regardless of station or ability, they are always in the forefront, always leading the confrontation and pursuit. If physical infirmity prevents them from physically engaging the enemy, then their time is spent sharpening the spears of their deities to assist those who can. These spiritual warriors do the primary work of calling our Ancestors and Divinity into battle with us. And regardless of how few we find in the trenches with us today, like Boukman, those who stand with us are our best models of a spiritual warrior's character.

A Healer's Spirit

Warriors are healers. To some, this may sound oxymoronic. But it is far from that in the sankofanized Afrikan mind. Even when employing our righteous rage to negotiate this insanity, the Afrikan mind clearly discerns that warriors, those who destroy threats, are, at the same time, preparing for reclamation and rebirth.

We are an intricate and indispensable part of the healing process. Equally so, we remove the threat and any obstacles it poses for the return of the Afrikan Way among our people. These two warrior responsibilities are inextricably intertwined. One cannot occur without the other, or neither will be done well.

For a people under genocidal assault, conscious, centered warriors are healers by default. It is those among us who work with others to further pacify us, who further open the way for their brothers and sisters destruction, who are not healers. They are the handmaidens of our destruction. They live to conceal or, at minimum, significantly moderate the identity of this world's vampires. And it is only within the collective delusion of a vanquished majority that they could possibility be made to appear as healers, while leading us into the fangs of death dealing "saviors" who need our blood sacrificed for their salvation.

In *The Healers*, Ayi Kwei Armah tells us of seven rules that the healers of our people must subscribe to if they are to be successful.[155] According to them, the healer does not:

1. drink or smoke intoxicants
2. use violence against human beings or fight
3. call upon his god to destroy anyone
4. go to the king's court
5. gossip or quarrel
6. waste the night, however, he
7. respects those older than himself.

Given cultural context and common Afrikan sense, a number of these require further explanation.

Although the second and third rules are similar in their exceptions, they must be dealt with individually. That the healer will not "use violence against human beings or fight" is reminiscent of the lifelong, unqualified, non-violent philosophy some in our community have held toward Europeans ever since we have been held captive in their destructive insanity.[156] Although we just analyzed this self-serving, mentacidal philosophy in the discussion on reverence, the prevalence of this active willingness in the face of violent threats makes it worth repeating.

Warriors don't pray that they lose their anger. Knowing that it is a righteous, responsible rage, they pray that it be correctly directed against their people's enemies. Warriors are healers called upon to do battle to open the way and clear the space within which their people's wounds can begin healing. Unless or until spirituality is connected to warriorhood for Afrikan men and women, it can find no permanent or meaningful home for them, except in pacifying them.

We should never confuse a true warrior's healing with pacifism. This is a contradiction peculiarly evident within individuals who are constantly declaring that we are at war, and even making credible points about european aggressions and inhumanity, but who possess no weapons to protect their families in a world of guns,[157] knowledge of the physical weaponry of war or methodologies of survival in an unpredictably unfolding chaotic anarchy.[158] The evidence of your mentality is in your action, or lack thereof. "If you are peaceful and give everybody in the world a guarantee that you are going to be peaceful and not hurt anybody, there's nothing you can be in this kind of world but a slave."[159]

"We are at war" is no slogan. It is a fact which those making this declaration must act upon, providing credible warrior models for those seeking liberation by any and every means necessary in a wholistic approach to the war effort. Peace must be an intelligent action predicated on operative definitions of what must be done to eliminate the possibility of others' incursions. Peace is kept, not bestowed at the whim of others.

As wise Afrikans have always pointed out, however, no one tactic or strategy applies in all times and places, especially during times of war. So, while it is important for healers not to be always poised for violent engagement, they must always be prepared and willing to do whatever is necessary to protect that which is right. The brilliant dialogue Armah gives us between the student, Densu, and master, Damfo, in *The Healers* brings out the importance and commonsensical nature of this qualification to nonviolence/passivism.

> "The principle sounds good," Densu said.
> "Would you obey it all the time, under every circumstance?" the healer asked.
> "When the circumstances are reasonable," said Densu.
> "Could you make yourself clearer?" the healer asked.
> "If the healer is attacked, surely he defends himself."
> "The attacker is a human being," the healer said.
> "Is a human being human under every circumstance?
> "When is a human being not human?"
> "Suppose a man turns killer. Is he not more like a beast then? Or if he invades your house, flashing a weapon?"

Densu asked.
"As one learning to be a healer," Damfo asked, "what would you do in such a case?"
"I would stop him."
"Violently?"
"Violently."
"Without killing him?"
"If that's possible."
"If it's impossible?"
"I would kill him," said Densu.
"That goes against the rule," the healer said.
"Not against its meaning, I don't think."
"What do you think is its meaning?" the healer asked.
"Respect for life."
"How can you kill out of respect for life?"
"If what I kill destroys life," Densu answered.[160]

The point has been made that Afrikans consider the intent of the law while Europeans follow its letter. Well, that is, they adhere to its letter when applying it against the dispossessed and uninformed, especially those they have identified as enemies. And while Afrikans first understood that everything is spirit and connected (and have since then lived by this principle, knowing that all is life and must be treated accordingly), we are also aware of our responsibility to protect ourselves from, correct or destroy (meaning using whatever force is necessary) any being that needlessly threatens or actively destroys other life.

It is inarguable that Yurugu has demonstrated a voracious appetite, an incessant passion, for wanton malevolence. This makes them the greatest living threat to life. Therefore, they call for the most severe and enduring correction. Through Damfo's masterful query, Densu makes this point well.[161]

The human logic that aggression should be defensive, not offensive, is the same qualification given with the exceptions in the 19th Oracle of Ma'at. It is only being responsible to Creation for conscious life to take up arms against any life that would selfishly, viciously, wantonly or even unwittingly destroy life.

To answer what is to be done, righteous Sisters and Brothers only need ask: How long have Europeans been incorrigible killers, savage beasts and heartless invaders of our houses? However we pose this question, if we are historically honest in our answer, we will inevitably conclude, forever. And that answer, unless the search has driven us into a traumatizing fear, will cause us to ask another question: How long must we respond passively to their aggressions as if our very salvation rested on absorbing their diseased assault and saving their lives?

The third rule, where healers are cautioned against calling on their gods to destroy anyone, bears the same qualification as the second and can be well matched to the 27th Oracle of Ma'at which states *I will not utter curses, except against evil.* To curse someone, or a people, is to call on Divinity to bring justice, in the form of whatever reciprocation Divinity feels is warranted. To do so is not wrong if life is at stake and correcting the aggressor is beyond the healer's known ability or power, for "Curses are the antidote for curses."[162]

Of course, we know the psychological dependency many Afrikans have developed in waiting on Divinity to do our work. It is a classic descriptive of how religion is practiced among the truly vanquished.

> The colored races are highly susceptible of religion; it is a constituent principle of their nature, and an excellent trait in their character. But unfortunately for them, they carry it too far. Their hope is largely developed, and consequently, they usually stand still – hope in God, and really expect Him to do that for them, which it is necessary they should do themselves. This is their great mistake, and arises from a misconception of the character and ways of Deity.[163]

Sadly, as we have noted, many of the initiated and uninitiated in our community have carried this same mentality into their practice of Afrikan spiritual systems.

But those of us who recognize that we are at war should know better than to expect Divinity to do our work. Healers are always the first warriors in times of chaos. And, at whatever point in the conflict they rise, our best warriors are always spiritualized warriors. Boukman Dutty, Nana Nanny, Nat Turner, Araminta[164] and Malcolm X are fine examples of engaging spirit in our battles against evil – of pragmatic spiritual warfare.

Warriors, themselves, are healers. Therefore, they call on Divinity to assist their charge, not fulfill it. Therefore, warrior healers should never call upon their gods to destroy anyone needing a punishment they are capable of administering themselves.[165]

The fourth rule tells the warrior healer to never go to the king's court. Never go "to any place where men go to seek power over other men."

> Whoever serves royalty serves the disease, not the cure. He works to divide our people, not to unite us, no matter what he hopes personally to do.[166]

This is the road to compromise. For such men and women will corrupt your very being in their effort to make you more like, and servilely subordinate to, them. Such is a fair criticism of many great minds born into our tradition who could have benefitted our people had they but distanced themselves from the king's court.

Masters (in the eurocentric sense) attract slaves. Ruthless power attracts the cowards and pretenders aspiring to ruthless power. However acquired, privilege entices intellectuals in need of security from the storm of their fears, disingenuity, mediocrity and who are in dire need of a validating attention. In the analytical end, association breeds assimilation.

Corrupted individuals, and those they honor for allowing them the favor of crawling around under the protection of their vile shadows, become quite uneasy in the company of spirits honestly in the service of the people, even those in what they would consider in lowly service to them. All in their presence must be changed into mirror images of them or removed from sight. Sadly, many wait in line for such spiritually bankrupt opportunities.

> The experience of being victims of oppressive power makes us dream of power before all considerations of justice....The dream of wielding power ourselves....Not changing places with the powerful, not overthrowing them, but joining them.[167]

Healers do not seek power over others. They seek power over self.

We are not here, especially in this time and place, and under these conditions, to waste time. Warriors who understand that they are healers must always be in thought. There is a natural order to the thinking that must occur before meaningful action can be taken to make it the most productive movement possible. First, there is the thought involved in choosing the right course of action given. This thought must consider the record of actions, responses and outcomes and, based on them, what choices remain of all reasonable options. Next, there is the thought that is given during action so that there is consistency throughout the action. And, finally, there is the thought given in evaluating the effectiveness of the effort and prepare for whatever exercises are needed to progress by building on previous activities.

Thinking is an art. It must be practiced to perfection. And, as Ivan Van Sertima so wisely stated, "You can't think easily if your life is a social thing."

In closing, for any who might feel the need to question the appropriateness of Armah's rules in this discussion of the character of Afrikans at war, I would argue that fiction reflects reality. One need only read his *Two Thousand Seasons* to know this. Fiction is a medium out of which truth is told, as believable, personal, instructive narratives. A people's mind is more visible in their fiction.[168] The story of a people can be captured in the fiction of an imaginary character who, in reality, is them. In the same way, the rites and guidelines of our healers, those warriors of the Afrikan Way who have always been, and will always be, with us, are told in a mythical format easily recognizable by the visionary imagination. The only requirement is that we believe in this ideal and recognize its power in ourselves.

The Akan Way

The Akan believe that the *sunsum* (spirit) plays a vital role in the development of good character.[169] From this, they have concluded that character, although developmentally a personal effort, is largely, at least foundationally, the fruit of one's sunsum. They also believe that all individuals are born culturally tabula rasa, i.e., with a blank slate upon which any culture can imprint itself. This latter belief, though, differs radically from the asilic concept of cultural origin and/or infusion where the individuals of a people are spiritually connected, i.e., there is a spiritual lineage which precedes the biological and/or cultural one.

Regardless of the beliefs Afrikans held about "human" universals like the ones we engendered before contact with Yurugu, a study of the goodness that has the possibility of developing in the european personality, in contrast with that which accumulates in the Afrikan one, would indicate that the European is born with a weak *sunsum*, whereas the Afrikan is born with a strong one. We can conclude this because the strength of the individual's *sunsum* is a critical factor in determining the quality of good character an individual can develop.

The "potential" for developing goodness in character is

the responsibility of the *sunsum*. For this reason, the weak *sunsum* offers the individual a limited ability in attaining a good character, while a strong one supports the development of a greater good character. This does not make the individual, or the people from whom he or she originates, innocent. (Future possibilities in the development of good or bad character become the function of original choices. And, we must remember that, at minimum, Europeans made their original choices over an unbroken period of 900 generations of progressively despiritualized cultural, mental and physical inbreeding.)

Here, though, we must recognize the importance of generalizations.[170] For, we know, assuming a divine origin for both the Afrikan and european populations, that some of us will be born with weak *sunsums*, while some of them will come with strong ones. Our concern here, then, is with proportions, as reflected in centuries of genocultural inbreeding and behavior toward others. Therefore, considering the historical and ourstorical evidence, we would have to conclude that the proportion of Europeans arriving on the physical plane with strong *sunsums* and the proportion of Afrikans coming with weak ones are equally small.

Thus, when judging Europeans in this, their manufactured, reality through our spiritual lens, historically adjusted to the record of their way, and doing so in terms of defining the deed, not the innate person, as having good or bad character, we have to be very, very careful. Here, both history, and "that was then and this is now" ahistorical apologies begging forgiveness for the pandemonium Yurugu has knowingly spawned and craftily left growing in its wake, are critical for understanding what must be done. If we are to follow the advice of those past and current europhiliac proselytizers who say we need to discard that which did not work and embrace that which will from our traditions in this dying world order, this is a key starting point. If our traditions are negotiable, as these confused Afrikans would have us believe, then we must use these selfsame arguments in keeping and applying those aspects of it which make ultimate sense for Afrikan people intent on living as Afrikan people when realistically assessing european thought and behavior and in determining how we should now treat them.

From this frame of reference, then, what history would tell us is that we must discard our tradition of solely defining good or evil based on deed, on the act and not the individual, with respect to the European. For, even beyond their incomparable, immeasurable record of evil, we would have to conclude that when they have done "good" deeds it has been for bad reasons.

Rather, acting on the courage that historical truth and awareness bring, we would logically be directed to adopt a more progressive, reasoned, humanist policy that protects good and stringently punishes evil. It would have to be an intelligent policy that weighs both the innate (genocultural) and the socialized equally. Otherwise, noting the extremes of evil historically evident among european people, and in their even more predatory relations with others, we should wholly adopt a scientific perspective based on a realistic theory of innate immorality, as the defining factor in assessing and dealing with them.

As stated, the logic behind this self-preserving philosophical and political stance is to be found in the fact that what we traditionally believe about how humans should treat each other is based on the experience of Afrikans interacting with Afrikans, not others. Some, set on turning our reality into something it was never meant to be, are determined to include Europeans and those like them, who were not present or in our presence as we developed our god, people or person concepts, in humanity as defined by our Ancestors. But they were not here during our developmental stages as a human culture and, therefore, because barbarity is their only authentic reality, do not deserve this honor. In fact, in the footsteps of their mythical father Yurugu forever in search of completeness because of his god-vying arrogance, they have forever passed over their own human possibility.

The Ancestors came into our truths through the scientific study of a Universe. It was a cosmos uncontaminated by any significant levels of imbalance and corruption. The study and enculturation of what we know was not centered around a selfish, hateful, anti-anything. It was without bias and human politics.

With our growing awareness of what Yurugu is, we can only conclude that what we assumed applied to humankind before them does not apply, and has never applied, to them. Or we have to modify our traditional theories to incorporate more genetics, more cultural influence and more (or less, depending on your perspective) of spirit so that we can make ourselves believe that we can be made more like them, i.e., that we and they are one and the same.

Often, in Yurugu's politically scientific studies, when a variable (or variable value) is introduced which does not follow the preexisting, understood patterns of thought or behavior, the assumptions prior to that variable are modified to allow its incorporation in order to obtain viable, testable findings. This is the western way by which science becomes an instrument through which the unnatural is made to appear natural.[171] An insecure, abnormal, power minority's lies/fantasies become a vanquished, submissive majority's truth, and the minority's oppression of the majority is validated.

However, we cannot afford to change obvious truths based on the insistence of some rogue variable (or variable value) when dealing with the yurugian anomaly. For, they represent a variable which cannot fit and has no explanatory power for humanity, except possibly as an irreconcilably different foil. Deduction, not induction, is the Afrikan Way.

Therefore, it is imperative to the development of an ancestrally-defined warrior's character that we not alter our understanding of our Ancestor's Way so that this anomaly can be made to fit the human norm. We must seriously consider the substance of a being who can live and, in fact, thrives outside of natural order. We must know that this cannot possibly be us. Furthermore, to begin and grow in the Afrikan Way, we must be intelligent and courageous enough to consider the possibility of innate evil.[173]

Always, in the face of anti-Afrikan propaganda, whether of subintegrationist or supremacist sources, warriors must remember that we are not just some disgruntled "radicals" refusing to accept defeat at the hands of a new humanity led by pale apostles claiming some divine, universal insight. In contrast to what we hear, we are not simply bad sports unwilling to accept that we lost the game because we are weak or were naturally ill-prepared for it. We are not loose canons or rebels without a cause. We know exactly what we are doing and why. We are warriors in a battle far from finished. Without question, we are righteous in our cause against sworn, inhumane enemies.

Hence, as with the others included herein, the Akan interpretation of character does not apply to Europeans because they do not operate out of the same spiritual framework and have no definite, foundational moral grounding. They can have no moral or ethical boundaries and still be themselves. Using an Afrikan interpretation of reality, it can also be well argued that they come with a weakened shell (spiritual constitution), which is the only foundation within which whatever potential for good character they have has the chance to develop.

On Becoming Human

With respect to how character is defined by the Akan,

and generally by Afrikan people traditionally, a note needs to be made on the much larger concept of being human, an obvious prerequisite to having character. According to the literature, Afrikans understand that the individual is not born human.[174] Becoming human, just like becoming Ancestors, is a process, a long, tedious, struggle that moves us toward a Creator-like perfection.

Humanness is not a given at birth as Europeans would have us believe.[175] It is an acquired state of being, earned through a demonstrated practice of righteous words and behavior.

We can look at Anthony Ephirim-Donkor's *African Spirituality: On Becoming Ancestors*[176] as a guide to the tenets within this general Afrikan ideal. In it, he speaks about this humanizing process as being representable by a set of stages exemplified by the responses of an individual coming in contact with another individual in dire need. He points out that how far a person goes in providing needed assistance is reflective of the test Afrikans use as a measurement of ones being human. In the language of the Akan, *awerekyekyer* is the term that describes the behavior and attitude of one who has become human.

The following are stages leading up to this final outcome are called:

1. *Ayemhyehye*, is an ability to see or recognize that a problem exists combined with the capacity to emotionally feel that something is seriously wrong and should be corrected;

2. *Ahummobor* speaks to the conscious existence of compassion. The individual has reached the point where she or he thinks about what options will best produce immediate solutions. Here the individual is still thinking but not acting;

3. *Abadai* is the stage when the individual begins to act, albeit in a secondary fashion, i.e., she or he provides assistance without becoming involved with the victim. Although it serves to solve the visible evidence of the problem, it is still a service given distantly, from the "outside," without

intimate personal involvement with the victim/individuals in pain and agony (for most people who provide social services in the West, this is the extent of the involvement they are capable of); and

4. *Awerekyekyer* is the final stage where an individual acts in a primary fashion toward the victim. To reach this level, he or she must altruistically walk in the other person's shoes to the degree that you become that person and work with that person (on an equal basis) to create permanent solutions to his or her problem(s), solutions that are not dependency creating. It involves the deepest level of caring. Here we find the true human, which is manifest in the individual who demonstrates Creator-like qualities. Here we find Creator-like communities formed by collections of Creator-like individuals who dearly love and selflessly care for each other.

Of course, we know from looking around this western reality that most Europeans and an increasing number of Afrikans are unable to feel true empathy, much less experience heartfelt sympathy, the quality that is prerequisite for reaching *ayemhyehye*, the first stage in the humanization process. While some might argue that this is not true, as evident from the number of charity organizations in this country, we should note that there is a major difference between face-to-face service and simply throwing money at a problem hoping that it will go away, or at least remain hidden.

Quite obviously, even fewer reach the *ahummobor* level, which requires sensitive contact with those in need. A majority of individuals in the West do not reach this second state and even fewer go beyond it to *abadai* or *awerekyekyer*, for they require a spirit of communalism that is not innate or socially bred into Westerners. Therefore, using an Afrikan definition of being human, most Westerners, whether genoculturally european, or socialized to believe they are, never develop into humans.

oreover, we cannot have it both ways because these two cultural personalities are diametrically opposed. Their differences are irreconcilable and cannot compatibly fit in the same mind. Combining the two within one psyche would result in some form of multiple personality disorder (where the expression of one, at any given point, negates the expression of the other). Both could not be consciously dominant at the same time. An ultra aggressive predatorial mentality cannot coexist with an altruistic sympathetic one without the development of some form of serious neurosis, however concealed it may be. When deeply ingrained as part of the personality, neither of these mutually exclusive ways of thinking can be turned on or off at will at the conscious level. Predators cannot deeply care without ulterior motives. Altruistic persons cannot be wantonly predatory toward those around them without being pressured by a nonnegotiable threat to their or their loved ones' existence.

Furthermore, we must recognize that this sterile, selfish, aloof limitedness is directly counter to Afrikan interpretations of personal growth and development. For Europeans, and those whose greatest aspirations are to be like them, this is to be expected. What is becoming increasingly more evident as wave after wave of new age spiritualists[177] come on the scene is the subtle treason of Afrikans proclaiming a traditional Afrikan spiritual base. While loudly boasting of our proud traditions and our need to again become independently empowered, these individuals remain unwilling to relinquish the individualistic, self-serving "benefits" of an internalized, european-induced mentacide.[178]

Afrikans who falsify Afrikan spiritual systems by acting them out through their european mind are more damaging to our efforts to return to our Afrikan traditions than Europeans who are attempting to find themselves by imitating Afrikan spiritual practices. If Afrikans practicing these systems do not define and direct their newfound energies as if we are at war, then they are working against our past, present and future. They are not only working against our ancestors and the PanAfrikan community today. They are also working to continue our domination by Europeans and the eventual complete corruption and europeanization of Afrikan traditions.

We should agree that there are good and bad in all people. (Afrikans understanding that neither can be wholly eradicated, that both are necessary for change and creation). People make choices.[179] Whether the emphasis is toward the good or bad, people make choices. Whether they are consciously aware of them or not, people make choices.

If we could see individual disposition as grounded in conscious choice, we would be able to comprehend two other things. One is that people, taken out of their natural cultural context can easily be confused in their choices by determined external/alien forces, opinions or ways. The other is that individual choices reflect group choices. Individuals act within the context of the pressures of the group of which they are a part. Individual choices, most often, reflect group choices. And group choices, honored, nurtured and honed over numerous extended generations in time, naturally become embedded in that group's genocultural strain.

In traditional Afrikan society, in the individual's evolving humanity, i.e., her or his moving toward making fewer and fewer mistakes, i.e., her or his movement toward a perfect self, an advantage in choices progressively favoring the good is sought. Goodness is the natural aspiration. Morality comes to wholly dictate thought and behavior.

Not so for the European. Good or evil is irrelevant to personal gain over others and, therefore, group gain over others. Behavior dictates definitions of what is and is not moral and/or morally logical.

Afrikans, as an ourstorical people, know that a person becomes human through social and spiritual development. It is not an honor acquired at birth just because we come here (in the same way that a male or female does not become a man or woman simply because he fathers or she gives birth to a child). It is earned through learning and correctly practicing those qualities which universally define what it means to be human.

This makes it easier to understand why, wherever we go into the socialization practices of traditional Afrikan society, we find that good character is the first and most enduring lesson taught. A communal, respectful people rear their children to love self and act morally responsible to others. Understandably, this humanizing evolution in the individual can only occur within the context of an involved community.

Of course, this begs the question of whether Europeans ever become human, since even when these qualities are stated as admirable they are only practiced to deceive.

We know that the newborn is newly arrived from the spiritual realm, but what came into being in the physical realm must develop its mind toward a humanizing mission that develops over one's lifetime. If we progress correctly, we grow from being an ignorant child to a youth full of information to an adult whose experience has produced a great deal of knowledge to a wise elder and, from there, into an ancestor honored by our people. It can be argued that "a man's life from birth to death was a series of transition rites which brought him nearer and nearer to his ancestors."[180]

When we wrongly define what it means to be human we include people who clearly do not qualify. It is an extremely limited definition of being human when we say that it is characterized by a separation from and elevation above animals. To say that everyone birthed on this planet automatically qualifies as a human is as erroneous as saying that just because a European was birthed on the Continent s/he is somehow Afrikan. Being human as simply defined as being separate from animals is tantamount to definitions that speak to control over nature and mechanical technology. In human terms, or a human definition of what it means to be human, some would argue that the vast majority of animals are more human than many people who claim to be.

Proverbial Wisdom

A people's proverbs are one of the best reflections of their character's nature. In them we find the essence of their interpretation of reality, their worldview, what they consider to be the outcome of any and every possible course of human thought, speech and act. They embody their innermost philosophical self, their reason for being.[181]

Very seldom if ever do a people's proverbs contradict their belief system or actual behavior. Given this, they can be considered an accurate explanation and expression of their spiritual, cultural, social self.

Undoubtedly, self is a communal creation for Afrikan people. So, knowing our proverbs (or at least a representative portion of them) and, through them the creative thought our Ancestors mastered in defining what reality is and should be, is to know our Ancestors.[182] And to know our Ancestors is to know ourselves.

The normal means by which the Afrikan's interpretation of reality has been passed on from one generation to the next has been oral or word of mouth. This is a natural way for an honest people to communicate.[183] Their literature is on their tongue. Their character is bound by what they say.

Language is their literature, written in memories far surpassing the activated capacity of so-called literate peoples. And this "literature" is so expansive in the consciousness that it covers mental dimensions only imagined in the written word.

> Oral literature is not what is written in a book. It is a live, dynamic, participatory experience. Even if one were to read all the anthologies of African oral literature and all the theoretical and analytical works about it, without ever witnessing and participating in a performance of oral art, the one would be illiterate as far as oral literature is concerned.[184]

In many ways, people who do not write to record their knowledge can easily be defined as being intellectually superior to those who do. There is more truth involved, more practical understanding of the making of civilized, human relations, more wisdom. It is only because literacy, as politically defined in the western[ized] mind as written words, is equated with intelligence, and oral literacy (spoken word) has been taken out of ourstorical context and forced into an alienating, lying historical one, that it is deemed inferior. Therefore, people of the oral tradition cannot be illiterate, except using alien definitions and measurements of civilization and intelligence.

Wisdom, also, is best conveyed orally, whether carried through time or transferred immediately. It travels from mind to mind and heart to heart through proverbs, stories, riddles, sayings, through nommo, the spoken word. Information, knowledge and wisdom[185] are passed on in an effort to make the developing individual think and be better, to know more of one's true self.

Proverbs, in fact, are wisdom.[186] Proverbs are the eternal thoughts of a people or an ethnic group within that people (which is still that people) precisely distilled into succinct kernels of profundity. These quintessential gems of their timeless genius reflect that people's deepest understandings about life, reality and divinity. We say that "it is through other people's wisdom that we learn wisdom; a single person's understanding does not amount to anything."[187] Proverbs are communal.

Proverbs reflect the accumulated wisdom of a people in a way that all of that people can understand it. They give individuals, whatever their age or level of intellectual development, what they need of their people's way to know why they think, speak and act as they do.

Though, in balanced minds, quality always outweighs quantity in measures of intellect, in many ways the number of proverbs a people has created speaks to the depth of their functional insight into universal order and the meaning of life in their everyday conversation.

Another point to consider is that proverbs are only the product of a settled people.[188] They come from a people who already have a well-developed habit of taking the time to use their experience to contemplate the obvious and enduring. They are the byproduct of continuous, intergenerational contemplation along the logical, unbroken lines of a people's cultural personality. This is one of the primary reasons we find so few, comparatively speaking, among european people.

Unlike logic, though, which can easily be made to serve good or evil intentions, all proverbs, at least all Afrikan ones, are designed to more positively develop the individual's character and intellect. Naturally, caring for each other's minds is something embraced in a communal, obligatory society as a benefit to everyone. So, in knowing the universal presence of proverbs among Afrikan people ourstorically, any systematic, culturally encoded use of logic to manipulate each other's thoughts could not possibly have been a normal practice.

Proverbs can fool some because of the simplicity of their wording. Yet, these *nyansasem* (wise words) are one of the most sophisticated ways of thinking. The depth of the sagacity hidden in such small numbers of words is unparalleled in human speech.

Ourstorically, proverbs have been critically instrumental in developing better thinkers by challenging them to find deeper meaning in what they see, hear, say, feel and, therefore, do. They bring out the best of the possibility in our thought, word and deed.

To gather insight into the depth of what these rather terse statements about life, gathered and evolved over millennia, say about the general thinking ability in our traditional communities, we must ask ourselves what kind of mind evolves in a reality where proverbs are a normal part of everyday conversation? What philosophical, commonsensical insight is produced in individuals who think in proverbs? What profundity of intellect thrives when the conversation's cadence is ruled by wisdom?

In answering these, we must bear in mind that proverbs

both exercise and massage the mind, continuously and progressively challenging it to produce higher level thinking about even what, to some, appears as the most mundane of things. In our effort to grasp this, it may prove beneficial for us to imagine the life and conversation of children totally engaged and at ease in constant intellectually stimulating interaction with each other, adults, Elders, the Ancestors and Divinity.

Unknown to so many Afrikans today raised in the rote, unthinking memorization european culture misdefines as thinking (where intelligence is judged much more on mechanical recall than thought), to be brought up in a society where proverbs, riddles, parables, and the like are as commonplace in conversation as cursing is in western society compels everyone to greater intellectual heights, no matter their given talents. Imagine being brought up in a world where everyone spoke to you in a way that made you think more critically about the importance of everything and where every adage was given in a relevant context, not just spoken to be said. Imagine the level of inquisitiveness that would go into every thought in every child, in every adult, in every Elder, progressively,[189] before speaking, in a place where the distinction between information, knowledge and wisdom were understood qualitatively. Imagine the general level of intelligence. Imagine the fear and disquiet of fragmented, insecure, creatively incompetent, intellectually limited minds who suddenly found themselves in the presence of a people whose children were even wiser than them.

Imagine critical thinking occurring as casually as speaking and where, in fact, one did not go without the other, where the silence in between words was golden because individual thought held such high value. Imagine this traditional space as a joyful reality, not as one would today through eyes that see any form of productive work as drudgery, where thinking was recognized as the only known way of being and becoming your Ancestors. This is the world that proverbs played a substantial role in creating.

> [Akan] children were also encouraged to acquire the skills of decent and presentable speech. Children were therefore taught proverbs which they were requested to use appropriately in everyday speech....the educated person was the one who could back his arguments with appropriate proverbs. Akan proverbs constitute an important mode of communication; used to develop the child's reasoning power and skill. It had to be mastered if a child was to be fully developed and be able to cope with the various occasions when they had to be used...a value is placed on beauty of speech that might well appear extraordinary to other people. Beauty of speech here refers not just to beauty of delivery but also, and more particularly, to a characteristic speech deriving from both logical and rhetorical factors. Beautiful speech is one that develops a coherent and persuasive argument, clinching points – and this is crucial – with striking and decisive proverbs.[190]

In some places, places still not fully contaminated by the trivia glorification of western media and education, such a reality still exists. And such places stand as models of timeless Afrikan progress. They epitomize the way that Afrikan people should live in the Centers we build as we return to our Way.

In terms of a warrior's character, we have the guidance of so many thought-provoking proverbs: "A good tree grows among thorns;"[191] "A man and his character – even rain cannot wash it off him;"[192] "An empty bag cannot stand;"[193] "Character is good, according to the way you behave it supports you;"[194] "Character is a line on a rock"[195] and "Work on your reputation until it is established; when it is established it will work for you."[196] Interestingly, certain proverbs that speak to the kind of warriorhood discussed in this book are, for the most part, conspicuously absent from collections of proverbs made available to Afrikan people.[197] In the proverbial records which have trickled down to us through their hands, there are few if any proverbs that hint at the reasoning or wisdom that would naturally have evolved in ancestral realities where warriors were given profound cause to consider their responsibilities as exacters of justice and the care they must take to focus that energy specifically and sufficiently against their enemies. And, because of this, one might get the impression that fighting or military operations (military training, combat, righteous rage and vengeance, kwk) were lacking or absent in traditional Afrikan society. However, we should know better.

So, given the multiplicity of sources pointing out the warrior presence among our Ancestors, it is safe to assume that people are trying to conceal and/or erase this memory. It is as if they are trying to make us believe that, except for the bickering between Afrikan "tribes" (i.e., tribalism), we never openly challenged attempts by outsiders to confiscate our resources, occupy our spaces and/or steal our bodies. Either that or, when convenient, they imply that we were all like them, aggressive imperialists,[198] but without their talent for turning destruction into dominance or a desire for turning chaotic habits into wisdom. What is this omission of warrior proverbs but retrofitting the "happy slave" mentality[199] to our "discovery" by Yurugu?

Something is terribly imbalanced and wrong about this emasculating, other-oriented, humanist propagating presentation of our oral tradition. There are ample proverbs which incite thought about every institution (family, education, political, economic and spiritual) except the military. Except among those determined to remain powerless subjects of others' will, the military is known as an institution vital to any viable people, regardless of its form or degree of formality. The cause of this absence of evidence of military thought in Afrikan proverbs should be a worthy and much needed point of serious consideration by warriors.

4. The Range of Possibilities

> It must be understood that the essence of a thing defines its destiny....It must be understood as well that a thing's essence is, in turn, defined by its origin.
>
> *Daudi Ajani ya Azibo*

The range of cultural possibilities of any given people is no different than the set of possibilities available to all other peoples. And, it can be intelligently assumed that the range of these possibilities and their possible combinations are infinite, given the known universe of what we can experience in this manifestation.

Still, the most pertinent qualifier of this point is that of all the possibilities, those clusters of thought and behavior a people select and practice systematically and meaningfully fit together in such a way that they are noncontradictory unto themselves. Any given people find themselves and define themselves within certain cultural parameters. They are/become who they have determined themselves to be.

For example, an extremely aggressive, selfish people does not normally exhibit altruistic or generous qualities (except to deceive others as to their true intent). A gentle people does not value interpersonal violence (except when forced out of their natural minds). The cultural attributes of any particular people logically cluster together at a certain point along a continuum of attributes that capture the behavior of all human possibilities.

Nonetheless, we must accept that human behavioral patterns, while vast, have limits given the bounds of human thought and behavior. This is only reasonable. Therefore, there are limits to the possible forms that different cultures can take. Willie E. Abraham summaries this point well.

> When one speaks of the unity of African cultures, one does not thereby imply any uniqueness. One does not necessarily wish to say that there is a certain minimal complex of significant elements which are common to African cultures and which are such that they have never been seen elsewhere before in the history of mankind. Such a claim would clearly be preposterous. After all, at the level of fundamentals there are only a few alternatives which face mankind. A culture of man is either essentialist or not, lineages are either matrilinear or patrilinear or mixed. There are logical limits to versatility and creativity. Bearing in mind the fact that the world must have seen quite a few tribes in its time, one is not really surprised if at some time somewhere outside Africa, a people have arranged things in ways fundamentally identical to those in Africa. For the unity of African cultures, it is enough that the cultural complex should occur in sufficient areas of negro Africa. Unity does not imply uniqueness.[1]

And although his statement does not allow room for (1) issues related to the chronological order of various cultures' origins, (2) the extent of their maturity as reflected in the degree of completion of, or even actual participatory involvement in, each stage of social development, or (3) their differential longevity, we are willing to accept that there may not be a complete uniqueness of any cultural formation in its entirety.[2] However, we do accept the importance of credible and meaningful, original and longstanding, contrasts in the cultural thought and behavior of Afrikans and Europeans.[3]

As a noteworthy aside, we must also point out that just because two distinct populations exhibit similar collections of qualities (out of the total possibility of human thought and behavior) at a particular point in time does not mean that these choices were the outcome of accident, fate or natural selection. What we see on the surface is not always what lies in the heart. The deep and abiding mentacide among Afrikan people is evidence enough of this.

Nonetheless, this does not negate the fact that particular populations make conscious selections out of the range of human possibilities as to what fits them, at least initially when their autonomy (self-definition) is unobstructed. These selections fully reflect who they now are, have always been and will always be, regardless of a self-selected or imposed facade. Therefore, in the case of cultural sovereignty, as well as in cases where two peoples are diametrically opposed in their qualities, we are forced to look beyond just being human (assuming, for the moment, that we are all human) for cross-inferential causal factors. For, if just being human was the reason for such choices, then all peoples would essentially be[come] the same.

And, as we have already noted, we also have to consider the fact that some people find themselves acting in opposition to their nature. In other words, they end up thinking and acting against what they ourstorically or historically have always been. This schism between actual self and staged self must be analyzed exactly for what it is, the consequence of some form of enforced duress which has compromised their asilic connection. Having been convinced that the Way of their Ancestors is backward and detrimental, they are in a reality diametrically opposed to their innate will (though they may be completely oblivious to it being so) where they cannot express themselves as they truly are.

Cultural deprivation (removal from self as a result of being systematically kept away from true self), if extended over generations, can lead to the point of chronic, extreme "cultural amnesia." In such a state, people easily come to forget and even violently reject and attack any thing or person even remotely resembling who they are naturally. Instead, they find themselves lost in pursuing and perfecting the ideal image of themselves as seen through the eyes of their suppressors, and/or trying to change their destroyer's image of them in order to become more appealing to and, hence, better accepted by them. In doing so, they stop existing in their natural state. They become, in this alien reality, a people "originating" only after contact with alien aggressors – created by them, shaped by them, preserved by them.[4] Cultural denial, leading to cultural distance, forgetfulness and, eventually, unconditional rejection, characterizes the intensified, advanced stages of this lost, misidentified mental state.

Ourstory and their story tell us that nations of people do not willy nilly change who they are or what qualities of all human options they honor, embrace and emphasize. Far beyond environment, a people's spiritual and psychic orientation will determine which end or point on the spectrum of all possible thought and behavior (ranging from pure good to pure evil) they will choose to select for themselves.

There are many possible significant factors contributing to intergroup cultural personality differences. Indeed, if we cannot understand the importance of these differences between where we and they are relative to each other at this time, in the future and with respect to our original traditions, then this whole discussion becomes pointless.

The main point is that where a people collectively sit on this cultural personality continuum (ranging from good to evil) was a well-reasoned choice made long ago in their origins. It is a pattern followed in an increasingly more complex and sophisticated fashion as they encounter the unpredictable challenges of their physical environment and the antagonistic social and cultural encroachments of other people throughout their evolution as a people. A people's culture and traditions tell the psychology of their story.

We must deal with this truth of choice if we are to correctly deal with our enemies. And we must also defend ourselves against the self-serving "We're all human" arguments of Europeans (and their subintegrationist, subassimilationist, subamalgamationist watchdogs), knowing that, in terms of the theory of one human lineage, if it were so, they are indeed an "aberrant strain" (or a miscreation, socially grafted from this strain). Such apologetic, self-serving arguments justify the consistent patterns of inhumane aggression by europeans as no more than a human extreme caused by conditions beyond their control. They make Afrikans and Europeans appear as *only* variants of each other (or, rather, in the political science of Europeans, of Afrikans being simply a variation of the european norm). As evidence, they often attempt to find isolated incidences of similarly insane, normative european behavior among Afrikans or similarly sane, normative Afrikan behavior among Europeans. From the "truth of choice," we can but conclude that the real and substantial differences we find between the personalities of peoples have tangible, spiritual origins and logical cultural evolutions. And, most importantly in the here and now of surviving as an Afrikan people, we have to realize that these personalities are defended by the cultural personality of each people by any means necessary and every means available.

Cultural personalities and, therefore, peculiar cultural

behaviors are not accidental. They carry historical or ourstorical intent. Therefore, they are not subject to change, except through the force and power of overwhelming external pressure. And, even then, they tend to do so only superficially, providing an illusionary image until, and only until, they can be returned to their rightful preeminence, a point accentuated in reference to Yurugu in the proverb "A snake will shed its skin, its poison never."[5]

If these innate qualities become corrupted or begin to become altered in fundamental ways, they will fight to regain ascendancy or will fall victim to destruction because culture is practiced. It does not exist without active, integrated, loyal participants. Therefore, "if we do not know our history then we do not know our personality. And if the only history we know is other people's history then our personality has been created by that history."[6]

When looking at the character of individuals, we are saying that even the individuals who are members of different (ethnic or subcultural) groups which are indigenous to or originating within a given culture are more similar in terms of their actual practice of virtues and vices than those individuals and groups of other cultural groups.

The deeper sociological understanding of this become evident when we locate the power and identity of culture within its parent asili. When approached in this theoretically inspiritualized way, scientific analysis of cultural differences as the basis for explaining various people's personality takes on a less commanding role.[7]

Though it may sound contradictory, the habits that reveal a people's personality, in the same way and at the same time, also account for the variation in preferences at the level of individuals. Other than imperialist multicultural propaganda which tries to give the appearance of true diversity, there is no reason to believe that variations among individuals necessarily negate a core commonality. The possibilities, as to where a people could be concentrated, even covering a wide field of virtues and/or vices, are endless.

No matter where on this spectrum they sit, or the range of this spectrum that they cover, they are one. A people's thought and behavior are directly reflected in the thought and behavior of its individuals, no matter what insignificant idiosyncracies in language[8], attire, diet, kwk. that may be observed here and there. It is said, "Whatever cloth one finds on the vulture belongs to it."[9] Individuals are microcosms of their people.

Deviations do occur within a cultural matrix. However, they do not violate its spiritual, cultural or social boundaries without being isolated and destroyed, or they will subvert the culture. And we know that culture operates as a defense mechanism for its originators, so it will not freely tolerate significant deviations.

Some will argue that, of the universe of virtues and vices, every virtue and vice can be found among all people. And, with few exceptions such as homosexuality[10] and atheism,[11] they may be right. No people is perfectly good or bad in absolute terms. But, relatively speaking, in the differences as to what end of the moral to immoral continuum they favor we can see extremes that easily allow us to place them into realistic, pragmatic categories of good and bad.

People looking for excuses to make Europeans more human or Afrikans less so will use the fact that we find evidence of almost all virtues and vices among each to promote either or both delusions. However, we are taking a more reasonable approach to such classifications. What we are focusing on here is the point of proportion, of concentration, of peculiarity, of higher or lower aspiration. We recognize that, whatever preferences exist, they are rooted in the asili.

What we would call "human universals" can become severely distorted (whether exaggerated or minimized) in one people or another through hundreds of generations of relatively exclusive genocultural evolution. Again, depending on the people who created and are created out of the asili/culture to which they are genoculturally tied, emphasis will always be given to certain virtues and vices over others. That is the nature of choice, whether in the context of individuals or groups.

Those virtues and vices which fit their asilic personality are those which are most profoundly emphasized by each people. Those virtues and vices which most easily allow them to continue to be themselves with respect to each other and other peoples are the ones most honored and practiced. This is evident, regardless of what personality they publicly claim.

And this last point is one which warriors who walk in the tradition must thoroughly comprehend. The distance between what a people says it is about and what it actually displays is a significant statement about the nature of its asili. Indeed, it is a scientific statement about its asili's preference for righteous thought and behavior (noncontradictory truth in the face of other people) or depraved thought and behavior (contradictory, self-serving lies against other people).

A truthful asili genoculturally produces a truthful people who remain like this, even when forced to appear otherwise by imposing, antagonistic forces. A lying asili genoculturally produces a deceitful people, regardless of how well it publicly manage its duplicity.

In that we are focusing on Afrikan people in a world culturally dominated by Yurugu, we have to remain cognizant of the fact that when a people is psychologically severed from its asilic roots and made to believe that it is an appendage of another, it will "naturally" adopt the unnatural (for it) thought and behavior of those practicing the predatory asili's ways as if they are their own. And they will even defend to the death that alien asili's thoughts and behaviors as normal and natural to itself, and even all humanity.

Happiness is a normal human aspiration, a true virtue, at least for the vast majority of humanity. Pleasure is the goal for those falling outside this circle.[12] When happiness is unattainable, pleasure is sought. If pursued long enough, such lower aspirations become an ingrained habit and continue to be the ideal, even in the presence of the real possibility of happiness.

In the western reality, vices are so much easier to practice and lose oneself in than virtues.[13] It is a child's world, designed to be lacking in any meaningful, lasting discipline. A virtuous reality requires internalized self-discipline. It demands hard, honest work. Vices, on the other hand, are open to even the weakest of people. Anyone, even the most intellectually lacking, can exploit. But not everyone will give.A mind without sound cultural roots is easily twisted by the questions and "facts" that others, as well as those among their own who think in the interests of aliens, pose in defense of their so-called humanity. "A mind attacked and conquered is guided easily away from the paths of its own soul."[14] So, even in understanding that Europeans, as indicated by all of their history, are genoculturally evil, some would still argue that we are all made out of the same human genetic matter. They would have us believe that, even if Europeans are more evil, it is only because of accident of the environment conditions of their "cradle." They would even offer the excuse that it is no more than a result of having evolved in a different, cruder, much more savage environment than others.

Eureason would have us believe, if we judge them guilty beyond reasonable doubt, that the way they are is still not their fault. Therefore, it is the mission of those who recognize the error in european ways to help them correct it. How different is this, outside of the more generalized and genetic component, from the servile religious mentality embraced by so many Afrikans? It still keeps Yurugu at the center of our recovery as human beings – i.e., we heal them and, *then*, they heal us. Within eureason, regardless of religious or secular ideology, the result and permanent solution are the same for us.

This brings us full circle to the fact that we are at war, from the asilic (what many rightfully call "spiritual warfare") to physical levels. And, given this, we have to agree that what we will be identifying here as what we should and should not do and be as individual Asafo and Jegna, what should be normally considered as warrior virtues and vices, is based on the ideal aspiration ourstorically practiced and formulated within the mind of traditional Afrikan culture and society.[15]

Because of this, and our knowledge of the irreconcilable differences that naturally exist between Afrikan and european interpretations of reality,[16] we have to acknowledge that those social and cultural traits which we identify ourstorically as the virtues and vices of Afrikan people are not those of Europeans, at least not in the same order or degree of emphasis. In fact, those Afrikans who work to be their ancestral selves and try to make logical, ordered, human sense out of the vices and virtues as they are actually practiced by Europeans in their fabricated, unnatural reality, if not careful, can be reduced to states of confusion and emotional distress. For, in the West, the unnatural can feel natural.

The main source of this confusion and emotional distress comes from the way Europeans so easily practice vices while claiming virtuousness. For conscious Afrikans, these patent contradictions are beyond reason. Yet, when we look at the historical record of how Afrikan virtues, or what should be called human virtues, have been trounced upon, all the while flaunted as their ideal by Europeans, we see that this poses no dilemma for them.

Western and westernized minds see no contradiction here. Vices are only vices when one is caught in the act and cannot lie his or her way out of it. And virtues are only characteristic of them for so long as they can fool others into believing this fiction. It should go without saying that if they truly believed in practicing Afrikan virtues there would be no contradiction to speak of.

As a matter of fact, in the attempt to euroversalize and normalize the exceptional presence of vices among themselves, Europeans have crusaded to euroversalize them as uncontrollably human, accompanied by the use of political science in a campaign to redefine the vices[17] they have no self-control over as "diseases."[18] Doing so completely distracts us from their passionate and genoculturally rooted devotion to vice and exonerates their deadly spirit as the innate cause of their moral weaknesses. Whether institutionalized as human or reclassified as diseases, these thoughts and actions become beyond their control, the product of an insurmountable "original sin." They classify anything they do not feel like exercising a reasonable constraint over as being human nature. Regardless of their disarming rationalizations, we know, just by looking about at the depth and pervasiveness of mentacide in our community, that the expression of weakness, like that of strength, is a choice.

This genoculturally rooted inability to admit to engaging in evil thought and behavior, unless caught, is a very important point to bear in mind. Without knowledge of how intensely this is related to their spirit, many of us make the grave error of mistaking Europeans for Afrikans, in the human, anthropological sense. Several thousand years of unerringly practiced contradiction, in our presence and against us, should tell us our Ancestors were quite sound in saying "The snake may change its skin but stays a snake. It has always two tongues."[19]

For Afrikan people, virtues are divine. They include such admirable qualities as being selfless, kind, considerate, generous, attentive, humble, caring, respectful, merciful, xenophilic and conservative of that which is good, creative and healing. These qualities speak to a generosity of one's spirit and heart toward others, especially those one does not know. They reflect an honest desire to work toward maintaining a peaceful, harmonious, reciprocal order within the macro- and microcosms of the Universe.

None of these take away from the strength of the warrior spirit. For this spirit knows that war and peace call for different attitudes toward foes. Fear and hate should not be the normal, constant way of thinking. However, predators and anarchists naturally view conscious, calculated deception as a most appropriate and effective tactic against such an open-hearted cultural personality.

In contrast with the above virtues, thought and behavior demonstrating that one is self-centered, mean, thoughtless, discourteous, miserly, inconsiderate, insolent, heedless, arrogant, remorseless, xenophobic and promoting of any and everything evil, perverted and destructive in existence would be considered vices. They are everything that Afrikans have ourstorically been socialized not to be. In fact, it is understood that to consistently and consciously be any of these things takes away one's humanity. It causes that individual to be removed from the embracing circle of family, friends, community, nation, Ancestors, Spirit and the Creator, our most distant Ancestor.

Qualities such as being intelligent, ambitious and/or efficient are neither virtues nor vices in and of themselves, for one can be any of these in the practice of their virtues or vices. The merit of these qualities should only be gauged by whether they are righteously or wrongfully applied.

The kind of character one has is gleaned from the evidence of her or his individually practiced vices and virtues. What a person says and does, and what others say about what she or he says and does, tells us about the quality of his or her character. If there is greater evidence of righteous thought and behavior in this individual, then we characterize him or her as being of virtuous or good character. If the opposite applies, we look upon this individual as having bad or questionable character.

Character speaks to your quality as a person, as a living, breathing, socially interactive being. Your character, as evidenced in what you say and do, tells others of what and how you think, of your worth in the Universe.

Character is the mirror to your soul. It tells what kind of a person you truly are. It identifies the affections, yearnings and moral and ethical sentiment of your spirit. And it is best revealed in times of difficulty and crisis because it is then that all convenience and privilege are removed. Not only does adversity reveal this about ourselves to each other personally but, when studying the quality of the character of those around us, we will also discover the depth of the ancestral truth that "one does not discover the heart of a brother if one has not begged from him in want."[20] When we pay close attention, what adversity shows us of ourselves gives us much of the direction we need to better build within. According to the wisdom of our Ancestors, "hardship reveals personality."[21]

A Study in Irreconcilable Differences

When looking to understand the political nature of Afrikan people and the society we naturally create, it can be insightful to study the reason and way of those who are opposite us in the most fundamental of ways. So, let us take a moment to examine a concrete example of the character we know to be so irreconcilably different from that of our Ancestors. Niccolò Machiavelli's *The Prince*[22] can prove instructive in this effort to better apprehend ourselves and what we must remove from power over us.

Machiavelli was a statesman of the european Renaissance who remains highly lauded for his articulation of the heart of his people's interpretation of reality. His magnum opus, *The Prince*, was specifically designed to provide direction to individuals who were born into the royal bloodlines of inherited european rulership, hence the title. This book has long been considered a western classic because of the truth that it reveals about yurugu's mind and experience to themselves. Through it we, too, are able to observe the political side of this being's spirit and indivinity.[23]

In practical terms, *The Prince* captures the spirit of the

european's belief that most, if not all, people are innately weak and sinful. This utilitarian assumption of intrinsic moral and ethical inferiority of the masses gives way to logical conclusions about what should be the normal personal and social response of those responsible for governing (politically, economically, religiously, kwk) toward the weak and sinful. This assumption, along with the conclusions it engenders, is self-serving, self-affirming/validating of mean and dominative attitudes by the haves toward the have-nots. They logically lead to the conclusion that those of greater power must mentally and physically manipulate those made subordinate to them in order to control the reins of social order. This quality of dominance and subordination thinking is evident in the concept of an "original sin," a thesis found dominant in european philosophy throughout barbaric and "civilized" european time.

Any European, or europeanized other, who expects to be successful in this abusive reality needs to have passionately studied Machiavelli's notorious treatise and/or those who zealously practice its principles. They need to have meshed its ruggedly individualistic, zero sum[24] properties into every aspect of their private and public being. Those who do not are bound to fail through their (acts of) goodness. One of Machiavelli's most quoted statements from *The Prince* reveals the depth to which interpersonal savagery is built into his peoples "civilization."

> ...it appears to me more proper to go to the real truth of the matter than to its imagination; and many have imagined republics and principalities which have never been seen or known to exist in reality; for how we live is so far removed from how we ought to live, that he who abandons what is done for what ought to be done, will rather learn to bring about his own ruin than his preservation. A man who wishes to make a profession of goodness in everything must necessarily come to grief among so many who are not good. Therefore it is necessary for a prince, who wishes to maintain himself, to

> learn how not to be good, and to use this knowledge and not use it, according to the necessity of the case.[25]

Of course, thinking Afrikans might feel compelled to raise the question of why any European would have to learn how *not* to be good when that is the underlying nature and most universal expression of their worldview. Surely, there can be no question of this asilic personality, as it is distinctly reflected in their treatment of themselves and, especially, all others. Certainly, we know that their propagandic public presentation of self must always present them as human. So, again, we know that *The Prince* is merely a systematizing outline of their natural way of thinking. Sometimes, who you are is so matter of fact that it takes penning it for the day-to-day, mechanical practice of it to register as a uniquely conscious, cultural temperament.

Webster defines Machiavellianism as "the view that politics is amoral and that any means however unscrupulous can justifiably be used in achieving political power"[26]...."the principles of government...in which political expediency is placed above morality and the use of craft and deceit to maintain the authority and carry out the policies of a ruler....[as] subtle or unscrupulous cunning, deception, expediency, or dishonesty."[27]

Machiavellianism, as passed down to its privileged inheritors (as well as aspirant masses), emphasized the importance of theft, cheating and oppression of others, frugality/hoarding of one's own resources while exhausting that of others (while viciously silencing any who dare complain), arrogant self-aggrandizement, cultivation of relations for purposes of exploitation only, force and brutality as a normal response to challenges from others and an obsession with military pursuits, whether developing them during "peace" time or exercising them during war, and pretending to be good while being evil.[28]

Lying is a key factor to the Machiavellian theme. It is Machiavellianism's most practical application. And although this practice is pervasive in every European social institution from the family to the church, the institutionalization of lying[29] in the political arena is where it is the most conspicuous. Indeed, this is a liar's paradise.

Niccolò Machiavelli's instructions to the governing european elite exemplify this asilic predisposition to prevaricate at every possible opportunity. His thoughts, as evident not only through their continued general popularity but also complemented in so much formative and foundational European scholarship, developed directly out of the genocultural context in which he was born and reared. This ideal was not his invention.

However, lying, in and of itself, is not the primary focus for us here. It is the magnitude, pervasiveness and natural acceptance of lying that is most important for our in-depth, lasting[30] analysis of their immorality or "rhetorical ethic."[31] While it is suggested that his entire work be read, the following quote is a representative example of the cultural rationalization of lying found throughout the book.

> Therefore, a prudent ruler ought not to keep faith when by so doing it would be against his interest, and when the reasons which made him bind himself no longer exist. If men were all good, this precept would not be a good one; but as they are bad, and would not observe their faith with you, so you are not bound to keep faith with them. Nor have legitimate grounds ever failed a prince who wished to show colourable excuse for the non-fulfillment of his promise. Of this one could furnish an infinite number of modern examples, and show how many times peace has been broken, and how many promises rendered worthless, by the faithlessness of princes, and those that have been best able to imitate the fox have succeeded best. But it is necessary to be able to disguise this character well, and to be a great feigner and dissembler; and men are so simple and so ready to obey present necessities, that one who deceives will always find those who allow themselves to be deceived.[32]

In other words, within the European experience of law and order, lying is a necessary evil in a reality given life through innate deceivers, manipulators, exploiters and fools.[33] Those who can only be themselves through the controlling, arrogant, unobstructed exercise of power over others can have no moral or ethical boundaries. Having power over others is Europeans' prime directive. As they discovered in their origins, in order to ensure their success, they must tell others, not the truth, but what they want them to hear. And this, at the same time, must be made into what these other individuals like to hear in the way they like to hear it. As reflected in the words of Francesco Vettori, a "contemporary and friend of Machiavelli,"

> I thought to myself with what means, with what deceptions, with how many varied arts, with what industry a man sharpens his wits to deceive another, and through these variations the world is made more beautiful.[34]

In the wrong hands, "beauty" becomes ugliness. This quote underscores how the reality we subsist in today misconstrues beauty – in terms of power over others and the cold-hearted and violent order that it cultivates. This is the mentality we are contending with today, have had to contend with since our captivity within european society and will have to contend with as long as we are floating around "like corks" lost from each other in a tempestuous sea of "other-oriented" insanity.

The life's philosophy, the cultural personality, the asili that Machiavelli captured in *The Prince*, promoted the glorification of, and personal and national investment in, self-centered, extreme individualism. Machiavelli explicitly stated that individual Europeans, once in power, must maintain it at *any* cost. Having subjects fear you is considered much more important than having them love/honor you because while people can be controlled by the former that cannot so easily be manipulated by the latter.

He made it clear that power, in and of itself, was the most important personal goal for, through it, all of worth was derived. In this pursuit, and the maintenance of this advantage over others once achieved, individuals should accumulate at others' expense, while selfishly hoarding their own resources. What they have taken from others they have exploited should provide the means for exploiting them even further. One's own resources should not be utilized for this.

Machiavelli pushed the art of pretense, of conscious, practiced deception, a way of thinking well deserving of the rhetorically ethical character Marimba Ani assigned it.[35] And, in this, "impression management"[36] is a critical skill. That is, those born of Yurugu, as well as the devotees they have among others, must deftly be able to have others see them in whatever way they need them to see them, without exposing their true hand.

The masters of dominative power must be good enough to fool others into believing in their goodness, all the while practicing their evil craft against them. If such minds are to be secure in their domination, they must always look out for and honor self above everyone else, no matter the relationship. Practices toward weaker others, such as being wantonly brutal and using excessive force, indiscriminately cheating and stealing from them, and mercilessly killing them and waging war and all forms of violence against them, all the while being cautiously reserved toward stronger others (until they can be subdued or overthrown), are considered essential to survival and elevation in power for the Machiavellian-minded.

Others are to be used and abused. And, continued use and abuse requires, at the very least, the destruction of their righteously grounded egos. At most, it entails disconnecting them from their spirit. In yurugu's mind, power is an accumulation. And, as a rule of thumb, this accumulation must not come at one's own expense.

However, again, we must point out that Machiavelli himself is not at fault. And on this point we must be perfectly clear, so as not to encourage the few bad apple theorists among us eager to make him an anomaly. He was only a messenger. And although well known and one of the most famous articulators of their way, he was only one of many such messengers of the european ideal.

So, possibly above all else we know about Machiavelli, we have to acknowledge that there was no contradiction in thought between him and his people. They were, and remain, one. He is simply responsible for an eloquent account of the political logic behind the truth of this nation of pathological liars. He explained the political and personal politics of his people well. Last, but not least, in this statement of the universal applicability of Machiavellian principles among european people, we must emphasize that these are asilic traits, still as powerful and evident in the european psyche as they were before and during Machiavelli's time.

We also have to bear in mind, as was discussed before about generalizing, that there are always examples of individuals among a given people that deviate (*or, at least appear to deviate*) from their norm. But, we must not let those aberrations distract us as we look to identify that norm, those long established, characteristic ways and political arrangements which cut across their ethnic groups and give them definition culturally and, therefore, asilically.

Still, regardless of how specifically we look at individuals among the people of the Caucasus, we should be able to see that they have created a society within which they can freely and justifiably be their deviant selves, a society where goodness, simply because it is the right way to be, is abnormal and an undesirable aspiration for those who wish to succeed. Success, in western society, as measured by the expanse of one's power (relative to others), naturally requires conscious deceit and callous predation. And it abhors *adiama* (reciprocity), not to mention generosity.

Machiavelli's *The Prince* reveals eureason for its patent negativity, and the drive to suppress and inevitably destroy whole, humane lives. It is the literary equivalent of the european mind.

As they have geographically[37] and in so many other calculated ways, the people whom he speaks of have turned the world of truth upside down in order to make their way appear right and normal. All they do, regardless of what they say, is the opposite of that which promotes humanity and the peace and happiness that it would normally bring. As Afrikan nationbuilders, we must always be cognizant of what exists as actual practice in this reality in contradistinction with what the voices championing this aberrant reality say.

Our contact with Europeans has reduced our belief system, an incorruptible one maintained through Ma'atian respect for each other,[38] our environment and the Universe, into entities which appear naturally European. And because, as thinking humans we need to believe that we are not thinking and acting wrongly, we have fallen for and are now diligently promoting the fabrication that what is really the european way is some kind of world culture.

We have come to embrace Machiavellianism as if it were our normal state of being. And this transformation has increased intergenerationally.[39]

5. The Quality of IWA in War

It is my deep conviction that all peoples wish to be free, and that the desire for freedom is rooted in the soul of every one of us. A people long subjected to foreign domination, however, does not always find it easy to translate that wish into action. Under arbitrary rule, people are apt to become lethargic; their senses are dulled. Fear becomes the dominant force in their lives; fear of breaking the law, fear of the punitive measures which might result from an unsuccessful attempt to break loose from their shackles. Those who lead the struggle for freedom must break through this apathy and fear. They must give active expression to the universal longing to be free. They must strengthen the peoples' faith in themselves, and encourage them to take part in the freedom struggle. Above all, they must declare their aims openly and unmistakably, and organize the people towards the achievement of their goal of self-government.

Kwame Nkrumah

The question here is simply one of treatment, of respect. It is one of how we should treat our enemies and how this is different from how we should treat our friends. Before stepping onto the battlefield, we should know exactly how we should behave toward those people(s) who have systematically proven their genocidal intent against us. At the same time, as warriors under the pressure of an ongoing genocidal assault, we have to have a working blueprint on how we should treat each other in war and "peace" because solidarity should be even stronger during the former when the assault is much more evident.

The following two discussions, one on Kwame Nkrumah's rules for guerrillas and the other about Zak A. Kondon's guidelines for students, are offered as guidance for answering both of these questions.

A Guerrilla's Rules

Throughout his *Handbook of Revolutionary Warfare*, Kwame Nkrumah maintained that "discipline comes from inner conviction."[1] In the spirit of this timeless truth, we will here look to Kwame Nkrumah's "Rules of Discipline"[2] for guidance as to a warrior's character. His rules are as follows:

1. Obey orders in all your actions.
2. Do not take a single needle or piece of thread from the masses.
3. Turn in everything captured.
4. Speak politely.
5. Pay fairly for what you buy.
6. Return everything you borrow.
7. Pay for anything you damage.
8. Do not hit or swear at people.
9. Do not damage crops.
10. Do not take liberties with women.

11. Do not ill-treat captives.
12. Keep your eyes and ears open.
13. Know the enemy within.
14. Always guide and protect the children.
15. Always be the servant of the people.

Of these, there are at least seven which need to be brought to our attention as they pertain to a warrior's relations with family, immediate and extended.

The first, "speak politely," establishes the ground rule for verbal communications. Respect expressed through one's words toward others must not only be heard. It must also be felt at the emotional, spiritual level. However, because of how european cultural imperatives have been so well infused in us, as we move to change this reality by setting the social framework within which a humane, Afrikan one can be built above and outside of it, many will inevitably find this a most difficult assignment.

In the current reality, it is always easier to be disagreeable and contentious than civil and peaceable to others, especially, given a deep and abiding mentacide, other Afrikans. Sincere politeness is absent in the West. Even when polite acts are expressed, they are superficial and manipulative in nature. Lack of any conscious awareness of one's deception does not alter this fact.

So, disrespect is strongly encouraged. Feelings of an overly anxious, powerlessness, induced by a suffocating self-hatred (to include all who look like you or remind you of your true roots), systematically trickle down[3] from the have-nots to those having even less in the form of an insensitive, pain-giving, displaced anger. Recipients of pain from above seek release from this maddening victimization through passing on their pain to those below them in even more dispairingly, violent forms.

Subconsciously, they believe that the pain and discomfort they feel can only be exorcized by passing it on to those in even lesser positions. Release is achieved through an unrestrained exercise of a mean-spirited power over others. We call this "trickle-down disrespect."

Trickle-down disrespect is most evident publicly among those socially and culturally depressed groups who view themselves as the least powerful.[4] It is the nature of the social relations they subsist in, and a cultural predisposition calling for the deliberate oppression of others, that makes them so easily lean toward venting their frustration over being oppressed on those of their own who are even less able to defend themselves from those who should be the first to love them. In their fear-ridden minds, they dare not confront their oppressors.

In other words, the blatant disrespect expressed by the dominant group toward the disempowered in a supremacist based social and cultural hierarchy is held up as the norm for human relations by those desperately in search of identity and self-control to an even greater degree than the empowered. What is used against the relatively most privileged of the disempowered group is, in turn, practiced in its worst possible form against those like them whose relative disadvantage permits their disrespect.

Disrespect and arrogance become the primary unspoken means of gaining and elevating one's self-esteem among the disempowered. Wave after cascading wave of disrespect crushes down on more and more victimizable layers of wretched victims. It is mentacide's killing fields.

Of all forms of society, Yurugu's stands as the best model of this progressive downward depression of sympathetic human spirit. For it is here where we find the world's most definite, devastating record of pervasive arrogant, privileged, brutal (wanton and controlled) domination through an institutionalized venting of frustration against those made to believe that they are less powerful. And, it is here where we find a deliberate, unbroken record of less powerful groups and individuals releasing their pent-up anxieties against any groups or individuals viewed as less powerful than they, and so on and so on and so on.

But, this is to be expected. Logic would dictate against any other course for relations in a despiritualized, mindlessly predatory, individualistic, materialistic society.

Interestingly, the reasons those at the top vent is quite different than those at the bottom. Those above act to maintain their supremacy and privilege, while those below act to gain worth and identity. Amos N. Wilson well explains this tendency at both ends of the privilege spectrum well in his introductory chapter of *Black-on-Black Violence*. Though, along with his other works, it should be read in its entirety, here he explains this phenomena:

> White supremacy by its very nature and intent requires the continuing oppression and subordination of African peoples and, in time, may require their very lives. Subordination of a people requires that that people in some way or ways be violated, dehumanized, humiliated, and that some type of violence be perpetrated against them. The violently oppressed react violently to their oppression. When their reactionary violence, their retaliatory or defensive violence, cannot be effectively directed at their oppressors or effectively applied to their self-liberation, it then will be directed at and applied destructively to themselves.[5]

As warriors representing the interests and vision (whether recognized or not) of a largely socially, culturally, economically, educationally, politically disempowered group, we have to bear the force and misdirection of this blind, unfulfilled rage in mind as we work against the enemy within ourselves, our community and beyond its walls. We have to set the standard while, as the Kemetic neophytes had to learn, remaining free from "resentment under experience of wrong" from our own. The lessons must be by example. And the lesson here is that "if you want to be treated with respect, be polite."[6] Righteous warrioring was never meant to be facile.

The sixth rule, "Return everything you borrow," should be common sense in our community. At one time, even in this place, it was. But time, deculturalization[7] and subassimilation have eroded our practice of returning what has been borrowed and, when possible, returning it in better shape than when it was loaned.

Warriors tend to be on fixed incomes or have very limited resources. And, therefore, much of what is at our disposal comes from those within the community. Generosity should not be disrespected, especially when it comes in the form of something that must be returned.

Being trusted with another person's books is a prime example of where this subtle disrespect can be found so widespread within the conscious community. For those of us without extensive libraries, but having a hunger for the revolutionizing ideas deciphered in books found in our private libraries, often, what we are able to read comes at the benevolence of others in our circles who see our thirst and feel the obligation to share. They honor us with their trust and generosity because they know these books will not be found in public libraries for obvious reasons.

Yet, borrowing these invaluable resources, materials being collected and preserved for those yet to come, without returning them is probably the most common offense committed by both aspiring and seasoned warriors.[8] Regardless of the misguided logic that might lead one to feel that the owner does not need his or her book, we are in no position and have no right to judge the value of that object to its primary guardian. Since when do warriors consider stealing from family a worthy character trait? Inconsiderateness destroys from within for "Respect depends on reciprocity."[9]

If we cannot be honest with each other how can we develop trust? And if we cannot develop trust, how can we build anything together of lasting worth?

It is sad, but for good reason, that Marcus Mosiah

Garvey advised us to "never lend anybody the book that you want. You will never get it back."[10] Unfortunately, this has been the experience of all too many conscious bibliophiles. It speaks to an undeniable record of loss and how this sad experience has forced many of our warrior scholars to defensively guard their hard earned and cherished libraries against a theft by those who otherwise should be most trusted with them.

That these, of all his words, adorns many of our bookshelves should tell us that Garvey was not fomenting distrust. He was being responsible to the future by giving those who were building our children's libraries a reasonable warning, knowing of the corruption of the honesty of the Afrikan warrior's character in this moral cesspool.

Set the righteous standard. Rebuild trust through honesty. As we were taught in days of old, return what you borrow. In fact, "If you borrow an axe, return it with some of the ribs it has cut."[11]

The concern with the correct treatment of others is also seen in the eighth rule, "Do not hit or swear at people." No one has the right to hit or swear at innocents. This should especially be the case in the relationship between warriors and their people. Those who are best prepared to wage war should be least apt to use their physical and mental strength against those they have been called on to defend against others' aggressions.

Indeed, in times of escalating terrorism and fear, in a world of ever increasing selfish extreme individualism, an uncommonly respectful courtesy toward other Afrikans should be the hallmark of our warriors. All of our rage should be righteous. And every ounce of it should be directed against our people's enemies.

As with the eighth rule, the tenth rule, "Do not take liberties with women," which specifically addresses our Brothers (but should not be taken to exclude Sisters who would sexually take advantage of Brothers), should not require explanation as to its appropriateness or relevance. However, recognizing the manipulation and abuse which has become so normalized for Afrikans in the chaos of this cultural and social insanity, it needs to be stated.[12] We need to be sure that we are crystal clear about what is right and what is wrong. (Thankfully, since we are talking to warriors, it goes without saying that Brothers should not prey on Brothers and Sisters should not prey on Sisters.)

That said, Sisters are some of our most valuable resources, not possessions. We are not a people who define ourselves through our ability to dominate others through manipulation or might. This is not in our nature, except when exercised to return order to the willfully disordered.

Therefore, it is an absolute violation of a warrior's oath to his Ancestors to use his position, knowledge base, resources, threat of violence or any other means to take from any Sister that which she does not willfully offer. It need not be said that rape, an unforgiveable offense, moves the warrior beyond treason into the realm of sheer sacrilege.

Circumstance has made intersexual exploitation primarily a male issue, though trends indicate that soon this may be otherwise. Nonetheless, it needs to be made perfectly clear to our Brothers, by our Brothers, that assuming the needed role of being a personal guide and model to the children of a Sister who wants a man in the lives of her children, but does not have one in her immediate home, in no way entitles the Brother to anything physical or material from her. Her giving you the right to help rear her/our children does not give you the key to her bedroom. The reciprocity is in the honor accorded in considering you a worthy baba. "The reward of generosity is gratitude."[13] Giving freely of oneself is supposed to be the meaning of voluntarism. It is supposed to express selfless acts from the heart.

At the same time, the dire circumstances of Afrikan men, and the dearth of them relative to their families and our sons (and daughters), should not be an excuse for Sisters to act as enablers to this highly destructive, extremely individualistic pattern of behavior of sexual exploitation in the community for the sake of their/our children. If a complementary relationship should happen to develop between a jegna-in-training and his teumari's[14] mother, then it should be taken very seriously. Commitment must precede all else. Such relationships, as in every complementary coupling of Afrikans, should have a long-term, family-stabilizing focus and not one of being a whimsical, ephemeral episode in a game of serial monogamy.

Along with the concern with others, warriors should be concerned with ourselves as noted in the thirteenth rule, "Know the enemy within." Here our focus ought to be brought directly to the word "within." The greater expenditure of our mental energies must be applied toward eradicating the enemy within. Though our situation requires that we fight on both fronts, clarity within removes the confusion which leaves us unclear as to who and what is the enemy without.

Most of us have experienced the hell of being unAfrikan in our thought, word and deed. Ignorance of who we are is pervasive in the Afrikan community. And warriors, diligently working to recover from european addictions, are not exempt. Deeply embedded , other-oriented neurosis, psychosis and the personality defense mechanisms that evolve to preserve them take time to recognize, stop and reverse.

Fear is also one of these critical internal obstacles which must be defeated if ReAfrikanization is to successfully occur. Certainly, it is normal to fear pain in whatever form it comes. Enemies know this. And this is why it is the main tool they wield against us. Fear kills, literally and figuratively. But it can only do so if it is not understood. Ignoring it will not remove the danger, threat or its use against you. No matter how much you may wish it away, when the source of your fear still exists as a deadly power, then the fear remains. At best, it is only temporarily suppressed. But, when we understand our enemies, the fear disappears. Be clear, our understanding is what they fear most. And, for warriors, if the understanding is there, the solution is there. Resolute aggressors must be removed. They cannot be ignored. Conquering fear requires completely subduing/removing its source. This applies for a people even more so than its individuals.

To "know thyself" as an Afrikan living in this anti-Afrikan reality, we have to be fully aware of our faults. We have to reach the point of psychological lucidity where we can understand the chaos we see within, and all about us in the community, as a reflection of us functioning in another's reality. We must reach the point where our higher mind is systematically engaged in mortal combat against the yurugian insanity determined to define and consume us. Warriors must evolve into our higher consciousness or devolve into agents of chaos through the internecine wars which will evolve within.

This is an intergenerational struggle. And, just as we used to recognize working twice as hard as anyone else as a critical, predictive factor of Black "success" in the white world, we must recognize that this normal philosophy of extraordinary success still applies for warriors. In warriors, the vision (definition of success) may have changed (from subintegration to liberation, empowerment and sovereignty) but the reality it is achieved in has not. In fact, because of what we believe and how we have reconceptualized success, we must work even harder than those who strove so hard for subintegration.

At the core of this victory lies self-forgiveness. We have to recognize our systematically ingrained mentacide for what it is and be willing to forgive ourselves for thoughts, words and deeds committed in ignorance. This is a task of epic proportions, for deep and tragic is the mentacide and what it has led us to think, say and do against ourselves and our people.

All things considered, the greatest measure of our success and our resolve to become honorable reflections of our Ancestors, a measure which offers justifiable reason for self-forgiveness, is the degree to which we work to correct these flaws in ourselves. In this effort, it is instructive to note, as our Kemetic Ancestors taught, that when a reed is bent too far in the wrong direction, it has to be taken even further in the other direction in order to be righted. This must be understood within the framework of progressively removing the possibility of Yurugu returning to haunt the generations to come.

And this naturally leads us to Nkrumah's fourteenth rule, to "always guide and protect the children." Here, he is telling us to make a life's mission of safeguarding our children's minds *and* bodies. If they cease to physically exist, or exist as simply uprooted, isolated bodies sadistically mangled by the insane, they become useless to our liberation. Even worse, they will serve to operate against it by even more viciously inflicting what was done to them on the generations they bear. Whether consciously engaged against us or not, if they cannot see themselves as Afrikans at war for our humanity and survival as a people the result is the same.

Carter G. Woodson told us that "the real servant of the people must live among them, think with them, feel for them, and die for them."[15] This is in line with the fifteenth rule which tells us to "always be the servant of the people." In the context of warriorhood, to serve means to seek out those obstacles to the empowerment of Afrikan people and remove them. It means that we have a sacred duty to be the first line of defense against anything (from hunger to agents of aliens' states) that would do harm against our people. Warriors are here for one purpose – to protect and serve Afrikan people – nothing more, nothing less.

Student Guidelines

To be a student of higher Afrikan education in western society is to be at war with the educational system. It is to be engaged in a battle to remain intellectually connected with Afrikan people, the masses, and to gather and defend the truth of ourstory and Way for them.

Zak A. Kondo's guidelines for Afrikan students go a long way in this effort to politicize and strengthen the warrior's intellect. They give serious direction to conscious warriors who, in developing as young adults, have found their way into the more intensely intellectually mentacide-inducing arena of negro and european institutions. They must maintain their sense of Afrikanity and the additional responsibilities to community that comes with the privilege of being educated, a difficult task in and of itself in such settings.[16]

Kondo's list is long and extensive, so we have selected only those which most closely reflect the focus of this book. Still, because the number we have chosen is considerable, their explanations will be brief. Those selected include the following:

- *Love yourself* – The afrism that you cannot love others until you love yourself is absolutely true. Forgive yourself for all that you think went wrong of your own doing (before consciousness and during your earnest effort to overcome the habits ingrained during your deepest days of mentacide) and work to make yourself into who you know you are. Love of self will bring you home. Look back and see what you have overcome to reach this point. "You've passed the most difficult test if the man in the glass is your friend."[17]

- *Maintain strong families* – Appreciate and build on what you already have and extend it outward to embrace those without. Where blood ties lack the substance you need to uphold a beneficial sense of family because of a unrelenting disrespectful rejection of your ReAfrikanization, fill the openings with family of like mind from the wider Afrikan lineage.[18] No matter where we find ourselves, family is core. Build complementary relationships, thoughtfully procreate and rear warriors of better character than yourself. There is nothing upon which we cannot improve.

- *Stop exploiting members of the opposite sex* – Move away from the european model of oppositional, exploitation-based, attraction. Building stable, trusting and loving relationships must become our primary, and only ulterior motive, when approaching members of the complementary sex. Read books on Afrikan relationships.[19] Think, speak and act in accord with our traditions.

- *Take care of your mind and body* – Remember that you are what you eat, just as you are what you think. Work to replenish what you most need. Drink clean water and follow healthy diets. Remember, your temple comes first. Without it, you are no good to anyone except the enemy.

- *Act and dress in a dignified and respectable manner* – Present yourself in such a way that it commands the respect of other Afrikans. This is not an expensive venture, nor is it one that requires a full Afrikan garb. It only requires using what we have that reflects the Afrikan personality to the best of our abilities.

- *Learn to discipline yourself* – Discipline is the warrior's way, for without discipline the determination to do the right thing becomes easily compromised by distractions which grow into obstacles and keep one's true power just slightly beyond ones grasp. Never stop doing what needs to be done. In this way, you will find discipline. We spend a lifetime fighting that within us which is nonAfrikan. For warriors, *that* is the development of discipline. *That* is the ultimate test of character in this reality.

- *Do not be afraid of being labeled radical or militant* – Radical, militant, revolutionary, warrior – all of these should be normal designations for Afrikans held captive in western society. These are badges of great honor among a people kept from their power through fear. It should be an insult to be viewed in any lesser light.

- *Share your knowledge with your people* – Do not be selfish with what you learn in academia. Give our people what they ask for, in the amounts they ask for, studying further when their questions surpass what you currently know.[20] You have a responsibility which they will define for you if you but listen. And,

> Do not be proud and arrogant with your knowledge. Consult and converse with the ignorant and the wise, for the limits of art are not reached. No artist ever possesses that perfection to which he should aspire. *Good speech* is more hidden than greenstone (emeralds), yet it may be found among maids at the grindstones.[21]

- *Politically educate and organize your people* – Define politics personally. Define politics in actively engaged working terms. Define politics as being your work in organizing a community for action and as acting with them. Do not misdefine it as the work of a proxy. Do not misdefine it as the process/act of giving some unaccountable person with glib, necessarily compromised words the responsibility for doing your communal work for you. Politics is not a vote on a subintegrationists ballot. It is not a choice of the lesser of two evils.[22] Know the historical record of electoral cause and effect. Learn the politics of revolutionary action and make them your modus operandi everywhere you go in the community.

- *Be loyal to your people and never compromise their interests* – Know who your people are and never betray their trust.

- *Strive to be the best* – Never do less than your Ancestors. Measure your progress against our Ancestors' heights. ("The mountain can only be measured by the clouds."[23]) Consider the logic of "Black Firsts"[24] and leave them in the wake of this knowledge. Struggle against enemy forces to build the inner strength our people need in their warriors.

- *Respect and consult with our elders* – Book sense does not outweigh common sense. Look to those who have acquired knowledge in whatever way was at their disposal and who used it to serve Afrikan people. Look for those Afrikans whose wisdom is reflected in a life of action and answers they have given to build integrity into our community. Define elder correctly,[25] for an old negro, regardless of the information that may be extracted from him or her, is no more than an old negro. Elders have an uncompromising record of exclusively serving Afrikan interests. Honor the elder's role in our nationbuilding effort. Read Fu-Kiau and Lukondo-Wamba's *Kindezi: The Kôngo Art of Babysitting.*[26]

- *Rely on resources in our community* – No matter where you are enrolled, stay connected with the Afrikan community. Find those in it who are of like mind.

Find what they have to offer and use it, returning reciprocally. Build that set of trusting communal relationships that so easily facilitate the acquisition and exchange of whatever goods and services are needed to nationbuild.

- *Correct the mistakes of those before you* – Spend the time that others waste criticizing those who came before them, without understanding ourstorical/historical context, making sure that you are improving on the work of those before you who moved our people toward the Afrikan Way. Do not get caught up in an eternal critique that enables our progressive spiritual, cultural and social degeneration. If the conversation produces no constructive action, excuse yourself from it.

- *Practice what you preach* – A student of character is not a contradiction. Do not promise what you are unable, or unwilling, to do. And, when you do something (everything you do should be of significance and in some way contribute to our ReAfrikanization[27]), make sure that you understand why you are doing it (be able to intelligently explain it to yourself beforehand).

- *Become a serious thinker* – Thinking is an admirable quality in warriors. Knowing ourstory, history, the reason behind this reality and intellectually delving into what would be required to rebuild the Afrikan nation, requires serious thought. And deep thinking requires sober and consistent practice. Read thoughts of substance. Build impressive internalized and material libraries.

- *Eliminate negative values and practices* – Stop doing what you know, as a conscious Afrikan, you should not be doing. No longer allow the dysfunctional appetite others have tricked you into developing to rule your choices.

- *Learn to defend yourself* – Martial arts are not optional for warriors. Warriors who cannot use their mind, body and environment to defend themselves are not warriors.[28]

- *Be a positive role model for Afrikan children* – Never let your guard down on your image. The children are always watching. Always be the best Afrikan possible. Always make your Ancestors proud. Appreciate why we were sent. You never know who is watching, who is studying you in search of something positive to emulate or, regrettably, something negative to imitate and use in dismissing the entirety of that which you claim is Afrikan.

- *Teach our children to love and identity with Afrikan traditions and features* – Become involved in the lives of Afrikan children in the surrounding community, not for the sake of your institution's name, but for that of our nation. Help give them an appreciation of their roots through exposure to everything Afrikan with the understanding that they are their Ancestors and, if they love their Ancestors, they will automatically love themselves.[29]

- *Make the education of our children a priority* – We are a people, extending over uncountable generations. If we do not make the time to educate those coming after us with the best of what we know then we have no character and are committing treason against our people. There is nothing more important to a people's future than its progeny. Of course, "You cannot teach what you don't know and you cannot lead where you won't go."[30]

Air differences behind closed doors – Omowale Malcolm X said,

> Instead of us airing our differences in public, we have to realize we're all the same family. And when you have a family squabble, you don't get out on the sidewalk. If you do, everybody calls you uncouth, unrefined, uncivilized, savage. If you don't make it at home, you settle it at home; you get in the closet -- argue it out behind closed doors. And then when you come out on the street, you pose a common front, a united front. And this is what we need to do in the community, and in the city, and in the state. We need to stop airing our differences in front of the white man. Put the white man out of our meetings, number one, and then sit down and talk sharp with each other.[31]

Nothing could be clearer. "Settlement of family matters is carried out by those who are familiar with them."[32] We could learn much from our Ancestors who sought to have resolution, not "winners," in disagreements.

Treat your brothers and sisters with respect – A people who love themselves act in loving ways toward each other. To complement another Afrikan is to complement self. To do for another Afrikan is to do for self. To show any form of respect to another Afrikan is to do the same for self. To love another Afrikan is to love self.

Identify yourself first and foremost as an Afrikan person

– If you are not your Ancestors, then you are no one. Let no one define you outside the boundaries of Afrikan people. Be the Afrikan our people need. It is only when the study of ourstory takes on a revolutionary purpose that it bestows power on the student.[33]

Be always at peace and in harmony with nature – Stay grounded mentally and physically. Our Ancestors talked of the priority of physically keeping in contact with Asase Yaa, i.e., being grounded. Keep others from harming that which sustains us.

6. Complementarity: The Quality of IWA in Love

> If a man sees a snake, and a woman kills it, what matters is that the snake does not escape.
>
> Yoruba proverb

Ideally, apparent evidence of the rightness of an Asafo's character can be found in his or her advancement through the sequentially ordered rites and stages traditionally intended to more firmly anchor individuals into their society. In this specific Afrikan context, the beginning of a warrior's adulthood is initiated through and defined within a mature heterosexual relationship. Adulthood is defined by the intimate attachment that can only truly exist, in any *Afrikan* reality, between a complementary man and woman.[1]

Character is found in following established traditions of what makes righteous people in the Creator's eyes. It is understood within the context of knowing that the millions of us who became honored Ancestors passed down the best expression of our humanity for us to emulate.

Character is developed through following established tradition because we recognize the value of time tested wisdom and the inevitable ignorance and arrogance of youth. And, by youth, we are referring to both age and time. For, as our children are youth to us, we are merely children to our Ancestors. We know that those who came before us know more about who we are than us, and we are neither intimidated nor made insecure by this fact.

Character becomes meaningfully defined and positioned to be transferred to the coming generations when it is molded through the rules, rites and thought processes that our Ancestors left for us to shape it in the Afrikan Way. To observe tradition is to build character because we are following what has been proven generation after generation after generation.

The tradition which builds the character of a boy into that of a man begins at the rite of passage into manhood, which symbolically allows the boy to shed his childish immaturity and sets the stage for his manly responsibilities to all who make up his community – Spirit, those yet to be born, the living (children, adults and elders alike) and the Ancestors. Over his lifetime, a man's character is tested and honed through his interaction with his age group (peers), complement, children and, finally, community and circle of Elders.

The tradition which builds the character of a girl into that of a woman begins at the rite of passage into womanhood, which symbolically allows the girl to shed her childish immaturity and sets the stage for her womanly responsibilities to all who make up her community – Spirit, those yet to be born, the living (children, adults and Elders alike) and the Ancestors. Over her lifetime, a woman's character is tested and honed through her interaction with her age group (peers), complement, children and, finally, community and circle of Elders.

No sane Afrikan would disagree that discipline builds character. And being complements and building family together bring greater discipline to the individuals involved because these duties require them to humble themselves and relinquish their selfishness for a more mutual benefit. Discipline is one of complementarity's most important, but least acknowledged, benefits.

In this character-building relationship, there is a natural sequence of developmental stages. In their correct order, from the beginning of the first stage to the point in the last when the roles and responsibilities of grandparenting and eldership take priority, they are Choosing, Marriage, Sex, Procreation, Family and Rearing Warriors.[2]

1. *Choosing* is the stage where potential complements are located and studied for suitability.[3] It is here when a warrior-in-training's character is challenged to rise in honesty and maturity with respect to her or his own weaknesses, abilities and vision because this will be a deciding factor in the quality of choices made. Here, individuals and their families search for someone who will strengthen the whole.

2. *Marriage* follows this process. It formally unites the complements' families. The married couple understands that they are merely extensions of their lineages.[4] Therefore, their coming together represents a joining of these two families, a joining that is vastly greater than the union of the two individuals, though they are the focus of the marriage rite and celebration.[5]

In culturally-grounded, practical terms, families, not individuals, are married. Unlike those caught in the west's individualist, me/us against the world mentality, Afrikans do not see this as a negative. The complements do not see this as detracting from their personhood. In fact, they recognize that it enhances it immeasurably. In terms of character, the quality of their relationships with others, individually and as a legally sanctioned unit in the community, reflects not only their individual character but, more so, the character of the distinct and newly combined families.

In marriage, the characteristics of patience,[6] sharing, self-reliance, self-control, thoughtfulness, caring and humility are given more room to safely develop in each individual as life's challenges test their limitations and flexibilities more and more in these areas. Our Ancestors understood that "woman without man is a field without seed" and "no man is complete without marriage"[7] in the context of character.

3. *Sex* is a consensual experience honoring marriage. It is the most spiritual, intimate use of productive energy between and within two people. Above all, in submitting ourselves to universal order, it is requisite for procreation.

Sexual violation, on the other hand, is rape. It is a spiritual tearing, damning the rapist and dehumanizing the survivor. Rape is unacceptable as a tendency in a warrior's character. Beyond the irreparable damage done to the person violated, rape is the worst kind of treason against our Ancestors.

Within complementary relationships, the Afrikan woman should be the only safe harbor for the Afrikan man. Therein, for the Afrikan woman, the Afrikan man should be the same.

4. *Procreation* is the prime directive of Afrikan families. We are a family centered people. Therefore, marriage is consummated through children. The complements' mission is to issue in Spirit's glorious, cyclical return through new births into this physical reality. It is our responsibility. Without procreation, family would cease to exist and there would no longer be the possibility of nationbuilding. Only in a nonAfrikan reality could children become a burden, a restraint on the parents' upward and/or spatial "mobility," an abortive choice.

5. The creation of *family* is the outcome of marriage and procreation. It is within family that a woman truly becomes a woman and a man truly becomes a man. Here, we must learn who we are to each other and how to make what each other lacks and possesses work interactively to successfully benefit everyone involved. Here, the tests of character development become intensified, and the most honest, enduring qualities of each complement's character become evident. Here, also though, criticisms can range from the unreasonably harsh or gently constructive and, as a result, respectively, lead to excuses to become less than we are or motivations to enhance our personal power. Here, we discover just how true are the Afrikan proverbs that "Only the woman knows the husband" and that "Other men can see her beauty, but only her husband knows her faults." Moreover, "It is a woman that gives birth to a man"[8] and a man brings out a woman's strengths.

6. *Rearing*[9] warriors is the final test of character for complements. And it exists without end in traditional Afrikan society because the order of relationships never change. The parents will always be the parents and their children their children.

Just as one never stops learning, one never stops developing one's character. The Afrikan goal is to become an Ancestor, an honored spiritual force in the life of one's lineage. Such an honor requires that parents continue to set the best possible standard for their offspring to follow. It requires that they have the best of character for whatever age set they belong, as long as they are here, using that as the primary qualification for their right to instruct and guide their progeny into their power and responsibility to their family, community and nation.

Europeans have no greater fear in the contemporary setting than the consciously centered Afrikan family. They recognize its threat to their standing hegemony and aspirations to global supremacy. That is why we must build family on the frontline. For Afrikans, this building progressively occurs through the struggle of choosing, marriage, sex, procreation, family and rearing warriors.[10] In these, we seek to refine our individual and collective warrior character. In order to reap the benefits, we must grasp the magnitude of both the struggle and the power this building potentially offers.[11]

> ...we must ask ourselves "What does it take for (and from) one person to choose to confront madness?" "What does it take for (and from) an individual to confront an overwhelming assault against his or her being?" "What kind of inner strength is required for one to be willing to risk death to visualize and work toward a sane reality?" Another critical question here is, "What does it take for two such individuals, each already individually assaulted beyond reason, to allow themselves to be targeted for even greater assault by yurugu's reality in an ongoing effort to extract themselves from insanity?" Even more critical a question is "Why would they be willing to procreate knowing full well the hateful, sustained assault that awaits the offspring they have sworn on their souls to provide for and protect." "What kind of commitment, strength and uncompromising vision does this goal of Afrikan family require of complements?"[12]

At this closing juncture, we should address a noticeable discrepancy among far too many of our frontline fighters, something that is critical for the survival of the warrior class. This is an inconsistency that exists between their visionary ideals for us and their personal choices which should reflect them. Some of our fiercest, most dedicated warriors, workers who are steadfastly modeling themselves as examples for those looking for personal guidance as to escaping and living beyond this cultural wasteland, are without complements.

However, this recognition is not to blame warriors for this predicament. Most welcome the idea of complementarity and search ardently for it, struggling to find a suitable warrior mate whose operative definition of consciousness is centered on our ancestral Way. It is the nature of this anti-Afrikan reality, hell-bent on keeping Afrikan men and women from uniting in family, that is at the core of this problem.

Regardless of the forces arrayed against it, while we can discuss the necessity and merits of warriors giving their undivided attention to *Abibifahodie* ("Afrikan Liberation")[13] we cannot debate about whether or not complementarity lies at the center of being Afrikan. It does. And it is not a question of a choice between the two. Warriors must find a balance between the two.

Along with the depth of our spiritual connectedness, Afrikans are the most family/child-centered people on the planet. We place nothing above our children, except that which will bring them into existence and allow us to rear them in the way of our Ancestors. This does not happen without complementary coupling and commitment.

Generally speaking, the two most important variables in this effort to produce and rear warriors are national sovereignty and family. However, families cannot exist as whole, sane, progressive, empowered forces capable of maintaining a sovereign reality without the complementary coming together of men and women. And, to have the possibility of success, these individuals must have committed themselves to each other as lifelong couples sworn to build children powerful enough to sustain their society.

If we are truly nationbuilders, we have to honestly ask ourselves what is the best model of who we want to be that we can/should pass on to our children? But, not really, because we already know the answer. Nationbuilding begins and ends with complementarity. It can only sustain itself and create a viable future through the balanced pairing of women and men into married couples[14] whose priority is family/children first. To do what is right for the children is to build a whole future.

In this respect, those who are setting the revolutionary standard need to ask themselves if their priorities are truly being set in accord with the will of our Ancestors.

7. The Character of Revolutionary Community

The task of nation(alist) building is an intentional and continual process and those persons and institutions that have committed themselves to this task must be assessed not necessarily in terms of success or failure, but in terms of their contributions to this process. Furthermore, this process is not a step-by-step procedure but the focused and conscious application of collective resources, energies and skills to the task of liberating, maintaining and developing the psychic and physical space we identify as ours. Africans in America reside in a social order wherein the terrain of our minds is a contested area. Therefore, this "contested area" is a life and death struggle to maintain and develop a sense of sanity whereby our psyche becomes a territory that is unoccupied by the destroyer's and predator's thoughts and images. The assaults of European images and cultural thought are relentless and, by necessity, African efforts to be defensive as well as offensive must also be unyielding.

Kwasi Konadu

The reciprocal, selfless qualities that characterize warriors in complementary relationships should also be evident in their relations with others in the organizations, institutions and communities we build, inhabit and maintain. These characteristics should define and emanate from the very spiritual and psychological foundations of these institutions and be naturally reflected in how they protect and nurture their members.

Social-Moral Codes

An excellent effort in this direction was The East Organization.[1] It formed out of a collection of student and educator warriors determined not to continue suffering the classic intellectual and identify suffocation Afrikans experience at the hands of the West. They created an institution which evolved into a communal center of education, child care, youth rites programs, entertainment centers, business enterprises and annual festivals. It effectively grew into a whole, self-respecting, self-defining, self-determining community that stands as a model of what is possible with farsightedness and work. Even given its flaws, it is a worthy study in ReAfrikanization and nationbuilding.

Following in the Kawaida tradition[2] and adhering to the *Nguzo Saba* principles,[3] they established sets of rules and standards designed to regulate, until fully internalized, the thought and behavior of its community members. In terms of the men, the following specific "social-moral" guidelines were given in the form of a set of codes.

1. Brothers should greet everyone who comes into the Mashariki[4] in a pleasant and warm manner.
2. We give praise where praise is due.
3. We function with each other in the spirit and reality of Umoja
4. We believe in Ujamaa and the concept of the extended family. We must put this belief into practice.
5. Although we believe in Ujima, each Brother is

responsible for his well-being and the well-being of his family. Each small unit is another aspect of the organization. If each small unit is functional, the larger unit will be a success....

6. Brothers must be sensitive to the needs of Sisters. We must strive to perfect the workings of the household.

7. Brothers in leadership positions must make their households examples for others to learn from.

8. All Brothers should be actively involved with a Sister who seeks or has the potential for growth as related to our Doctrine.

9. We are not players or creepers but Blackmen, therefore we should not seek to play or creep. Playing creates bad feelings and bad images.

10. We cannot misuse or abuse Brothers and Sisters outside of the Mashariki family structure...

The East Organization wrote this family-centered list as a "brotherhood code." These directives speak well to how we should respond to others in our centered spaces as well as broader community. They make an explicit statement about the level of respect that members should have for each other and the quality of the moral character that warriors should normally exhibit. More than anything else, they promote the creation and sustenance of family and its elevation as the center of Afrikan community.

However, there is absolutely nothing about this list that does not apply to Sisters. A companion and corresponding list could easily be composed. Most rules would call for no more than replacing the word "Brother" with "Sister." In pointing out the ease with which this could be done, number eight would require the most attention because "Brother" would have to be switched for "Sister" and "Sister" switched for "Brother." Only number seven would require a more extensive, delicate modification because of the leadership

Sisters have and should expand on. Here we need to look back at our traditions for guidance.

Traditionally, the role of Afrikan women has been very different from that of european women or Afrikan women indoctrinated into westernized gender roles. We must be careful not to allow those tenacious fragments of our westernized egos which have us viewing what men and women do in hierarchical terms, placing value and rank ordering where it has no place, to cloud our judgements of each other and each other's possibilities. "You lead based on ability. You respect skill and ability rather than gender."[5] Leadership is just a word if every individual in the family and community is performing his or her understood role/function. And common sense tells us that the voices in front are not always those who are leading.[6]

The ourstorical record is clear that we had a gender division of labor based on sound, egalitarian reason. In times of immediate physical threat, men are the first line of defense against the enemies of our people.[7] In every compound, village, town, city, territory, nation, the perimeter or periphery was under the watch of the men who were necessarily more mobile and whose occupations created the kinds of danger and toxicity to others that they were naturally located on the community's boundaries.[8] They patrolled the society's boundaries not only because of greater upper body strength or muscle mass but also because they were not physically or spiritually designed to birth, nurse, raise and nurture the children as women are uniquely qualified to do.[9]

Women are one of our most valuable, our most precious, natural resources. Without them there are no children, and we have no balance without either. Therefore, they must be protected at *all* costs. In the words of the Asanti, "If the men are not slain, the women are not carried off."

Yet, our women were no less formidable a defense for us. Their communal responsibilities placed them in the perfect position to protect the interior or core of the community. This division of defensive labor had no sexist component or basis until the advent of the relatively recent historical social disruptions and transformations on the Continent and their insertion of foreign thought and behavior into the minds of Afrikan people. Then, and only then, did an anti-Afrikan way become grafted onto what is intrinsically Afrikan.

Before this, the division of defensive labor was but a sensible extension of the naturally balanced, different abilities of men and women. And these were lateral, not vertical, divisions. Role differentiation had functional, nation-sustaining/building reason. They were not dominative, ego based. Ayi Kwei Armah has drawn us an uncomplicated picture of the natural order within this concentric model of village life and the layers of protection involved in it.

> The core of the town belonged to children. The next ring belonged to old people. Young adults lived in the third ring. The last ring was for military youth.[10]

The primary role of Afrikan men is that of warrior thinkers who seek to map out, defend and heal the nation's perimeter. Like Herukhuti, Shango and Ogun, Afrikan men who stand in this manner are charged with the life's mission of vigilantly operating as a unified, although at times solitary, guard roaming the edge of our community seeking to repel or destroy intruders. Like that of Ogotemmêli's ironsmith,[11] it should be a proud, selfless and productive role that enters struggle easily and willingly.

The primary role of Afrikan women is as warriors and scholars who define, defend and keep the nation's interior pure. Like Sekhmet, Oya and Yemoja, Afrikan women of this tradition see themselves as warriors whose mission it is to gather, unite and safeguard the children, Elders and each other, as well as the men they love. They walk along the paths of countless queens, without concern for what difficulty or harm this brings to themselves. They are our mothers.

Of course, these only speak to two dimensions of leadership. There are many in a family and community, enough to go around for all.

Nepotism

The revolutionary core of a people cannot begin to rebuild within itself without its individuals selfishly, collectively supporting each other. Marcus Mosiah Garvey is legendary for encapsulating this mandate in the self-explanatory declaration "Race First." And John Henrik Clarke also often spoke of this fundamental component of sovereignty. Both heavily emphasized this ageless need among self-loving Afrikan people to be "selfish" with ourselves without allowing it to turn into the xenophobic hatred it naturally devolved into in others.

Any collectively institutionalized effort in our centers of communal power cannot continue indefinitely without the spirit of its self-interestedness gradually expanding as rivulets into the great social rivers which feed the transcendent ocean of Afrikan people. Empowerment is a progressively dynamic process.

It makes no difference whether we look at this essential economically, educationally, politically or within any of the other interdependent social institutions sustaining a given people. Consciously, collectively working to sow and enrich the talents, resources and energy, first and foremost in a responsible, visionary closed circle, precedes all other priorities. And, at the heart of this collective sharing lies a personal, deeply ingrained, obligatory sense of connectedness which calls each individual to give the greatest weight to mobilizing, distributing and circulating assets, while identifying, containing and removing liabilities, among members of their group first.

That this sense of undivided loyalty is especially lacking in the Afrikan community is most evident in the economic realm. We buy so much, but so little from each other. We create immeasurably profitable enterprises and self-fulfilling jobs only to sell them to the lowest bidder. More than ample evidence of just how outrageous our economic suicide is can be found everywhere. Every comparatively racial national and international economic variable is a glaring indicator of how well we have made an intergenerational practice of setting ourselves up as open game in a capitalist system. It is shameful how hard we work to make each successive generation even more dependent than the former on the consumption of others' cheap quality, overpriced goods and services for their self-esteem.[12]

It is obvious from our disorganized, debilitated, divided condition that we exist as an anepotistic aggregate. Here, we are defining anepotistic as being against nepotism (which is the systematic hiring and buying from our own to the exclusion of others) in a self-destructive fashion. Unfortunately, we are against nepotism in a world where nepotism is a positive, inclusive norm for Europeans, although it is politically misdefined pejoratively for us by our enemies.

Being anepotistic means blindly operating within a false state of "fairness," a state of mind which prevents a group from favoring and working with its own in a beneficial, systematic fashion in the face of overwhelming competition from others. Worse still, most anepotists prefer working with these others and favor them as the more important investments of their time, energy and resources.

In the case of thoroughly misguided Afrikans, this condition leads them to mentacidally serve as models of ethical behavior for Europeans. They blindly do this in what, to those with sight, is a permanently racially nepotistic reality intentionally created by Europeans to serve their self-preserving ends. They do this in high hopes of reforming it to the point where they can be invisibly absorbed into the other group.

The word "aggregate" indicates one of the anepotism concept's most defining social characteristics. For aggregate, in contrast with "group," specifies nothing more than a collection of individuals brought together for a particular purpose (here, service to others). Their relationships do not obligate them to otherwise associate (though conditions may enforce their social proximity) with each other. There is no sense of a need for economic, or any other social, accountability. They are together only because those in power force it and they do not have the ability to influence those with power to accept them as equal. Otherwise, their self-hatred would be much more pronounced.

Apparently, we are a people who, having been corralled together against our will by a society needing a sizeable target to hobble, exploit and vent its frustrations against, have devolved into one which willingly works to sustain this imbalanced, unfavorable relationship. Despite hundreds of years of serving as the doormat for numerous ethnic groups of various nations who keenly recognize themselves as one and who actively pursue their self-interests against us, we continue to act more favorably toward others than ourselves in every area of social power. And we do this with an amazing level of precision and devotion.

It is as if by divine edict we have been cursed to serve as the world's scapegoat. We continue to be others' springboard into prosperity, solvency and security in this reality by treating them more as family than our own. And we do this even while complaining of our mistreatment by them despite our family-like overtures toward them.

We exist as an aggregate unable to see each other as one (except as a necessary convenience until we are allowed to return to the fantasy of yurugu's individualism). We exist as pariahs unto ourselves who see no need to embrace a favoritism based on the commonsense of genocultural kinship. It is not simply that we ignore the universal practice of nepotism. We outright reject it as a viable means of upliftment. We work completely against it, an attitude that undeniably earns the label anepotistic.

Regardless of excuses rationalizing why, or rhetoric suggesting the contrary, the evidence is in the outcome – our fragmented condition. As a people we refuse to see ourselves as a nation whose self-interests should override those of other peoples. We refuse to see ourselves as family and act accordingly in those areas where self-interest is best pursued.

For so long we have been misguided into believing that nepotism is wrong. This is not accidental. We have been socialized to not see ourselves and act as family by a nation fearful of our unified power.

Family is created. And nepotism is a natural outgrowth of family because it establishes a self-preserving preference for kin.[13] This, of course, works against the divide and conquer strategy of those who work to keep us beneath them and ours traditional selves.

We have contributed our fair share to this centrifugal fragmentation by pretending each other's invisibility. As with our distrust of genetics because of its historically racist use against us by western political science, we reject the idea of nepotism's good because of its racist record in western society (in particular) against us. And, for so many blindly adhering to their so-called humanism, the burning desire for subintegration severely undermines any possibility of personal self-love, a prerequisite for operating at a concerted group level.

Warriors, on the other hand, are far too historically knowledgeable to be deceived by the mystifying trap of assessing european thought and behavior at the individual level. We see a nation at work against us. Therefore, we have to recognize that nepotism is woefully inadequate as a concept for capturing the heart and heartlessness of the social network Yurugu has nurtured to hold power and resources exclusively within the ranks of their nation. What their "nepotism" discloses is a paneuropean system which enables them to internally circulate and/or hoard what they have stolen among themselves in ways which preserve them as a sovereign people without giving the appearance of conscious intent.

The terms "genocultural favoritism" or "exclusionary nepotism" would more appropriately describe how they selfishly think and act for themselves *and, especially, against others* for a competitive advantage in the global arena of nationalist, imperialist competition.

Though often hidden from untrained eyes, a racist, genoculture-based nepotism, or rather race-based favoritism, is universally rabid among Europeans. Only in a relatively few cases where a benevolent integrationist/multicultural image is more politically judicious publicly is it not evident. Any lineage (a spirit-bloodline of genocultural descent) with an insatiable taste for the ill-gotten power of racist supremacy, far surpasses the simple concept of nepotism. Such a lineage consistently moves in a warlike fashion in its dealings with all others.

If we are to survive and nationbuild alongside this aberrant, caustic reality, we must be inclusionary among ourselves first and foremost. Being the most targeted for exclusionist policy and practice by Europeans, and every other nation or ethnicity which has no ethical issues with capitalizing on the "trickle down disrespect" of Afrikan people sanctioned by the european lead, makes this offensive-defensive strategy toward Afrikan progress not only logical but necessary.

At the same time, because we are not extreme individualists, adopting a self-interested approach to national solvency requires the rejection of any individually self-serving nepotism within the ranks of the revolutionary Afrikan community. And, in order for this to occur, there must be an absolutely unqualified accountability among warriors to the nation and sense of fair play between each other.

These must become qualities fundamentally

characteristic of the new vanguard. When these character traits are prized and honored at the individual, familial and communal levels, the unfair privilege and unequal distribution of duties and responsibilities that can accompany nepotism in a world of self-interested disorder would not be allowed to flourish.

The same selfless/selfish fundamentals apply to whatever organizations and institutions we collectively build to facilitate our nationbuilding efforts. Revolutionary Afrikan organizations and institutions are not members of some aggressively competitive corporate club with the goal of winner takes all. Our organized efforts must be designed to pursue the ourstorically collective vision of our people while serving the immediate and long-term collective missions of their particular constituencies. This cannot be done without us exclusively focusing on us.

In adopting a social, communal nepotistic mentality toward each other, we strengthen the conviction of our reciprocal obligation. In favoring each other above others in the accumulation, management and apportionment of goods, services and information, as well as prestige, power and influence (fairly distributed based upon skills and demonstrated abilities), we insure our victory.

This is political organization in its highest form. And, any group who expects to succeed in this reality must be very politically organized, or expect defeat at the hands of those who are. Resources collectively concentrated are much more effectively used toward decided ends than dispersed ones.

Therefore, and without question, there is a definite need for benevolent, mission- and vision-oriented nepotism among warriors. But, it must again be emphasized that we need the grassroots development of an organic, nationalistic "nepotism." For, nepotism, thusly defined, is just as righteous as nationalism and, in fact, is inseparable from it.

If we just take a moment to look around, we can see that everybody actively practices this but us. Only Afrikan people have come to misinterpret self-love as reverse racism[14] and an open message to Europeans that we are being unfair to them. This confusion is most evident in the fact that most of us will hire them, even over our own, when they will not hire or promote us (relative to their overall advantaged power, income and status), in an effort to demonstrate our love for (i.e., obeisance to) them. It is no more than a public display of social masochism designed to impress upon them that the historical proven need for rebellion and/or separation is farthest from our minds.

Accountability

The importance of accountability to revolutionary organization cannot be discounted. If the members cannot be held accountable, there will be no guarantees that they will not, for whatever reason, begin working in the service of our enemies.

We can neither debate nor doubt this. There are far too many examples of this treasonous weakness among so much misleadership within the Afrikan community during the long night of our captivity in this cultural wasteland. Politicians who ran on platforms of community loyalty forget their constituency. Ministers, many entering that priesthood because of the plethora of opportunities to physically and economically exploit their flock and the harem they so meticulously maintain within, empty their congregations' coffers to satisfy personal vices without conscience. Even independent of their benefactors' direct commands, school and college administrators institutionalize the tracking of their own children/students, already disadvantaged by a fully operational genocultural nationalist racism, into dead end fields and occupations which are out of competition with the children of their masters. Grassroots radicals defend counterrevolutionary ideological alliances with aliens and the gender-confused in unchecked gestures of loyalty to the whiteness and perversion with which they have fought so long to consort and sleep. "We don't sleep at one side and fight for the other side."[15] Therefore, "a scholar whose lifestyle is inconsistent with the implication of his work and the collective achievement of our people cannot be taken seriously."[16]

Accountability must be written in the stone of any revolutionary organization if it is to remain intact, strong and effective at all levels, places and times. Compromise is inevitable in any organization formed against the powers that be, if the members are held together by a common appearance and oppression. Experience has taught us that time and difficulty can often weaken and undermine both as revolutionary motivators. Therefore, there must be a system of enforced accountability to accompany the heart and will of the members.

> The next time, if fate is kind enough to present us with a next time, we'd better know what makes a nation. We'd better deal with our traitors. I advocate the re-establishment of the old African Blood Brotherhood with an accompanying sisterhood – an internal security force. We don't take you to the white man to be punished. We will punish you so well that we won't have to do it too many times. When you do wrong and see us coming, you'll run to the white man because his punishment will be much less than ours. If you talk nation-time, you've got to think nation-time.[17]

What makes a system of accountability imperative at this time, in this reality? Things happen. Finances crumble. Strong workers are imprisoned or assassinated, leading to their movement families becoming emotionally devastated and financially crippled. People's loved ones become chronically ill or their "security" is threatened. Pre-consciousness indiscretions become tools of extortion against those vulnerable to a debilitating shame over their erstwhile ignorance. All the while, accomplished enemies sit in wait to tempt the weary, disgruntled and/or avaricious. Consciousness, often, does not discipline one's personality to the extent that it does one's reason or sense of purpose.

Only a deep and abiding sense of accountability to universal truth, one's Ancestors, Elders, peers and progeny prevents whatever happens to their sense of security, others' loyalty and fair play from turning warriors away from their oaths. It leaves thoughts and behaviors which occurred in a former dead, lost time incomparable and irrelevant to a dedicated record of consciousness and loyalty. Accountability's establishment as the practiced norm makes Afrikans into the kind of warriors we can positively count on in the best and worst of times.

Revolutionary Tithes[18]

Ethnicities, religions, churches and other formally organized groups and institutions are not primarily supported or sustained by occasional superficially considered contributions. They extend their functional existence over lifetimes through the financial sacrifice of their membership. The systematic expression of commitment by their constituents through privately or publicly promised and fulfilled monetary and energy donations over very extended periods of time is their life blood. Revolutionary, nationbuilding movements are no different in their need to be consistently and selflessly financially supported by those they serve. Time and condition do not change this fact.

Tithes is the term commonly reserved for such beneficence. It can be thought of as a form of self-taxation. Those members who selflessly, though selfishly, accept and act upon their obligation to sacrifice a portion of their income to their chosen organization or association do so in order to help support its larger effort/vision.

Whether done in public view or hidden behind closed

doors, tithes keep visions alive. For this reason, if no other, every warrior must accept it as a personal duty to commit him or herself to some form of "revolutionary tithes."

All of these individuals and organizations that we speak of with such pride because of the work they do and the example they set need our assistance. They cannot do our work and be beholden to someone else at the same time.

Have we not yet learned the lesson of economic extortion into political conformity by "benevolent liberals" and so-called "apolitical" institutions and organizations that are owned and controlled by others?[19] *Every* contribution carries a price.

Even those "revolutionary tithes" which come from centered Afrikans has conditions attached, and rightfully so. Those warriors who give of their resources have every right to expect it to be fully used to do the work of liberating Afrikans. Nationbuilding revolutions can only be funded, without compromising their intent, activities or vision, by those of like mind. It is imperative that warriors identify and study[20] organizations or individuals in training/planning before supporting them. And, if the study proves them to be worthy, warriors must selflessly provide them with financial, material, physical and emotional support. Any amount devoted each month to such a cause is not unreasonable to ask. Though inclusive of more than the financial, Hannibal Tirus Afrik's question "What are we willing to sacrifice when our people are in crisis?" is appropo. The measure of quantity is truly in the quality of the warrior's intent. If we want the best, *we* have to help build the best.

8. Character Flaws

Everyone is silent about it. The whole land is in great trouble. And none are wise enough to know it; none are angry enough to speak out and every day one wakes to suffering. Thus, my suffering is long and heavy. The weak and wretched lack the strength to save themselves from that which overwhelms them. It is painful to keep silent about what one hears and yet it is of no use to answer the ignorant. People only love their own words. Everyone builds on crookedness and right-speaking is abandoned.[1]

The Book of Khakheper-Ra-Soneb

To whom shall I speak today? Brothers and sisters are evil and friends today are not worth loving. Hearts are great with greed and everyone seizes his or her neighbor's goods. Kindness has passed away and violence is imposed on everyone. To whom shall I speak today? The one doing wrong is an intimate friend and the brother with whom one used to deal is an enemy. No one remembers the past and none return the good deed that is done. Brothers and sisters are evil and people turn to strangers for *righteousness or affection*. To whom shall I

> speak today? Faces are empty and all turn their faces from their brothers and sisters. Hearts are great with greed and there is no heart of a man or woman upon which one might learn. None are just and righteous and the land is left to the doers of evil. To whom shall I speak today? There are no intimate friends and the people turn to strangers to tell their troubles. None are content and those with whom one used to walk no longer exist. I am burdened with grief and have no one to comfort me. There is no end to the wrong which roams the earth.[2]
>
> *The Book of Dialog with the Soul*

No one is perfect. But, as our Ancestors so beautifully taught us, that is no reason not to strive for perfection. Of course, if done well, there is order to this striving. Internal purification precedes external cleansing. In the following, we will delve deeper into some of the internal issues that affect this internal striving for perfection and, therefore, the possibility of warriorhood.

The Enemy Within

James Forman lists twenty negative forces that work against a revolutionary organization's success.[3] Avoiding or correcting each is necessary if it is to become stable and effectively remain on the frontline. These negative forces include the following:

1. Lack of practice and day to day work
2. Loss of morale
3. Laziness
4. Failure to study revolutionary theory and the experiences of other revolutionaries

5. Failure to engage in criticism and self-criticism
6. Liberalism
7. Failure to exert leadership
8. Lack of initiative and imagination
9. Lack of discipline and individualism
10. Elitism
11. Lack of internal democracy and authoritarian actions
12. Egotism
13. Jealousy
14. Sectarian attitudes and actions
15. Isolation
16. Adventurism and romanticism
17. Male chauvinism
18. Reactionary nationalism
19. Police infiltrators
20. Lack of administration

Of these "enemy forces," with regard to what has not already been addressed to some degree within these pages, our attention needs to be drawn specifically toward warnings which speak to those flaws in individuals which can undermine the stability of revolutionary organizations. The warnings given in numbers two, four, five, six, seven, eight, ten, twelve, thirteen, sixteen and seventeen fall into this category.

Loss of morale: Without morale there is no incentive to win. One's mental state is the most important factor in determining the level and intensity of the energy and work available to complete tasks.

In addition, morale is a critical factor in developing immediate plans, especially those whose victories and defeats will be useful in extending any revolutionary work against a "bitter enemy" forward in a dynamic fashion. With respect to warriors in our community, whether our morale is high or low is primarily a question of our receptivity to the propaganda of our enemies in contrast to the strength of our inner conviction and integration into a dynamic, functional Afrikan centered community.

Several variables seem to have the greatest impact on our morale and, in turn, that of those around us we love. As I outlined in *Centered: Building Afrikan Realities*, they include the degree to which we feel isolated from our blood relatives and/or socially created family, whether or not we feel we are part of a global minority or majority, how militarily empowered or disempowered we believe we are, our interpretation of our financial solvency or future economic survivability, the extensiveness of our study of our Way and revolutionary ourstory, having an equally dedicated complement and children (both biological and social), having ample, existent evidence of the imminent genocidal threat against us and being in the presence of an operational warrior class and collection of accountable, proven Elders/Jenoch.

Morale tends to be high when warriors have a deep respect and appreciation for those they are fighting for and know that they are loved by them, know who their enemy is and believe not only that they can but that they are winning. It tends to be considerably lowered when any of these beliefs and conditions are in doubt.

Failure to study revolutionary theory and the experiences of other revolutionaries: In this warrior's estimation, what is critical here, is not the absence of study but the overindulgence in the revolutionary theory of others, especially that sanctioned by (the leftist) european mind. Even a cursory look at the politics, platforms and philosophy of the majority of "revolutionary" "Afrikan" organizations, as well as their ancestral leadership (or sources of the ideology of those leaders) makes this clear. Though in many ways their ideologies are devised from or built upon the communal/socialist mind of traditional Afrikan society, they are bereft of the unfiltered revolutionary Afrikan mind. This point is well stated by one of our jegna Ancestors in looking at the decolonization movement while thinking about the Haitian Revolution.

> The leaders of the more recently successful and still continuing armed struggles in Southern Africa apparently have ignored the Haitian Revolution. These revolutionary Blacks seem to be more inspired by the Russian, Chinese, Vietnamese and Cuban revolutions than the one truly successful Black revolution in modern history. They apparently never quoted Dessalines, although they have found much inspiration in the words of Marx, Lenin, Mao Tse Tung, Ho Chi Min and Fidel Castro. They do not preach "death to the whites," rather they speak of expelling the imperialists. They do not vow "Conquer or Die," rather they fight to force the colonial power to negotiate. They do not execute the white assassins of the Black race, rather they ask many whites to stay and help rebuild the country.[5]

Again, naturally, the vast majority of those who initiated or served as the ideological figurehead of such organizations are grounded in others' philosophies. We see that in the literature and language they use to describe radicalness and revolution. Most of this literature and language is borrowed (was given) from the dispossessed european left. For example, "comrade," not unlike "nigger," is a eurocentric concept made Afrikan as if without historical referent.

We will never be the warriors our Ancestors are as long as we subscribe to someone else's interpretation of reality, a mentality philosophically embedded in their politics, no matter how revolutionary we may think them to be. This is especially the case at that end of the ideological spectrum where class analysis reigns over racial determinism (i.e., power prescribed by an overriding, permanent nationalist racism) in explaining inequality.[6] If nothing else, class-based interpretations of human relations and social evolution attribute european dominance to a select group of evil geniuses and not to a nation deeply rooted in evil.

For Afrikans, our wretched condition on this planet and our increasingly near total absence of exercised power cannot find resolution in siding with one brother, frustrated and angry over his dispossession (relative to his empowered brother), who is looking for needy, mentacidal dupes to man his rise to power within their family. These alter-elites want nothing more than to unseat their rivals so that they can supplant them in ruling over others. Even though studying our participation in their socialist/communist organizations is instructive, the confusion of those of us who followed John Brown (volunteering as soldiers of one of the enemy's dispossessed warlords versus our own interests and *still* holding him up as a hero for revolutionary Afrikans) is worth consideration. Here is a prime example of our use as others' political fodder because we saw freedom as one thing for "all of u,s" while they understood it as the securing of power over others for only them.[7]

We have to remind ourselves, even in the most desperate of situations, that no matter this or that yurugu's rhetoric/politics, he or she is still their blood, their family. This applies regardless of how similar his/her economic state may appear to ours or how humane or unifying his/her philosophy may sound to those of us gullible enough to believe it.

Afrikan victory requires the study of the strategies and tactics of Afrikan warfare. It has to come, as Jacob H. Carruthers so brilliantly argued, through the mind of the Haitian Revolution as seen through Boukman's, Dessalines's and the whole host of other Afrikans who valiantly fought in the spirit of "The Irritated Genie's" eyes.[8] Our victory can only come through the military mind of Afrika.

And while there should be no doubt that it is important to study others' methods and reasoning, we do this so that we will be better prepared for confrontation with them, not so that we can ape what they know by heart and can more easily be seen coming. Unless our minds are of the european (or arab or asian) asili, then we cannot dynamically expand on their philosophy of confrontation and aggression in the way that they can. In changing times, where frontlines and battlefields fit a different mode of warfare, what Afrikan minds call for is

Afrikan reasoning to devise that which will better work for us under these conditions, not a surrender to an insanity we can never hope to master.

Failure to engage in criticism and self-criticism: Before critiquing others, warriors must look deep inside to see where their faults lie. Once found, these shortcomings must be ordered in terms of their destructive history and capacity and attacked. Yet, they should be corrected one at a time. The worst should be targeted first because removing the habits most damaging to one's character first systematically works to unravel the fabric binding all the others to it.

Warriors must also be humble enough to listen to the criticisms from those around them most concerned about their well-being, as well as those expressed by the larger community and nation (even those who mean us absolutely no good because even ignorance and hatred can teach – as our ancient Kemetic Ancestors taught us, "Everything teaches"). A Tsonga proverb says that "if you do not accept criticism you must look after yourself alone."

Warriors cannot afford this vulnerability of arrogant self-knowing any more than that of a harbored self-loathing, whether actively engaged in combat or not. On the battlefield, or off, we are best positioned when we have our backs protected by each other. Respect is strengthened through knowing that those critiquing you have your best interests at heart (a friend is someone who will tell you the truth even when that may cause a loss of friendship). Knowing this requires that we earnestly listen and value the critiques, regardless of how we respond.[9]

In a reality where extreme individualism has led so many of our children, as well as too many of our adults, to believe that they know everything already, where criticism, no matter how small, is considered a personal insult, and where placing oneself in the position to be able to disdainfully dismiss/ignore criticism is considered a positive measure of one's intelligence or superiority, the criticism necessary for warriors to constructively self-evaluate their character and steadily mold it into something better has only limited space. In such a falsified reality, it takes a mature warrior's strength of humility to seriously consider the value of ancestral wisdoms such as the Tshi proverb which cautions: "If someone says, 'Watch your conduct,' she has not insulted you." Most importantly, "A nation builder should not be touchy."[11]

At the same time, while many are highly skilled at criticizing others (a habit often subconsciously designed to distract attention from their own faults by projecting them onto their victims), they quickly become quite intolerant of others' evaluations of them. Ignoring or avoiding criticism is an understandable, defensive posture to adopt toward enemies or those looking to divide us from within, even though, as was stated, lessons for building character can even be found in the words of fools, if we listen carefully. But the same measuring rod for their criticism should not apply for those who stand shoulder to shoulder with us on the frontline. Those who best follow in the footsteps of our Ancestors are most qualified to offer us constructive instruction. And the love and tolerance with which these ancestral aspirants critique those beside, behind and in front of them will evince the depth of the respect they hold for their fellow nationbuilders.

One more note must be made with reference to the enemy within because of what those newly moving into the circles and centers of consciousness logically assume about those around them who have and will make this leap in thinking. Becoming "Afrikan" changes our cultural orientation and politics (to varying degrees) but, more often than not, not automatically our character/personality.

Changing our cultural orientation is the least challenging of this work. Changing our politics is a little more difficult because politics defines how we actively respond to threats from without and within. But the most difficult thing to change is our character/personality because it is the most deeply ingrained, having served a life's adaptive/survival/defensive function for the owner. And herein lies the problem for many warriors who would be Afrikan but who cannot relinquish those developed and/or inherited personality traits which go against the Afrikan grain. Most often, becoming Afrikan culturally and politically will not automatically change a nasty or selfish or envious attitude. Of course, this would mean that the cultural and political change was only superficial because a full transformation would also entail at least beginning to move one's character/personality within a range of communally acceptable Afrikan thought and behavior. And, of this, there should be evidence.

Liberalism: Every Afrikan voice is not worthy of our ear. Particularly notable in their contradictions, many grassroots organizers seeking widespread, popular support welcome constituency from any Afrikan willing to commit some time to service and ideological obedience. These "leaders" cannot afford to turn away anyone willing to sign up for the liberal draft. Their need for numbers to intimidate aliens into offering them a seat at the negotiation table in the "City of Privilege"[12] is too great. So, they conveniently mention the consensus required in communal decisions among traditional Afrikans as an excuse to accept any willing voice.

However, this is extremely problematic in a world where the spirit of Cointelpro and its descendants live along with those fleeing eurosupremacist racism but not yet strong or determined enough to stand in our centers. Many such individuals bring a dedicated, undying compromise, if not an easily compromised "consciousness," to the organizations claiming to promote liberation.

If we are to move forward as one in following the path laid before us by our Ancestors, we cannot tolerate voices intent on dragging us away from this Way. It is far too late in the war to negotiate the preservation of insanity within. We cannot afford to be what is defined/labeled as "politically correct." We cannot allow mentacidally compromised Afrikans to command any part of our decision-making circles. Everyone's voice cannot be welcomed because a considerable portion of those voices are inherently anti-Afrikan.[13]

Liberalism is neither practical nor possible in any revolution, except the liberals be instruments of dissension against their own in service to the victors. If an Afrikan world revolution requires the input and participation of all of Afrikan ascent, then it will never happen because the cultural misorientation[14] of most makes them worse than useless.[15] Henry McNeal Turner's observation about the revolutionary uselessness of a significant portion of our people still rings true. As he said, "Two-thirds of the American negroes would be of no help to anyone anywhere."

We cannot be Afrikan and European at the same time. These are irreconcilably different realities.

Failure to exert leadership: In the words of our Ancestors:

> This is the precept: Do to the doer that he or she may also do. It is thanking one for what one may do, blocking a blow before it strikes and giving an assignment to one who is skillful. Be a shelter and make your shore safe. See how your wharf is covered with crocodiles. Let your tongue speak straight and not go astray.[16]

Responsible leadership requires a heartfelt appreciation of the privilege of leadership. It requires that leaders be workers, examples, givers, models of what is right in the tradition of their people. In no way should this honor be misinterpreted as the right to take from those whom one is responsible to or deceive them with irrelevant fantasy.

Always remember that leadership requires knowledge and consciousness and that knowledge and consciousness by default require action. Leadership is work, not leisure. Never speak without acting on those words. To do so is harmful for your people and a positive for those who work to break them.

Lack of initiative and imagination: Warriors must have the vision of a people, the vision of a nation already locked deep inside their souls. They must have the visionary aptitude to understand nationbuilding as an extensive, protracted, intergenerational phenomenon to which they are significant contributors. They must know this with or without tangible evidence of our revolutionary progression.

Given this, warriors must be self-motivated. The energy spent by one person to galvanize another is energy wasted to the struggle. We must find ways to do what needs to be done using our own inner strength and kuumba (creativity). We should not have to be told what to do when we encounter novel problems. Our spirit, study, Elders and common Afrikan sense should be adequate to give us the answers we need.

Our imagination grows within the scope of what we know/believe we have done since the beginning of our existence. It is derived from what we know/believe to be our capabilities based on the testament of what we have tried and accomplished as a people relative to our curiosity and the challenges confronting us. We measure the immensity and potency of our vision, as well as our capacity to fulfill it, by appraising our responses to the greatest, not the least, of our curiosities and challenges.

Without this gauge, the physical, intellectual and religious boundaries others have established for us become what circumscribes our possibilities. With it, having millions of years under our belts, we know our true limits, or limitlessness in this form and consciousness.

Elitism[17]: Under no conditions should warriors be elitists. Elitism is stolen (appropriated), undeserved, arrogant privilege, maintained at the expense of others in the community. Elitists believe themselves superior. They believe themselves the only ones of their people or group capable of understanding the nature of problems and providing fitting solutions to them. They imagine themselves as above the masses in intellect and "breeding" and the best qualified to know and speak truth. The fact of the self-serving, subjective estimates of their intrinsic worth notwithstanding, they see themselves as the talented tenth, five percent or whatever small fraction of the population they declare themselves to be. Mostly, their privilege is inherited and/or delusional, like the claims to royalty of those unwilling to do the sacrificial work to declare themselves kings and queens. There is no evident justification. Among the dispossessed, elitism, like colorism, is a "pathetic imitation" of the elitism Europeans practice among themselves and, as a people, against us.[18]

For Afrikan people, elitism presents a very, very wrong order with very, very negative consequences. In our tradition, only humility deserves privilege. And that privilege does not come at the expense of others. It comes as a sacrifice by those given privilege who have earned the distinction of being obligated with greater duties and responsibilities to others because of it.

The presence of elitism (financial, intellectual, credential), however disguised in revolutionary organizations, is clear evidence of deeply embedded trends in them toward greater inequality, idle, counterrevolutionary chatter and arrogant, invidious hierarchical divides. It is evidence of control, without appearing to be so.

If elitism were present at its inception, it never was a revolutionary organization. If it were not present at its inception, but is present now, it is a ready sign of its impending decline as being a revolutionary organization because the privileged status it brings a few signals political impotence for the masses as far as their functional interests are concerned.
We must be especially careful of intellectual (credential, esoterica) elitism, disguised behind cultural attire and disconnected, loquacious jargon. Interestingly, it is particularly prominent in grassroots organizations, in that the leadership manipulates their following by convincing them that

they are fulfilling "the people's" will, that of the "masses," and not that of those in charge of the organizations. Indeed, the intellectual elite

- base their authority and irreplaceability on mastery and control of esoteric terminology (unexplained, and often unexplainable in a truly meaningful way by the speaker, verbiage conceptually "above" the membership, e.g., terms such as "scientific socialism," "hegemony" and "dialectical materialism").

- are elevated above the "masses" based on credentialism and expertise, even if not displayed as part of their public titles

- are skilled in the use of rhetoric and propaganda to manipulate and control the agenda and aspirations of the membership

- define organizational interests through in-group (clique) organization and coercion; although they claim egalitarianism and equality (usually propagating the idea that they are simply the appointed or anointed leaders of the "people's" organizations) of all voices, they systematically work to remove any dissenting voices that question the correctness and authority of their external or self-centered interests

- pursue the interests of external, more powerful interest groups, such as feminists, marxists and homosexuals (external and infiltrated) as if they were their own (which, in some cases, they are)

- exhibit a greater tendency for cooptation, disguised as liberalism or alliance creation

- exist half inside, half outside the movement and, last but not least,

- are subject to the whim of the financial (usually alien) supporters of the organization who deal directly with them, usually without the knowledge or consultation of the membership.

In no way aspirationally different from the negroes they

decry, those in "revolutionary" positions of power or influence acquired, maintained and/or validated through elitism will protect their privilege, and that of their children and others they may bring in, at any costs. Compromising the interests of what exists as no more than their constituency becomes standard operating procedure in the effort to gain greater leverage over those not in the inner circle. Truth in procedure and decision-making must be made secret, which works to lock the people out of an active participation in their future.

Egotism: Egotism is marked by having an "excessive conceit or excessive preoccupation with self-importance. It is the tendency to overvalue, in a rather obvious manner, personal actions, qualities, possessions, or achievements."[19] Evidence of this among so-called leaders within the Afrikan community comes in the form of high sounding titles, grandiose trappings and settings, and an insatiable desire for meaningless, distractive debate and the media attention that goes along with them.

This is most evidenced through the presence of their bloated egos. An ego is a defense mechanism. And when it is magnified beyond what is normally required to keep one functionally interconnected within the social circle of life, it reflects a deeply troubled personality, a well-hidden, frantic insecurity. The greater the insecurity, the larger the ego. Therefore, knowing the enormously inflated ego of the European, and the evidence of it in those of us who have come to don that personality, we can fairly well guess what level of insecurity lies beneath the facade of the self-assuredness many flaunt.

Interestingly, but to be expected, the need to be seen is exaggerated among those individuals among oppressed people who have the talents of public presentation but not the self-respect to actually work toward uncompromisedly liberating their people. It is an insatiable, possessive neediness, combining a narcissistic desire to be seen and rule over others, much in the style of what western social scientists call the Napoleon Complex.[20]

Not only is their ample evidence of this in the conscious community in general, but we also see the resulting conflict that prevents unification in the *centers* of our conscious community. No one is always right and, if we are being Afrikan, no one is more important than anyone else. Ego-ridden individuals and families are driven to do anything that appears radical or revolutionary just so that they can hear the sound of their own names. But that desire and effort does little more than blemish what good work they could do by actually being seen doing something constructive.

Something we must understand is that the personal qualities that deeply reflect eurocentric peculiarities are often not relinquished as individuals decide to follow the Afrikan Way. What we must overcome in moving toward a revolutionary mentality involves more than just diet, appearance and media consumption. It also significantly has to do with the importance with which we view ourselves relative to others.

Warriors have no use for dysfunctional egotism. Counter to what we have been led to believe, it is not a prerequisite for excellence in thought or warriorhood. Though we, like any other human, need social recognition and attachment, we cannot afford to be emotionally needy. Whether conscious or otherwise, allowing oneself to be continuously burdened with feelings of being severely neglected cripples productivity. Revolutionary nationbuilding is not a show and we are not on display.

Jealousy: Jealousy, like elitism, is extremely divisive. And western-style, invidious individualism exacerbates jealousy. Among nationbuilders whose explicit focus should be on combining the best of their individual talents into a formidable collective effort, this vice is definite evidence that some have yet to master their personal insecurities. As such, it foments unnecessary anger, frustration and distrust among the group's members.

Whether it is over power, possessions, love, favoritism, longevity, honor or whatever (for there is no relationship in which it cannot surface), jealousy only produces distance and infighting. It is a major factor contributing to the breaking up of organizations into factions hatefully pitted against each other.

As is to be expected, these internal squabbles are not over which "philosophy" is best suited to liberate Afrikan people, but over who is "most" right. Even more importantly, most often in such struggles, group philosophy becomes subordinated to individual or special interest opinion. Socially, at the level of organization, these squabbles devolve into subgroupings of individuals organized around alpha individuals in close competition with other individuals organized around another such individual or, cliques against cliques. Consequently, the vision suffers. And the people agonize, as does the grass beneath tussling elephants.[21]

Adventurism and romanticism: War is no fantasy. In all real probability, there will be no oscar award-winning final gunfight showdown where you go out blazing on the silver screen as the last martyr dodging a hail of enemy bombs, booby traps and bullets, while shooting so skillfully that every one bullet you expend, while in flight, somersaulting and diving through enemy lines sporting a full length, gold-lined, mudcloth trench coat flapped open to reveal an oversized neon ankh dangling from an necklace of roped bronze plated cowry shells atop a bulletproof vest made of hardback Afrikan literary classics, picks off ten of their best black ops trained attackers. Revolution is not play. It is no game. It is not showtime. It "is not a gig for crybabies"[22] or daydreamers.

There is no great adventure in which to find yourself. There are no new uninhabited, untamed frontiers to discover and plant your bendera.[23] Only your imagination will be allowed to run wild, if that. No ticker tape parades will welcome you. People will not be shouting your name out in awe. No front page will feature your exploits. And, if you do happen to appear on any page, it will not be out of gratitude. At best, your character will be assassinated, with you portrayed in the image of a beast against which they can more easily rally the people. You will not find a celebrated, perfect love and/or lover to whisk you off into la-la land.

As noted before in the critique of egotism, a revolutionary Afrikan organization is no place for the severely emotionally needy. It can offer no sanctuary for those without esteem who are hypochondriacally nursing scars needing the attention pity brings. "It's an obsession for a grown-up – ...the slave yearning to be revealed a king[24]....the need to be royal is a sickness of the slave soul."[25] We need warriors who are not driven by the attention others give them.

There are no self-created heroes or sheroes, fantasy or otherwise, in revolution. That is a community prerogative. Revolutionary nationbuilding is work. You do your work, "your best work,"[26] without question, without doubt, without regret.

If you are sincere, there will only be you, and others like you, doing the work of freeing our people. The cause drives us. "Sometimes work itself gives us energy. If it touches us where it matters."[27]

How you see being honored and rewarded for this necessary work will determine how effectively you perform your role in this great movement toward Afrikan liberation. Service is the watchword.

Male chauvinism: Male chauvinism strengthens misogyny, the fear, envy, distrust and hatred of women inherent in western and westernized patriarchy. It inflates male egos and demeans our Sisters' complementary contribution to our organization as a people. It negates the invaluable presence of the womanist spirit in our tradition.

If nothing else, the reality of sexism in our community should cause us to question why any conscious Afrikan man, knowledgeable or not of ourstory, would have to demean those closest to him in order to elevate himself. Of course, male chauvinism demonstrates a definite lack of ourstorical insight because, with self-knowledge, Afrikan men would never imagine themselves superior to Afrikan women. There would be no logical reason to do so.

We are one. We are in this war together. If we cannot respect ourselves as equals, we will surely lose this war.

Of course, a number of so-called revolutionaries, not true nationbuilders because of their primary reform and "we're all human" orientations, have taken this issue too far and have embraced feminism.[28] More and more we hear of Afrikan males calling themselves feminists. They study and mimic the thought patterns of women who have turned to women for bedfellows because of bad relationships with men and/or their desire for a man's power in a patriarchy gone mad.[29]

In whoever's hands, feminism is no better than male chauvinism. For feminism is the positioning of women over men, not the binding of women and men as equals. So, the misandrous (hatred of strong men) reaction of feminists is as destructive to revolutionary Afrikan organizations engaged in nationbuilding as misogyny.[30] Neither male chauvinism nor feminism is Afrikan. However, with respect to our traditions, womanism and motherism are elemental.[31]

> In understanding that culture molds and impacts males and females equally, and understanding the violent and highly competitive historical relationship between the sexes in European society, feminists are characteristically European. It is natural for hate to dominate Western power relationships. Womanism, being an Afrikan tradition, has an almost exclusive Afrikan membership. In fact, logically, a woman cannot be both feminist and womanist. For a womanist is one who seeks absolute equality with men. She is one who requires that there be mutual respect and equally shared power between men and women engaged in defending and building their community against those who would destroy it and them. She knows that white supremacy sees no sex or gender, as it sees no religion, political party, educational credential, income, occupation or age in its racist assault

on Afrikan people, except as a matter of expediency when dividing to conquer.[32]

Doubt Drains[33]

War is about bloodshed. And any good warrior, firmly committed to the liberation of his or her people, knows that death is nothing less than an opportunity seized in the effort to remove the threat to his or her people's ability to be themselves. War is not a stage or playground for vainglorious cowards in need of attention for an unearned glory. It is not a platform upon which one makes grandiose declarations about freedom, revolution and martyrdom without operational substance. It is the place where one applies oneself toward these ideals.

There is a beautiful quality of fearlessness in a mind ever rebellious against assault. Warriors do not choose to die. They choose to live. And it is because they choose to live that sometimes they must die.

So, warrior, have faith in what you do now, here and now, right now, at this very moment. Bear no concern for what you have done or intend on doing, or what has stood, or may stand, in your way. *Know* that we are winning and that there is no room for doubt, for doubt drains.[34]

Advance. Never accept where you are as a resting place. Never stop until you have become your Ancestors in all their glory, goodness, splendor and wisdom. Advance until we have returned the Afrikan reality to power. For, "where there is power there is no opposition."[35]

Enemies within and without have made a point of introducing/injecting demoralizing lies into the ears, eyes and hearts of earnest warriors. Our world is saturated with stories exaggerating and even glorifying the horrors, defeats, psychosis, self-hatred, willful betrayal and general misidentification and lostness of Afrikan people. We see them everywhere we look, everywhere we feel.

This is no more than propaganda designed to demoralize warriors and misdirect our energy against ourselves and each other. And well planned streams of calculated lies are highly effective tactics of war. Between Europeans and us, there is nothing less. If we don't understand this, we understand nothing. If we are to personally overcome this mental onslaught, we must recognize that everything conveyed by them, and the confused among us, are lies until those we trust with our story and contemporary geopolitics tell us otherwise.

No one's view is more important than that of our Ancestors' (which is a direct reflection of our oldest Ancestor's, Nana Nyame's, since they became Ancestors as a result of becoming godlike) and the children's (to whom we are most accountable in the here and now). No one else, excluding all of the other uncompromising Afrikans in our midst, counts. No one else should have any meaningful kind of influence in our thinking as warriors with respect to our roles and responsibilities in the Afrikan community.

> Let no voice but your own speak to you from the depths. Let no influence but your own raise you in time of peace and time of war. Hear all, but attend only that which concerns you.[36]

The idea that you can address an individual warrior's flaws, motivation and achievement independent of family, community, nation and spirit is completely foreign to the Afrikan mind. Similarly, the idea of individual doubt as something separate from communal uncertainty is foreign to Afrikan thinking. Just as Afrikan psychology looks to all individuals in the person's nexus in an effort to resolve mental illness/disorder,[37] the same must apply when we are forced to analyze the vestiges of doubt which may surface within individual warriors.

Certainly, taken as an impartial piece of literature, *As a Man Thinketh*[38] can be a useful piece of literature in the psychology of achievement motivation, be that progressive or regressive motivation.[39] But it is far from a complete text for purposes of motivating the Afrikan mind to lose a sense of doubt over one's ability to overcome all odds and create a better personal world through thought and affirmation because it wholly misses the point of the deeply socially intertwined nature of the normal Afrikan personality. Definitely, it is capable of directing Europeans and culturally misoriented individualized Afrikans solely focused on gaining success in a european reality, that is, to a degree. But it is ill-equipped to guide Afrikans toward their most fruitful expression of self because neither self nor success is detached from others. It is an understood afrism that "a person is a person because of people."[40]

One cannot be or win unless the others in the community experience the same. "A single person is not a warrior."[41] Individuals win because the community wins.

Adopting passivity or peace as a life's philosophy is distinctly characteristic of Afrikans who subconsciously dwell in doubt alone, even when congregating. They do not believe that Afrikan people are powerful enough to rise as a nation. In willful ignorance, they want peace as they are destroyed.

So, instead of publicly admitting to their obvious vanquishment, these doubting Thomases pretend that they have risen to a higher calling, which is nothing more than a submission to the brutal machinations of evil. Defeat, disguised as victory, mars their effort to fabricate a visionary humanity, a higher existence they argue that the corrupters of all of human worth are somehow bound to eventually respect and also embrace as their life's philosophy.

"Peaciers," as some have come to sympathetically call them, try to find shortcuts to love and respect from their destroyers that override the need to confront their relentless inhumanity. Hope is their all-in-all, their panacea.

Akil is one who deftly spoke about Afrikans claiming a personal philosophy of nonviolence but who, in reality, were only nonviolent toward Europeans. Unable and unwilling to recognize or confront their true assailants, their growing rage and frustration is taken out on their own.[42]

Initiatives by Afrikans toward the disarmament of the oppressed and the promotion of nonviolent philosophies of life are the work of those seeking to be immortalized in European myth. They are the programs of sheep blindly seeking a place of comfort among shepherding wolves.

There is no such thing as innocence in the West. And to act as if this society is not as predatory as it is invites destruction by it.

Those who would disarm themselves, relying on agents of the state to protect them from agents of the state or a mentacidal 3AM intruder, are faced with the prospect of slipping into a more debilitating insanity that is only a break-in away. How can a man explain to himself and his kin (not to speak of his Ancestors) that his self-centered nonviolent philosophy allowed another man to enter his home and rape, sodomize, beat, torture and/or even kill his family, while he was forced to watch at gunpoint because a so-called higher calling to the subservience of other men led him to lie down without a weapon strong enough to deter or repel an intruder? He would then have to live with his alienated self at an even greater psychologically mutilated state.

"He who lives by the sword dies by the sword" and other similar sayings are only warnings to those already petrified into inaction by the fear of pain. Like the many other sayings and verses selectively and systematically pumped into our community to keep us passive and dying to remain dominated by those who we are told "know not what they do," this warning should be taken as a challenge.

If you have to go, will you go alone or, like "Robert Charles, the Black paladin who faced down a mob 20,000 strong, and sold his life at the cost of death and wounds of some twenty lynchers,"[43] take your proportionate share with you? Serious warriors, i.e., those willing to die for the people, take martyrdom as a given. Only "the chicken says, 'life is fear.'"[44]

In times of war, when one is charged with gaining the freedom and respect of his or her people, one does not look for intellectualizing or over-moralized excuses to passively watch and/or participate in the carnage. The warrior's "destiny is *not* one of trying to become a member of this gang of thieves, but to end its existence here on earth, to inhibit its rapacious ways and to bring this group of people to heel!"[45]

What can Yurugu do to you that is worse than what you see about you? Warriors fight to the death. When all is said and done, everyone who goes to the frontlines does not physically return. This, warriors accept.

The only question is, "Was the fight in vain?" Did their individual efforts count toward the victory? Will we call out their names as among the honored warrior Ancestors as we continue to march on into victory? Did they handle their fair share? We must daily affirm it so.

In times of war, when innocents are being furiously aggressed against, when others are trying to slay their family, institutions and nation, true warriors are either on the battlefield or have made their transition battling on it. The myth that there has already been enough bloodshed and, therefore, we should seek peace at any cost, even at our continued expense and eventual total destruction and removal from planet Earth as a people, should be taken by Afrikans for as ridiculous a statement as Europeans consider it. Retirement is not a warrior's option until total liberation and sovereignty are achieved. We do not practice a consciousness of convenience.

The ourstorical record shows that, among Afrikans, it was not until the creation of the negro, afraid of dying at the hands of Europeans, that pacifism[46] and nonviolence against sworn enemies became a normalized way of life among some

Afrikans. It takes those who have truly become vanquished, that is those fully accepting their defeat at the hands of those they believe to naturally be their superiors, to alter their ancient and traditional commandment from "I did not kill unjustly"[47] to only read "Thou shalt not kill" (except on behalf of they master). Just as this commandment of justice was bastardized to fit the spirit of the truly vanquished, negroes dilute moral commandments or select rules that will not antagonize Europeans in their sacred "fight" to be subintegrated/subassimilated with them.

To conclude this discussion, the subject of a warrior's patience must be addressed. For, no matter how we look at it, warriors must come to grips with the fact that they cannot escape the need for patience.[48] It is part of a warrior's durational sustenance. Patience with war can come by force or choice. If not, the lack of it becomes a progressively more destructive obstruction in the warrior's vision.

If you are running away from western religious institutions, which is a highly desirable goal, in hopes of releasing oneself from the requirement of patience with enemies and destruction in order to gain a heavenly salvation or reward, be warned that warriorhood is not a quick fix. The same long-suffering disposition (love and devotion), the same tenacious patience that they demand from Afrikan men and women in service to Europeans in order to enter their otherworldly paradise is required of us by our Ancestors in service to the coming liberation of Afrikan people. So, if patience is your issue, prepare to be tested.

Spoilage[49]

No social practice is a greater evidence of the perverted, destructive presence of european influenced, mentacidal insanity in the Afrikan home and community than the spoilage of our children. That we have accepted this practice as our norm says volumes about how little we care about them and our future as human beings and as a people.[50]

Though also evident within yurugu's community,[51] spoilage manifests its most devastating forms in ours. It is evident that those who want their children to lead revolutions and revolutionary society do not spoil them, unless they, themselves, expect to become the dominant power in society and have their grown, incompetent children simply fill in the privileged, decisionless positions they establish for them as Europeans have successfully done for their own. But, that is a fantasy unbefitting today's warrior. As I was taught by those who reared me in a disciplining love, "You do not spoil a child who will be brought up in a world trying to destroy him."

For Afrikan people, spoilage is a most wretched mental condition to be in, whether you are the victim/recipient or perpetrator/contributor. To be spoiled is to be without self-discipline.[52] It is to be at the center of everything socially defined as being of conspicuous worth but possessing nothing of intrinsic value. Spoiled individuals exhibit qualities of an extremely questionable, malleable quality because of uncontrolled appetites, limited inner strength and an insatiable lust for all they do not possess.

We could question the origin of spoilage and these qualities. However, since we know that all humans have the potential for both order and directionlessness, the real question is of why the latter has become so magnified and even celebrated among Afrikans who, otherwise, would be today's warriors. One of the most critical determining factors is our childhood. Amos N. Wilson reminded us that

> One of the most profound things that we've learned in psychology is that the most powerful forces that shape human behavior are those factors that are consciously *not* remembered by human beings, that are unknown by the person, are those experiences the individual can swear he's never had. That is one of the paradoxes of human behavior, that the very things that shape us and make us

> behave the way we do, see the world the way we see it and relate to people the way we relate to them, are those things that occurred in our lives at points we cannot remember or recall.[53]

Among many of our adults, but more impressively among our youth, we are witnessing the third generation of a general trend toward the spoiling of our children. It is a virulent form of spoilage adopted by Afrikan people in an attempt to follow the child-raising directives of an alien, though dominate, people who

(1) do not know how to raise their own children,

(2) fear public exposure about how badly they have historically treated their children,

(3) have been experiencing what they are promoting as an unprecedented economic boom that has dramatically increased their wealth, credit access and discretionary income at others' expense and

(4) have created an empire that has enabled them to ensure their children's success over others in the labor market. Though we are keenly aware of the last two factors' decline in the capitalist world, none of them significantly apply to Afrikans now or over the last half millennium.

Yet, how we think, and speak, about and practice the art of bringing our babies into adulthood is no different, minus our inability to protect their present, future and ancestral memory, than how Europeans do. In imitative, trickle down fashion, we have allowed ourselves to gradually (or selectively) incorporate their child raising methods to the point where they have become wholly ours. This fact is obvious to any ourstorical observer studying the way we now bring our children up in this reality.

We have mistakenly interpreted their psychology as our psychology.[54] And, in doing so, we have done our children a great disservice. We have done our best to spoil our children, to allow them to experience personal "freedoms" and material excess without restraint in a world without humanity, to impress them with "this way of life on total exhibition"[55] and unpreparedly release them to subsist in and find a mentacidal identity within Babylon.[56]

And they, in turn, have responded to this eurocentric voice of insistent demand as only children would. For, in this atmosphere where children are taught to exploit, and even extort, their parents' and other adults' resources, "A child can cry so much until you do everything they say."[57] They have become socialized into needy, self-centered, arrogant, aggressive, impatient, predatory, disrespectful, destructive youth who have matured, at least chronologically, into "adults" totally in love with this capitalistic, individualistic western culture and society.

Spoilage teaches our children the art of demanding. It teaches them to prioritize self above all else, except when that may mortally endanger self (and, even often then, the demand often overrides the threat). It is not a socialization process that begets generosity, benevolence or concern for others. That must be forced by prevailing conditions or necessity and, even then, it only temporarily works to selfishly serve one's own emotional needs.

Spoilage is instant gratification in the extreme. It cultivates insatiable appetites. In western-style child raising, it is claimed to translate into higher aspirations. This may be true in an immoral, materialistic social context but the downside is that reasonable limits to desire are thoroughly suppressed and a competitive avarice produces selfish, hedonistic, callous individuals blindly in pursuit of fame and fortune.

As individuals blindly wrapped up in a eurocentric, over consumptive show and tell, they are completely oblivious to the causes and consequences of their love for excess and waste, and disdain for anything Afrikan. They have submerged themselves in a mentality that does not allow them to appreciate anything that they have. So their insatiation continues, refusing ancestral intervention. In a reality created by inhumanity, they are fed by fantasy inducing machines that turn their loyalty against themselves. Their appetites have been formed and are controlled by others.

For our youth, who are trying to break into (gain a "rep" within) this insanity, the question has become who can I disrespect the most and get away with it. At whose expense can I become somebody?

We would have to be blind not to see what exists, and more so what is coming. "What the childhood of a generation is will be what that generation becomes in its adulthood. A ruined childhood is a ruined society."[58]

By definition, spoilage means rottenness. Spoiled things contaminate and transmit rot to whoever and whatever they touch. Spoiled individuals do this by bringing additional disorder into situations where we are fighting for a semblance of order so that we can move forward. They are a naturally corrupting internal force who often cannot see themselves as the problem because all they can see is themselves. They cannot relinquish their european ways because they have a vested interest in maintaining them.

There is no "we" in their "I." Or, if so, as in the regurgitation of popular proverbs, only a superficial pretense that shields a persistent self-centeredness. As we should know, "He who has no manners does not care about others."[59]

Very unfortunately, this confusion over who we are, how we should be Afrikan in rearing our children, is also evident in some of those claiming to be members of the Afrikan centered community. Even here, for those unable to divest their minds of a spoilage priority, sanity remains locked up in creating an Afrikan world where their grafted european self is acceptable. These are people who hide their pale insanities behind the mask of an Afrikan center. And those of us who have learned of this europeanizing process, who recognized that they have personally been victimized by it, yet do nothing to alter their thought and behavior against it, are immeasurably worse than those who remain ignorant of their mentacide.

Those who claim to be warriors but who refuse to do the hard work of relinquishing their highly individualistic european imperatives, especially in misrearing our children, do more damage to our movement than negroes, lost souls or, even, Europeans.

Exemplifying this is that collection of "conscious" parents claiming to be warriors in the tradition of our Ancestors, but who have wholly embraced this crass, eurocentric individualism. They are proudly raising children as if being Afrikan is reading, recitation, song and dance, diet, attire, name, kwk, versus a way of being, of which these are only constituent parts. Those who have confused what it means to be Afrikan with show and tell, catering to their unchallenged fears and weaknesses, rightfully suffer. Our Ancestors were right in saying, "Slaves deserve slaves for children."

Unknown to most pointing accusatory fingers at the children, though, it is not their fault. They did not raise themselves.

Equally sad, because we are affected by the act of any person of Afrikan descent, we have to suffer along with their children. We have a dire situation here. However, as with any condition we find ourselves in, we have a choice. We can either do what is necessary to save our children, regardless of cost, or surrender to the pressure and release them to the insanity rushing to engulf them.

Again, what we are now witnessing is a cultural and social degeneration through multiple generations of progressively regressive spoilage. There has been misguided spoilage in our community before but the kind, degree and rate of its popularization that we are witnessing today have no precedent among Afrikan people. Again, it is a selfish, hedonistic, willful, needy, arrogant form of spoilage which comes with no sense of benevolent, humanistic responsibility to others whatsoever, unless some form of reward is offered. Those inflicted in this way have no desire to work or accomplish anything of substantial, intergenerational worth, except possibly when it affords the opportunity to gain more individualistic things (physical, mental and material) and/or satisfy a needy attention.

Afrikans victimized by their own in this way have no respect for others except for those with the will and means to punish them when disrespected. Those who reward them without this capacity are taken from, taken for granted and dismissed accordingly. "The child hates the one who gives him all he wants."[60] With this new form of spoilage, the outcome for the victims (both children and adults) has worsened and our community's potential to defend itself from external assault and internal discord has lessened.

Another way spoiled individuals corrupt revolutionary Afrikan organizations and communities is that the virus they carry corrupts and limits our return to an uncontaminated Afrikan way. No matter our progress, we will continue to be pulled in the direction of whiteness by the voice of their confusion because their psychological need to think and act as Europeans compels them to find creative ways to compromise our progress with european ideas and things. To have anti-Afrikan ways and ideas infused in a Way that is completely and totally incompatible with that which is european begs compromise within it. This condition is analogous to a body unaware of a predatory germ's presence in it that, if it remains unchecked, will gradually, but eventually, make the whole body sick.

In this degenerate, immoral reality, it is much more common for evil to corrupt good than good to impede evil. And, throughout this reality, a reasoning, deliberate, insatiable evil is free to be fruitful and multiply. Spoiled individuals bring european germs that they feel they cannot live without into the conscious Afrikan centered community and those organizations designed to empower us. Once in, if the uncontaminated members do not take on the hard work of distancing themselves from this corrupting force (something spoiled individuals are fiercely adverse to), they will negatively impact our thoughts and actions and, therefore, Afrikans possibilities.

Moreover, because of this, spoiled Afrikan adults provide extremely bad models for Afrikan children. In an anti-Afrikan world, even a number of consciously reared children are constantly studying us for contradictions so they can have an excuse to be "free" of this order we know of as the Afrikan Way.[61] Because of the weakness this reality encourages in the minds of many Afrikans in positions of responsibility and leadership, and because this alien culture teaches our children that our Ancestors' path is constraining, disciplining them beyond reason and taking away their individualism, the ones who have become or have always been determined to be free of their Afrikan selves are intensely looking for contradictions which will easily allow them to proclaim that we are no more worthy than those we criticize.[62]

Specifically, in terms of the communal spirit of Afrikan people, spoilage does not allow one to freely give to others. It does not permit one to have or act on a vision of selflessly benefitting others, an admirable trademark of traditional Afrikan society. It does not empower them to sacrifice their time, energy and/or life for the good of the community.

Something greater, more than what is due, is always expected in return. Their individual selves sit at the center of all their thought and actions, even though their words may at times indicate otherwise.[63]

Not surprisingly, because of this me-centeredness, spoiled children and adults have great difficulty following instructions. Although functionally immature, they can be told little, thinking they know everything already. According to our Ancestors, "A bad child does not know how to take advice." Therefore, instructions and instructors are an affront to their egos, and are interpreted as degrading and meaningless, except, temporarily, upon the possibility of a reward.

Our judgement of them, however, must always be tempered fairly. They are being no more or less than how they have been socialized to be because "If you are given bread for being stupid, you may learn to despise instruction."[64] And they have been trained well through the rewards received for thinking and acting selfishly.

Spoiled individuals are also not respecters of rules. They are socialized to aspire to dominate others. For them, rules are simply another useless thing to be broken. But warriors of our tradition know that rules define and dictate a necessary order. Without order there is no true civilization, no consciously directed people's power.

The ageless Afrikan priority of acquiring and cultivating land is also seriously undermined by spoilage. Both require difficult, though fulfilling, work. Spoilage fosters laziness, a quality anathema to the labor required for agricultural and other land cultivating pursuits.[65]

We find the same problem when it comes to the defense of our land and people. Being on post requires being at attention for its own sake, not for some immediate, personal reward. It should go without saying that spoilage negates ReAfrikanization.

That is why it is so astonishing to see "conscious" parents spoiling their children. Parents who claim to follow and outwardly evince our traditions should be the last to disarm their progeny. They should be offering leadership in this area by giving their children an Afrikan model of order. They, who should know far better than the negroes and lost souls they are virtually indistinguishable from in this area what we are up against. Knowing what they know, they should least desire to sabotage our children's power, integrity and centeredness. They should know what quality of children we must produce if we are truly nationbuilding.

Even more confusing are those knowledgeable Afrikans who often permanently damage our youngest warriors because of their panic-stricken fear of losing them to the glitter of the enemy. They would have us believe the eureason that we cannot live in this world without being in the company of Europeans and their insanities. Therefore, exposing our children to insanity under "Afrikan centered" supervision and guidance, in anticipation of their freely moving about in its midst (something these *eurationalizers*[66] argue is unavoidable anyway), is better than keeping them from it. This is no different, and definitely no better, than those willfully ignorant "parents" who sit with their children while watching pornography or getting high or drunk, saying they will have to encounter it sooner or later, and that it is better that they do it with them and/or in their presence so that they can manage its introduction. The Ancestors taught us that "The ignorant praises his own ignorance."[67] How sad to be confused and frightened, still believing they can fight the european way using eureason.

It never ceases to amaze me the number of community children who publicly talk back to their parents, interrupt them,[68] tell them they "hate" them,[69] unrelentingly make "demands" from them until their wishes are fulfilled, "pull away" from them, hit them and even throw tantrums to express their dissatisfaction with them. This is not parenting, except maybe in an unnatural, convoluted context of role reversal where the child is training the adult.

Children raising parents or parents improperly raising their offspring is counterrevolutionary at the least and anti-nationbuilding at best because the [re]creation of a powerful people is an intergenerational process. With the young ruling their parents and a constant and fierce battle raging between the generations, there is no ordered intergenerational continuity. All meaningful, powerful transmission of self-definition is lost, or is in the process of being so. Unless spoilage and intergenerational disconnection is the choice of an autonomous, self-defining people, which is logically impossible, it is destructive to that people's existence as a people. Only a people can choose to functionally disconnect their generations. Only a suicidal people would map out such a genocidal path for themselves.

Spoilage is not an act of ReAfrikanization. Spoilage is not the practice of nationbuilders. There is nothing revolutionary about it – counterrevolutionary, yes, but not revolutionary.

It is self-destruction in its meanest and most subtle form, the kind of suicide where Afrikans thoughtlessly, carelessly, selfishly, take an innocent mind along with your own. As such, it is an apt description of Afrikan children being raised by Afrikan adults who do not want to release themselves from their dependencies on european ways. In truth, among Afrikan people, it is a reactive disorder created in the minds of those who live in fear of acting against that which they know makes no sense. It is the result of perfecting survival strategies which allow one to eternally live "securely" within fear. It is the willful reactive thought and behavior of Afrikan adults who do not have the strength or will of mind to provide the order and discipline their children need in the face of destruction.

As far as warriors nationbuilding in the tradition of our Ancestors are concerned, though, the reasoning/excuses misguided Afrikans give as to why they systematically work to bring disorder into our children's lives is irrelevant. The results are the measure of this phenomenal self-hating effort.

Self-discipline and the ability to create order within chaos simply because it is right are two of the most important character qualities we need in our warriors to become successful as a people.[70] We need Afrikan minds which see and feel the need to put Afrikan people first. We need warriors who voluntarily, altruistically are willing to give of their time and energy to help rebuild the spiritual, psychological and physical infrastructure of the Afrikan nation.

We need Afrikan warriors who know themselves well enough to have identified their particular talents in an effort to find better ways to improve the quality of life for those around them, knowing that this effort will automatically improve theirs and set the stage for an ongoing improvement through forthcoming generations. We need conscious individuals who are willing to die for each other, the Elders who are the repositories of our traditional wisdom and maintainers of peace and order in our community,[71] and the children who are returned spirit and are our future.

9. The Primary Qualities of Respectful Warriors

They never learn...and We will never give up.

Akua Njeri

What qualities are built into a warrior of good character (as if there is such a thing as a true warrior who does not have, or is not earnestly aspiring to, good character)? What is the true reflection of her or his essence? What are those qualities which define the thought, word and deed of any claiming to be their Ancestors and uncompromisingly intent on reestablishing our order?

Taken from what has already been explained, what follows is a discussion of some of the more virtuous personal attributes. As implied, these are not all of a warrior's character traits. However, they should suffice as a beginning for those in search of the godlikeness evident in those ancestral and living elder jenoch who have always manned our frontlines.

With that said, warriors are:

- *Disciplined* - Dead Prez lyricized the revolutionary thought-action sequential connection in "my mind is the place where I make my plans. The world is the place where I take my stand."[1] Planning and standing each requires discipline. Neither ordering study in such a way as to make ready for practical application nor holding one's ground in the face of determined, antagonistic forces occurs without a practiced self-rule. Without it, weakness in thought and/or action prevails.

  Discipline is a process of self-honing. It is the strengthening of self which comes from defeating the experience of failure through trying and trying again until success is achieved because "A person always breaking off from her work never finishes anything."[2]

  Warriors know this. They know that, in order to constructively nationbuild, they have to build within first. Inner struggle begets outer struggle. Inner strength begets outer strength. And, given focus and vision, the intensity, difficulty and duration of the struggle determine the quality of the outcome. So, only a limited amount of inner strength is generated without exerting an extraordinary effort to overcome that which others consider insurmountable. Those who do this work intimately know why they stand, regardless of the odds.
- *Studious* - Warriors are never without a challenging book or constructive thought. Ever vigilant in intellectually refocusing their vision and mission, these indefatigable workers know that they must mentally be better prepared for the battleground than our enemies. No mental time goes wasted, no revelation unstudied, no wisdom unheeded.

> Be diligent as long as you live, always doing more than is commanded of you.

> Do not misuse your time while following your heart, for it is offensive to the soul to waste one's time. Do not lose the daily opportunity to increase that which you have. Diligence produces gains and gains do not endure when diligence is abandoned.[3]

That "the wise person who ceases to learn ceases to be wise"[4] is common knowledge in the tradition of a people who prize the learning process from birth to transition. We understand that life, more than anything else, is a wasted journey without learning. Only through learning can one understand self and others.

- *Worldly* - Active students of the Afrikan Way are acutely knowledgeable of others' ways as they relate to Afrikan people. Historical parochialism is uncharacteristic of this self-chosen few. However, analyzing the world begins and ends in our Afrikan center.
- *Frugal* - Although this applies to speech also (as in always trying to being as succinct and concise as possible), we do not waste resources. Frugality in the disbursement, as well as stockpiling, of sources we have is critical for warriors in many ways.

  One, in particular, which many eager to protect our sacred spaces may have not considered, is in the collecting of weaponry. Warriors never arm our enemies. For instance, knowing that sometimes flight is necessary in order to better prepare for the next engagement, they would never have more weapons than can be easily carried. In the case of an unplanned escape, you take only what will not weigh you down. All that is left behind falls into enemy hands, augmenting their already plentiful arsenal.
- *Polite and Courteous* - Respect is not a given in this reality, even in our general conscious community where it should certainly be. Western society makes it an

individual prerogative. People choose to be polite and courteous, or not. This, like so many other socially divisive insanities, has been reduced to the level of individual choice and, therefore, is not socially reinforced.

However, this should never be an option for warriors within our community. For us, being polite and courteous is a given, at least toward those who are not disrespectful toward us. Being nice and helpful to those around us is second nature.

- *Generous* - We know that manning the frontline and serving those behind it is a collective effort among warriors. Therefore, what we individually have that is in any way useful to our nationbuilding effort must be shared so that it can be collectively beneficial to our individual missions.

Among the warrior class, none should be working against any other(s) because of limited resources. This would feed internal dissension and division, empowering exploiters and genocidists. We must freely give to each other what we have so that comradery is built at the same time as our communities are.

When generosity is attenuated, greed flourishes. And greed divides any community into suspicious, deceitful individuals unable to trust each other in any meaningful, revolutionary way. "Where trust breaks down, peace breaks down."[5] What then becomes of nationbuilding?

> Do not be greedy lest your name send forth an offensive odor. Greed brings conflict and fighting in a house. It takes all sense of shame, mercy and trust from one's heart and it causes turmoil in a family. Those who are greedy do not like to give to those who gave to them. They do not consider tomorrow, for they

> are only concerned with the moment. There is no end to the wrong done when money and greed are together.[6]

We must give to each other all that is needed, without disgruntlement, without regret.

- *Loving* - Love means instinctively putting others before self. It means doing and caring for them better than yourself and making sure that they are able to be who they naturally are without obstruction. Without a naturally occurring, unconscious selflessness, without an internalized gratitude for others that ultimately fosters altruistic sacrifice, there is no love, only pretentious, ostentatious sentimentalism.

Love is voluntary and involuntary, even instinctive, if you will, given normal Afrikans in an uncompromised Afrikan reality. There is no calculating forethought. It cannot be coerced or forced by either the giver or recipient. If so, it is not true love. This applies whether we are assessing complementary, familial, community or national interpersonal relationships.

Time is the greatest evidence of love. Only when our durability is revealed through the difficulty of sustaining the bond that evolves between individuals and those whose happiness they have assumed personal responsibility for has love's primacy been truly tested. Only time reveals true love.

Love does not always appear kind. In fact, for one corrected through "tough love," it may appear downright cruel. And, for those who love their people and are cognizant of the hateful, merciless war that has been raging against us for thousands of years, what must be done to the offenders (both initiator and accomplice) to arrest this assault is an act of undying love for Afrikan people and humanity. This is not about revenge. It's about justice, no matter how similar they may look on the battlefield. And this, as history has shown, is far beyond the understanding of those needing correction. A warrior's love for self, complement, family, community and nation is immeasurable and without qualification for we willingly sacrifice everything for victory.

- *Truthful* - Warriors distinguish between others' realities and the one modeled after our Ancestors, which we have established and maintain in our sacred spaces. We recognize that, while we cannot speak truth to enemies because they are enemies and look to know what we know so it can be used against us, we do not lie to those with whom we are working to build a lasting trust.[7] Those of us standing on the frontlines know that "confiding a secret to an unworthy person is like carrying grain in a bag with a whole."[8] And, it is because of the enemy's imperative and our family's security that the warrior is most discreet.

  Truth must be kept. So, silence is a very critical virtue where a people's liberation, empowerment and sovereignty are concerned. "Better are those whose knowledge remains inside them, than those who talk to their disadvantage."[9]

- *Righteously Enraged* - We, warrior scholars, are fully entitled to our righteous rage. It is a cumulative gift, built up over centuries of mental, physical and spiritual torture. This unique combination of time and intensity have given us the confidence of knowing, and stamina to defeat our enemies. And, it is the greatness of this gift, and its inherent responsibility to think, speak and act in terms of remembrance, that requires its constructive application by us. Carrying the conviction that comes with being righteously enraged means that, even though you have the will to stand alone, you know that you will never be so. "Gonna find a few, always walk with you,"[10] no matter where you are on the frontline.

- *Resilient* - People who live with and/or welcome physical and psychological challenges bear new difficulties much better than those whose lives have been sheltered from them. They have learned that discomfort is a necessary ingredient for growth, for elevation, for a deeper connection with one's higher mind and spirit. They believe "God sends misfortune only to purify us."[11] Throughout time, our greatest revolutionary leaders and workers are the best evidence of this unquestionable fact. Malcolm X, Fannie Lou Hamer, Jean-Jacques Dessalines, Queen Mother Moore, Sundiata and Ida B. Wells are all glorious examples of this afrism.

  Warriors gather strength from hardship. Hardship strengthens the mind and body and opens us better to our spiritual endowment. It tempers the determined. Without it a resilient character, one that will assuredly rise no matter how many times others attempt to crush it into the earth, cannot be built. Dedicated revolutionaries know that "there is no cure that does not cost." Therefore, we must savor our victories. We must study our defeats.

  On the same note, an oppressed people believing that they are saved by being in an enemy's presence and aping their imperatives and doctrines, and who are subsisting in the lap of leased comfort, cannot grow into themselves without experiencing incredible levels of pain. There is no easy way out of submission. And that is where warriors who know the Way come in. Someone must be there as they awake to guide them through the gauntlet of their return.

- *Humble* - Humility is perhaps the most telling quality of warriorship. When one lives without arrogance or undue pride, the work that needs to be done is apparent and taken on without complaint or frustration. It is recognized for the preeminent life's work that it is and undertaken accordingly. There are no self-centered thoughts of regret, loss or quitting because the people are larger and more important than self. At the same time, humbleness, because of the greater commitment it brings to ensure the well-being of others over that of oneself, pushes involved individuals to surpass what they might consider possible in self because of the demands of this indisputable obligation and duty to one's Ancestors, children, fellow workers, Elders, ascendants and Spirit.

- *Observant/Cautious* – Experienced warriors constantly scour their environment, something which has become second nature through practice, something which does not take away from our happiness and living because of its second naturedness. On the surface and within, warriors are never boisterous, undisciplined or lackadaisical in hostile situations. Rather, they are always quiet, thinking, studying, planning, applying. There is a warrior's wisdom.
- *Military Minded* - Warriors prepare for any exigency. No attack should catch us totally off guard.[12] We are the first and final line of defense against the enemies of our people. In this reality, if you are unable to defend what you have built and/or have, it's not yours. Bloodshed is an inseparable part of this responsibility for "blood is the sweat of heroes."[13] As Omowale Malcolm X correctly chastised so many of us, "You haven't got a revolution that doesn't involve bloodshed. And you're afraid to bleed." And, given that warrior is a derivative of the word "war," warriors know that their primary calling is to draw the blood of their enemies.

We can dress it up any way that we want but militaries have one mission, and that is to kill. All other responsibilities are secondary and carry within them that preeminent threat of enforcing the will of those they serve through killing. Those who claim warriorhood must know this and have no question as to what it is they are here to do.

- *Dedicated/Committed* - The Ugandans say, "A promise is a debt." In declaring ourselves warriors we have willingly incurred such a dept. We have promised to liberate Afrikan people from the unwarranted spiritual, mental and physical shackles of european domination. We have committed our lives to the promise of Abibifahodie (Afrikan liberation). Warriors do not break their promises.
- *Fearless/Intrepid* - The warrior affirms: "Nothing can or will stop the volition of my power. No man, no nation, no conditions, no history, no threat, no obstacle, nothing, ever, will deter me from liberating Afrikan people. I will always stand my Afrikan ground." This is clearly in line with Amos N. Wilson's assertion that

> The true nationalist is intrepid. Not that the nationalist does not have fear, but he learns to operate *in spite of* fear; fear does not paralyze him. He uses the fear as energy to move forward and to confront his enemies.[14]

"He who is in the right shouldn't be scared."[15] The ancestral wisdom that "...a strong heart in the midst of difficulties is an ally to its owner" should go without saying.[16]

Women Warriors

After laying out a solid foundation explaining "The Stages in the Development of an Afrikan Woman,"[17] Jegna Marimba Ani lists those qualities of Afrikan women which speak to good character. Afrikan women of character must:

- be life affirming
- be in partnership with an Afrikan man
- be a political organizer
- function as part of a collective
- exert influence
- speak for the Ancestors
- be an advocate for Afrika
- be a mother who does whatever is necessary to protect her child
- teach
- be a healer
- represent the continuity of Afrikan people
- represent the stability of the Afrikan family
- maintain and pass on Afrikan culture
- organize and direct the Afrikan market, enabling our people to understand the spirit of economic exchange ad distribution of our resources
- be a scientist of the sacred
- be a spiritual leader
- be an intellectual
- be Divine

There is no doubt that an Afrikan woman exhibiting these qualities is in supreme standing in our community and holds an honorable place in the Ancestors' hearts.[18] And even though they cannot be explained with the clarity and force Ani does in her essay "To Be An Afrikan Woman," we will attempt to summarize the individual and collective significance of each.

In being "life affirming," the Afrikan woman must develop and sustain a positive, generative outlook toward the Afrikan possibility. She is obligated to promote life and those things that create and sustain it in its optimal peaceful, loving state. At the same time, she must work to remove whatever brings unnecessary pain and disorder from our space. In recognizing that the Universe is about procreation, and that they are human incarnation of this never-ending, divine miracle, Afrikan women have a spiritual calling to ensure that life continues under their nurturing guardianship.

Following universal order naturally calls Afrikan women to form loving, lasting "partnerships" with Afrikan men. The Ma'atian principle of complementarity dictates that those with a dominant female energy and intuition (women) and those with a dominant male energy and intuition (men) be brought together for balance, procreation and the building of a reality modeled after divinity. This is not an easy task; rather it requires much give and take and, in this alien world, a mutual strengthening to soothe past scars, current frontlines and future victories.

In answering the call of the Akoben, Afrikan women must be "political organizers." Like any good leader who recognizes that she is primarily a worker, these knowledgeable Sisters instinctively position themselves to become an intermediary organizing our community's vast talents and directs them toward healing. She must also hold herself responsible for bringing to her complement, offspring, family, community and nation those issues upon which our reAfrikanized nationbuilding depend.

Afrikan women of consciousness enter family disputes fully intent on resolving them to our benefit. They do not shy away from problems which have the potential to disrupt the solidarity of our primary relationships. They are no less aggressive in confronting those affecting our societies and nation.[19]

And, like Yaa Asantewaa a who stood against Yurugu when the men would not, Sisters are no less responsible for demanding, on no uncertain terms, that Afrikan men stop this genocidal war against us. According to one of our honored grandmothers:

> So I call all real African women to the forefront. Let us declare war on the society that is destroying our sons, our men, and let us lead them into another direction. *It is the tradition in African societies that when things get so*

> *terrible, the women call for war.* Yes, it will be an arduous and dauntless journey, but what else do we have to do for the rest of our lives? I have nothing else to do but to liberate my grandsons, my grand-daughters and try to talk to the men. The men can be very stubborn, and sometimes, they fail to act in their own best interest and the interest of the entire family and the entire race![20]

Women walking in the tradition of our Ancestors know that we organized ourselves in the best human social form for harmonious cooperation and individual expression. They know that this expression is best manifest in the "collective," a working fellowship of individuals joined together in a common spirit, mind and body. In collectives, we provide for each other's social and personal needs within the context of a deeply ingrained, selfless sense of shared responsibility. All within are united as one without alienation, competition or arrogance. Women are the keepers, the collectors, of our community.

In the spirit of the most fundamental of all Afrikan characteristics, altruism, the warrior women who are committed to building and sustaining a functioning, communalism willingly submit themselves to the will of the collective. They do this knowing that the result of their duties will improve the quality of their individual humanity and that of every other member.

"Influence" is an Afrikan woman's prerogative. This goes without saying in Afrikan society. It is exerted because it is knowing and just. It does not dominate or burden. It works to unite all equally.

The Ancestors created our traditions out of their accumulated wisdom. But, because of our social and cultural dislocation, our knowledge of these ways and why they fit so well our spirt is very limited. This, however, does not stop Afrikan women from unquestioningly fulfilling their directives. Therefore, thoughtful, loyal Afrikan women think and "speak out of this collective mind." Ensuring everyone's adherence to the knowing will of our Ancestors and protecting it from alien, destructive ways is in good character.

We know that without their roots trees become deformed and die. We know that without the mother the child does not thrive. Afrika is our Motherland. PanAfrikanist, conscious, committed Sisters "advocate for Afrika." They are knowledgeable of the alien onslaught, others' abuses and our contribution to our instability and relative powerlessness globally.

Such women also know that, while the father is a defining factor also, the condition of the children has ourstorically been determined by the health, welfare and vision of the mother. If for no other reason, we know this because, in a normal Afrikan reality, the mother is the first teacher, discipliner and nurturer. No righteous Afrikan should ever questioned the point made by so many of our jenoch that the quality of our Nation depends on, and is reflective of, the state of Afrikan women. This understanding of the role of motherhood in our future guides the female warrior's activities toward the Continent.

Children are the most sacred beings in any true Afrikan community. Nothing in an Afrikan woman's character would ever prevent her from "protecting" them first.

No one is better qualified to "teach" Afrikans than Afrikan women. If the measure of what should be the best characteristics of our educators is an undying love for our children, fearless, uncompromising study and presentation of the truth and unqualified self-sacrifice, then women in the Afrikan tradition unquestionably qualify.

Being a "healer" is evident in the elemental make-up of all of these qualities. Afrikan women heal all of us through being our Ancestors, through doing what they would do, through returning us to our Way. They love us in ways other women do not have the spiritual depth to imagine.

We are the culmination of the Afrikans who came before us. And, because we honor, love and take pride in our Ancestors, we do the same for ourselves. This, what should be a self-evident continuity of what is Afrikan, must be manifest in each conscious Afrikan, in each generation. Being part and parcel of a self-respecting people and tradition, Afrikan women are called to dynamically and progressively "represent the continuity of Afrikan people." It is through this self-actualization that we identify, internalize and practice those qualities that characterize the strength of the Afrikan line.

Character is more than a individual function. It is also a quality of families/lineages, communities and nations. When we see adults, those responsible for rearing our children and providing stability, we know the quality of the family they represent. Even more than the Afrikan man, because she is more in the center of public life in our spaces, the Afrikan woman must *blacknificently*[21] "represent the stability of the Afrikan family." She is the primary reflection of our families' ability to maintain our cultural integrity.

There is no greater measure of the depth of a Sister's good character than the seriousness and accuracy with which she "maintain[s] and pass[es] on Afrikan culture." If virtuous character is defined and enacted through the thinking, speaking and acting of one's culture (recognizing that different cultures have different definitions of what constitutes worthy and unworthy character), a culture that evolved through the interactive, unfolding lineage of that people, then the degree to which one's character is virtuous is determined by how well one maintains and passes that culture on.

There are reasons why "the marketplace" is ourstorically the domain of Afrikan women. More than any other public venue, it is here where Afrikan women empower "our people to understand the spirit of economic exchange and distribution of our resources." As Amos N. Wilson reminded us, the economy is a set of relationships existing between people that sets the stage for how and why goods and services are distributed among that people.[22] Such an established social network precedes the production, exchange and even consumption of goods and services. Therefore, the basic nature of these relationships, of how our people naturally communicate with and treat each other, is most purely reflected in the market among the women who jointly "own" and control it.

Each Afrikan woman must "be a scientist of the sacred." A scientist studies, searching for solutions and truth, two indistinguishable intellectual aspirations. Such a use of energy requires that Afrikan women make second nature a number of exemplary rules neophytes to the Kemetic Mystery System had to make a normal operating part of their very being. True scientists work to govern their own minds, to elevate themselves above unreasoned bias[23] and be devoted to a vision of truth which can only be gained through conscious study. Truth is sacred and it can only be extracted through scientific study. And rightly so, to our Ancestors, the finding of scientific order was only available in the study of what is natural.

It is because of this mission of scientifically searching for our sacred truth that each of our Sisters becomes "a spiritual leader." Again, genuine leaders are workers, recognized as leaders by the community that knows their worth. Spirit is inextricably intertwined into everything Afrikan. And spirit defines the basis of one's moral stand, how one treats the world and others. So, to be a leader, in the Afrikan mind, is to be a spiritual leader.

The goal of every Afrikan woman must also be to "be an intellectual," not in the sense of study for study's sake, but to know truth so that it imbues practice with purpose. The Yoruba use the term *eko* when referring to this character building way of thinking about learning and the subsequent application of knowledge acquired in this way. To use Elleni Tedla's words,

> The Yoruba word *eko* – which translates as education in its widest meaning – conveys the Yoruba aim of developing one's spirituality, intellect and oral literature, as well as one's skills in agriculture and crafts, and physical strength and agility. Above all, *eko* aims at developing a person's character and wisdom. In other words, it is concerned with the discipline of all the faculties of the learner...[24]

The Afrikan woman who lives *eko* reflects a wholistic character modeled after the balance so evident in the Universe. Like our Sister goddess Ma'at, she lives and breathes a material/spiritual, manual/mental, self/others synthesis.

All of this culminates in the Afrikan woman being "Divine." And this means far more than it suggests. The Afrikan woman's divinity is locked in her procreative gift. But equal to this is her responsibility of exemplifying a goddess likeness.

Aspiring to divinity is the ultimate Afrikan quality. It is clearly evident in our scientific understanding of the cycle individuals follow when moving out of the wholly spiritual into the physical, being tested and honed, and then returning from the physical into the spiritual again that characterizes the human/spiritual being throughout our recorded time.

Military-Mindedness

The military is the institution charged with the responsibility for defending the people from any physical threat, without or within,[25] which would deprive them of being themselves. Whether a standing army or one organized with citizen-soldiers at a moment's notice, it is the armed extension of any whole society and culture waging physical battle against any aggressing group or other nation whose hostility in some way prevents the people from being self-defining, self-empowering, solvent and sovereign.

Regrettably, it has primarily become a policing agency

or, better yet, an occupying force within the majority of our societies on the Continent and around the world. In most of these situations, they are there to prevent rebellion by Afrikans against further exploitations by outsiders through their strategically placed, "elected" or imposed, henchmen.

The military is not just a minor appendage of society in comparison to the other institutions. This has become increasingly true as "war and rumors of war" have become an everyday sign of the times everywhere.[26] In this aggressively more volatile context, the military rises as the most important institution in repelling invasion, assault, occupation, domination or other harmful violations from outside (as well as any rebellion and anarchy triggered internally). At the least, it should become any physically threatened people's preeminent priority. For it is a normal and natural defense mechanism any viable people use to protect themselves.[27]

Any sovereign people, conscious of being threatened or attacked, mobilizes for defense and retaliation to repel and "school" the attacker. It is only a people who has become vanquished into a submissive pacification who does not respond militarily to invasion, assault, occupation, domination or other harmful violations from outside.[28]

Vanquished people often try to appeal to the "humanity" of their destroyers as a means of lessening the assault. They often promise (whether spoken or implied) to not retaliate against those who have committed every imaginable evil against them in exchange for a "kinder, gentler" domination and/or destruction. Is this the legacy we want to pass down – that of a doomed, pacified people? Is this how we want to be remembered?

Resorting to passivity as a means of arresting an unspeakable and ongoing murderous rampage, does not work to appease the perpetrators who directly benefit from their offensives and have every intention of continuing to do so. Their heartfelt plan is to instill a crippling fear and pain. Reducing their victims to frightened, mindless objects who believe themselves incapable of defending or fending for themselves, is not an aside or afterthought easily surrendered with the victims' plea for mercy. These social states are installed by design.

At no point in history is there any credible evidence that supplicating tyrants works. Such policies only serve to protect, secure and encourage aggressors as they continue to find more sophisticated ways to violate and exploit those who allow themselves to remain subject to their whim. Such policies have only made sense and function correctly to maintain harmony among people and in societies where everyone's humanity is prized. They can only work where civilization, correctly defined in human terms, prevails.

Warriorhood calls for an approach completely different from that of supplicants relative to the enemies of our people. It demands that we act against them as we know, deep down in our hearts and souls, warriors do.

It is different when we are ignorant or afraid. But knowing conquers fear. Fearfulness is not in a warrior's character. Fear cannot carry the burden of war.

Our knowing and intrepidation make it impossible for us to seek the back road to a delusional peace. They force us to stand in the face of our enemies and command victory and justice.

There is no other way. There is no gray area to hide in. There is only vanquishment or victory for warriors with a just cause.

To this end, we must build armies. And, more than anything else learned from successfully operating from a disadvantaged position within the enemy's camp, we should know that building liberation armies requires a thoughtful discretion. There can be no slogans, no mottos, no insignia, no ranks, no dues, no broadcasting or public proclamations of intent, no evidence outside concrete results, no visibility.

The single, most consistent piece of evidence that a guerrilla is a guerrilla is that the enemy, within and without, does not know he or she is one.

Revolutions are done. They are not a point of conversation,[29] except to discuss strategies and tactics for immediate implementation. "Two men in a burning house must not stop to argue."[30] Revolutions are not something for tomorrow. They are to be done now.[31] What possible questions are there when you *know* your enemy and *know* this foe will never stop until there is no longer any evidence of your existence?

It is Ptahhotep who reminds us that

> The trusted man is one who does not speak the first thing that comes to mind; and he will become a leader. A man of means has a good name, and his face is benign."[32]

On the other hand

> The fool who does not hear, he can do nothing at all. He looks at ignorance and sees knowledge. He looks at harmfulness and sees usefulness. He does everything that one detests and is blamed for it every day. He lives on the things by which one dies. His food is evil speech.[33]

Afrikan men and women coming into consciousness, full of a dormant righteous rage brought to life by conditions and contradictions, expect to find an army to work with, not a bunch of loud, insecure personalities debating what we do and do not, can and cannot, will and will not have. This is confusing and demoralizing.

Of course, Europeans know this morass of contention and inaction is what they will find. In fact, they depend on us having, at most, nothing more than a rag tag militia without a concrete mission other than within a vision of a european-created anarchy from which we can benefit. As romantically revolutionary as anarchic opportunism may sound to some, this mentality is still european-centered because the focus is on waiting for the contradictions of european culture and society to implode.

Nonetheless, there are many serious questions that need to be well answered before attempting to raise an army in enemy occupied territory. At minimum, they should include inquiries into the following:

- Where would you recruit the best, most experienced, conscious warriors?

- By what means would you persuade them to walk with you? And why should they? Remember that warriors who cannot follow cannot lead. Warriors who cannot listen, who do not hear anything but their own voices, cannot constructively instruct others.[34]

- How will you determine who is an enemy infiltrator?[35]

- How will they be able to tell that you are not a front for the enemies of Afrika, a recruiter looking to gain the confidence of and betray those most qualified and prone to real revolutionary action?

- How would they sustain themselves and their families, and how would their method(s) of gaining sustenance tie them to you?

- How will secrecy be maintained from the moment of recruitment?

- How do you assess their abilities and usefulness?

- Will they unquestionably submit to a direct order, a master plan?

Of course, it is always easy to criticize any set of questions which force us to take a logical revolutionary stand, questions which bring us face-to-face with the insecurities and fears of actual, definitive, uncompromised nationbuilding. We can always argue that this or that point is overemphasized or missing. We can turn another potentially revolutionary act into an endless, dysfunctional debate. We already have so much extensive practice at it. Or we can choose to ask and answer only those questions which cause us to act and direct the action toward the liberation, empowerment and sovereignty of our people. Healers with vision will only momentarily allow themselves to be distracted by the ramblings of those who are about nothing, but who eagerly criticize what is actually being done to build real, flesh and blood, liberation armies.

The Purpose of War

We are at war, pure and simple. Some have tried to dress it up in a plethora of disarming ways. But, the truth be told, based on indisputable historical and ourstorical evidence, we are at war.

And, whether we like it or not, we are at war under the conditions of battle imposed by others because the Afrikan way of war holds no logic here. There are no ground rules except destruction. There is no functioning moral base or ethical guidelines. And there is no escape.

Therefore, if we are to win, we must understand these genocidal conditions as they have been brought to us or continue to misinterpret their meaning and lose. If we are to apprehend what we must do, we must understand the purpose and nature of war for europeans in its asilically fulfilling function.

An easy way to grasp the significance and interrelatedness of war, violence and domination to the european mind, is to look at their vision of the future. Where a people sees itself going tells you a lot about where it has been and toward what it is now directing its greatest energies.

For Yurugu, war is a casual pastime as well as a passionate vocation. It is what they do, playfully and in all seriousness, as you would a never-ending game, hobby or collection for which there is no possible end until you cease to exist or all is consumed in or by it (an impossibility as long as you exist). The phrase "state of perpetual war" often used in the historical literature to describe their interpersonal relations and ethnic conflicts/cleansings during Medieval times, is characteristic of all their time. From their beginnings to the end game they dream of, they have aspired for "a war that will last forever." And, in this pursuit, they have created a world of untold horrors, a world they cannot fix, and cannot risk changing for fear of losing what little they have of themselves and, therefore, must make appear normal so that history will not hold them uniquely at fault.

So, "peace," whether advertised in eternal or transitory terms, is the rhetorical ethic fed those among us who do not have the capacity to fathom the necessary permanence of their alien dreams of all-consuming violence.[36] It is a well-wielded lie to distract others from the genocidally supremacist intent of a people who live to destroy.

Toward this end, at this point in their warmongering evolution, they have been able to successfully use their political science to ideologically define their war as one of the modern, progressive world against the old, regressive one. Many of us have fallen for this tactical politico-military propaganda and believe that their battle for control, global domination and the establishment of an irresolvable, eternal state of internecine conflict is the normal state of human relations on every square foot of the planet, minus their heavily protected, demilitarized zones.

Under no condition should we succumb to the myth of this carnage as a war of good against evil, except they be the evil. Through the intelligence of a warrior's insight, it can be readily exposed as a war waged by evil against the possibility of there ever being good again.

There can be no end to this violence against human sanity until there are no longer individuals aspiring to absolute power over others. Yet, we must be keen enough to know that such a naturally peaceful disposition is an impossibility for those born and bred of the european asili. So, the idea that this chaos (state of perpetual war) will cease when they have won is as ludicrous as the notion of negro aspirants selflessly returning to assist their communities after having "made it" in others'. It is an impossibility if they or their followers continue to lead.

When studying the implementation and trajectory of yurugu's genocidal vision of us, we can see that removing the enemy is a real possibility in their mind. Even though we know their greatest enemy lies within, they have projected it onto us to defend their fragile egos. And the only way they can defeat or find release from that enemy is through mass suicide. The dictates of one's asili cannot be indefinitely suppressed. The killing rage will continue as long as they do.

Rightfully, many call for reparations to correct for the damage done to Afrikan people. But these calls cannot be couched in limited analysis or demands. If there is to be correction, it must be absolute[37] for "what is a gift from the powerful if not a cut from property stolen from the people?"[38]

First, we should determine the crimes for which we should be compensated? This war against Afrikan people has been in progress for centuries. It is not limited in time or space to the Ntoreasee Otuko, our enslavement in this particular land or the colonization of the Continent.

The scramble for Africa continues. The mentacidal propaganda of white innocence[39] and Black complicity continues to find disciples. The Maafa continues, unabated. Nothing in our enemies' war against Afrikan people has stopped. It has done nothing but escalate.

Knowing this, even given one aspect of what has been done to Afrikan people, "They owe us more than they could ever pay."[40] How would we begin to calculate the cost of this repair? All that has been taken must be returned – nothing more, nothing less.

> In one estimation, by no means overblown, between 1619 and 1865, slaves just in the United States were forced to perform 222,505,049 man-hours of unpaid wages. The claim for reimbursement for those wages (arrears with interest) devolves on us their descendants, to whom the debt is now owing....[one estimate given for this is] the 1983 value of the slave labor expropriated between 1620

> and 1865 from Black Americans ranged from $96.3 billion to $9.7 trillion, depending on whether a 3 percent or a 6 percent rate of interest is applied....[Another lesser estimate] figured the 1983 value of slave labor performed from 1790 to 1860 at between $2.1 trillion and $4.7 trillion....[from another angle, another estimate] set the white benefits from labor market discrimination against Blacks from 1929 to 1969 (a short 40 years) at $689 billion in 1972 prices, compounded at an interest rate of 6 percent per annum. Adjusted for inflation, the 1983 total came to $16.3 trillion. In view of these and similar calculations, David Swinton concludes that it would take more than the entire wealth of the whole United States to compensate Black folk fully.[41]

None of these estimates considers the destruction wrought on the Continent from the collection of Afrikans for enslavement and just general resource theft, the coffle lines (where one in every three of us were murdered), the dungeons (where four in every five of us were murdered), colonization (where millions of us were murdered) or the millions upon millions of Afrikan lives which never came into existence because their would-be descendants were murdered before they had the chance to be conceived. The value of Afrikan lives is almost never taken into consideration in equations attempting to calculate reparations to Afrikan people. Not that it does not have merit, but compensation is always oversimplified into economic terms, into labor, production, hours, kwk. As difficult as it may seem to some, this is the easy way out.

In "Mentacide: The Ultimate Threat to the Black Race," Bobby E. Wright closed the debate on a simply material reparatory compensation (a mentality we have fallen into as a result of our submersion in a capitalist system). In his challenge to warriors, he said:

> Our Black mission is clear, [Afrikan warriors] are men and women of destiny and their task is to develop a social theory which will liberate the minds and bodies of their

> people. They must take the unequivocal position that if the Black race is to perish, the world must perish with them. Blood debts must be repaid in blood. Blacks must never accept money and privileges as repayment for the mistreatment of their people. The past Black generations who suffered for no other reason than the color of their skin must be avenged not because of hate but for justice.[42]

They owe us all, minus an insignificant deduction for a limited, ignorant complicity.

Bear in mind, though, that our war, though largely centered around them, is not strictly with Europeans. Our argument is with all people, all nations, who have been and are at war with Afrikan people and continue to benefit from past and/or present aggressions against us. And this obtains whether they pretend to be ignorant of their offensives or not. Our righteous rage is directed against any and everyone who wants what we have and, in the process, seeks to prevent us from being Afrikan.

For centuries, this motley crew of enemies has included Europeans, Asians, Arabs and negroes. This should be obvious. But for a people brought up with a fear of personal destruction and neediness of validation by their destroyers, it is not so easily discernable.

Regardless of the degree to which we all recognize it or not, we are at war. And people who do not recognize that they are at war when others seek to destroy them will always be ill-prepared, reactively defensive and bound to lose. Such a position is patently unacceptable to warriors.

Forgiveness? Forgetfulness? Nowhere is there a statute of limitations on murder. We are dealing with blood debts. Righteous rage, i.e., acts against them, be they on paper or the physical battlefield, is justified. They have made their beds. Now, they must lie in them.

We are not a warlike people, but we have never shied away from addressing aggression. No matter the nature of the assault, we respond accordingly.

Ourstorically, Afrikans have understood that war should not focus on bringing destruction. It should return peace to the land. It entails the restoration of a balance which produces harmony. *This is the basis and science of Afrikan militarism.*

Therefore, in the tradition of our Ancestors, we have an responsibility to bring peace to the land by disarming the disrupter. This chaos will not stop until they are stopped.

This is a difficult task for those new to the frontlines and who have only learned to visualize war in the here and now and in the way that Yurugu has dictated it on this planet. Because so many of us have learned to see war only through the eyes of warmongers (and have even assimilated *their* rhetoric of war to bring about peace – i.e., war to insure their continued imperialistic/expansionist empire), and because we do not conceive of social reality in terms of a framework of Ma'at, we do not study war as having a naturally healing function. Nor do we see warriors as being our first line of healers.

In fact, those interpreting the reality of war in others' warmongering, unnatural way, much unlike our Ancestors, see warriors and healers as diametrically opposed mentalities. We have allowed the connection of being both a man of God and a man of War to become severed and oppositional in our thinking. They have forgotten that "the priests go to war with the warrior. They do not stand at the rear trading beads."[43]

Because we blindly and patriotically see european priorities as ours we have become oblivious to the fact that Europeans not only pray for victory at the inception of and during hostilities, but they also generally pray for war. Because we embrace their propaganda, we do not see that they have never separated church and state (e.g., "God bless America"). Their church always sanctions and gives their god's blessing to their imperialistic aggression.

We must remember that warfare is spiritual. Whether we consciously solicit it or not, Spirit is fully involved. So, it is not a question of divine intervention. It is a question of the degree to which Spirit is actively solicited and the righteousness of our cause.

Therefore, it stands to good reason that we can be no less relentless than those who hunt us. People must be spoken to in a language they can understand. So, those who have historically proven that their primary form of communication (even in the false pursuit of peace) is violence have to be answered in kind in order for them to get the message.

The misthesis that "revenge will only bring more bloodshed" holds no logic here, for justice is not revenge. Either way, our blood flows more. The ability to commit violence is no character flaw. In fact, for a people under physical attack, or existing in a state of oppression out of which they cannot break free without violence because their oppressor understands no other language, violence can be a commendable virtue. In such settings, violence tends to be one of the warrior's greatest weapons.

Ourstorically, violence has been a necessary part of the warrior's combative arsenal. It must be readily available at the slightest provocation in order to nip enemy incursions in the bud. There is nothing about the reality we find ourselves in which should make us believe otherwise.

Those who truly want lasting "peace and goodwill toward all men" should be able to recognize that this ideal is not possible in a situation of institutionally enforced chaos. So quickly, in our drive for peace at any cost, we forget that the european personality is not conducive to such a humane state of affairs. Only ahistorical, mentacidal, masochistic fools with a deathwish[44] would believe that they can rise up from being the preferred prey by being nonviolent with those who see them as their eternal enemy.

Along with this misthesis, warriors must throw out the

politicized notion that you cannot kill (every one) of your enemy. The same people who teach us this nonsense operate with the opposite conviction. As this instruction was originally conceived in the Afrikan mind, it was a statement of universal law in the context of those who acted as humans.[45] When Europeans and other aliens moved onto the world stage, this no longer remained the operative rule in war.

Moreover, the vanquished are in no position to proclaim that they will end the bloodshed by ceasing, or working to end, all violence. They have already been pacified. The most they can do is work toward disarming the rebellious within their community so as to make their destruction easier.

Only an equal, empowered to enforce this resolution at the international level, can authoritatively make such a declaration. Lasting negotiation requires equals and, even in peace, the maintenance of that equality. Only one in a position to be victorious can proclaim to pursue absolute peace and have others believe that it is of his own ideological volition.

So, even though they have claimed intergenocultural peace as their divine mission, negroes, lost souls and the like have no power to declare an Afrikan peace with Europeans, or anyone else for that matter. That is only a choice possible for those who have never left, or have fully returned to, their Ancestors' Way. And, even then, it can only be enforced from the seat of power.

Preparedness and Security[46]

Members of the centered Afrikan community need to establish and consistently demonstrate to ourselves a model of preparedness and security on par with the best of what our traditions evince of our abilities in times of war. We need to militarily grow to the point where we instinctively feel compelled to establish a defensible parameter and practice the righteously enraged mentality that goes along with its creation and maintenance. And we must stop tiptoeing around and onto the frontline as if enemies do not see us coming.[47] Similar to the characters in the movie *They Live*, you can see and they know that you can see. It should be obvious by now that they see and hear us loudly and clearly.

Using the insight gained through a judicious hindsight and a visionary foresight, we should be able to see that what is possibly more critical than anything else within the context of war is our need to seriously take on the responsibility of training our children in this duty to defend our right to be Afrikan. And, since experience has taught us that children are prone to do more of what they see than what they are told, especially in the face of the contradictory expression of thought, word and deed, we must provide them with exemplary, uncompromised examples of warriorhood. This includes tirelessly scrutinizing Asase Yaa, as well as this insane reality, for teachable moments from which they can intuitively learn what we already know must be the life's work of countless generations to come.

In this respect, ants can be very instructive. If even a small hole is made in their hill (community abode), especially on warm, sunny days when they have brought their eggs near the surface for the warmth, they *immediately* come out, in force, searching for the destructive threat and effectively deal with it. There is not even a moment's pause to contemplate or debate what to do or the consequences of dealing with the threat, in some cases, obviously powerful enough, in one blow, to cause significant damage to their home, if not wipe them out. They instinctively act.[48] "Instincts" can be socialized into humans. We call these responses second nature.

In the animal kingdom, even when there is an apparent fear of a mortal threat to the adults, the safety of the offspring takes priority over inaction. There is no retreat, no negotiation, no conversation, except to express immediately backed up warnings and threats. Those among the two-legged vanquished, however, have no such shame. They insistently claim that such defeatist, regressive inaction is a mark of their greater reasoning and sense of humanity. But warriors know that they are doing no more than grasping at excuses which will allow them to redefine manhood and womanhood along thoroughly subdued lines.[49]

Not long ago, a video about some water buffalo on the Continent was circulating on the internet under the title "Battle at Kruger."[50] One of the calves from this herd was captured by some lions determined to make a meal of it. At first, they continued on, distancing themselves from harm, seeing if the calf had the strength to escape of its own volition. But then to the lions' chagrin, after realizing that it could not free itself from their grasp, the water buffalo returned to reclaim their own, using their horns and hoofs to attack the pride and even using horns to jettison a lion. The lions retreated and the water buffalo continued as before, liberated calf in tow. We should be as furious and spontaneously courageous in our acting against what others are doing to our children and families as we are in complaining about it.

Vigilance about potential threats to the community is the prerogative of those who have decided that they have a special role in securing Afrikan premises.[51] Sentries by choice, these mobile warriors are aware of each other's presence and body language. And they spread themselves out well enough when we gather so that anything "odd" or "out of place" is easily detected, surrounded and removed as a threat without alarm to the other participants.

Such conscious courage leads seasoned warriors and those in training to automatically make sure that their vehicles are always parked with the side of the individual(s) most deserving of defense in the brightest light and facing the destination so their vulnerability is limited. They are always identifiable as those defenders who open the door and step out of the house first to recognize and confront any external threat (a reverse of the showy nonsensical european chivalry of putting the female in front on defenseless display). The same reconceptualization of what defense should be in the Afrikan community applies when a couple or family is coming around a blind corner. Warriors should always be on point.

Socially retarded defensive displays are also prominent in situations where misguided gallantry leads Brothers to usher Sisters down the stairs first in front of them so they can be "viewed." Equally ignorant are those of us who seat or stand our Sisters closer toward the direction from which harm can most easily come in a restaurant, classroom or meeting, kwk, than us, an ignorance not to be confused with those who need to guardedly face the doors and/or other openings.

At crucial, questionable or life-threatening times, a man placing himself before a woman does not constitute sexist thought or action. These calculated moves speak to the exact opposite quality. The protector should always be in the position to best break or soften the other's fall. He or she who defends always moves between the threat and the potential victim. Men warriors must think to place ourselves between our women and danger. Such practices only become problematic when an arrogant, egotistical misogyny, something entrenched and pervasive in western and eastern societies, accompanies this more intelligent protectiveness.

Our Ancestors' everyday normative practice of this basic level of security is no where more evident than in the following statement by Anthony Ephirim-Donkor.

> To underscore the protective nature of the paternal spirit the sleeping arrangement of the Akan is such that the male always sleeps in front of the female. The sleeping position must be such that if the woman has to get up she may have to go over or around her husband. What is meant here is that the man not only protects the woman spiritually but physically as well. In times of danger the man is the first to rise up to confront whatever the perceived danger or threat is. He must have unimpeded access to the door to arrest the threat, and by the same token be the first to be attacked.[52]

Unlike the many eurocentric (especially feminist) misinterpretations of the functionality of gender roles within our traditions, this statement gives contextual respectability to the Akan proverb that "a woman lies behind her man." Afrikan women want Afrikan men who will fulfill this divine purpose.

This same spontaneous protective courtesy for Afrikan women must become the normal expectation in every situation and under every condition Afrikan men find themselves in the presence of Afrikan women. At no time in public (i.e., outside of wholly secured sacred spaces where this would be a given) should there not be an inconspicuous circle/fence of Brothers around a gathering of Sisters. There should never be a time when the Sisters have gathered the children together when there is not a Brother present to insure security and discipline.

The womb must always be protected from every possible angle, including above and below. To this end, the concentric sphere model of defense and nurturance should always be in place. Because we are at war, under no conditions should it be relaxed.

As long as a Sister is in a Brother's sight she should be in his immediate guard. Nothing should override this or distract his attention from what enters within her space. (Specifically, in relation to complements, when in immediate proximity, a Brother should never allow anything alien/harmful to move between him and her.) The only thing that should distract our eyes and ears away from our Sisters is the assessment of a potential threat. And being out of ear and eyeshot is also no excuse for an absence of vigilance. Consideration of all possibilities is always a must.

We must also continue to remind ourselves that our warriors-in-training should not be exempt from internalizing the responsibility of this duty either. It still amazes me how much pride our young men take in inconspicuously physically guarding their sisters and mothers, especially before and after communal gatherings. When they are allowed, the seriousness with which they take the role of being "man of the house," even when real men are around, is astounding. To see them studying their environment for unsecured spaces and every potential weapon, and to see this evolve into second nature, is something to behold in those others would have us spoil into obsolescence. For observant adults in the community, these are points of Afrikan pride.

I am always proud when I see an elder leaving a function flanked by security, whether that elder recognizes it as such or not. In fact, one of the most powerful examples of warriorhood I have seen is of a Brother, himself an elder-in-training, who, instead of coming into a lecture and partaking of the sumptuous meal afterward, sat outside in the shadows across the street and watched for potential threats to members of the community who were coming, going and milling around the facility. He did this until the day's activities were basically over.

He reminded me of the blacksmith in some Afrikan villages whose residence was beyond the communal social space, but who saw no disadvantage in the solitary job of minding the perimeter for threats against that sacred space.[53] These sentries were keenly aware of the individual selflessness requisite for gaining, securing and perpetually sustaining sovereignty. And it is in this same spirit that John Henrik Clarke called on us to "produce a caliber of young people who can take on the loneliness of struggle."[54]

On a final note, what of evacuation and internal concealment? We have all kinds of plans and exercises to keep us safe in case of fire, weather and medical emergencies. But we come up severely lacking when it comes to managing a direct military/police assault or simply investigative presence at the door or entering our sacred spaces, our homes, schools and other places of activity.

We have no escape routes or plans for our children and elders. We have no code words to alert them or each other of an alien presence. We have neither established nor built places deep within our facilities to secure them. We have not identified and agreed upon points at which to rendezvous and collect ourselves and do a count in the worst case scenario. Our centers must be protected, militarily.

You cannot consider yourself at war without constantly working toward greater preparedness. Enemies are most easily able to overcome us when we are surprised or in panic, the result of a lack of thorough preparedness in all areas.

Battle Fatigue[55]

Battle fatigue is a very real and most serious spiritual, psychological, emotional and physical actuality for those Afrikans who have uncompromisingly, with clear sight and with firm resolve, taken the blood oath and chosen to accept the challenge of the frontline. The impact can be devastating, even among those who cannot, or refuse to, recognize what it is doing to them and us as they continue, without rest, without complaint, to carry the burden of a nation on their shoulders. Warriors must find ways to release themselves from the more harmful aspects of this burden or, in the end, they can do our movement more damage than good. If seriously contemplated in the spirit of comradery and love in which they are given, the following three statements should assist in facilitating a healing process for an ever present battle fatigue.

Still Waters

If I have learned nothing else from being a warrior scholar, I have learned that warriors become tired, too. Like everyone else, we need rest.[56] "Work is good provided you do not forget to live."[57]

I have learned that, if we are to operate at the peak of

our potential, we need regular and complete psychological and physical breaks from the battle lines. Five or six hours of restless sleep a night will not do. In order for sleep to work, there must be peace in it. Our bodies, minds and spirits require quality time in safe, demilitarized zones in order for us to continue operating optimally as Afrikan warrior scholars on the battlefield. Sound rest allows us to remain balanced while fending off the relentless assault against our humanity. Exceptionally arduous efforts require exceptional degrees of rest to keep the warrior balanced. Balance is critical to our maintenance of Ma'at. And, at the root, Ma'at is what makes us Afrikan.

Warriors often forget this. We often forget that work requires rest. Work and rest are complements. They move as one.

If we somehow forget this, sooner or later, the imbalance will affect us. After long periods without rest, even minor psychological and/or physical complications are pretty good signals that something is amiss. Sometimes these breakdowns are gradual, sometimes they occur suddenly, but they are always preceded by other subtle but recognizable warnings such as the following: We cannot rest even though we force ourselves to take days off. We isolate ourselves from community. Or we overexert ourselves even further seeking any form of peace. We unwittingly vent at family. We almost always feel overwhelmed. We cannot stop even when we can feel the extremes of fatigue.

Mostly, though, we don't pick up on the warnings until they are repeated so many times that we cannot help but notice them. War has an uncanny way of consuming all the time and energy that we ordinarily might spend on ourselves.[58] With all that is involved, it is hard for us to find the time to see that these signals reflect an unnatural state. And, even if we do notice them, the time needed to figure out ways to achieve inner balance is not deemed reasonable, available or, even, advantageous.

But, whether we find the time or not, without rest, eventually, we will meet with an often prolonged, painful and, sometimes, debilitating lesson about the fragility of our temple and sanity. Yet, even when we fully recognize the warnings for what they are, rest remains a hard lesson to practice. It remains very hard to stop and smell the roses when battles are raging all about us. We have solemnly promised the Creator and our Ancestors to stand tall as the indefatigable underdogs holding the victorious line. Time, study and conflict have taught us the value of remaining determined to win, and at any cost. Simply put, in order to be the type of warriors we have become, we have accepted that no sacrifice is too large or small for our people, even our health.

That, however, does not change the fact that we need quality rest. And, if we are to come to truly understand that rest is a tremendously vital part of our individual effort to battle well, we must seriously consider our military obligation within the context of several related factors. We must consider it in terms of how long this battle has lasted, and that it is far from over. We must consider it with the understanding that we are returning warriors of returning warriors. Our ancestors have been fighting Europeans, Arabs and Asians for millennia. And we are they. Further, we must consider our obligation with a real personal appreciation of the concept of durability. The length of time a warrior can stay on the battlefield before expiring from violence or a frustrated exhaustion is limited by his skill and internal resolution, or inner strength.

Skill, of course, is beside the point. We master the means of warfare by using common sense to do what must be done. We find a way because it must be found. Skill is dictated and revealed by necessity and refined by determination. But, and regardless of our enemies' terms for it, exhaustion of "internal resolution or inner strength" for us warriors is a *spiritual* burnout. Necessity and determination do not naturally prevent it. It occurs when warriors have used up their allocation of warrior energy for that time and are operating on mental and physical fumes, not spiritual fuel. Resolution is kinetic mental energy. It is mental energy in motion. And mental energy requires spiritual fuel.

In a desperate effort to win, now, and at any cost, we continue to take from self without allowing the source to replenish itself. Spiritual connection requires contact. Contact requires peace, prayer and meditation. And peace, prayer and meditation require conscious, concentrated quietude. Communing with Spirit is not accidental. It does not just happen because you are born Afrikan. It calls for deep, sincere, undisturbed thought.

Battling without rest, regardless of how long the road ahead or how desperate the situation is, is a linear approach to war. We have logically adopted it because of the ongoing, pressing demands of waging war against an enemy bent on our genocide. But Afrikans should fight like we have always done everything, in cycles, not dead-ended lines. We balance work with rest. We rest in between calculated conflicts. We may not choose our enemies, but we must choose when and how we will deal with them.

If we are to win against this onslaught and put a final stop to this process of deAfrikanization, we must recognize that the longer a warrior is able to remain on the battlefield the better a warrior he becomes. Experience teaches. Great efforts in great battles produce master warriors. The Shona of southern Afrika call those warriors who have mastered the art of war through defending our people's way *Mwene Mutapa*, which means "master soldier." That is our aspiration. Also, the longer we are on the battlefield the more opportunities we have to pass on our skills, helping to build better warriors to follow us.

No matter how hard we work to prepare ourselves individually, we have to constantly remember that this is not our battle by ourselves. It is our people's battle. We must win this as a people, regardless of dissenters and abstainers within. negroes will always follow whoever they see as the most powerful, whether their masters seek to destroy them and their family or not.[59] Individualized heroism cannot heal the wounded ego of soldiers so long without complete victory. Winning is the result of a joint action, of the effort of a coordinated army, an army of heroes. "The lone man cannot exhibit bravery."[60] We must understand this as self-chosen members of the warrior class who have willingly assumed our Creator-given mission as well as the nationbuilding responsibilities of others in the community who have chosen fear over their children's empowerment.

Warriors detest weakness among would-be warriors. That is only natural. However, when those would-be warriors become the majority of a potentially more powerful enemy's army, this detestation can become a distraction and sap the warrior's stamina and will. It is stressful to have to fight your own *and* the enemy in order to free your own from the enemy. No matter how hard we try, "One person cannot perform a task meant for a thousand."[61] Under such conditions, the battle within increasingly works to undermine the battle without.

Because war is a mental as well as physical action, the conversations that go on inside our heads influence the success of our actions. They determine the strength and focus of our energies. And when those conversations become unnecessarily laden with battles against external enemies, as well as those who should be fighting by our sides but have either turned traitor or apathetic bystander, our energy is drained to our enemies' advantage. As a fellow warrior scholar once said about Europeans as we casually conversed in a safe communal space, "They're not even here and we're battling them in our heads."

The same applies to negroes and lost souls. They create chaos in our minds even in their physical absence. We cannot allow ourselves to be sidetracked into a stress-inducing and psychologically arresting frustration over those among us who have crossed over to swell the ranks of our enemies.

Those thoughts must not be allowed to dominate even a fraction of our thinking. They destroy the clarity of our vision. When such thoughts are present, they must be exchanged for images of the small but phenomenal victories that tell us that, even if there are only two of us, we are winning.

Of course it would be easier to recognize and just live by Afrikan cycles of rest and battle if there were more soldiers to divide the work among. But, even given the superior quality of our Asafo, at this point, there are not. So, given that fact, we must find ways to still successfully wage war and attain an appropriate amount of quality rest even without sufficient reinforcements.

Again, sadly, most of us do not pick up on our need for rest until we discover that we have created a situation where there is little to no peace in our lives. We usually stumble upon this realization only when our health forces us to see that it is nearly too late to reverse the fatal wear and tear that doing the work of too many has on our minds and bodies. Exhaustion to the point of a debilitating dis-ease is a cancer that doesn't just hurt us. It weakens those around us. It tears into the loved ones who depend on us for companionship and security. The Afrikan warrior spirit is an energy positively or negatively affected by all who do and have contributed to its existence. Restlessness, vented inward or outward, disturbs or, rather, disrupts its movement toward victory.

Although a true and lasting peace during war is not an option, being at peace with being at war is. We need rest to achieve this. And, therefore, a fair share of our energy must be directed toward finding time to meditate (without reliving and critiquing confrontations), sit or lie down (without editing a mission statement or reading ourstories of rebellion), be in nature (without allowing our thinking to wander about the environment looking for possible guerrilla lessons), feast (without confusing eating utensils with weapons) and laugh (at more than just our enemies' mishaps). In other words, we need to make the time to completely distance ourselves from the frontlines. Even if only momentarily, we need to mentally and physically find peace so that true rest and relaxation are possible. Regularly submitting our entire being to enjoying our community and playing with our wives and children must become an ongoing ritual. We must find times for rest and rejuvenation from battle so that we can return with an invigorated, refocused fury. So, in moments of rest, be patient knowing that "still waters run deep."

Morale

When most of what you seem to hear and see is bad news, shocking realizations about those around you who you thought were clear about their Afrikanity, painful news about those you honored because of their words and/or nationbuilding efforts that epitomized warriorhood, scary stories about "everyday" Afrikan people in mentacidal anarchy, and when what you hear and see is no exaggeration, what do you do to maintain your sense of direction and keep progressively moving forward? This is a question of morale. And it is a question asking how do warrior scholars, whose vision is not limited to their personal glorification and individualistic accumulation of knowledge, keep their morale when, seemingly, all around them there is nothing but deceit, suffering[62] and signs of military inferiority and vanquishment.

A defeatist attitude attends a logical consideration of the "fact" that Europeans have a massive destructive arsenal and means of gathering information. Propaganda is a weapon of war, though. Therefore, we cannot consider their truth in their terms.

There is no Afrikan logic in the eureason they spread across the battlefield. Their propaganda is meant to undermine the Afrikan possibility and break our will to exercise Afrikan power. A weapon's efficacy is relative to the user's vision and determination, not merely its destructiveness.

How many times can we count our rising into victory in the face of being incredibly outnumbered and outgunned?[63] We know the answer to the question "What makes a soldier ride alone into battle?"[64]

Yurugian media outlets stage reality for those susceptible to their brainwashing. It is presented in such a way that their prey can come to no conclusion except that they will lose if they try to rebel against their oppression. Yet, too, there is an obvious factor that has stood the test of Afrikan time. Odds have never been a deterrent to a determined warrior.

Nothing is impenetrable. Nothing is indestructible. No people is irremovable from a tyrannical seat of power. No rule is unbreakable. Therefore, it is obvious that our fear is evident in our inaction. Ample evidence of this is recognizable in our self-destructive action also. These two reactions are the same. Knowing the deceit and dominative spirit of Europeans, warrior scholars holding a victorious vision for Afrikan people must determine what spiritual, mental and/or physical martial assault against this enemy can produce meaningful, progressive, cumulative damage now and/or later, rather than submit to defeat.

In general, though, loss of morale among warrior scholars is the result of a combination of factors, most of which can be found entangled in the social sediment all about us. It is the result of painful dejection and feelings of insecurity from those who should be closest to us in this fight. These demoralizing factors include:

- feelings of isolation and doubt as to one's individual capabilities,
- separation from birth family and peers (conscious and unconscious),
- questioning one's own rightness in the face of preponderant condemnation and denouncement by the majority of people, even Afrikans,

- feelings of being militarily overwhelmed and
- doubts about economic security and survival (for self and others in the community).

When issues of sanity and survival are in question, especially when we fear that what may be coming will undermine them even more, morale can reach an incapacitating nadir. At that point, a soldier's effectiveness can become seriously compromised by states of seemingly unbearable despair.

Sometimes, shrapnel from these issues can be carried in the wounds of unsuspecting warriors into the Medial Zone and, even momentarily, past the border into the Innermost Sanctuary of our Centers. And, even if it is quickly contained, it still can have an impact. With each new vanguard, the impact of this intrusion must be aggressively confronted with every resource and energy at our disposal until it ceases to threaten the Center's harmony.

If warrior scholars working toward the Center take a moment to reassess just how far they have come from their pre-ReAfrikanized, demoralized state, they will be able to compile an impressive collection of moralizing factors which have a demonstrated record of countering yurugu's physical and mental assault against our being. This collection of factors has proven quite effective in keeping despair, for all intents and purposes, at bay. These essentials include:

- a knowledge of self and a commitment to the study and practice of a righteous Afrikan philosophy of life (spiritual, mental and physical)
- a fully functional integration and assimilation into the conscious community,
- economic independence,
- the support of immediate or significant (sanguine or social) family members,
- an equally dedicated complement,[65]

- having and rearing children (biological and social),
- the highly visible presence of internal and external threats to the enemy and knowledge of frontline imperatives and
- the audacity and sense of accountability expressed by Jenoch and other Asafo.

All of these we find nestled comfortably at the Center nurturing those present and awaiting those yet to arrive.

Progress

We are warrior scholars in recovery from addictions to pale appetites. As such, we are still susceptible to the demoralizing tow of propaganda specifically directed against our efforts toward liberation.[66] Therefore, we must take care to reconceptualize how we measure our progress so that it positively reflects this imbalance to our advantage. Everything is relative. So, this measurement must be grounded in our assessment of the relative psychological density or fluidity of those who occupy the layers of our Centers.[67]

Sometimes, it may appear that all our revolutionary struggle is for naught.[68] It may appear as if Europeans are still effortlessly winning over the minds of Afrikan people, while we are struggling to maintain the attention of our own children. We, ourselves, may also unwittingly fall victim to the morale battering of a thoroughly anti-Afrikan society that has severely infected those who most need to heed our warnings.

We can find ourselves resigning, feeling that we are doing no more than documenting our demise as we speak Afrikan truth to and about our people. Often we come to this conclusion when writing or speaking revolutionary truth because we are unable to find evidence of any immediate or emerging change or positive growth in those who claim that they are listening. In fact, at times, despite our best efforts, our conditions and mentality can look as if they are worsening for the community as a whole.

However, deep down in our spiritual core, we know better. With studied hindsight, we know that change at the personal level, which precedes change at the communal level, is a slow progress. Afrikans knowledgeable of our legacy of effective struggle know that this progress must take into account the fact that mentacide is a progressive disease. And mentacide must first be slowed down, then stopped, and finally reversed. Becoming Afrikan is a transformation that is ongoing and generally takes many, many, many determined years.

So, before we judge other Afrikans or become impatient with family (especially those making a serious, concerted effort to understand what is wrong) we have to ask ourselves how long it took us to progress to this point on our path. With sincere empathy, we have to humbly make the effort to look deeply inside to see just how very far we have yet to go.

In our reactionary despondency over our generally collective submission to eurocentric style progress, we also have to recognize that progress must be redefined. On the one hand, we know that being a shadow of the European means that we are moving in the direction that european culture is willing us. However, on the other hand, we must understand that not moving in that direction does not mean we are standing still or failing.[69] Instead it means that we are *progressing* in another direction.

Simply rejecting european culture and society *is* progress. And the more forceful and determined the rejection, the greater the advancement away from yurugu's reality. The problem here for most of us is that we are measuring our advancement based on our perception of the failure of the Afrikan community in general to detach and distance itself from the european mainstream. Even though the western media are currently the primary causal agents, we see evidence of this "failure" at the personal, interpersonal and genocultural level in a wide variety of suicidal acts of self-hatred.

It manifests in subtly suicidal acts such as bad diet, drugs and alcohol, physical inactivity, violence, over consumption, kwk, set in motion by our interpretation of reality through the eyes of our enemies. It is the outcome of the genocidal acts systematically committed by others against us, such as disease, diseducation, encarceration, birth control, disarmament, kwk. Many of us consistently overlook the fact that this "failure" is also propagated by the western media as the victory of western progress and the relative weakness and decline of our Afrikan foundations.

A more accurate, psychologically beneficial, Afrikan centered measurement of the progression or regression of the Afrikan centered community would be in seeing how far our thought and action are taking us away from where they want us to go. The greater the distance between us and their way, the greater our progress.

Afrikan centered progress is not complicated. When conscious, our rejection of them is an appreciation of us.

Most of us just do not know to interpret this deliberately rebellious movement as progress. Mainly, this is because, most often, Europeans still command the center of our interpretation of reality. We still base our success or failure on whether or not we think they are winning against us, not on whether or not we know we are winning against them. We forget that the Afrikan Way and the european way are irreconcilably different.[70] We forget that any Afrikan movement against them, away from them, is a progressive movement toward our empowerment.

Three profound thoughts come to mind when dealing with these sometimes debilitating distractions. First, a quote from an author unknown to me defines obstacles as the "things that you see when you take your eyes off of your goal." Obstacles are things that awaken your potential as you overcome them. Second, an Asante proverb directs us to "act as if it is impossible to fail." And, third, in the context of the specific role of warriors in the war for our solvency and humanity, the insightful Afrikan writer Ayi Kwei Armah guides us to see that:

> Endless our struggle must seem to those whose vision reaches only to the end of today[71]....The present is where we get lost – if we forget our past and have no vision of the future[72]....A healer needs to see beyond the present and tomorrow. He needs to see years and decades ahead. Because healers work for results so firm they may not be wholly visible till centuries have flowed into millennia. Those willing to do this necessary work, they are the healers of our people.[73]

Afrikan progress entails empowerment. And empowerment is a mental, physical and spiritual strengthening that parallels a decline in the european influence over our being. Ignoring for the moment the European's taste for using duplicitous manipulation, public demonization, institutionally sanctioned force and systematic, brutal, inhumane violence against those who refuse to mentacidally submit to their lies, the only way that strong, tradition honoring, self-defining Afrikan voices cannot be silenced is if they are completely independent of european sponsorship, censorship and, therefore, ownership. To be Afrikan we must be free to do so.

Declarations of Warriors

Every warrior needs guidelines, a set of unbreakable rules adhering to one's mind and soul at the same level of seriousness that blood oaths do.[74] The bond and threat to one's life and security must be felt so deeply that they remove the possibility of confusion in the heat of battle, when the enemy is the closest and most effective. We know we are at war, we know we are right, we know this is a battle to the end.

> This is a battle for the mind and souls of our people, and like any sustained battle, the advantages and ultimate victory lies with the morally righteous, the best prepared and the most determined.[75]

Below is a collection of commandments which, if thoughtfully followed, will provide any given Afrikan warrior with the necessary "advantages and ultimate victory" because they provide the psychological artillery needed to ward off questions of purpose, motivation and character. Warriors are, of course, encouraged to add those which more specifically apply to their unique frontline situations.

- I will not be intimidated by an enemy. I will show them no fear.
- I will not compromise the spiritual, cultural or social integrity of our people.
- I will not retreat from battle except as a tactic to gain a decisive military advantage.[76]
- I will train my mind, body and spirit in the warrior methods of my ancestors. I will study others' warrior methods only as a means of determining how to more decisively defeat them. I will remember that those we consider the masters of "death, destruction and domination" could never have defeated us without the assistance of traitors.
- I will never vent my rage against family.[77]
- I will protect my elders, complement and children to the death.
- I will show my people's enemies only the mercy they demonstrated toward my Ancestors (for they are their ancestors as I am mine).
- I will listen to no other propaganda than that of the Afrikan warriors who came before me and who now stand at my side because I understand that "one of the characteristics

of revolutionary propaganda must be truth."[78]

- I will not individually judge my enemy. Enemy is understood in the context of nations at war.

- I will *always* be on guard.

- I will *always* be prepared.

- I will *never* lower my eyes from the enemy.

- I trust only worthy Afrikans. (A person cannot be your friend and enemy at the same time. Dismiss contradictory Afrikans. Every warrior has to prove his or her loyalty and worth. The history of treason is well rooted within our compromised community.)

We must be clear about our need for a set of guiding warrior's declarations. *All* writings by serious Afrikan warriors, by Afrikans who recognize that we are at war with a mortal enemy, are war manuals. Everything said, which we take seriously, should galvanize us on the frontlines of battle to victory.

Play follows work. It doesn't precede it. We are at war. Therefore, until we are victorious, we must never cease engaging in combat with those who never cease trying to destroy us. "They never learn...and *we* will never give up"[79] is a warrior's motto. This is no less so when applying pen to paper than when laying down fire with an automatic.

We must remain conscious enough of ourstory, and their history, to know that this is not a temporary situation for us or a whim for them. Wielding power over others through terrorizing acts of "death, destruction and domination" is their nature. It is fundamental to their definition of themselves and the world they covet. We can never assume that they will change because of any goodness purported to be lying dormant in their hearts. History teaches us that they never have and there is no reason now to believe that they ever will.

What's in a Name?

Whether we are speaking about your reputation or your proper name, what you are called by your community is a most important personal thing to an Afrikan. Traditionally, this was true of our ethnic groups also. Their names were given, and they were accordingly judged, based on what they did relative to their names.

Of course, as students of character, we know that there should not be a contradiction between your proper name (what you are called) and your reputational name (what you are known to be like). As with our Ancestors, hearing our names called should be a constant reminder of our express purpose here and now.

Afrikan names carried multiple layers of sharing, for our appellations included spiritual references, lineage namesakes and day names.[80] We were as collective in our naming of those following us as we were in naming all else in our reality. Just take a moment to consider the feeling and impact of oneness when everyone, or at least a significant number of people, in your community share the same name – yours. Imagine the affect on our children's minds of bringing that back to our priesthoods.

Names were also based on important ourstorical events, whether family or national. At one time, we understood the importance of literally connecting ourselves with ourstory through the names we carried which brought the memory of events to mind each time we called each other by name. We felt the need to be deeply connected to our "time." A simple numeric day of the year simply would not do. It was too limiting, too individualistic, too selfishly meaningless. Names had to carry communal, obligatory meanings and Afrikan names carried many meanings.

We also have insight into the depth of the importance of Afrikan names in the knowledge that our Ancestors are kept alive in our hearts and minds through the naming of their ascendants. Of equal measure in importance, we know that Ancestors remain alive as long as their names are called. We understood that their spiritual strength and, therefore, ability to assist us is determined by the number of people calling and number of times their names are called, with the earnestness of those callings being the decisive factor.[81]

As traditionally given, your name tells you and those of significance around you of your life's mission and lineal connection to your people. It gives you the opportunity of an entire lifetime to work at perfecting one's talents for the communal good, moving along a clear path. And, though choice is a human given, questioning the correctness of your given name, in all its facets, is unthinkable because it is understood to be the will (whether "negotiated" in the spiritual realm or not) and wisdom of the Creator. Being named as one arrives in this physical reality from the spiritual realm precludes the need to "find oneself," a crippling confusion so common among Afrikans today.[82]

Of course, we know that our "lostness" serves the diabolical ends of those who would destroy us. As long as we do not have our energies focused on our life's work, they can continue to mislead us into an active participation in their chaos. As long as we have no idea that we are without liberation, empowerment and sovereignty as a people and that each of us is responsible for honing our skills specifically for that purpose, we will continue to be guided down the path of our own spiritual, mental and physical destruction. As long as we are named by others, we will do all in our power to support and accelerate their station above us through the exploitation of our energies in service to them.

We also know that a person's first/original name(s) was augmented/"changed" over her or his lifetime. New names/titles were added and old names/titles designating completed missions were removed to make room for new obligations and duties as one advanced in age and acquired the necessary skills, knowledge and wisdom to fulfill them.

Ourstorical conditions have dictated our missions. And no other time in ourstory has been more critical for us to correctly, politically define ourselves, and affirm these definitions daily, than now. Indeed, the traditional naming of warriors is long overdue. Just imagine being in the presence of numbers of warriors sworn to ancient, proven, powerful names (in addition to those like Hannibal, Malcolm, Yaa Asantewaa, Araminta and Nat, renowned through rebellion against more contemporary agents of Afrikan destruction) like Adofo (warrior), Ajamu (one who fights for what he wants), Ajani (one who fights for possession), Akins (brave boy), Akinlana (valor), Akinsanya (the hero avenges), Akinshegun (valor conquers), Akinsheye (valor acts honorably), Akinshiju (valor awakes), Balogun (warlord), Bomani (warrior), Fenyang (conquerer), Gahiji (the hunter), Gamba (warrior), Hondo (war), Jabari (brave), Jalani (mighty), Kamau (quiet warrior), Kapeni (knife), Kefentse (conquerer), Ketu (female warrior), Kondo (war), Lisimba (lion), Lutalo (warrior), Minkah (justice), Nkosi (ruler), Nyatui (tiger fighter), Ojore (a man of war), Sefu (sword), Sentwali (brave one), Tau (lion), Thabiti (a true man), Tyehimba (we stand as a nation), Yero (warrior) and Zuberi (strong), names full of ancestral and ourstorical warrior meaning, who act on what they are called. Such names should be on every warrior's tongue as we call to each other for assistance, location, intelligence, technique and technology on the frontline. The title "Asafo" could also be used to strengthen the affirmation of these names.

Age Grade Statements

Every people, working to replicate themselves progressively, positively, intergenerationally, needs guidelines, affirmations as to who they are and what they are supposed to be considering, learning and practicing at each life stage in order to develop and maintain the quality of the character their ancestors possessed. And, because maturity, understanding and ability are different at different ages, that which serves as instructions must be tailored to fit each age group appropriately. What each age group must learn and do should build on what they have learned in their previous age group and firmly establish the framework from which their developing responsibilities can be fulfilled. If we understand natural law, we can easily see the epigenetic nature of a person's spiritual, mental and physical developmental stages.

These stages reflect a continuum in growth and development. Especially for a warrior's character, they identify what kind of person, based on those who came before who truly epitomize our traditions, we need to be in order to be true nationbuilders. In our traditions, these stages were identified by "age grades." These groups are cohorts of people who learn and grow together and, in doing so, develop extremely strong bonds of Brother/Sister loyalty toward each other.

Since this is a workbook about what constitutes a warrior's character, we have included the following pledges/statements for each age grade. They clearly reflect what should be the progressive development of an Afrikans faculties and assumption of responsibilities traditionally and within the ongoing context of war against those who would destroy us.[83]

BABULUNTU

(ages 71 and above)

- We pledge to grow closer to our Ancestors, so that we may hear their voices and pass on their wisdom
- We assume the responsibility of guiding our people and correcting them when necessary.
- We have the courage to speak truth, especially when it is not popular.
- We will tell the story of our journey living from our

Afrikan center, and of the lessons that we learned when we moved away from it.

- We know the ancient stories of our people and we live to tell them.
- We strive to live with integrity.
- We are accessible to our people. In this way, we serve them.
- We maintain our physical, emotional and spiritual health, so that we may live long lives and be whole human beings.

MBUTA

(ages 41 - 70)

- We pledge to provide leadership for our people.
- We provide a foundation for multigenerational family continuity, and intergenerational transmission of culture, history and mission.
- We love our parents and help them by passing on the best that they have given us and by not passing on their limitations.
- We heal with them as we meet the challenge of growing for them.
- We embrace the cycles of life and support each other and our grown children, by being models of continued growth and enduring responsibility.
- As grandparents, we teach our children how to parent their children, and we support them spiritually as they become parents.
- We always uphold an Afrikan concept of Divinity.

MBUTA BILESI

(ages 26 - 40)

- We are the mature warriors/builders of the Afrikan Family.

- We take the risks that those older than we are and those younger than we are, should not take.
- We use our energy and our resources to build and to produce for the Nation.
- We build strong families and are having children for the Nation.
- We educate ourselves and our children to take power and to control the resources of our people.
- We study and we teach what we learn.
- We listen to MBUTA and BAKULUNTU.
- We are spiritually healthy and have an Afrikan concept of Divinity.

BILESI
(ages 13 - 25)

- We are warrior/builders in training.
- We are spiritually healthy and we have an Afrikan concept of Divinity
- We commit ourselves to continual study of the ways of our Ancestors.
- We form complementary relationships in preparation for marriage and having children.
- We commit ourselves to fitness, health and survival training.
- We respect our peers male and female in our actions and our speech.
- We learn from MBUTA-BILESI how to challenge oppression.
- We strive to create positive media images that reflect and respect the values and culture of Afrikan people.
- We commit ourselves to study and to use our knowledge of Our Story to create and build the Afrikan community.

NTWENIA

(ages 7 - 12)

- We are beginning to learn the skills and acquire the tools that we need in order to become warriors for our people.
- We are learning as we play.
- We are learning how to think as Afrikans.
- We are learning Afrikan languages.
- We are learning science.
- We are learning math.
- We are learning music.
- We are learning dance.
- We are learning to live and do Maat.
- We respect our parents and their parents and their parents' parents.
- We know their stories and their best work.
- We love, honor and respect Afrikan people.
- We learn about our Afrikan Spirit, and know that we are Divine.

BANA

(ages 1-6)

- We know that we are Afrikan.
- We respect our Ancestors.
- We know our place in the story of our family.
- We can say the names of our parents and their parents and their parents before them.
- We have fun and we are happy as we learn.
- We see all that is around us.
- We love ourselves, and we know we are loved by Afrikan people.
- We feel our spirit.
- We love Afrika.
- We love all of our warrior Ancestors.

10. Returning to Our Way

We must advocate for the re-Afrikanization of Afrikan people, and we must lead a revival of traditional Afrikan practices. We must define ourselves and our children by Afrikan names complete with meanings that connect the past with the present and the future. We must become comfortable with the language and behaviors of at least one kinship group on the continent. We must engage in a campaign to redress the images of our families on the continent and make pilgrimages to meet with them in their space. We must become attached to our communities, beliefs, ceremonies, rituals, and festivals. We must return to the traditions of our ancestors; traditions passed on by the Dogon, the Asante, the Yoruba, the Mende, and others who have maintained *the way*. Traditions that ensure the beliefs, the ethos of our way. A way that guarantees our return to the natural rhythm of becoming one with nature. A way that determines the survival and development of our people.

Mawiyah Kambon

Character flaws internalized through a defective, eurocentric socialization notwithstanding, we, the ultimate expressions of what it means to be Afrikan, must become immaculate models of noncontradictory, "deyuruguized" nationbuilders. Europeans, negroes and lost souls can afford to make mistakes. We cannot. Our people do not measure us by the same rod. We are held more stringently to our moral code. And that is good. We should visibly be better.

The fairness of this double standard is not in question. Even though we know it gives us much more work and calls for an immeasurably greater discipline on our part, we *should* be held to a higher standard.[1] We should welcome this challenge, knowing that earnestly engaging better struggle hones our minds, bodies and spirits for the larger battles to come.[2]

Nationbuilders are trying to *build* a nation. In doing so, we have to take on the personal responsibility of establishing ourselves as the models of good character (that the other members of our nation) should follow.[3] As above, so it will be below.

Most of us, having suffered lifetimes of European indoctrination, find it extremely difficult to shed the ingrained insane, subconsciously operating, anti-Afrikan psychology that drives and defines the reality in which we live. However, if we are to again become Afrikan, that is just what must be done. If we are to be victorious, if we are to again become Afrikan, we must become our Ancestors. The Ancestor within must be liberated.

The European within us and our environment must be removed and that which is Afrikan built in its place.[4] We must shed much of what we have become and become all of who we have always been.

My mother used to say that you cannot tell Afrikans not to buy from european markets, unless you have given them a viable, reasonable Afrikan option. If that choice is not made available and they choose to follow your advice, they will starve or, more likely, eventually run back and hold on even more tenaciously to an inferior, disempowering retailer. What "we take or destroy, we must give or rebuild."

People seek meaning in their lives. And, if there is no other meaning provided for them that gives them a wholistic sense of being/self, they will return to whatever gave them a sense of security before. No matter how physically, mentally and spiritually alien and unhealthy this previous security was for them or their children and community, they will return because the human mind demands the security of order.

This is the european sway over many of our potentially conscious minds at this time. Those incomplete beings who so desperately work to separate us from the Afrikan within, have convinced us that what we were before them is inferior to what they have given us. Because we do not know who we were before them, and we believe that all society is the same (with their's being obviously superior, given its dominance), we see no need to return to our roots to gather around and into ourselves that which is ours.

But, we miss an obvious contradiction in our thinking, for, if no culture is superior to any other, then why are we still opting to follow one that does not reflect Afrikan interests? Why do we still choose the desert over the savannah, death over life? And, even having answered these questions, we seem befuddled over what steps can, and should individually and as communities, be taken to reverse the effects of so long trudging along the european way?

We also have to be realistic and come down to Earth in understanding exactly what we are dealing with. Europeans cannot be changed by the sheer will and force of our humanity. They are what they are. "Death, destruction and domination" are their all-consuming passion. And, in this passion, people are their ultimate "game." They kill, maim and oppress in an effort to convince themselves of their superiority.

We have to realize that we cannot reverse this madness

without completely changing, i.e., replacing the cultural technology that drives it. And, we have to remember that the asili is beyond change. It will persist until it is no more. Until we understand how the asili operates, we cannot modify the culture because the culture is simply the visible and felt expression of the asili.

Of course, if we seriously studied the ease and naturalness with which an asili structures and modifies the structure of culture and society with its essence, we would know that its imperatives are unchangeable. At least, they are not changeable by us. And, obviously, the Universe has no reason to change what it has created with divine reason. It is for us to learn why.

It is only with this intelligence that we should interpret any plans concocted to initiate revolutionary change within european culture and society. Europeans are the natural products of their asili.

Before considering the following suggestions, we also have to realize that we are not in Afrika. And, considering the abysmally low level of ancestral connectedness among so many Afrikans on the Continent, we must be even more acutely aware that this is not traditional Afrikan society. The rules of interaction that our Ancestors formulated for human relations were created in the presence of Afrikans who naturally thought and acted like Afrikans. There were no Europeans on the Afrikan continent at that time.

Therefore, because we understand these extremely important facts, facts people "in flight from themselves" are quick to overlook when dealing with nonfamily members, we cannot apply our ancestral rules of human interaction to Europeans as if they are Afrikans. *They are not Afrikan.* We can never make that mistake again, even after we as a people become fully liberated, empowered and sovereign.[5]

In addition to the commonsensical solutions thinkers will naturally derive from each chapter, the following ideas are taken from the established, evolving habits of Afrikans who have successfully found ways to restore order to the Afrikan mind. They are offered as suggestions for those who are truly searching for practices, techniques, rituals and affirmations that will help take them back home. In that, while still held captive within european society and culture, any movement in an Afrikan direction can feel like climbing out from an earthly abyss onto the moon, we offer the following wisdom written by Ngugi wa Thiong'o for support.

> The true seeker of truth never loses hope. The true seeker of real justice never tires. A farmer does not stop planting seeds just because of the failure of one crop. Success is born of trying and trying again. Truth must seek justice. Justice must seek the truth. When justice triumphs, truth will reign on earth.[6]

Therefore, in the warrior's personal pursuit of real truth and justice, the following suggestions are offered:

- ☐ Learn an Afrikan language.[7] How can we expect our Ancestors and the Afrikan universe to hear us in a foreign tongue. It is not a matter of simply being able to speak in an Afrikan language because that, in the european tradition into which we have been socialized, becomes no more than imitation or spiritless regurgitation. Change in how we see and construct a meaningful ReAfrikanized reality only fully arrives when we begin to think in our native tongue.[8] Speaking as Afrikans invokes a higher level thinking process which more explicitly (especially in practical terms of interpreting european culture for the irreconcilably different interpretation of reality that it is) connects thinking Afrikans to our native mind. Meaning and use in language more explicitly show differences between peoples than anything else because the spoken word is required for the creation and explanation of everything.
- ☐ Assume and embrace Afrikan names (with

nationbuilding meanings you can grow into) that reflect your mission,. Take full (first, middle, last and other) Afrikan names. And do not pay to have returned to you what was illegally taken.[9]

- ☐ Schedule a set amount of time daily to read about us.[10] Affirm and follow this plan.
- ☐ Read those who write for us first. Read those who love us first. Buy their books from our stores and build a library of them. Use the public library to access the writings of others.
- ☐ Place Afrikan literature throughout your residence and vehicles. Keep them ever ready for study.
- ☐ Watch and keep copies of enough intellectually stimulating and ourstorically telling Afrikan movies, documentaries and lectures to keep your mind occupied for at least a year.
- ☐ Listen to and collect every decent form of Afrikan music. You are what you listen to as equally as you are what you think. Feel our artists speak to the Ancestors and Creation.
- ☐ Wear Afrikan attire. Wear Afrikan attire, especially in our sacred spaces. When going into enemy territory be judicious in what you wear, considering your safety and the practicality of starting a battle. To what end does a true warrior, aware that we are at war with an unscrupulous, deadly enemy, conspicuously wear our "uniforms"/attire in spaces where our defenses are minimal and a lost battle would prove meaningless? Surely, given what we have learned about our enemies' insecurities and fears,[11] such display and losses make no sense, except for those hounded by ego-ridden aspirations to martyrdom, an honor best earned through humble, selfless service.
- ☐ Surround yourself (your home, work space, vehicle, person, kwk) with Afrikan symbolism (art, cloth, trinkets, kwk).

- ☐ Pour/speak libations daily. Call your ancestors into your space. Create libation using a revolutionary time line invoking the nommo of words such as integrity, uncompromising, empowered, resilience, vision, mission, ReAfrikanization, nationbuilding, reclamation, wisdom, kwk. Call on the Ancestors to remove enemies, within and without, from our path and presence.[12]
- ☐ If affirming works, and we know that it does, then there are things we should daily affirm to stop european aggressions against us and even remove the very presence on this planet of Europeans and every other people who act against us. Affirm "Abibifahodie." Affirm "I am an Afrikan warrior, a warrior scholar. I refuse to be at peace with anything less." As Marcus Mosiah Garvey taught, "You rule the world through your mind."[13]
- ☐ Turn your thoughts into meaningful prayers for your thoughts are your prayers. Pray always. That is our tradition.[14]
- ☐ Get a reading from a spiritualist in the community who knows we are at war, who has consistently demonstrated an undeniably firm record of revolutionary, Afrikan centered, righteous thought, word and behavior. You will know who they are by the stories they tell and their interpretations of what they see.
- ☐ Befriend Afrikans who have earned the title of Elder. Honor them with your presence. Ascertain their needs. Fulfill them as best you can. Reciprocate wisdom with deeds. Place the children at their feet.[15]
- ☐ Connect with warriors of like mind globally. Militarily, PanAfrikanism must become more than a catchy concept lost in a world of words. Warriors without borders should be our mandate.
- ☐ Acquire land. Build solvent, protected, self-sustaining

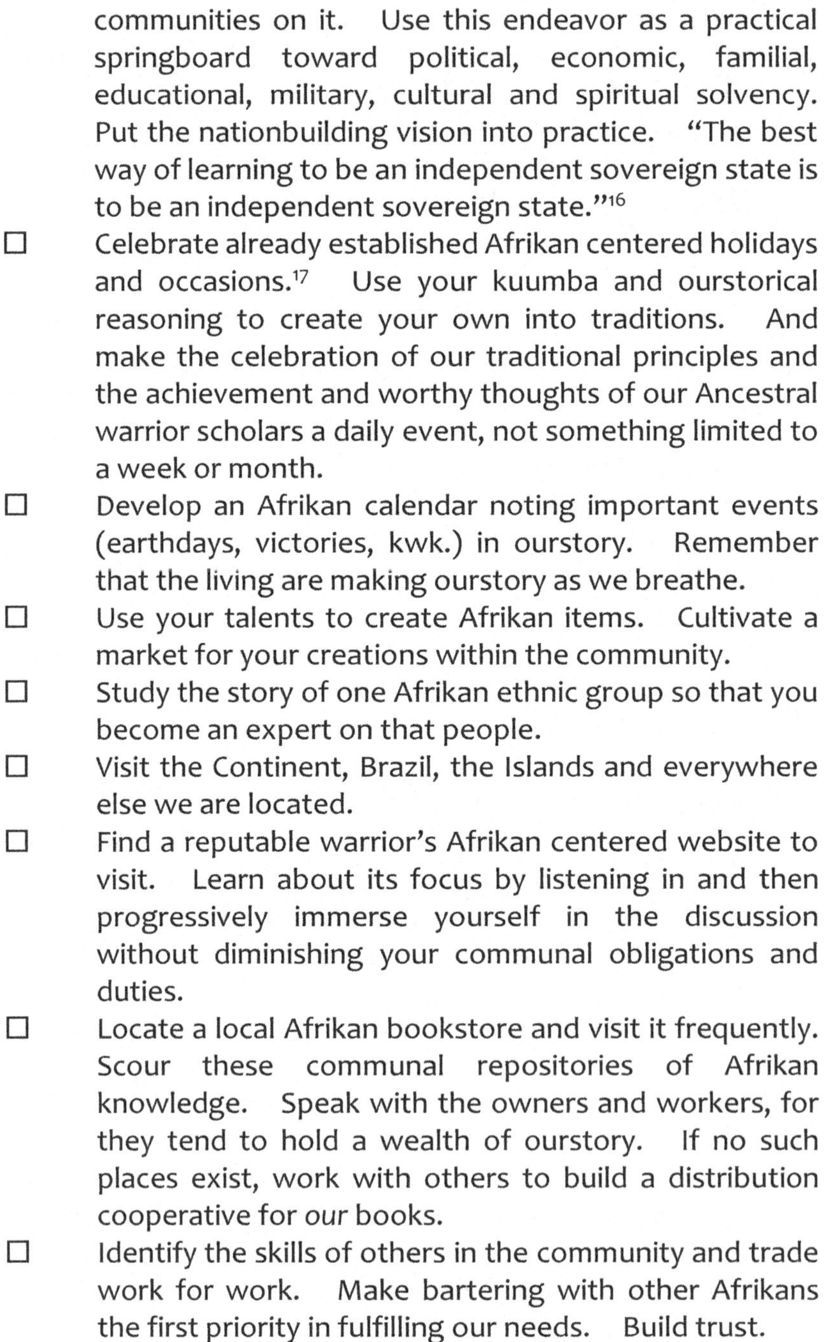

communities on it. Use this endeavor as a practical springboard toward political, economic, familial, educational, military, cultural and spiritual solvency. Put the nationbuilding vision into practice. "The best way of learning to be an independent sovereign state is to be an independent sovereign state."[16]

- ☐ Celebrate already established Afrikan centered holidays and occasions.[17] Use your kuumba and ourstorical reasoning to create your own into traditions. And make the celebration of our traditional principles and the achievement and worthy thoughts of our Ancestral warrior scholars a daily event, not something limited to a week or month.
- ☐ Develop an Afrikan calendar noting important events (earthdays, victories, kwk.) in ourstory. Remember that the living are making ourstory as we breathe.
- ☐ Use your talents to create Afrikan items. Cultivate a market for your creations within the community.
- ☐ Study the story of one Afrikan ethnic group so that you become an expert on that people.
- ☐ Visit the Continent, Brazil, the Islands and everywhere else we are located.
- ☐ Find a reputable warrior's Afrikan centered website to visit. Learn about its focus by listening in and then progressively immerse yourself in the discussion without diminishing your communal obligations and duties.
- ☐ Locate a local Afrikan bookstore and visit it frequently. Scour these communal repositories of Afrikan knowledge. Speak with the owners and workers, for they tend to hold a wealth of ourstory. If no such places exist, work with others to build a distribution cooperative for *our* books.
- ☐ Identify the skills of others in the community and trade work for work. Make bartering with other Afrikans the first priority in fulfilling our needs. Build trust.

- ☐ Find a warrior skilled in what we need and apprentice under her or him.
- ☐ Start an afterschool, weekend or full-time school program and uncompromisingly teach our children our truth. "Teach the children. Teach the babies."[18]
- ☐ Develop long-term rites programs. ReAfrikanize the lineage.
- ☐ Make the study of military strategies an intricate part of rites of passage programs.
- ☐ Encourage self-defense classes for *all* members of the community.
- ☐ Study the war strategies of Afrikan armies and great military minds.
- ☐ Practice at firing ranges. Or, better yet, find space in rural areas where firing on private property is not illegal and create our own ranges.
- ☐ Teach our children chess.[19]
- ☐ Join an Afrikan centered organization. Investigate it thoroughly beforehand. It is not difficult for charlatans to "look" Afrikan or appear so on a mission statement or website.
- ☐ Tithe one to ten percent of your income to an Afrikan centered organization you believe has the same vision for Afrikan people as you do. Commit yourself to consistently give "revolutionary tithes."
- ☐ Create a family/individual mission statement and read it daily.
- ☐ Create community councils of elders to arbitrate internal problems and set penalties for violations.
- ☐ Create an agency of responsible adults to enforce correctives assigned "lawbreakers" in the community.
- ☐ And, finally, something that applies to each of the above at the most fundamental level of character, be who you say that you are, for "the word that you speak stands and waits for you."[20]

Finding, institutionalizing and safeguarding the Afrikan Way is not as impossible a vision as many of our own would have us believe. Living within the mind and spaces claimed and defended by our enemies is not a requirement of living. Compromise is not something we have to live with in order to be ourselves in peace.

Only weak-minded Afrikans or saboteurs try to convince us of the impossibility of returning home, that we cannot recreate an Afrikan world outside and above the constraints of european culture and society. It is only those Afrikans who subsist within a deep-seated vanquishment, whether in the Diaspora or on the Continent, whether knowing or ignorant of ourstory, whether dressed in our traditional garb, speaking our traditional languages, eating our traditional diets, claiming our traditional names or not, who would seek to undermine our ReAfrikanizing nationbuilding efforts by convincing us that the odds against us accomplishing something of this magnitude are too great for a people define humanity and created civilization. Remember that "obstacles are things that you see when you take your eyes off of your goal." And, as my mother schooled me, "*Can't* died before you were born."

Therefore, logically, if we are to survive and build as Afrikans, there is only one way to stop yurugu's rampage.[21] And that "final solution" has already been well reiterated by Kamau Kambon.[22] Long ago, their unprovoked and barbaric terrorism moved beyond the point of being ignored or questioned. A policy absolute intolerance and removal toward the "harbingers of death" is not an unreasonable approach for warriors to take. "If the scorpion stings you mercilessly, then you have to kill it mercilessly."[23]

Prayer, alone, is not a viable option. Unaccompanied by physical and mental action, prayer hasn't a prayer against them.

The warrior character that is required to destroy this unforgiving and unforgivable menace to life and order is the focus of this discussion. If we cannot build an army of warriors of character who understand both the concepts of enemy and community and progressively act on them, then the future's historical record will clearly show that the best of us spent our time and energy engaging in meaningless and distractive debate about and/or recording the cause and events of our genocidal demise.

ENDNOTES

Chapter One || Introduction

1. Warrior will be used instead of warrior scholar throughout for the sake of economy because only an individual seriously studied in the way of our Ancestors could possibly be a warrior useful to us. And, by "studied," we are referring to quality, not quantity. Centered warriors must know who they are, and self-knowledge requires study. And, for warriors, study, of course, is only effectively meaningful when it is put into practice against enemy incursions. "Determination is not the same as actually going to war" (Akan proverb). By definition, a warrior scholar is an Afrikan who fully commits her/himself to politically develop her or his intellect, by studying the traditions of our people and the ways of our enemies, in order to more effectively engage those who would seek to destroy us in mental, physical and spiritual warfare. Politics rule a warrior's life. Every decision is based on its benefit for (or liability to) Afrikan people. This is an operational, i.e., applied, working definition, not endlessly disconnected planning; a practical application, not reform-oriented armchair "negotiations." Equally important in our use of the warrior concept is the premise that, because we are at war, all Afrikans of consciousness, by default, are warriors. So, given a centered consciousness, the word warrior is interchangeable or synonymous with Afrikan. Warrior is also used here rather than soldier because of their political, mental and spiritual differences. There is a clear difference of depth at which the righteousness of the battle is internally understood between the two. Warriors are at war for the liberation of their people because they have no choice, whether they want one or not. They are spiritually charged with relinquishing their people from the pain inflicted on them by oppressors. The role of the warrior is understood. Soldiers fight for the thrill of killing, because they have been

drafted into another's ambitions or in order to survive financially. In other words, the soldier's cause is his employer's cause. The justness of the cause is irrelevant (whether soldiers have psyched themselves into believing it is just or not). Soldiers believe in their leaders in the same way that house negroes believe in their masters. They do not think for themselves as to cause and effect. Like slaves, they fear questions. And "too much fear creates slavery" (Swahili proverb). They are historically and ourstorically unaware. They do what they are told. Mercenaries are a special variety of soldier. They are almost always fighting for someone else's cause and could care less about their target, even if it is one of their own. Some mercenaries, psychologically and actively, fall into the category of serial killers. Given that combat is a natural part of their existence and that war is the root word of warrior for good reason, if we wanted to be simplistic, we could say that warriors are soldiers. But it is not a given that a soldier is also a warrior. Warriors also, in our tradition, study who they are and what they must build when the fighting ends. Warriors are fearless because there is no room for trepidation in a war to permanently arrest the assault against family/community/nation. They do not compromise. Warriors do not attack or exploit innocents. They are gentle with their own. Warriors respect the work of their Ancestors and Elders. They are primarily defensive in their natural posture. Their primary function is to protect their people, excluding the treasonous. Though still essentially defensive, their military functions only become offensive when they must take the battle into the spaces of those who initiated the confrontation. Throughout their existence, the warrior is prepared for any exigency, military and otherwise.

2 . Yurugu, like Caucasian or white, is another name for Europeans. Marimba Ani brought this name to our attention when she imparted the Dogon myth of Yurugu and titled her magnum opus after it. Also known as the pale fox, Yurugu is a severed male spirit or principle. He is incomplete. His female half is absent because of a selfish and childish Creator-vying act. Because he was so determined not to wait for the Creator to finish creating him, he did not receive his female "side" before arrogantly completing himself. Therefore, it was lost *forever.*

Yurugu will remain forever incomplete, destroying all in his path in an effort to find completion in the only way he knows. This myth helps us understand the nature of the European as a function of a spiritual disconnectedness that is uncorrectable by us or them and, therefore, leaves us with a realistic base from which we can reasonably assess options for solving the problem of his blind, unrelenting destruction.

3. In Kwame Nkrumah's timeless words, "The secret to success is to have no fear." It is also worth noting early in this discussion that warriors' worst fears are realized first in their own minds. Afrikan proverbs teach us that "man often suffers most from the suffering he fears" and "fear is worse than the blow." Fear, like courage, is self-created.

4. Being uncompromising and being intolerant are not the same. They carry very different connotations on the frontlines. The former implies a refusal to tolerate anything that takes or keeps us away from the Way of our Ancestors. The latter means to not be understanding of difference. As a people, Afrikans are known better than any other for our tolerance of others and their ways (something many with clear hindsight now cogently argue has been a leading source of our demise as a world power). But our tolerance of difference never insinuated or directly meant our voluntary embracing of it.

5. Succinctly, Ancestors are those individuals who were born before you and have transitioned from the physical world and returned to the spiritual realm. Warriors must carefully select those we call Ancestors based on their work during their lifetime here. Those who committed treason against our people or those who oppressed them are neither honored as Elders while here nor as Ancestors upon transition. In the words of one of our revered Ancestors,

> The Ancestors are our ancient foreparents who determine what we are. They will help us when we remember them and deter us when we don't. It is the Ancestors who venerate our soul and give us inspiration to emulate and embellish their deeds and accomplishments. It is because of them that we desire to become a part of destiny and strive to create better societies. They help us to build great people, great communities and great nations. It is extremely important that we consecrate a part of our daily lives to them. (Nana

Yao Opare Dinizulu, *The Akan Priest in America*, Long Island City, NY: Aims of Modzawe, 1974, pp.3-4)

6. Mwalimu K. Bomani Baruti, *Centered: Building Afrikan Realities*, Atlanta, GA: Akoben House, 2009.

7. Bobby E. Wright, one of our most insightful Ancestors, in *The Psychopathic Racial Personality* (Chicago: Third World Press, 1984), defined "mentacide" as a form of insanity that leaves many of us thinking out of the mind of the European as if it were our own. It is the state of being psychologically brain-dead and having one's thoughts replaced with alien ones, a state akin to being a zombie. "Mentacide" is derived from the root word *menta*, meaning "mental or thinking," and *cide*, meaning "to kill." "Mentacide" means to kill the mental process, to kill one's normal thought processes, essentially, to kill one's own mind. In that there is still a thought process at work, "mentacide" also means that an artificial, alien collection of thoughts and way of thinking have replaced what has been altogether suppressed or removed. (See Harold Pates, *Notable Quotes of the Living Bobby E. Wright: A Primer on Western Civilization's Racial Dementia*, Chicago: Kemetic Institute, 2002, Olomenji, "Mentacide, Genocide, and National Vision: The Crossroads for the Blacks of America (An Essay of Commentary)," in Daudi Ajani ya Azibo (ed.), *African Psychology in Historical Perspective and Related Commentary*, Trenton, NJ: Africa World Press, 1996, pp.71-82, Kwabena F. Ashanti, *Psychotechnology of Brainwashing*, Durham, NC: Tone Books, 1993 and Mwalimu K. Bomani Baruti, "Mentacide," in Mwalimu K. Bomani Baruti, *Mentacide and other essays*, Atlanta, GA: Akoben House, 2005, pp.5-10.)

8. A prime example of this is Kemet until corrupted. It made conquests to establish a wider perimeter to safeguard the order within the society from further attack.

9. Kwame Nkrumah worded this so eloquently in *Africa Must Unite* when stating that "we are fighting to *construct*, not to destroy" (London: Panaf Books, 1998 (first published in 1963), p.74).

10. Of course, this compensation for others must be a realistically measured assumption about what would constitute others' responsibilities and duties if they were conscious and not fighting against us. As in the game of chess (a game we should all learn

because it is ours and for what it can teach and hone in us), if you spend an excessive amount of time and power defending a vulnerable piece, you will become so encumbered by trying to save what is already lost that you will be unable to successfully defend your position generally or launch successful offensives of your own. In the same way, overextended pieces, pieces attempting to guard too many other pieces, are easily defeated or, at minimum, undermined and taken away. So we have to be careful in our commitment to do others' work, especially when they are already working against us. That "one can only do some of the things to be done in the world and not all" (Twi proverb) is a word to the wise from our Ancestors. (See Mwalimu K. Bomani Baruti, *Chess Primer*, Atlanta, GA: Akoben House, 1992 for an introduction to the game of chess.)

11. Akoben is the Adinkra symbol which calls people into preparedness for war and righteous, communal decision-making. In *The Adinkra Dictionary* (Washington, DC: The Pyramid Complex, 1998), W. Bruce Willis explains it thusly:

> **Akoben** (the war horn) is a symbol of readiness of war, or a call to action. The war horn was usually an ivory horn with an opening cut at the smaller end. It was side-blown and made a low, loud, earthly sound. In precolonial days, an Akan village and its surroundings might constitute a very large area. Tending crops in the field or in the nearby forest chopping wood, the people might be scattered throughout the village during the course of a day. Because the defense of the town was a collective and voluntary act of the townspeople, the *akoben* alerted the townspeople that an enemy was near or that they should assemble for a task for the common good. Thus, the sound of akoben was a battle cry and a call to arms. In modern times the symbol has been associated with a state of readiness for a common task, a common endeavor or communal unity for the common good. (p.67)

One variation of the Akoben symbol can be seen at the base of the spine of a number of Akoben House books. The recognition that our children and nation are under assault is the reason why the publishing company is named Akoben House. Similarly, our educational institute that includes our homeschooling program, adult lecture classes (on site and one-line) and other educational outreach activities is named Akoben Institute. "If you hear the war horn, it means trouble has come" (Akan proverb). And it is our belief that we have a responsibility to continue sounding the alarm until there is trouble no more. Warriors must recognize that it is our gradual, progressively declining sensitivity as a people to being destroyed that we, "in modern times," have lost sight of the fact that the enemy has never left the vicinity, the threat remains and, because of this, many are either not blowing the Akoben Horn or are blowing it for the wrong reasons.

12. In the words of Amilcar Cabral, "Be aware at every moment of the situation of the struggle." (*Unity and Struggle*, NY: Monthly Review Press, 1979, p.224)

13. Queen Mother Audley Moore, "What's the Hour of the Night?," July 27, 1950.

14. Sojourner Truth, Fourth National Women's Rights Convention, 1851.

15. Mwalimu K. Bomani Baruti, "Gratitude," in Baruti, *Mentacide*, pp.153-155.

16. As Ella Baker maintained, "If there is any philosophy, it's that those who have walked a certain path should know some things, should remember some things that they can pass on, that others can also use to walk the path a little better."

17. We can *never* overemphasize the importance of tradition. Our traditions are all that have come to work for us. They reflect our human essence, our interpretation of the Universe and are the most apparent manifestation of our deepest imperatives. In contrast to what those who work to bend our minds to their will have taught us, being traditional does not mean being archaic, outdated, outmoded, primitive, backward, useless or out of sync with reality. For tradition is no more or less than all of the intellectual, mechanical and metaphysical technology which naturally maintains a people as they have come to see themselves. It is the result of untold generations consciously working together to correct their errors and perfect those corrections. Tradition is the culmination of all that has been tried and proven true through the experience of a people. It defines that people's worth and existence. Without tradition a people cease to exist. For these reasons and more, we must get over the idea that *our* traditions, in and of themselves, but especially relative to europeans', are bad, dysfunctional, useless or burdensome. We must stop allowing

others to convince us that most traditions do not make sense and therefore can be discarded at will.

18. Yurugu would have us think that our problem is that we refuse to accept the natural progression of "human" social evolution. Otherwise, we would not fight the destiny of our europeanization. It would suit their unfulfilled supremacist desires perfectly, if we would just stop rebelling against what they consider to be their inevitable ascension and submit to the lie that they manifestly know where we are headed, and admit that we do not. But we have been at the work of liberation for far too long to succumb to the delusional nature of their desperate psychopathologies. We are not backward. We are not blind. We are fully in sync with reality, ours, not theirs. We are not insane. We know. We know who we are and what they have always been. We know what has been done to our bodies, psychologies and spiritual connection. We know that some find it so much easier to sleep, to play in the deadly games of this anti-Afrikan nightmare. We, however, are willful insomniacs. We walk the day and night, forever. We are not separable from our Ancestors. We are they, for we are the warriors we have sent to finish the work we started.

19. Since they are superior to no one, "white nationalism" would be a more appropriate descriptive of what Yurugu has manifest. As Autum Ashante so eloquently reminded us, "White nationalism is what put [us] in bondage." However, beyond that, white supremacy will not be used herein, not because when stated in this way it forms an affirmation of something which does not, in reality, exist but because it is a euphemism (no matter how harsh it already sounds to many) for what most "conscious" folk still do not want to face. It is not so much white supremacy as the European (mind/asili). Blaming white supremacy is the easy way out, giving hope to something conceivably within the realm of change. This allows most who adhere to this philosophy to still keep Europeans (their ideals, society, way, people, kwk) at their center. ("...sometimes hope is the biggest weapon of all to use against us" (Edwidge Danticat, *Krik? Krak!*, NY: Vintage Contemporaries, 1996, p.19)). The problem would be more accurately stated, if you don't understand Europeans as a mind/asili, nothing else you come to "understand" will make sense

relative to the removal of their power over us. Racism is only one hateful manifestation of Yurugu and only through changing this incomplete being, an impossibility, can white racism, along with its other functional "isms" against humanity be brought to an end. (Still, in order to deal with it, racism must be understood as the thought and action of one genocultural race against another. To use the words of Stokely Carmichael and Charles V. Hamilton as a reference point, racism is "the predication of decisions and policies on considerations of race for the purpose of subordinating a racial group and maintaining control over that group" (*Black Power: The Politics of Liberation in America*, NY: Vintage, 1967, p.3). Also see Larry D. Crawford (Mwalimu A. Bomani Baruti), "Racism, Colorism and Power," in Larry D. Crawford (Mwalimu A. Bomani Baruti), *negroes and other essays*, Atlanta, GA: Ankoben House, 2000, pp.118-121. The attitude of supremacy should never be reduced to the individual level. It is a group function, a sense that who they are now and how they do things is the best of all possible ways, that even their errors are worthy. We make a critical mistake when judging those who act as supremacists individually. Those who are delusional enough to practice supremacy (racial arrogance) come in many different personalities, real and imagined, inbred and fabricated. For these reasons, it could prove useful to delve a little more into the definition of power itself. And, in analyzing our situation, a most valid way of thinking about what power is can be found in looking at the source of the power differential between oppressors and the oppressed. Because we can, with all seriousness, argue that power is not taken by oppressors. It is given to them by the oppressed. It is not taken. It is a function of acquiescence. If I refuse to do as you command, you have not exercised power. If I refuse to do as you command, and you beat me or kill me, you still have not exercised power. You have only exercised force and violence (Hannah Arendt, *On Violence*, NY: Harcourt Brace Jovanovich, 1969). If I refuse to do as you command and you fire me or, through your connections in the banking community, steal my house or other property, you still have not exercised power. I have not willingly submitted to your demands. Only when I comply with your wishes have you exercised the power. Power is a function of compliance. An aggressor without compliance remains powerless. This is not simply a play with words. The gun is not power, even though the thought behind it has the potential to extort it. A rebellion is not power. But the thought in the mind motivated to take it to the streets has designs on it. Power is a mentality that confronts another mentality responsive to its desire. It is the creative genius of two minds – one determined to convincingly compel, another destined, at least for the moment, to comply. Power cannot be had alone. It needs another to become visible, to be seen and felt. It is an act of consciousness that requires an act of submission to be fulfilled. Trepidation or submissive caution must be strong enough in one group for another group to intimidate it into domination, to exercise power over it. Otherwise, given superior destructive might, the would-be oppressor is reduced to simply acting out violence, of carrying out a frustrating, ignoble genocidal effort where the would-be oppressed are either totally annihilated or forcibly interned or banished. As an extreme form of this power imbalance (which, interestingly, combines annihilation and banishment), slavery requires the active participation of slave and master. Technically, both are at fault, even though it is ludicrous to imply that the enslavement of Afrikans hurt the European as well. It was we who were enslaved, not them. There is no sensible comparison. Regardless, *enslaved* Afrikans were not powerless (Vincent Harding's *There is a River*, NY: Vintage Books, 1983). And, in effect, their enslavers were by no means powerful; inhumanely violent, yes, powerful, no. Only those thoroughly confused Afrikans who felt they were rightfully slaves succumbed to that level of vanquishment. Only those who lost sight of home gave their masters power. Slaves accept their destruction. Enslaved Afrikans never submit. They never give up.

20. Yoruba proverb.

21. Lee Miller (ed.), *From the Heart*, NY: Alfred A. Knopf, 1995, p.164.

22. Dinizulu, *The Akan Priest*, pp.1-2.

23 . Afrisms are truths that Afrikans have ourstorically commonly accepted. While there are truisms that can be found to cross cultural boundaries, the body which is unique to Afrikans, and usually in conflict with european truths, can be considered to

be the central body of Afrisms, since Afrisms are conceptually used to illustrate fundamental cultural differences in perceptions of truth and untruth between Afrikans and Europeans. However, the entire body of Afrisms includes both those that distinguish Afrikan truth from european truth and those which are generally shared by the indigenous peoples of the world.

24. By "crippled" (or rather circumscribed) I am referring to minds trained to both emotionally feel for their destroyers and see their people's, especially their Ancestors', pain as irrelevant.

25. "Genocide" is a word made up of the root word "geno," meaning gene or genetic, and the suffix "cide," meaning to kill, resulting in a word meaning to kill off the genes, genetic structure or substance, of a people, i.e., to remove from reproductive existence, to exterminate a people, to extirpate them, to kill them off forever. The indigenous people of Tasmania and Australia and the Arawaks are prime examples of genocide. In the same way, our genocide is an intricate part of the European's vision, for genocide is simply the procedural framework through which they operate to win war. And war, for them, is to completely destroy another people. If this people cannot be immediately annihilated, then they must be made to internalize a subordinate status until they can be. To this definition we must add the fact that such mass destruction, by default, assures the obliteration of that group's cultural base because to destroy a people's sense of self through erasing or seriously distorting their story beyond their recognition (historicide) causes them to unwittingly and willingly allow their own genocide. With time and an ancestral disconnect, the fear that makes genocide possible ensures that people will actively assist in the implementation and perpetuation of their own destruction. Europeans are fully cognizant that their racial insecurities have firmly placed them on the global offensive. They have no hesitation in taking whatever steps are required to make them, in their bloodied minds and bloodless eyes, supreme gods in this reality. When all the above holds true, genocide must be defined in the context of war. War is inherent in any attempt to erase a people or race from historical memory. When you start to dabble in the real numbers of the Hellacaust, the Great Suffering, the Maafa, you are able to see that it is the systematic removal of people of color from the planet, not just an enslavement

or conquering. When we realize that they are doing this to us, and not us to us (even though we may in some capacity unwittingly or knowingly assist), things will dramatically change. In order for us to correctly engage European culture, we must see our relationship with them in the context of war. As long as Afrikans in the heart of Babylon are portrayed and see themselves as a few individuals rightfully captured by foreign enlighteners and taken from a family that did not want them in the first place, there will be no cause for alarm. In our reconceptualization of genocide along Afrikan lines, we must also consider three other factors. First, their United Nations' definition of genocide includes "forcibly transferring the children of [one] group to another." Second is the exponential impact of historical and immediate genocide in the context of the ongoing genocidal war against Afrikan people. In other words, when a young Afrikan male or female who has not yet procreated is murdered, he or she is not the only one murdered. Every individual that person was ever to produce through the end of the line of his or her generations is murdered. In the long run this is a hidden genocidal accelerant because this intergenerational genocide does not show up in the immediate statistics. Here, genocide is not even detected or defined as genocide because those who are murdered are never born. Third, by definition, what happened to european Jews does not qualify as a holocaust because it was internal. It was an act among Europeans, not between Europeans and other people. It was not one people trying to kill off another people. Genocide and suicide are two different things. European Jews are Europeans. What happened between the Germans and european Jews during europe's second major spike in its ongoing war against the world (otherwise known as World War II) was not one people trying to decimate another, except in the minds of misguided Europeans who want to claim that this european ethnic group somehow makes a distinct racial group within the european nation because of the religion they claim is theirs. The historicide parenthetically mentioned above is also an act of one or more people against another people. Historicide accompanies genocide and is the process of killing a people's memory of self. And, to kill a people's story is to obliterate their past, their origins, originality and worth, even their very existence (contributions) in meaningful terms. Or, equally destructive, historicide serves to reduce a people's record to relative obscurity in comparison to other peoples' social and cultural litany. Killing a people's history involves removing or renaming/reoriginating (attributing them to an alternative or alien origin) virtually all material and intangible evidence of their existence as independently thinking, self-empowered, dutiful people who contributed to the development of the human potential. Their past is erased. Historicide is the successful (at least temporarily) negation of everything positive that a people accomplished to the point where all that they did is credited to others or deemed inferior mental, physical or spiritual efforts. This denial of a people's value also involves degrading their uniquely functioning methods for living into acts of inferiority relative to others' techniques/technology, even while both accomplished the same ends. For example, the Afrikan's oral tradition has been ignominiously subordinated to the western and eastern's written ones, even though Afrikans had numerous forms of literature and their oral tradition required a vastly more in-depth thinking ability and memory. Through historicide, a people become nameless. They are made to feel that they have made no meaningful contribution to human society and civilization, that they have no worth outside of grafting themselves onto others' accomplishments and cultures. In the end, because they believe their people have never had worth, they do not, and do not want to, see themselves as a people. Achieving individual recognition and validation within a "superior" cultural construct, and being able to claim its history as their own, becomes their highest aspiration. Another concept mentioned above which bears explanation is Maafa. This Swahili term was presented to us by one of our most honored Afrikan centered warriors Marimba Ani. The Maafa refers to the entirety of the effort Europeans (and other aliens) have put into trying to destroy the Afrikan continent, Afrikan culture and Afrikan people. Even though its inception predates the systematic invasion of Afrika by Europeans by about 840 years when Arabs began their enslavement of Afrikans for themselves and exportation to China and other points in Asia, the european nation is our focus because they expended by far the greatest amount of energy aimed at bringing about our physical, mental and spiritual destruction. Ourstorically speaking, the

Maafa is a massive, protracted "crime" against *our* humanity. In fact, to even use the word crime as descriptive of it is a gross understatement, severely minimizing the pain and devastation it has brought to Afrikan people. Holocaust is not even sufficient enough of a word. Be that as it may, the Maafa includes the unprovoked wars of invasion and clandestine instigations to capture and subdue the Afrikan continent, the violent dispersion of Afrikan peoples across all the other continents, except one, the missionary efforts to remove us from our spirit, the consciously arrogant undermining of Afrikan cultural activities and sensibilities, the colonization of Afrikan political systems, the balkanization of formerly peaceable ethnic groups and mass theft of Afrikan resources, the confiscation of Afrikan lands and relegation of Afrikans to infertile soil, the global dehumanization of Afrikans, and the brutalization, rape, torture and murder of hundreds of millions of Afrikans and all the ascendants those murdered individuals would have produced. It is important to note that most Afrikan centered warriors recognize that the Maafa is a genocide in progress. It did not stop with the official end of our enslavement in the western hemisphere (noting that the enslavement of Afrikans on the Continent by Arabs continues to date) or the termination of colonization on the Continent through revolutionary warfare (noting that an advanced state of neocolonization still plagues virtually every Afrikan state). The continued efforts of the european nation to terrorize Afrikans into nonexistence and the ongoing psychological effects of our past enslavement (referred to by various terms such as psychic trauma, post-traumatic slavery syndrome, cultural misorientation, mentacide, kwk.), as well as the ongoing ruination of the Motherland under a heartless alien and alienating, paternalistic, capitalistic imperialism, are clear indicators that this has been and continues to be one, indivisible "Great Destruction." We must also emphatically note, however, that this definition is not to imply that this atrocity is near completion. On the contrary, it is to provide the broadest picture and give a clear understanding of what happened, and is happening, so that conscious Afrikan people will understand the magnitude of what we have committed ourselves to reverse and, in the process, the traditions and sanity to which we fully intend to return.

26. The warrior's view of progress must be reconceptualized from our Afrikan center. It must be a measurement of where we need to be relative to our current status. And this measurement must be grounded in a proactive assessment of our movement away from where others would oppressively or mentacidally lead us.

> In our reactionary despondency over our generally collective submission to eurocentric style progress, we also have to recognize that progress must be redefined. On the one hand, we know that being a shadow of the European means that we are moving in the direction that european culture is willing us. However, on the other hand, we must understand that not moving in that direction does not mean we are standing still or failing. Instead it means that we are *progressing* in another direction. Simply rejecting european culture and society *is* progress. And the more forceful and determined the rejection, the greater the advancement away from yurugu's reality. The problem here for most of us is that we are measuring our advancement based on our perception of the failure of the Afrikan community in general to detach and distance itself from the european mainstream. Even though the western media are currently the primary causal agents, we see evidence of this "failure" at the personal, interpersonal and genocultural level in a wide variety of suicidal acts of self-hatred....A more accurate, psychologically beneficial, Afrikan centered measurement of the progression or regression of the Afrikan centered community would be in seeing how far our thought and action are taking us away from where they want us to go. The greater the distance between us and their way, the greater our progress. Afrikan centered progress is not complicated. When conscious, our rejection of them is an appreciation of us. Most of us just do not know to interpret this deliberately rebellious movement as progress. Mainly, this is because, most often, Europeans still command the center of our interpretation of reality. We still base our success or failure on whether or not we think they are winning against us, not on whether or not we know we are winning against them. We forget that the Afrikan Way and the european way are irreconcilably different. We forget that any Afrikan movement against them, away from them, is a progressive movement toward our empowerment. (Baruti, *Centered*, pp.97-99)

As warriors, this is how we logically assess our probabilities and possibilities for success because, "you measure a people's chance for achieving liberation by how different their culture is from the oppressors" (Amilcar Cabral). No matter what we are doing or how we are doing it, if we are going to legitimately measure our progress, we must measure what we are building against what we are destroying, internally and externally.

27. The stages of moving from being purely mentacidal into a committed state of consciousness are outlined in the "To Become Afrikan" chapter of my *Asafo: A Warrior's Guide to Manhood* (Atlanta, GA: Akoben House, 2004, pp.163-171). "Focused rage" is the final stage in this spiritual, psychological, physical *Sankofan* evolution. Sequentially, the preceding stages are "Encounter," "Denial," "Shock," "Anger," "Search" and "Study." Psychological interpretations of this process are manifold. The best are brought together and well critiqued as to their explanatory liabilities and assets for us in Kobi K.K. Kambon, *African/Black Psychology in the American Context: An African-Centered Approach*, Tallahassee, FL: Nubian Nation Publications, 1998, pp.269-314 and Daudi Ajani ya Azibo, *Liberation Psychology*, unpublished manuscript, Chapter 7. With reference to "Sankofan" as used above, Sankofa is one of the many Adinkra symbols of the Akan people of West Afrika. It literally means "go back and fetch it." The Sankofa symbol, drawn as a bird with its head turned toward what is behind it, is designed to remind us that we have to investigate and understand our past in order to correctly interpret the present. With this wisdom we can then make determinations as to which direction we should move in the future so that we will be guided toward our traditional ways of thinking and doing.

28. Bobby E. Wright, "Mentacide: The Ultimate Threat to the Black Race."

29. Afrikan centered has become a catch-all designation, much the way "Black" did. Any and everybody with a predominately, or even significant, Afrikan student body, workforce, constituency or following can call themselves Afrikan, even when what they do and say is totally contradicts this claim. As the label Afrikan centered becomes more diluted, in terms of what it represents, the more it becomes overused and misinterpreted. As more of us have become attracted to this term, more of us seeking clients or popularity have self-interestedly abused it. It can be expected, and, in a number of cases, is evident now in everything but

genocultural attributes, that predominantly european, as well as european led negro and lost soul, organizations, will place "Afrikan centered" in their title or description, without challenge or effective censorship from the Afrikan community. The mind of subintegrationists is a case in point of this trend because they are so desperately searching for any sign that Europeans don't hate us anymore that any effort by Yurugu to commandeer more of our essence is a credible evidence of their love.

30. Kwame Agyei Akoto, *Nationbuilding*, Washington, DC: Pan Afrikan World Institute, 1992, p.186.

31. Akan proverb.

32. It is most interesting that with the Akan, "if it is found that one died while running away from battle or retreating ignominiously from the enemy, then one is obliterated from historical memory." (Kofi Asare Opoku, *West African Traditional Religion*, Jurong, Singapore: FEP International Private Limited, 1978, p.36)

33. Ibid, p.154 and J.A. Sofola, *African Culture and the African Personality*, Ibadan, Nigeria: African Resources Publishers Company, 1973, p.99 and 118-119. The Akan refer to this as "Suban." To the Akan,

> Morality is generally concerned with right and wrong conduct or behavior and good and bad character. We speak not only of a moral act but also of a moral person; we speak not only of an honest or generous or vicious act but also of an honest or generous or vicious person. When a person is generally honest or generous the Akans judge him or her to be a good person, by which they mean that he or she has a good character ..., and when the person is wicked or dishonest they judge him or her to be a bad person, that is, to have a bad character. It is on the basis of a person's conduct...that the Akans judge one to be good or bad, to have good character or bad character. According to them, the character of a person is basic. The performance of good or bad acts depends on the state of one's character; inasmuch as good deeds reflect good character, character (*suban*) appears as the focal point of the ethical life. It is, in Akan moral thought, the crucial element in morality, for it profits a society little if its moral system is well articulated intellectually and the individuals in that system nevertheless have bad character and so do the wrong things. A well-articulated moral system does not necessarily produce good character; neither does knowledge

> of moral rules make one a good person or produce good character....According to the Akan thinkers, to be able to act in accord with the moral rules of the society requires the possession of a good character (*suban*). (Kwame Gyekye, *An Essay on African Philosophical Thought: The Akan Conceptual Scheme*, Philadelphia: Temple University Press, 1995, pp.148-149)

It is interesting to note that IWA, like Ma'at, is female.

34. NY: Wazobia, 1994 (first published in 1962), p.154. And although many Yoruba practioners explain that "IWA Pele" is the term used in reference to good character, IWA will suffice for our purposes in that we are simply defining a warrior's character.

35. Yurugu has separated ethics from good character by removing morality from its universal source and making it the individual's prerogative. Whereas before good character and being ethically sound/morally correct were the same (i.e., had the same measuring rod), now there is no basis for judgement beyond the individual in a cultural order where individualism is the ultimate priority. Although he gives "science" the volition of an agent independent of genocultural interests (i.e. speaking of "men" as if the asili [spiritual connection] is not a distinguishing factor between Yurugu and us), Willie E. Abrahams offers a sound, but euphemistic, explanation of the decline in universal law as the guiding principle of morality in modernity.

> What the growth of science does is to anthropologise morality and politics. Morality comes to be based on that complex which suits men in their present circumstances, or on the consensus of human opinion. A sort of utilitarianism and naturalism in ethics would then be almost inevitable. (*The Mind of Africa*, Chicago: The University of Chicago Press, 1962, p.47)

36. Molefi Kete Asante, *Afrocentricity*, Trenton, NJ: African World Press, 1988, p.viii.

37. Genoculture is the term we use when referencing cultural traits that are genetically encoded in a people. In terms of those areas where people do have choices, genetics, beyond basic instincts, is culturally bound. It has yet to be accepted by the European scientific community that most thought and action they claim to have a biological origin were molded within a cultural genetic structure. And culture is molded within an asilic genetic structure. One could even say that the asili is the mind, and

culture is the materialization of that mind. When we use that description and our basic common sense, culture can be recognized as a living entity. So there is no reason to believe that it, any less than any other living thing, does not have a genetic makeup. Beyond the elemental drives of seeking water, food, warmth and shelter, the human genetic structure evolves from a people's adaptation to their social and physical environments. Habitual behavior comes from the refinement of adaptive strategies which, in turn, become biologically locked into the genes. When a people have done something in a particular way for uncounted generations, it becomes natural, it becomes genetic. And, as culture evolves, human biology (genetics) adapts. (See Mwalimu K. Bomani Baruti, *Homosexuality and the Effeminization of Afrikan Males*, Atlanta, GA: Akoben House, 2003, p.125.)

38. "The Book of Phebhor," in Maulana Karenga (ed.), *The Husia*, Los Angeles: The University of Sankore Press, 1984, p.67.

39. Asa G. Hilliard, Larry Williams and Nia Damali (eds), *The Teachings of Ptahhotep*, Atlanta: Blackwood Press, 1987, p.21.

40. Mwalimu K. Bomani Baruti, *Yurugu's Eunuchs*, Atlanta, GA: Akoben House, 2008, endnote 29.

41. "negroes" (and "negroettes") are those persons of Afrikan descent whose loyalty lies with Europeans. These individuals do not see themselves as Afrikan to any degree, except as a hyphenated version, which allows them some degree of protection against their destroyer's psychological molestation. negroes have intent in that they are consciously anti-Afrikan, doing all in their power to sabotage any self-determined, empowering PanAfrikan or race-based, politico-economic initiative, organization or individual effort. They share a deep and committed state of racial confusion and self-hatred, as well as an exceptionally strong and determined denial of their ancestors against whom they take great pride in committing treason. (See "negroes" in Crawford (Baruti), *negroes, The American Directory of Certified Uncle Toms*, NY: CBIA & DFS Publishing, 2002 and Baruti, *Centered*, pp.50-51.) There is, of course, the worn-out argument that our critique of negroes is only because we do not have the validation and things that they do, that our jealousy is the issue, not their treason. With this, we completely and

emphatically disagree. Warriors do not hate self-haters. That would be a self-defeating waste of energy. In fact, accusing warriors of hating segments of our people is nothing more than a propagandic, political weapon (similar to labeling Afrikans homophobic or racist) designed to force those who should know better, but whose sympathetic humanism makes them question what they know, to accept anti-Afrikan thought and behavior in Afrikans as reasonable and, therefore, acceptable.

42. Eureason is the entire body of logic/reasoning that drives the european interpretation of reality into others' minds. It is the confusion that gives the illusion of a universal order to european thought and behavior. At the same time, for us, it is the Afrikan "genius" that, having accepted their thought as universal, determinedly seeks to rationalize the world as it has been organized by Europeans as normal for us based on this interpretation. It is the using of one's Afrikan genius to rationalize the world from the european interpretation of reality. Succinctly, it is what makes Afrikans believe they are correct in willingly thinking and acting as if they are Europeans and act/react against anything, unapproved by Europeans, that is Afrikan.

Chapter Two || Vision and Mission

1. Such a solution must, first and foremost, explain the very nature of what we are dealing with.

> It is the essential nature of western-European society that threatens our existence – not just its mechanism, not only its exploitative nature, nor its white racism (anti-Africanism) alone. There is no single aspect that accounts for its dangerousness. Western society means chaos to the African spirit. In order for that spirit to thrive, order must be restored. (Marimba Ani, *Let the Circle Be Unbroken*, NY: Nkonimfo Publications, 1997 (first published in 1980), p.49)

2. N. Xavier Arnold put it this way: "...when we lead we represent humanity at its best, when we follow we demonstrate humanity at its worst." (*The Genocide Files*, Marlow Heights, MD: Tana Lake Publishing, 1997, p.331)

3. Discussions of this consensus-reaching model among Afrikan people can be found in Willie E. Abraham's, *The Mind of Africa*, Chicago: The University of Chicago Press, 1962, pp.76-77 and K. Kia Bunseki Fu-Kiau's, *Mbongi: An African Traditional Political Institution*, Roxbury, MA: Omenana, 1985.

4. Our weight, and that of those who want to be Afrikan, is enough. "No one carries a sick person on his back when going to war" (Akan proverb). It is gratifying to know that this wisdom reverberates in the minds of the new vanguard. They tell each other to "strengthen the weakest link in the chain or get rid of it." (PreciseScience, "Love & Sacrifice," *Heart Chakra*)

5. Akan proverb.

6. An Elder is an older person in the community who has accumulated a vast working knowledge of her or his people's traditions (normalized, functional beliefs and behaviors) and, because of a lifetime of demonstrated commitment to these principles and practices, is sought out for the wisdom that maintains the integrity of the family, community and nation. Elders are beyond reproach and held in high esteem. Among Afrikan people, being an Elder is indeed an honor. (Mwalimu K. Bomani Baruti, *Centered: Building Afrikan Realities*, Atlanta, GA: Akoben House, 2009, pp.131-138)

7. "Jenoch" is the plural of "Jegna," a word taken from the Amharic language of Ethiopia. It refers to those who are altruistically committed, out of an unqualified duty to their people and nation, to teach our children the art and science of a politically conscious adulthood. Or, as articulated by Wade W. Nobles,

> *Jegna* (*Jenoch*, plural form) are those special people who have (1) been tested in struggle or battle, (2) demonstrated extraordinary and unusual fearlessness, (3) shown determination and courage in protecting her/his people, land and culture, (4) shown diligence and dedication to our people, (5) produced an exceptionally high quality of work, and (6) dedicated themselves to the protection, defense, nurturance and development of our young by advancing our people, place and culture. ("From New Afrikans Ezaleli to the Jenoch," in Lee Jones (ed.), *Making It on Broken Promises: African American Male Scholars Confront the Culture of Higher Education*, Herndon, VA: Stylus Publishing, 2002, p.181. Also see Asa G. Hilliard (Nana Baffour Amankwatia) *African Power*, Gainesville, FL: Makare

Publishing Company, 2002, pp.18-20.)

When honoring these Afrikan individuals, "Jegna" should be used instead of "mentor" because "mentor" is derived from the mythical greek character Mentor, whom Odysseus left to care for and educate his son Telemachus in his absence. As with every other "mentor" in ancient greek society, a significant part of his role as teacher and guardian was to personally introduce his ward to a homosexual sexstyle. (Mwalimu K. Bomani Baruti, *Homosexuality and the Effeminization of Afrikan Males*, Atlanta, GA: Akoben House, 2003)

8. This is understandable because we are socialized in this social context. Historically in western society aging has been associated with uselessness. Today, that still obtains, but is masked by the glorification of retirement and assisted living homes, which give the impression that these individuals essentially remain independent and are a contributive part of a youth-fixated society. Old age is simply regarded as an extended period of retirement, for those who live long enough. For Afrikan warriors who can see beyond the veil, this impression does not conceal the prevalence of gerascophobia, or irrational fear and/or hatred of aging, and gerontophobia, or irrational fear and/or hatred of the aged, that historically, without break, curiously characterizes yurugu's culture and society. With this gerontophobic backdrop, it may be helpful for the reader to understand the rise of the American Association of Retired Persons (AARP), the largest lobbying group in this society, as an aggressive reaction to agism, in the same way as feminism came into being and evolved as a reaction to western patriarchy and its characteristic misogyny. (Irreconcilable differences in the way that Afrikans see and treat elders versus that of Yurugu is pointed out in J.A. Sofola, *African Culture and the African Personality*, Ibadan, Nigeria: African Resources Publishers Company, 1973, pp.76-78.) Ironically, in the same way they are running away from the past that reveals them for what they are and are not, Europeans and those they have culturally subassimilated are always looking back in time for happiness as they age. Even while arguing that progress is God, Europeans long for the "good ol' days" and have us doing the same thing, forgetting that this is not our culture and that our cultural orientation toward time and satisfaction was quite dissimilar.

(Traditionally, for Afrikans, happiness comes in the here and now and increases as one ages.) Part of the problem, of course, is that Europeans equate life's satisfaction with pleasure (physical). Afrikans, on the other hand, associate it with happiness (mental). In the European mind, beauty and personal power (as potency) wane and pain/discomfort increases with age and these bring dissatisfaction to the European mind. Europeans do not want to see their elders, or others in illness or deformity, (ergo the effort of elders to remain healthy and attractive) because it is an outward sign that

1) they are not as perfect as they would like others to believe

2) they do not know all (cannot explain or cure all maladies)

3) they are not the gods they pretend they are which would be clearly indicated by possessing everlasting life.

9. We say "traditionally comprised the warrior class" because age is most often the primary factor in who actively, physically stands on the frontlines, especially during times of peace (i.e., when they are strategizing but unable/unwilling, in calculating the right moment, to actively aggress against us). During war, while they still may comprise the majority of the active, physical forces, everyone is a participant.

10. Most Afrikans in western society assume that integration is a two-way process of equal "give and take." After all our hard lessons, the "melting pot" delusion is still alive and well in our community. Too many of us also assume that so-called integration is a positive and something to which we should aspire. However, integration is not what has happened. The Afrikans and Afrikan ideas and things that Europeans have allowed to be absorbed into their culture have assumed a lesser or subordinate importance and status, or at least have been given the impression of such. Therefore, in using the word integration, we may be using the correct dictionary denotation, but it is the incorrect connotation for Afrikans in the western reality. That being the case, we need a term that more appropriately fits this reality. *Sub*integration includes not only the basic ideal definition of integration but also the way in which Afrikans (and those ways and things Afrikan) are introduced and incorporated into (and

recognized by) western culture and society. Be mindful that we are not here speaking of those ancient and traditional Afrikan ideas and things that were stolen and distorted into the foundations of european thought and behavior because those Afrikanisms are not accepted or admitted as Afrikan within european culture, thought or society. Of course, discerning minds question the idea of integration based on the serious thought they have given to the question, "Who are they that we would want to be equal to them?"

> Remember equality is a fool's target devised by lesser men to rob you of your potential, men who cheated, lied, and murdered to get their place in the world. All of you are better than that. We are better than that. We were here first, understand that and know what that means. God made us first to lead, not to follow. There is a flame that burns in each one of us. Not five hundred years of hatred, murder, rape, or slavery could put it out. It burns purer now, it burns hotter because of our suffering and tribulations. It could light up the world again if we would let it....There is an old European saying, "God's first green is gold." It means God's first work is His most perfect work – the purest, the best. It is the mold, the template, the standard by which everything that comes later is measured. The Europeans understand what we are, and what that means. Until we, until you understand that, you will remain zombies trapped in this twilight, this purgatory of Western civilization, chasing a dollar rather than creating a vision. As long as you do that, you will never reach your true potential. It's really very simple: there is no middle ground. It comes down to this, you can be niggers or you can be Africans; the choice is yours. (Arnold, *The Genocide Files*, p.136)

13. Inferiorization is the process of forcing/leading individuals or a people to believe they are less than that of which they are capable. It is the process where individuals or a people are made to feel that they are the intellectual inferiors of others and that this state of being intellectually or morally less is beyond their control, i.e., they are born that way. If this thinking is repeated long enough or fully internalized, those made to feel inferior often come to accept their position as a fated, Creator-given handicap. Almost always used to rationalize oppression and exploitation, inferiorization is a social fabrication which, if left unattended, would reveal its own contradictions. If this were not so, the process would not require the continuous, cyclical manufacture of

scientific "proof" or its institutionalized reinforcement built into the social system. Most telling in this tactic of inferiorization are we Afrikans, who cannot yet be left to be inferior of our own accord. Still, millions and millions of dollars and timeless energy must be put into scientifically "proving" our intellectual genetic inferiority because this theory of white supremacy holds no water. If biology, and not racist society, were the key, suppression would not be necessary because we would naturally fall to the bottom without any help on their part.

14. Dehumanization is the process whereby the attempt is made to make an individual or group less than human. The desired goal is described thusly:

> People are easier to kill if they come from nowhere. If they have no names, no fathers or mothers....Nothing has been lost, no crime committed. Rather, a kind of harsh but impersonal justice has been served, the wheel of historical inevitability has rotated, as it must, as it has countless times before, without malice...The dead, the piles of corpses are nobodies who began nowhere, go nowhere, except back where they belong. Nowhere. No-count. Nothing. (John Edgar Wideman, *Fatheralong*, NY: Pantheon Books, 1994, p.77)

It reflects the homicidal (at the individual level) and/or genocidal (at the group level) tendencies of those who desire to dehumanize others, for dehumanization is meant to do more than enslave. It is meant to spiritually, mentally and physically devastate to the point where an individual's identity, defined in terms of being the culmination of one's people, is obliterated. At best, the victims remain consciously aware of this assault, rejecting it in every possible way. At worst, it is affectively internalized and manifests itself in the fragmented shell of a being who truly believes in this grossly inferior label.

15. Also called scientific racism, this is the western political science which studies and propagates the idea of innate differences in intelligence based on race. It is the white supremacist study of racial differences in physical and intellectual outcome based on genetic causation. (See Allen Chase, *The Legacy of Malthus: The Social Costs of the New Scientific Racism*, Urbana, IL: University of Illinois Press, 1980, Russell Jacoby and Naomi Glauberman (eds.), *The Bell Curve Debate*, NY: Times Books, 1995 and

Claude S. Fisher, et. al., *Inequality by Design*, Princeton, NJ: Princeton University Press, 1996 – the list is virtually endless). Also see my "A Godless Reason" (in (Mwalimu K. Bomani Baruti, *Eureason: An Afrikan Centered Critique of Eurocentric Social Science*, Atlanta, GA: Akoben House, 2006, pp.63-109.). Even when it is in front of our eyes in the form of undeniable similarity in attitude, predisposition, preferences, kwk., across multiple generations of offspring, most Afrikan people do not want to consider the possibility of genetic influence (beyond looks) because of the bad name given us through it by eurocentric political science.

16. See Baruti, *Homosexuality and the Effeminization of Afrikan Males*, p.125.

17. This point is well stated in Calvin R. Robinson, Redman Battle and Edward W. Robinson, Jr., *The Journey of the Songhai People*, Philadelphia, PA: Pan African Federation organization, 1987, pp.222-228.

18. A comparison of the Afrikan and European geopolitical cradles is outlined in "Irreconcilable Differences," in Baruti, *Eureason*, pp.201-241.

19. The primary reasons I have given for almost exclusively addressing Afrikan men and boys have been:

> First, men fear men. Therefore, Afrikans who will become men need to be reared by Afrikan men in such a way that they will be adequately prepared for contact and confrontation with mentacidal (negro and lost soul) Afrikan and nonAfrikan men. Afrikan boys need to be trained to deal with other men more efficiently than those men will deal with them.
>
> Second, men teach boys how to be men. Therefore, it is the responsibility of Afrikan men to be the primary teachers of Afrikan boys in the ways of manhood.
>
> Third, men provide primary and last resort discipline in the home (and community by extension). This unique responsibility calls for men who understand the reason behind, and correct application of, this important socializing tool.
>
> Fourth, European culture has taught our youth (especially the boys) to absolutely disrespect women (increasingly including mothers). Women do not incite a healthy enough fear in boys as they grow older and stronger. Therefore, men must also assume responsibility here,

providing women with the safe and controlled space and environment to remain effective teachers and nurturers. (Mwalimu K. Bomani Baruti, *Asafo: A Warrior's Guide to Manhood*, Atlanta, GA: Akoben House, 2004, pp.v-vi)

20. Akan proverb.

21. Laini Mataka, "It's All Right To Let Some People Into Yr Vestibule, But Never In Yr Livingroom," in Laini Mataka, *Never As Strangers*, Baltimore, MD: W.M. DuForcelf, 1988, p.14.

22. Kenyan proverb.

23. What this means is that a good husband is one who prevents any external force from obstructing his wife's self-actualization and he, himself, does not interfere with her being herself. The happiness of a wife with a good husband is radiant. Otherwise stated, a man's harshness or gentleness expresses itself in his complement's countenance.

24. It is easy to see this Afrikan appreciation for women's power in the words "The true worth of a race must be measured by the character of its womanhood" (Mary McLeod Bethune) and "A nation can rise no higher than its woman." (Elijah Muhammad)

25. Nyansasem (pronounced n-yawn-say-sem) is a Twi word meaning "wise words."

26. Akan proverb. In contrast, the Akan say, "It is only the fool who needs a proverb explained to him," or "When you quote a proverb to a fool, you also need to explain it."

27. Akan proverb.

28. Nonetheless, I have addressed the vision our daughters should have of themselves, our sons and ourstory and people. See "Groundings with My Daughters," in Mwalimu K. Bomani Baruti, *Mentacide and other essays*, Atlanta, GA: Akoben House, 2005, pp.113-120.

29. "Shrew" being one of the many derogatory terms european males have created to voice their loathing for their own (and others') women, "taming the shrew" indicates the need for males to directly and oppressively control females in order to keep them manageable in a male-ruled culture and society. Other such terms originating in the european mind in terms of their utilization against females include wench, slattern, hag, harlot, prostitute, jade, rig, tart, trollop, slut, bawd, hooker, hussy, tramp, virago, moll, hex, grisette, cow, sow, termagant, bag, spinster, vixen,

piece (usually "of ass/tail"), punk, demirep, cyprian, broad, minx, crone, trick, floosy, nymph, amazon, hen, nympho, nymphet, easy, slag, quean, doxy, frump, sloven, harridan, loose, beldam, streetwalker, butch, battle-ax, whore, strumpet, adventuress, bat, trull, baggage, floozy, jezebel, skirt, drab and bitch, to name a few.

30. Regardless of what we credit this to, it is not an exaggeration to state that, historically, matriarchal societies have been more egalitarian and peaceful while the balance in patriarchal ones tilted toward violence and domination. And this is not a function of one thriving in a state of "primitiveness" and the other having evolved in a time of enlightened reason. It is a function of having a deeper appreciation of the value of life because of one's intimate and long-term involvement in the creation of it and the temperament this produces. Let us not in our ignorance and/or arrogance dismiss this as feminist thinking. For, by their words, deeds and agenda, feminists are simply androphobic (man-fearing), misandristic (man-hating), vaginacentric, phallophobic, penis-envying european females who want to be mistaken for european males.

31. The term "euroversalization" is a reconceptualization which more aptly than "universalization" describes what is going on culturally and socially in this world/reality. Instead of the politically neutral, blameless "universalize"/"universalized"/"universalizing," "euroversalize"/"euroversalized"/"euroversalizing" indicates the specific source and direction of this process. Universal locates its truths in the Universe, whether that be all that exists or the ourstorical evidence of normalcy in this planet's humanity. This is a deductive science, logically inferring from that above to that below. Euroversal is the truth according to the imperatives and limits of the european mind. It is an inductive science, extrapolating from the limited to the unlimited. It operates based on the assumption that others' cultures are simply deviations of one norm, theirs. And although some warrior scholars prefer the term globalization over universalization, for all intents and purposes they are the same. They are one in the same generic macro process of imperialistic geographical, cultural and religious conquest and empire building through the supplantation of one people's way over that of all others for purposes of unmitigated

exploitation. However termed, in their mind, this process leads to only one desired end for european people – global domination with the consent of the systematically oppressed noneuropean. For this reason and the fact that Europeans are this reality's imperialists, we will use the political reconceptualization of euroversalization to identify this process. We must remember that everything has a source, an initiating energy. As time goes on, the source may become more obscure because what that source has affected/infected has come to take on the traits of that original source. But the true source does not change. This is especially relevant to our understanding when the source is nefarious and continues to benefit materially and image wise from those it has wrongly acted upon and altered into its image of them in its mind. Therefore, in order for us to correct ourselves we must remove ourselves from that source so that it can no longer instigate the thought and behavior it is compelled to (and systematically benefits from) in us.

32. The power of Afrikan women in battle is fittingly pointed out by J.A. Rogers in *The Real Facts About Ethiopia*. As quoted by Runoko Rashidi

> [T]he Ethiopian woman "goes with her husband to war, and often becomes his avenger, should he fall. Usually she is fiercer in battle than the man. Europeans sometimes kill themselves, rather than fall into the hands of the African woman." ("The Life & Legacy of Joel Augustus Rogers: Chronicler of a Glorious African Past," *Global African Presence* website, http://cwo.com/~lucumi/rogers.html)

Also see Filomina Chioma Steady (ed.), *The Black Woman Cross-Culturally*, Cambridge, MA: Schenkman Publishing Company, Inc., 1981, John Henrik Clarke, "African Warrior Queens," in Ivan Van Sertima (ed.), *Black Women in Antiquity*, New Brunswick, NJ: Transaction Publishers, 1984 pp.123-134 and Elleni Tedla, *Sankofa: African Thought and Education*, NY: Peter Lang, 1995, pp.139-140. No Afrikan man who understands the pivotal role of Afrikan women in our struggle would disagree with Yosef ben-Jochannan's statement that, "I have so much time to praise and worship Black women, to kneel down and thank the heavens they are here!" (in John Henrik Clarke (ed.), *New Dimensions in African History*, Trenton, NJ: Africa World Press, 1991, p.48).

33. Mwalimu K. Bomani Baruti, Atlanta, GA: Akoben House,

2004.

34. Baruti, *Complementarity*, back cover statement.

35. Excerpt from the poem "Just How Traditional Do We Spoze To Be," pp.44-45, in *Never As Strangers*, Baltimore, MD: W.M. DuForcelf, 1988.

36. Familialphobia is an irrational fear and hatred of creating and/or being a part of and participating in sustained, meaningful (primary) family structures. Familialcidists systematically work to undermine and eradicate the family as a natural, viable, foundational social institution.

37. This familialphobic, familialcidal asilic predisposition is why orphanages, childstealing for labor in other places and great legal debates about the State taking full responsibility for raising the society's children have dotted much of the social and intellectual landscape of european society since they became organized enough to form centrally governed societies.

38. Mwalimu K. Bomani Baruti, Atlanta, GA: Akoben House, 2002. My *Complementarity* and *Homosexuality and the Effeminization of Afrikan Males* also address this at multiple, interspersed points.

39. A good deal of this discussion has been taken directly from my book *Asafo*.

40. If we are to understand this in the way that Bobby E. Wright did, we have to know that it is in the european personality to blame any and everyone else except themselves for what they are and do. I.e., to blame all *others* for their faults and misbehavior is an intricate part of the european genocultural self.

41. Amos N. Wilson, *The Falsification of Afrikan Consciousness*, Bronx, NY: Afrikan World InfoSystems, 1993, p.74.

42. Amos N. Wilson, *Blueprint for Black Power*, NY: Afrikan World InfoSystems, 1998, pp.97-98.

43. G.K. Osei, *The African Philosophy of Life*, London: The African Publication Society, 1970, p.11. Using the Akan as a specific example to counter the eurocentric idea that, originally, naturally, "people lived solitary and uncooperative lives, with undesirable consequences that in time led to the formation of society," Kwame Gyekye makes the point that

> Akan thought...sees humans as originally born into a human

> society..., and therefore as social beings from the outset. In this conception, it would be impossible for people to live in isolation. For not only is the person not born to live a solitary life, but the individual's capacities are not sufficient to meet basic human requirements....Consequently, the individual inevitably requires the succor and the relationships of others in order to realize or satisfy basic needs....Human sociality, then, is seen as a consequence of basic human nature, but is it also seen as that which makes for personal well-being and worth. Because community life is natural to man, the kind of society that permits the full realization of human capacities, needs, and aspirations should be communal. Communalism as conceived in Akan thought is not a negation of individualism; rather, it is the recognition of the limited character of the possibilities of the individual, which limited possibilities whittle away the individual's self-sufficiency. (*An Essay on African Philosophical Thought: The Akan Conceptual Scheme*, Philadelphia: Temple University Press, 1995, pp.155-156)

He goes on to say that

> [I]t is implicit in communalism that the success and meaning of the individual's life depend on identifying oneself with the group. This identification is the basis of the reciprocal relationship between the individual and the group. It is also the ground of the overriding emphasis on the individual's obligation to the members of the group; it enjoins upon him or her the obligation to think and act in terms of the survival of the group as a whole. In fact one's personal sense of responsibility is measured in terms of responsiveness and sensitivity to the needs and demands of the group. Since this sense of responsibility is enjoined equally upon each member of the group – for all members are expected to enhance the welfare of the group as a whole – communalism maximizes the interests of all the individual members of the society....[Society's] intricate web of social relationships tends to ensure the individual's social worth, thus making it almost impossible for an individual to feel socially insignificant. In a communal social order like that of the Akan, this assurance is already provided; the individual feels socially worthy and important because his or her role and activity in the community are appreciated. The system affords the individual the opportunity to make a meaningful life through his or her contribution to the general welfare. It is thus part of the doctrine of communalism that the individual can find the highest good – materially, morally and spiritually (psychologically) – in relationships with others

and in working for the common good. (pp.156-157)

44. Anthony Ephirim-Donkor, *African Spirituality: On Becoming Ancestors*, Trenton, NJ: Africa World Press, 1997, pp.75 and 109.

45. Kikuyu proverb.

46. Mwalimu K. Bomani Baruti, Atlanta, GA: Akoben House, 2004.

47. Asafo is the Twi word for warrior. An Asafo is an Afrikan who fully commits her/himself to politically develop her/his intellect, by studying the traditions of our people and the ways of our enemies, in order to more effectively engage those who would seek to destroy us in mental, physical and spiritual warfare. For a detailed definition see Baruti, *Asafo*.

48. Asa G. Hilliard, Larry Williams and Nia Damali (eds), *The Teachings of Ptahhotep*, Atlanta: Blackwood Press, 1987, p.34.

49. Afrikan proverb. Of equal value to warriors are the words of one of our newest Ancestors, Hannibal Tirus Afrik, who says, "Words are wonderful, but deeds are divine."

50. It is interesting and, even at times, comical how vanquished people (defeated, broken individuals who feel that their defeat and brokenness is deserved) come up with and thoroughly research and practice into oblivion any and everything (e.g., religion, crystals, astral projection, drugs, alcohol, food, forgiveness, effeminization, interracialism, humanism, intellectualizing, music and dance, sports, video games, sex, wholistic health, yoga, kwk.) to avoid seeing their destruction, except removing their enemy.

51. Baruti, *Centered*, pp.117-119.

52.

> It is good character that is man's guard. The bad people, or people of evil character are they who fear needlessly, for it is their sin that haunts them and cause them to fear needlessly. (Sofola, *African Culture and the African Personality*, p.123)

"He who has done evil, expects evil" (Guinean proverb).

53. The Xhosa people of Azania (S. Africa) beautifully pose this afrism as "I am a person because there are people." Medase Bandele Gwamanda.

54. Tunisian proverb.

55. Ìdòwú, p.157. In Ptahhotep's words, "The character of a righteous person is an honor to him or her and a thing of value which is long remembered." ("The Teachings of Ptahhotep," in

Maulana Karenga (ed.), *The Husia*, Los Angeles: The University of Sankore Press, 1984, p.47)

56. Tshi proverb.

57. Also see Sofola, *African Culture and the African Personality*, pp.93-100.

58. And this truth applies whether they came from us or not because over 900 generations on a glacier created substantive, irreversible, irreconcilably different, genoculturally grounded differences in mind and personality ("Irreconcilable Differences," Baruti, *Eureason*).

59. *Intellectual Warfare*, Chicago: Third World Press, 1999, p.26.

60. "A few bad apples" is the idea that there is a good majority whose image is being spoiled by a minority of bad/wayward individuals. In the context of western culture and society, this is the politics of projecting their racist core, structure and interaction with others onto a few so-called confused, backward european scapegoats. This is our most common apology for them. It permits us to see the vast majority of Europeans as good and humane. The minority of perpetrators are either insane beyond help or, with greater exposure to us, would "see the light," too. Not surprising, this logic explains our support for the failed busing program initiated by the liberal democratic government to cure the "race problem" with proximity, i.e., to give Afrikan people an equal opportunity to become whiter. In keeping with this logic, we attempt to identify and single out the small number of overt and usually physically aggressive, declared racists in such a way that the European community at large is in no way indicted by association or ideology. Simply stated,

> A serial killer or child molester or drug addict don't exactly stop being what they are between crimes...Yet we address white prejudice and violence directed at black people as a series of unfortunate instances, deviancy from an enlightened norm. (Wideman, *Fatheralong*, p.108)

61. By definition, primary relationships are those among close friends and family, whereas secondary ones describe the (primarily utilitarian) associations that exist between all others who regularly interact, e.g., coworkers, classmates, providers of professional services, kwk. Some might classify this as a

distinction between friends and associations, respectively.
62. That Afrikan couples are heterosexual should go without saying. But, in view of the homosexualizing assault on Afrikans, including a number who claim a nationbuilding agenda, we must be clear that we are defining family as Afrikans. And Afrikans only define family heterosexually. Homosexuality and pedophilia (which is the predominant form of homosexuality in European society historically) cannot exist in a society where the family is sacred, where women are loved and honored as wombs of ancestral spirit and children are loved and honored as gifts from the Creator. They can only thrive where children are seen as the natural sexual prey of men and women. And they can only take root among those who abhor it and see it for what it is if that community has been pacified and is fearful and self-hating enough to welcome the abnormalities arrogantly imposed from outside and brought in by members of its own community who have been spiritually and psychologically broken. See Baruti, *Homosexuality and the Effeminization of Afrikan Males*. And so it is in western society; the pedophiles are out in force, transforming our community into a pedophile's paradise. Children fear the monsters that lurk in the closet. They are out now. Western society is out of the closet. The pedophiles no longer need to hide in the dark. They are openly in our children's bedrooms. And the label pedophobic awaits those who dare confront this assault.
63. Serial monogamy is defined as the situation of "marriage" or temporary couplings in which an individual goes through multiple relationships one after another. One marriage or coupling occurs after the next in an unending sequence. Of course, this must be understood in an anti-family, anti-marriage cultural context. So, the phenomenon of serial monogamy, popularized in the social science literature of the 1970s as the latest trend, has "progressed" into what have become called "starter," "practice" or "trial" marriages. These are "marriages" in which a number of months to a number of years are contractually designated as the marriage time frame with a general agreement of (producing no children, even though that has changed as their supremacist aspirations have awakened to growing fears of genetic annihilation because of their negative population growth rates and the positive global

population trends among people of color). At the end of the contract the couple can decide whether they want to renew the contract for an additional period of time or not. Serial monogamy become the preferred option for those who feel open marriages are too constraining (except as a "respectable" means of practicing bisexuality, and/or freely participating in any form of sexual activities without concern for it interfering with the legal status of marriage), and, for those who dismiss the institution in its entirety. In short, serial monogamy has been essentially reduced to serial sex. Marriage is naturally dying as an institution in western society and being replaced with a normal individualism that abhors children (negative population growth occurs when a people is not producing enough children to replace themselves) and promotes even greater selfishness and lowers propensities toward compromise with intimate others. Of course, in the highly individualized West where relationships are not relationships without polarized power struggles pitting the "strong" against the "weak," where the balancing dispositions which normally characterize two complementary individuals in long-term, intimate relationships become naturally construed into manipulative terms, where a superior must dominate an inferior, the solution to this problem, for those who see it as a problem, is to redefine marriage and lessen its importance and demand as a social institution.

64. Reconceptualization is the process of searching out and/or creating more appropriate terms and, especially, meanings to terms that better fit the logically self-interested, nationbuilding politics of our research and agenda. It is the first act in functionally politicizing language.

65. "Sesh" is an ancient name for the uncompromising warrior scholars who held dominion over the art of writing and recording and was considered to be foremost among all librarians. The word is derived from Seshat, the goddess of the library and records. These dedicated recorders of Ourstory and the Afrikan Way have been honored as our greatest workers because they are our people's memory and vision. Because we have been forced to use the european's language for so long that we have been misled into calling them "scribes," a european word of Latin origin. Be that as it may, "sesh," a Kemetic term, is the correct

terminology for these eternal students of truth and wisdom whose chosen profession it was and is to study and record the essence of our people. It is still a most honorable calling, a mission passed down through the generations from seasoned master to aspiring neophyte. It is still designed to ensure that time does not dilute, confuse or lose the traditions of our people. (See Mwalimu K. Bomani Baruti, *Sesh: an Afrikan centered guide to writing and self-publishing for warrior scholars*, Atlanta, GA: Akoben House, 2007.)

66. No people is perfect. But there are things which we are not. And, of all these, the greatest is european.

67. *The Destruction of Black Civilization: Great Issues of a Race from 4500 B.C. to 2000 A.D.*, Chicago: Third World Press, 1987, p.310. There is an echo of familiarity in the Angolan proverb that "some smile with hatred in their hearts."

68. Ntoreasee otuko (pronounced pronounced n-tor-ah-ee-see oh-too-koh), is an Akan term for expressing a truer meaning for what we have come to call the "Middle Passage." For a detailed account of this tragic piece of ourstory see Mwalimu K. Bomani Baruti, *Kebuka!: Remembering the Middle Passage Through Our Ancestors Eyes*, Atlanta, GA: Akoben House, 2005. Ntoreasee Otuko is a Twi (a dialect of the Akan people of West Afrika) term which is used to describe part of the most horrific event in ourstory. Literally, *Ntoreasee Otuko* means a "genocidal forced emigration/exile/captivity." This fits the depiction we are seeking because it speaks to both intent and process. The way in which we were captured and brought here was against every fiber of our will and fully intended to destroy all psychological and genetic memory of ourselves. Of course, it makes no real difference whether we use this particular Afrikan term or another. What is important is that we use Afrikan terminology.

> Many of us recognize that the term "Middle Passage" is no more than a euphemism softening the horrendous psychological feeling that part of the Maafa spent on the Kemetic Ocean naturally brings. We know that for untrained ears it subconsciously feels more like a mundane leisure cruise than the horrid journey that it was. "Middle" in no way connotes the horror Afrikans experienced. It is a neutral word indicating nothing more than location (middle – between Afrika and this land), while "passage" indicates only

a place traveled. (Baruti, *Kebuka!*, p.74)

69. A balanced discussion of both the treason and our rebellion are given in Sylviane A. Diouf's edited *Fighting the Slave Trade* (Athens, OH: Ohio University Press, 2003).

70. Baruti, *Kebuka!*. The Kemetic Ocean is what we now call the Atlantic Ocean. We unapologetically make this declaration using our Afrikan reason. European "old world" maps label the Atlantic Ocean as "Oceanus Aethiopicus" (Ethiopian Ocean). "Ethiopian" was a greek label for Kemites (Afrikans), meaning "burnt skin." It is the oldest known greek word for the Kemites (Afrikans). However, since we are not these protoeuropean Greeks or their descendants, we should not use greek words to characterize and describe the Afrikan reality/worldview. Yet, at the same time, calling the Kemetic Ocean the Ethiopian Ocean speaks volumes about how the Greeks saw the world. Calling this enormous body of water Afrikan, which means they possibly changed it into a greek name that reflected earlier Afrikans calling it by an Afrikan name, indicates both the respect that ancient Greeks had for the names Afrikans had given to places in the world as well as the fact that Afrikans had already named this world. Therefore, moving back in time to our original thinking, if anything, we should call the ocean that changed from being the Ethiopian to the Atlantic (also a european[ized] term) nothing other than the Kemetic Ocean. This would be ourstorically consistent.

71. Ibid, pp.77-79.

72. Because Europeans always become an occupying force (be that occupation spiritual, mental or physical), one of their prime objectives has always been to kill the messenger. We have far too many examples of this to debate this truth. It is obvious. Oppressors automatically do this against a vanquished, messianic-oriented people because they know that killing the messenger usually crushes the movement or, at least, its life's energy. Once they have done this, they can install a dysfunctional misleader, subintegrationist at heart, who possesses absolutely no threat to their domination.

73. Akan proverb.

74. Moreover,

> Expect not a friendship with they who hath injured thee; those

who suffered the wrong may forgive it; but they who doth it, never it be well with them (Kemetic proverb)

75. Naturally, the same applies to debates with Europeans or any other nonAfrikans with a demonstrated record of working against us. Unless the debate is leading to some immediate, useful, concrete action on our part, it is meaningless. "We don't take important matters to play with" (Akan proverb). While we talk, they destroy. And, because they have us in this mostly reactive, war torn, defensive position, they can converse with us in between rampages against us and while deciding who would be the next most strategic target within our community and how to best neutralize it.

76. Once we realize this, what they (along with those among their masters claiming liberalism) are attempting to do to us becomes quite obvious. When they are successful, we have become like the lion who was so busy chasing the hyenas away from his feeding ground that he died from exhaustion and starvation. All the hyenas needed to do was pretend to be separated from each other and individually encroach/attack from everywhere to create the endless distraction which, given the power and skill of the lion, was their greatest weapon against him. Once the lion had removed himself from the feeding ground, together, the hyenas were free to come in and feed at will.

77. Ayi Kwei Armah, *The Healers*, Popenguine, Senegal: PER ANKH: 2000 (first published in 1978), p.42 (pp.31-32 in the Heineman edition).

78. Ourstory is critical because just knowing what defines war is not enough. For Afrikan warriors, war must be understood within the context of how Europeans have warred against us. Our ancestral "War Correspondent" Nana Kuntu (Del Jones) is well qualified to describe their mentality relative to us.

> A war-like people they are, who advanced war technology to dangerous levels. They have developed "higher forms of killing" that go beyond war, beyond genocide and into the realm of madness. In this reality there is no room for liberalism. The smoking gun is still loaded and pointed at the Afrikan, while still in the sweaty palms of professional mass murderers...it's a horror! (*The Black Holocaust*, Philadelphia, PA: Eye of the Storm Communications, Inc., 1992, p.8)

79. Amos N. Wilson, *Afrikan-Centered Consciousness Versus The New World Order*, Brooklyn, NY: Afrikan World InfoSystems, 1999, p.53.

80. We have been broken into adopting an individualistic analysis of events and conditions in the lives of Afrikan people as we do for things in our personal lives. Even now, when examining Afrikan phenomenon progressively and from an Afrikan center, many of us misdiagnose the nature and magnitude of our problems because of this narrow sight. Our enslavement is but one example of this limited analysis. For, as atrocious and horrific as the crimes committed against individual enslaved Afrikans were, we do not give the tearing apart of us as a people the far greater emphasis it deserves. Too many of us see these "individual" acts as special, specific and in the singular. Because of this individualistic analytical oversimplification on our part, we tend to focus more on the pain of the damage (whipping, breaking, drowning, twisting, starving, experimenting, murdering, kwk.) done to individuals than the tearing, ripping apart of Afrikan people and community, a process of more profound and far-reaching effects. This error applies everywhere we think. Too often, we make the grave mistake of personalizing assault. We become angry with the actor who is the bad guy, the police officer who pulls the trigger, the politician who makes a racist statement, the banker who cheated us. What has been, and continues to be, done to us is almost always attributed to the immediate actor or business or organization, who is but an agent of a nation on a genocidal warpath against us. Almost always, our righteous rage is deflected away from its nationalist, culturally and socially institutionalized source and onto mere action figures, puppets, scapegoats, tentacles of a killing machine on a feeding frenzy for Afrikan minds, bodies and souls. The whole is not without intent.

81. Lost souls are the unconscious, passive equivalent of negroes. They have serious problems with the Afrikan centered interpretation of reality, but choose to ignore it rather than attack it. Their lot, as far as individual politics goes, is to seek out the safety of the status quo. They remain busy about the business of quietly being as European as possible without drawing too much attention to themselves. And they make no attempt at self-definition beyond that which their appointed leaders sanction.

Because of a lack of awareness of their Afrikanity and an uncritical interpretation of european propaganda, but more so because they intensely fear "rocking the boat," most lost souls will follow wherever negroes or white noise leads them. Lost souls live in fear for their lives, livelihood and borrowed quasi-liberty because they, too, know the European. They, too, know his tendencies and capabilities. Thinking of lost souls reminds me of a statement I recently saw on a Sister's shirt which read, "I don't suffer from insanity. I enjoy every minute of it." Regardless of superficial differences, because both work against the liberation, empowerment and sovereignty of Afrikan people, negroes and lost souls are little more than scavengers in the desert. To children, and immature, mentacidal adults, the mind of insanity is so terribly seductive. It is the easier way. (See "negroes" in Larry D. Crawford (Mwalimu A. Bomani Baruti), *negroes and other essays*, Atlanta, GA: Akoben House, 2000 and Baruti, *Centered*, p.48.)

82. Infamous for his bug-eyed acts of comedic self-hatred on the program *Mad TV*, Orlando Jones plays a character who makes this irreverent, evidently mentacidal statement in the movie *Primeval*. His outburst expresses the real feelings of so many negroes and lost souls. It sent a gratifying message down the subconscious spine of every Afrikan in denial and a chilling reminder to those of us who know the depths of self-hatred within mentacidal Afrikans. He played the perfectly subintegrated patsy. Some may argue that this statement has been taken out of context. Regardless, such a statement could never be taken out of context as the words of an Afrikan. An equally intelligent response would be that it may have been taken out of the context of that particular scene in that particular european media presentation, but it is not taken out of the western socio-cultural context, the dominant interactive context of Afrikans subject to european culture and society and its resultant institutionalized mentacide. Of course, even without this statement, this movie was one of the worst depictions of the Continent and our people, as well as the classic lie of a passionate european savior and sought after european female, I have ever seen.

83. I have made references to the point and utility of "Black Firsts" have been made elsewhere.

In our proud celebrations of "Black Firsts," we applaud Afrikans for *finally* repeating, or building on, the accomplishments already done by Europeans. We act as if we began here. While this criticism is not designed to negate any of our accomplishments while we have been dominated in this or any other land, it should force us to place them in the context of the accomplishments of, at the very minimum, 6245 years of advanced Afrikan civilization. (For those who would ask why I am counting today, we are still advanced. That is why they still seek to destroy us.) Do not misunderstand this critique of "Black Firsts." We must be clear about what, in reality, we are doing to our children. Making our children focus on individually being "first" in an area where none of us has been allowed to go before in the European world is, on the surface, an honorable success-motivating strategy. It motivates them into higher levels of struggle. And it forces Black-into-white subintegration by using our children as battering rams to invade areas, heretofore in this white supremacist reality, inaccessible to us. But, at the same time, and an even more significant issue for Afrikan warrior scholars working toward ReAfrikanization and nationbuilding, our children's misguided infiltration, subintegration and, ultimately, assimilation and amalgamation into whiteness, becomes the ultimate goal of "Black Firsts" themselves. The goal becomes to show Europeans that we are as good as they in whatever they do and, therefore, in proving our equality in all things, they should feel compelled to welcome us into their hearts and minds with deracialized, open arms. This agenda for the success of our children is no more than the subtle subintegrationist strategy of a vanquished people trying to conceal their sacrificing of their own children's extraordinary talents to their masters, so they too can be accepted as human. No matter how you look at it historically, their goal is still to convince Europeans, to influence them. Most of us still see them as holding all validating power that is socially and culturally derived. So our, and our children's, "Black Firsts," as measured against white progress, are designed to prove something to them, not us. (Mwalimu K. Bomani Baruti, *Asafo: A Warrior's Guide to Manhood*, Atlanta, GA: Akoben House, 2004, pp.85-86)

Of course, most of these anglo/europhiles are merely resting on the laurels of their glorified negro ancestors. They would never think to honor any Afrikan judged by western society as one who fought this racist system or who worked above and beyond the call of duty to move us away from an assimilated possession of european culture. The respect of negro historians is reserved for Europeans and those Afrikans who evinced some form of european validated success. The greatest collection of these historical figures fall into the category of "Black Firsts," epitomized by individuals such as Madame C.J. Walker, our first Black millionaire, who became rich by developing products to make our features look more European; or Crispus Attucks, who holds the distinction of being the first individual (Afrikan or otherwise) to lay down his life for the winning side in a european civil war that ended with the sovereign beginning of yet another racist european terrorist empire. negro scholars have to start and stop at piecemeal Afrikan "contributions" because any serious analysis of the lessons ourstory could bring us with respect to who we are as a unique cultural and traditional people, as well as the forms and outcomes of our interactions with others, might cause them to question the very foundation and reason for their false sense of security in the house of our enemy and be revealed for the intellectually impotent traitors that they are. (Mwalimu K. Bomani Baruti, *Notes Toward Higher Ideals in Afrikan Intellectual Liberation*, Atlanta, GA: Akoben House, 2006, pp.17-18)

84. They are aware of our genius and have used it as their dominative needs dictate once we lost control of it to them. Accordingly, our misguided genius has been coupled to their evil genius greatly enhancing their ability to generate universal disorder and chaos. Others have also been brought into the fray, through a much more subtle and pervasive brain drain, creating layer upon layer of support for the reality created of this unbelievably demonic, psychotic genius.

85. The use of "must" is in no way to say that it is choosing to do so against its wishes. In this case, it is a conscious, determined route.

86. Kenyan proverb.

87. Asase Yaa is Twi for Mother Earth.

88. Unfortunately, this was and is the personal intent of so many of our prominent scholars who spent their entire lives trying to prove that there is no such thing as races and that there is a common human origin. And many of us desperate to get the spectre of eurosupremacy off of our backs fell for this logic understanding neither the Europeans use for it nor the subintegrative agenda of many of our own scholars who, in many

cases, sought to be comfortable in their own subinterracialist confusions. Now we see and suffer the consequences of this contribution of the depoliticized science of Afrikans in the politicized world of european science.

89. Annexation is when a people add on their territory through appropriation/conquest. They seize part or all of another's space and militarily, politically and economically take control of it. To annex land is to commandeer space that lies outside one's legal jurisdiction, property that belongs to other people. The determination of the rightness or legality of such acts has historically fallen in the province of the annexationist, who usually has the overwhelming amount of power in the contest.

90. Colonization is the process by which one nation takes control over another nation or ethnic space for the purpose of directly exploiting it for its material and human/labor resources. Colonization is most evident when (1) the colonizers install (or overlay) their political and economic systems in order to systematically seize all power and remove control over any and all resources from the hands of the colonized and place them directly and completely in those of the colonizers, (2) the educational and religious orders of the subject people mirror and aspire to mimic those of the oppressors and (3) access to subsistence needs and fundamental truths lie is regulated by the colonizers. Remember that there is no room for truth in the politics of domination. Truth reveals oppressors for what they are and the methods by which they acquire, maintain and transfer their ill-gotten power and privilege intergenerationally. In practice, colonization is a modified form of absentee ownership because those who are colonized remain the majority in the colonized territory and, for the most part, man the political, economic, educational and religious machinery put in place and are governed by the colonizers. All of these institutions favor economic and cultural exploitation by colonizers. And, in the tradition of colonies and absentee ownership, all of this occurs while the colonizer holds absolute sway as the head of these institutions and administers the final decisions about their operation from their native land. Those colonizers who have been given the mission of overseeing the occupying force in the land of the colonized remain a minority backed up by an iron fisted military force, that is, until enough

time has passed so that the newly institutionalized ways of the colonizer have been internalized by the colonized. Once this has come about, i.e., once enough of the colonized are brainwashed enough to believe that what is being done to them and their way is progressive and beneficial for them and they reject their traditions and way as backward and harmful to their empowerment, the foreign military forces are supplemented by a native majority which then serves as a dedicated militia (organized mercenaries) loyally maintaining the colonizer's physical domination, even in his absence. Wade W. Nobles gives a more straightforward description of this in a list of the three methods of colonial reorganization:

> The first is that colonial reorganization always has to deal with the domination of the physical space....The domination of the physical space is really the ability of the colonizer to acquire, distribute, and exploit resources....The second method which colonial reorganization requires is the managing of the indigenous modes of production....[This] means that the alien integrates his own modes of production into the traditional natural modes of production....The third method...has to do with the reformation, or the reforming, of the African mind. Once the other two methods have been employed, the ultimate task is to replace the African mind with a European mind, which is done by replacing African indigenous education, religious, and psychological systems. (*Seeking the Sakhu*, Chicago, IL: Third World Press, 2006, pp.266-267. Also see Kwame Nkrumah, *Towards Colonial Freedom*, London: Panaf Books, 1979 (first published in 1962; first written in 1945), p.10)

91. Neocolonization is colonization without the presence of an official, direct control of the formerly colonized by the colonizer. Neocolonization occurs after the colonizer's social institutions have been made normal for the colonized, even though the colonized have rebelled and physically removed the aliens who were actually running the colonial machine from their space. Although their removal is not always a prerequisite for neocolonization to occur, ideally this is the case. This is not always so because the leadership of the newly independent country, usually trained and culturally loyal to the erstwhile colonizers, usually claims that (1) relations with the colonizing nation must be maintained to keep the economy from folding, (2)

the colonizers are the only ones who know how to make the political and economic order work so they must remain until enough natives are trained to replace them and (3) the newly independent government does not want to appear inhumane before the world to those who have become "citizens" of their country by having lived their entire lives there, using the illogic that they have as much right to remain the owners of that land as the natives from whom they stole it. We must note that there is usually only a short period of time, if any, in between when the colonizers relinquish control over the colonized and when neocolonization becomes the "new" reality. It takes time for those trained and loyal to the colonizer's way to have the power to functionally operate as agents of the colonizer. In the end, neocolonization is the state in which the exploitative colonial process remains in place, fully intact and operational, only now managed by those who were formerly dispossessed and held no prestige in it because they had not been allowed to make it their own in service to their beloved colonial master. We see variations of the neocolonial model in this society through examples such as Afrikan managers and executives of european businesses or Afrikan institutions of higher education exhibiting the illusion of independence all the while faithfully programming our children in the interests of a racist, supremacist, eurocentric educational system. In neocolonial situations nothing changes structurally. Only the color of the faces are altered. We should also note here, as in this and the above definitions, that all systems of exploitation of Afrikans, whether slavery, colonization, sharecropping, neocolonization, internal colonization are related (Robert Blauner, "Internal Colonialism and Ghetto Revolts," *Social Problems*, 16 (Spring 1969), pp.393-408 and *Racial Oppression in America*, NY: Harper and Row, 1972, Kenneth Clark, *Dark Ghetto*, NY: Harper and Row, 1965, Douglas Glasgow, *The Black Underclass*, San Francisco: Jossey-Bass, 1980, Manning Marable, *How Capitalism Underdeveloped Black America*, Boston: South End Press, 1983, Walter Rodney, *How Europe Underdeveloped Africa*, Washington, DC: Howard University Press, 1982, William K. Tabb, *The Political Economy of the Black Ghetto*, NY: W.W. Norton, 1970, Robert Staples, *The Urban Plantation*, Oakland: Black Scholar, 1987 and Eric Williams' *Capitalism and Slavery*,

Chapel Hill, NC: University of North Carolina Press, 1994 (first published in 1944)). They all not only steal our natural material resources, leech our labor and inculcate a self-deprecating, dehumanizing mentacide, but they are also disproportionately aimed at the genocidal destruction of Afrikan people. In an effort to apologize for Europeans or pretend intellectual authority in a specialized scholarship, many of us make the distractive mistake of overemphasizing differences between these selfsame forms of alien invasion. There is only a difference in form, not content. Each means of exploitative oppression systematically denied us our humanity, labor and resources, and negatively impacted Afrikan people cumulatively.

92. Interesting how easily they privately recognize and admit that war is "the most successful of [european] cultural traditions." (Robert Ardrey)

93. Ethnic groups are collections of people who share a common story and heritage usually over a great many generations. They tend to trace themselves back to a common origin/ancestor. Their relationships are mainly primary and close in nature. And, due to their sense of family, these allegiances extend over time as well as across living generations. Lineage, be it blood or marriage, with blood being key, is their principal bond. We are usually able to distinguish between ethnic groups based on language or dialect, location, attire, diet and to some degree appearance. Nations tend to be composed of a number of relatively autonomous ethnic groups functionally interacting with each other. Ethnic groups within any given nation also share a common core culture. Differences that exist between ethnic groups do not negate an equality of membership in the core culture. Assuming that there is no dominant ethnic group, then what would be considered status quo would be pretty much diffused throughout the ethnic groups. Also, in comparison to subcultures, ethnic groups are older, in time, have larger populations and usually carry more influence and power in society. (However, as europeanization spreads itself globally, these comparisons have increasingly become questionable.) Examples of larger ethnic groups within the European nation (culture) would be of the Europeans in places such as Australia, Azania (S. Africa), Israel and the United States. Examples of different Afrikan ethnic groups would be the

populations found in the diasporic Afrikan communities in places such as Brazil, Haiti and Australia. If we focused on the Motherland, ignoring the artificial borders imposed there by European invaders, we would see the Ewe, Yoruba, Masai, Ibo and Akan as separate ethnic groups, not distinct cultures. To make this point plain, we can refer to Molefi Kete Asante and Kariamu Welsh Asante's preface to their edited *African Culture: The Rhythms of Unity* (Trenton, NJ: Africa World Press, 1990).

> Africa...is one cultural river with numerous tributaries characterized by their specific responses to history and the environment. In this way we have always seen Europe after the Christian manifestations. England, Norway, Ireland, France, Belgium, Germany, etc., were one culture although at the same time they were different. Asante, Yoruba, Mandinka are also one, though different in the historical sense. When we speak of unity in Africa, we are speaking of the commonalities among the people. Thus, a Yoruba who is different from an Ibo or Asante still shares more in common culture with them than with Thais or Norwegians. To the degree that the material conditions influence the choices people make, we Africans share similarities in behavior, perceptions, and technologies. (pp.ix-x)

Molefi Kete Asante adds in his included essay "Afrocentricity and Culture,"

> Culture...means the accepted behavioral patterns of the African people. This represents the total organization and arrangement of African people's thinking, feeling, and acting. While there may be variations in action as well as in the physical manifestations of African people, the in-group variations are not as great as the group's difference from European or Asian groups. (p.11)

94. We find this same process currently occurring through a process called regentrification in those cities where Afrikans disproportionately live, especially in those where there has been a strong Afrikan presence. Gentrification, which is formed from the word "gentry" (i.e., those who were the nobility or elite in traditional France), occurs when the residents of a particularly desirable area/location who are members of a less organized, less powerful group, are targeted for removal and replacement by members of a more powerful group who have designs on owning and controlling it. Though this has historically been considered as an urban phenomenon, it is no different in intent or outcome

from what has happened in the displacement of Afrikan farmers by european landowners. The white flight from the cities to the suburbs in fearful response to the in-migration of Afrikans into "their" urban areas during the 1960s and 1970s is the most commonly known example of gentrification. What we are seeing now is called regentrification because the group which had previously occupied that territory, but had vacated it in order to distance themselves from the group that replaced them, is now determined to return and rout them out. Technically, they are trying to reclaim territory they only temporarily abandoned. In actuality, they are stealing back what they abandoned for greener pastures which have come to no longer be as attractive due to resource depletion or, because they have come to feel increasingly vulnerable in more open, difficult to protect spaces, they feel the need to consolidate their population in fort like fashion. Obviously, a calculated racial politics has played a major role in this "trend" because, at least psychologically, enough Afrikans have been confused into believing in the innocence and user-friendliness of yurugus that they are defending the right, and even desirability, of the removal of Afrikans from these spaces and the welcoming into them of Europeans. Our familiarity with regentrification has been gathered from the recent efforts of Europeans to forcefully (which does not always entail direct, physical violence, unless we are to include the increased police presence and accompanying ticketing and general harrasment, displace the Afrikan residents from their generations old urban housing stock in Harlem, Chicago, Washington, D.C. and Atlanta and so many other cities and claim this confiscated territory for themselves as if they are "saviors" who just happened to stumble upon or "discover" it. Once there, they raise real estate costs, construct physical barriers (in the form of buildings, circuitous travelways, white citizen councils, police, kwk) and laws (as in all forms of exorbitant taxes and unreasonable housing codes) that prevent any substantial return of these residents to the areas and housing these residents formerly occupied. As a thoughtful aside for warriors, though, this latest phase in their gentrification could be interpreted as a blessing in disguise. Strategically, their urban containment can be seen as a good thing. When you lock others out, you lock yourself in.

95. Ayi Kwei Armah, *KMT*, Popenguine, Senegal: Per Ankh, 2002, p.216.
96. Haile Selassie.
97. This asilic imperative could not be more simply put than in Boukman's observation that "the god of the white man inspires him to crime." (quoted in Carruthers, *Intellectual Warfare*, p.26)
98. This (xenophobic and crimogenic) society is epitomized by the european saying "Keep your friends close and your enemies closer," which speaks to a mentality of distrust and the drive to control this endless anxiety through mindful deception and surreptitious domination.
99. Ayi Kwei Armah, *Osiris Rising*, Popenguine, Senegal: PER ANKH, p.164.
100. Though eurocentric social science has attempted to clean up this sterile and very revealing theoretical conceptualization of yurugian society by arguing that, now, instead of people reluctantly giving up some of their rights to the state in order to be/feel more secure (a theory which they have described as a "consensus" model of society), Afrikan centered warriors can still see the connectedness between this term and the abiding extreme selfish individualism and immorality of Europeans, qualities which have never changed, though their humanizing propaganda would have us believe otherwise. Succinctly, the social contract, of which we speak when describing the social glue of european society, is the basis of their control of each other and domination of everyone else. Through social evolution (i.e., getting to practically know themselves, as well as their naturally xenophobic, covetous reaction to all others), they have come to "agree" to relinquish some portion of their individual free will in order to be regulated by a state which facilitates, protects and insures their continual invasion, violation and exploitation of the others' spaces, persons and resources for purposes of individual accumulation and gratification. Inherently volatile and truculent toward any and everyone including themselves, they have to keep internal discord at a minimum in order to dominate the world. This spiritual, constitutional and psychologically encoded agreement of group (against the world) solidarity is necessitated by the understood need for some form of cooperation for survival in a world that is a constant reminder of their inferiority. One

could of course argue that, in this way, we could say that they do have a consensus. But it is a consensus over the need for this social contract.

101. An apt statement of this expression is articulately given by John Henrik Clarke when he speaks of the European's propensity to "drain the diseased pus of their political sores on the lands of other peoples...to solve their propblems at other people's expense" (Marimba Ani, *Yurugu: An African-Centered Critique of European Cultural Thought and Behavior*, Trenton, NJ: Africa World Press, 1994, p.xvi).

102. In western[ized] society, collective coerced beholdenness based on having embarassing information on each other is the politics of virtually every bureaucracy or organized endeavor, including the church, media and academia. Secrets about others are kept as leverage against exposure of one's own misdeeds.

103. This was tragically demonstrated in Emperor Frederick II's experiment using a control group of newborns to disprove the thinking that "humans" are social creatures, that we need the contact of others to thrive.

> [H]e bade foster mothers and nurses to suckle the children, to bathe and wash them, but in no way to prattle with them or to speak to them, for he wanted to learn whether they would speak the Hebrew language, which was the oldest, or Greek, or Latin, or Arabic, or perhaps the language of their parents, of whom they had been born. But he laboured in vain, because the children all died. (quote taken from James B. Ross and Mary M McLaughlin (eds.), *The Portable Medieval Reader*, NY: Viking, 1949 in Ian Robertson, *Sociology*, NY: Worth Publishers, Inc., 1977, p.98)

Chapter Three || The Rules of IWA

1. A clear, defining example of this difference, in terms of culture, is the priority given good character in socialization. For Afrikans, good character was the first and most important lesson in a child's education. Its qualities are the first (and last) thing taught and modeled in traditional Afrikan society. Jomo

Kenyatta explains the distinction between the priority of character in the social development of Afrikan versus european culture/society while discussing comparative education agendas in *Facing Mt. Kenya.*

> The striking thing in the Gikuyu system of education, and the feature which most sharply distinguishes it from the European system of education, is the primary place given to personal relations. Each official statement of educational policy repeats this well-worn declaration that the aim of education must be the building of character and not the mere acquisition of knowledge. But European practice falls short of this principle; knowledge is the dominating objective in the European method of teaching in Africa as a whole and, as long as exams rule, it is hard to see how anything else can be given primary importance. While the Westerner asserts that the character formation is the chief thing, he forgets that character is formed primarily through relations with other people, and that there is really no other way in which it can grow. Europeans assume that, given the right knowledge and ideas, personal relations can be left largely to take care of themselves, and this is perhaps the most fundamental difference in outlook between Africans and Europeans. It can be safely said that, in the European system of education, school coordination, and especially social subordination, marriage, the family, the school, vocation, relation of people to the State, etc., are all regarded as things which have grown up of themselves, as historical forms which, however, are always capable, as such, of change, and over which the free man, namely, the personality must have authority. For freedom of personality is the highest good, and co-ordination with other people and especially mutual subordination are on the contrary something accidental. Here it is worthwhile to ask a question which seems very pertinent to our subject: "If it is true that the European system of education aims at individuality, is it then to be wondered at that Europeans educated in this way have some difficulty in finding the right place for the organic tribal relationships of the Africans?" We may sum it up by saying that to the Europeans "Individuality is the ideal of life," to the Africans the ideal is the right relations with, and behaviour to, other people. (NY: Vintage Books, 1965, pp.117-118)

As this Afrikan priority is found throughout the literature, apparently, our Ancestors believed that "a good character is worth more than money" (Akan proverb). To briefly take from another source,

The children were taught what was good and evil in the community. Education of the young ones inculcated a religious attitude to life. Traditional education was concerned with morality. They were taught to be generous, courteous and honest. Most of the things the children were taught, had a bearing on the life and culture of the community. (G.K. Osei, *The African Philosophy of Life*, London: The African Publication Society, 1970, p.58)

2. Colie Williams, "Ol' Soul For A New Day," Light Up The Darkness.

3. Of course, this statement must be evaluated in the context of the possibility of freely and peacefully living "your own" within the confines of a dominant, intolerant, predatory culture.

4. Miseducation, the term most are familiar with, is a term coined by Carter G. Woodson in his classic book *The Miseducation of the Negro*, "miseducation" names that learning which is irrelevant to one's empowerment. It means to be wrongly educated. In his book, Woodson explains how Afrikans in colleges and universities are being taught subjects, theories, agendas and philosophies that are irrelevant to the elevation of Afrikan people, but which makes them feel as if they are being highly educated because this is what european academia says defines the intelligent citizen and is critical for the continued development of their thinking and leadership skills. He points out that a miseducation leads the student and graduate everywhere they need to go, except in a direction of self-knowledge and understanding of what knowledge her or his community really needs in order to rise up and prosper as an independently thinking people. In many cases, it takes individuals so far away from the education they need that it becomes virtually impossible to move in that direction. We should add, though, that miseducation is not reserved for those who have participated in the college or university experience. It is a process that begins before the individual can officially enter the formal educational setting and is found throughout life, at all educational attainment levels, in all forms of media and all social institutions for those targeted before birth for failure or intellectual peripheralization. With miseducation, individual Afrikans become mindless clones of their eurocentric academic mentors, no longer thinking, no longer wanting to think as Afrikans. Unlike miseducation, which does teach an appreciation of learning,

although wrongful learning, diseducation leads the individual to despise the very idea of learning itself. Diseducation creates an anti-learning psychology within its victims that predisposes them to reject any information and study that requires them to go beyond what is required for basic survival or assimilation. Like miseducation, diseducation is a conscious, institutionalized process designed to make a people useless and even destructive toward themselves because they see no reason to want to learn. Diseducation is further related to miseducation in that it can be a direct outcome of the recognition that the individual has been miseducated if (1) one feels he or she has too great of a vested interest in the culture or institutions of those who miseducated him or her to suicidally move against them, (2) there is so much rage that it cannot be corralled and focused toward rejection of the miseducation, or (3) one feels that he or she has gone too far down the miseducation road to recover from it. Indeed, whether induced through miseducation, diseducation or both, "a mind is a terrible thing to lose."

5. The Kemetic-Kushite tradition is foundational to our analysis because it presents the most detailed, preserved evidence of our intellect, mainly before, but also after, the european-arab invasion. Given our knowledge of the Continent to date, these Ancestors produced the greatest literary record of all Afrikan ethnic groups. Nonetheless, we must consider why we more fervently embrace the Kemetic portion of our entire Afrikan intellectual root system. And the question would be why do this? Why, in the face of a dire need for the confirmation, elevation and glorification of ourstorical truth for ReAfrikanized nationbuilding, would any qualification be appropriate? And the answer is mainly because the cause of a good deal of what is admired of themselves in the minds of those subject to racist imposition is often not all for the reasons which seem obvious. As I have stated elsewhere,

> [M]any Afrikans around the world cannot get beyond Kemet (renamed Egypt) in locating the origins of Afrikan civilization [...because t]hey see that the *writing* there is acceptable to european definitions of civilized literature....[In addition, t]he Arabs who now occupy and claim Kemet as their (original) home are phenotypically more acceptable (aesthetically pleasing). The color and features of the people who now occupy Kemet after centuries of invasion, rape and

> amalgamative absorption are closer to those of Europeans than Afrikans. (Mwalimu K. Bomani Baruti, *Eureason: An Afrikan Centered Critique of Eurocentric Social Science*, Atlanta, GA: Akoben House, 2006, p.47)

Just many still find it psychologically comforting to separate this country and other of yurugu's states from Europe proper, some Afrikans find it expedient in the "salvaging of their wounded egos" to separate Kemet from the rest of the Afrikan continent,. Warrior Ancestor Amos N. Wilson, wise in the ways of kenteed negroes (i.e., Afrikan attire [kente clothe] on the outside, subintegrationist focused on the inside), poses a number of critical questions in relation to this mentacidal, other-directed selectivity relative to Kemet.

> Are we studying Egyptology to prove to the White man how great we were? And hope one day that when he acknowledges that Egyptians were Afrikans, that he will accept us as human beings? Is our study of Egyptology a personal and collective defense mechanism, a means of dealing with our hurt pride? As a means of trying to slip into the acceptance of White people by the back door? Is our hang-up with history and the exaggeration of certain of our achievements means by which we try to salvage a damaged ego? There is the ache of inferiority that never goes away. And we study, and we study, and we read, and we read, and we learn the hieroglyphics, and we still feel inferior – because we are pushed by the wrong reasons. And when we are motivated by the wrong reasons, even though we may replace the people who rule over us, we will end up being just *like* them. (*The Falsification of Afrikan Consciousness*, Bronx, NY: Afrikan World InfoSystems, 1993, p.84)

6. Numerous easily accessible sources are available with this sacrosanct listing. The more known ones include: Queen Afua, *Sacred Woman*, NY: One World, 2000, p.12, Muata Ashby, *The 42 Precepts of Maat and Their Foundation in the Philosophy of Righteous Action of the Wisdom Text Sages of Ancient Egypt Study Guide*, Miami, FL: Sema Institute of Yoga, 1998, esp. p.7, Anthony T. Browder, *Nile Valley Contributions to Civilization*, Washington, DC: The Institute of Karmic Guidance, 1992, p.91 and Johnson, *Seven Steps Toward Black Reemergence*, pp.199-201. Maulana Karenga has included the "Negative Confessions," or what he prefers to call "The Declaration of Innocence," as part of the *Book of Coming Forth by Day* in his translation of a number

of sacred, ancient Kemetic texts, titled *The Husia* (Los Angeles: The University of Sankore Press, 1984, pp.109-111). I have taken the liberty of copying two lists from his book here, without paragraph interruption, for the sake of the reader's convenience.

> I have not done evil against people. I have not mistreated my family and associates. I have not told lies in the court of law, the seat of Truth. I have not associated with evil or worthless persons. I have not done evil things. I have not begun a day by demanding more than I was due. I have not brought forth my name for praise. I have not cursed God. I have not defrauded the poor of their property. I have not done what is hateful to God. I have not slandered a servant to his superior. I have not inflicted pain. I have not caused anyone to be hungry. I have not made anyone weep. I have not committed murder. I have not ordered a murder or turned over anyone to a killer. I have not caused anyone to suffer. I have not stolen the offerings of the temple. I have not defrauded the divine beings of their bread offerings. I have not stolen the offerings of the departed. I have not committed adultery. I have not been unchaste in the sanctuary. I have not increased or diminished the measure of grain. I have not reduced the length of the palm. I have not encroached upon fields of another. I have not added to the weight of the scales. I have not tampered with the tongue of the scales. I have not taken milk from the mouth of children. I have not driven cattle from their pasture. I have not snared sacred birds. I have not caught fish with the bait of their own bodies. I have not stopped the flow of water in its season. I have not damed up water when it should flow. I have not put out a fire when it should burn. I have not violated the times of making meat offerings. I have not driven away cattle from the property of God. And I have not turned back God at His appearances. I am pure. I have not done wrong. I have not robbed. I have not been greedy. I have not stolen. I have not murdered people. I have not cheated at the measures. I have not committed fraud. I have not stolen the property of God. I have not told lies. I have not stolen food. I have not spoken curses. I have not violated the law. I have not killed sacred animals. I have not dealt deceitfully. I have not stolen land. I have not eavesdropped. I have not talked overmuch. I have not been angry with out just cause. I have not committed adultery. I have not been unchaste. I have not terrorized anyone. I have not violated the law. I have not been hot-tempered. I have not been deaf to words of truth. I have not stirred up strife. I have not been blind to injustice. I have not engaged

in unnatural sex. I have not been deceitful. I have not indulged in quarreling. I have not engaged in violence. I have not been quick tempered. I have not misrepresented my nature. I have not gossiped. I have not slandered the pharaoh. I have not waded in *drinking* water. I have not been loud voiced. I have not blasphemed against God. I have not been arrogant. I have not discriminated against others. I have not coveted others' property. I have not offended the God of my city.

7. The use of "stolen" is most the most accurate descriptive here. To say borrowed would be far too polite a misnomer in that borrowed implies that it was not stolen and the borrower is not lying about originality in order to cover up the theft. Any relatively serious student of ourstory and history is fully aware that all known evolutionary ordering of human intelligence places the origin of european rules of good human conduct far before the europeans ability to fathom a false divinity or project their incompleteness into it, less known read or write.

8. Yosef A.A. ben-Jochannan, *Africa: Mother of Western Civilization*, Baltimore, MD: Black Classic Press, 1988 (first published in 1971), pp.355-365 and 510 and Browder, *Nile Valley Contributions to Civilization*, pp.91-97. In a comparative chart, Kwame Nantambu also expounds on the Heru origins of Jesus (*Egypt & Afrocentric Geopolitics*, Kent, OH: Imhotep Publishing Company, 1996, p.19). Anther noteworthy statement about this parallel comes from Johnson in his *Seven Steps Toward Black Reemergence* (pp.189-193.)

9. This "audience participation" versus spoon feeding is also characteristic of the way information is disseminated to individuals at public gatherings in Afrikan versus european settings.

> *[T]he physical arrangement of traditional African oratory promotes social interaction.* In these traditional settings, the audience at storytelling and other events typically sits in a semicircle, where nearly everyone's face is seen, and each person is encouraged to participate in this truly collective activity....Whereas, the LECTURE MODEL speech-event does not encourage social and group interaction. At LECTURE MODEL events the seating is almost never arranged where everyone's face is seen, even when it is entirely feasible to do so. Rather, advocates of this model arrange the seating in typical Eurocentric fashion. They

arrange them in successive rows, where everyone is looking at the back of someone else's head, and all attention is focused on the individual speaker. The message in this arrangement is that the *individual* speaker is the most important person, and is therefore the sole focus of attention. This arrangement is the total opposite of that of African oratory, which organizes social events around the idea of collectivism and social participation, and as a result everyone's face is within view. (Manu Ampim, *Towards Black Community Development*, Oakland, CA: Advancing The Research, 1993, pp.149-150)

10. John Henrik Clarke is in agreement (*Who Betrayed The African World Revolution?*, Chicago, IL: Third World Press, 1995, p.90).

11. "Womb" is used instead of "Cradle" because the womb is the place of a person's spiritual-psychological gestation, while the cradle is where the infant begins its psychological-physical/motor development. While no one should doubt the formative influence of the cradle, starting a scientific investigation with it overlooks the even more elemental contribution of both conception and gestation. And, again, not that it is not of considerable significance but, *theoretically*, the concept of cradle as a human developmental stage ignores the seed's source, its formation and the bed in which it is first laid, instead jumping staight ahead into the plant's surroundings. While environmental forces carry significant weight in the development of a people's personality, the womb is where the possibilities of environmental influence are determined. Existing earlier in life, the womb precedes the environment and is the deeper determinant. The embryo is given life (identity, protection and nurturance) and matures in the womb. After birth, after the defining experience of the womb, the infant is placed in the cradle where it encounters and begins to learn from the physical universe. Therefore, if we are to assess the essence of a being, i.e., what are its probabilities and possibilities, the earliest source/origin is where we should always look. In this discussion, however, the environment is being interpreted as a womb because its impact on the personality of the people who evolved in it from their social and cultural beginnings is so much more spiritually, mentally and physically profound than what we would imagine simply *thinking of it* as a later cradle. It is

conceptual significance. Marimba Ani's video lecture "Yurugu: The Asili Analysis" (Baltimore, MD: Afrikan World Books, 2008) goes far in explaining why womb is the preferred term.

12. This set is taken from Maulana Karenga's translation of the *Book of Coming Forth by Day.*

13. Afrikan proverb.

14. Why would you smile at someone/a people who is/are consciously trying to kill you/us? Is it productive to try to befriend a determined assailant? It is only the fool who cannot believe his enemy is his foe and that this enemy is trying to kill him. It is only the fool who believes that conversation brings peace to sworn enemies or that predators are only sporadically predatory.

15. *Handbook of Revolutionary Warfare*, NY: International Publishers, 1968, very beginning of book.

16. Evolutionary theory is linear in its explanation of progress in that all change moves in one direction. Constant "progressive" change is defined as the motive force behind all social development. And, in that change is identifiable, it is argued to follow a unidirectional line. There is no stopping or turning to the side or going backward or repeated motion in linear movement. It is all in one direction, nonstop, straight ahead. Linear thinking views time as a never-ending line. You live and die on that line. For individuals, that means there is no cycle of birth, life, death, rebirth. There is no return. There is only life and death followed by heaven, hell or purgatory. What is behind is lost. What is ahead is to be found. Therefore, their fixation on time machines (and black holes, stargates and other portals that whisk people off into other dimensions of time; technology that bends space in such a way that crossing light years of time can be instantaneously done; and a whole collection of other fantastic theories that give them command over time), natural ("discovered") or manmade scientific technology that could transport them back and forth along an unchanging linear dimension, has remained a constant. There is no room for tradition in linear thinking, unless that tradition makes way for a more predictable and sustained progression into the future. Lineal thinkers run from the past in an effort to escape into the safety of an ideal future free of individual constraints and the pain of feeling inferior and insecure. For them, clearly, traditions (outside of their own genocultural ones) can have no lasting meaning because all

answers to today's questions and problems lie in tomorrow. Thinking linearly negates universal rhythm, cycles and time outside the dimension of human measurement/quantification. It negates the possibility of things beyond human comprehension. Linear thinking is the apt domain of Europeans and their intellectual zombies. (Mwalimu K. Bomani Baruti, "A Godless Reason," in Mwalimu K. Bomani Baruti, *Eureason: An Afrikan Centered Critique of Eurocentric Social Science*, Atlanta, GA: Akoben House, 2006, pp.101-102)

17. Circular thinking, on the other hand, is essentially not restrained by limiting conceptions of time that occur in thinking held captive by the day-to-day quantitative measurement of humans. (Here, circular thinking is defined as dealing in endless cycles and not the eurocentric definition of being basing conclusions on already assumed premises, i.e., pretending science by asking questions as if the answers have not already been given.) It is grander in conception. In it, there are countless cycles of birth, life, death and then, again, rebirth. Time repeats itself over and over and over again, ad infinitum. This optimistic and loving way of viewing reality as a place, a space, versus a duration, is based on a scientific study of the order and movement (procreative force) of the Universe. It is Afrikan in origin. Unlike what linear thinkers would have us believe, circular thinking is also progressive, very progressive. Only it is not so myopically focused on what is to come that it does not recognize that what is to come will always be directly the result of what has occurred. It acknowledges the validity of the universal rules which determine the outcomes of behaviors regardless of when the behaviors occurred in time. Circular thinking is a way of interpreting time and reality, which sees the progress of mechanical technology as an overriding theme in the cultural social and spiritual development of people as largely irrelevant. Time is not viewed as the framework within which some great technology race is run. Time is used to achieve spiritual perfection with technological, mechanical development as simply an instrumental means to that end. Minds that think circularly conceive of time as divinely having no beginning or end, while they also are able to see time in the cycles of its limited human existence. (Ibid, pp.102-103)

18. And we are not talking about a reactive concern over the future state of these resources after they have already gone beyond the possibility of replenishment so that you can save yourself and

deluding yourself into believing that you are scientifically more powerful than the Creator and, therefore, that what you wastefully exhaust you can create again or find elsewhere.

> Curiously, we see remnants of their efforts to save the environment everywhere they point us toward. The problem is that these are nothing but cruel jokes against Nature designed to fool others into believing that they are altruistic, and not politically motivated, acts. The heavy publicizing of these efforts indicates a conscious intent to make these lies truth. In addition, preservation initiatives, usually detrimental to the basic survival of indigenous peoples and which drives them into a european modernity, are meant only to save a captive Nature as a laboratory and museum for the viewing pleasure of their progeny. Even George Carlin joked about his own people belatedly coming to be concerned about this planet. He pointed out that they were only out to save themselves, not the planet. They have no where else to go, yet. As far as they are concerned, the only problem is that their ravaging of planet Earth has outpaced their science's ability to get them off of it. (Baruti, *Eureason*, p.92)

19. While the term global warming itself is quite euphemistic, it has been neutralized even more politically into "climate change" to distract from the truth. This newer euphemism in no way captures the desacralized nature of its initiating, primary, cowardly, other-blaming source or its devastating, irreversible impact for millennia to come, even if all contributors to this pattern were to stop immediately. (Hubert Henry Harrison puts this consciously deceitful tendency into a quite revealing reflection in asking, "What is this but a developing disease of the American conscience, to put the blinkers of a catchword over the eyes of the spirit?" (When Africa Awakes, Baltimore, MD: Black Classic Press, 1997 (first published in 1920), p.104)) Specifically, in speaking of the warrior's way, a quote from Che Guevara's *Guerrilla Warfare* can prove insightful and instructive to the Afrikan mind.

> ...the guerrilla fighter, as a person conscious of a role in the vanguard of the people, must have a moral conduct that shows him to be a true priest of the reform to which he aspires. To the stoicism imposed by the difficult conditions of warfare should be added an austerity born of rigid self-control that will prevent a single excess, a single slip, whatever the circumstances. The guerrilla soldier should be an ascetic. (NY: Monthly Review Press, 1961, p.43)

20. Interestingly, in the fashion of the western capitalist system, companies are fully exploiting this panic by claiming private rights and ownership over chunks of Arctic and Antarctic ice. The three things essential to human life, in order of importance, are air, water and food. Without air, you will die in a matter of minutes. Without water, it is a matter of a few days. And, without food, a couple of weeks is more than most could hope for. Free access to these is fundamental to a wholesome life at the most basic of levels. If not, survival becomes highly questionable. So, as Samuel F. Yette put it, "There are other ways to kill a people or colonize them, but none is more certain than the denial or control of their food." (*The Choice: The Issue of Black Survival in America*, Silver Spring, MD: Cottage Books, 1996 (first published in 1971), p.100) This, they have virtually accomplished and are well on the way to controlling our water. The logic of yurugu's mind tells us that air is next.

21. Yoruba proverb.

22. Ward Churchill and Jim V. Wall, *Agents of Repression*, Cambridge, MA: South End Press, 1988 and *The Cointelpro Papers*, Cambridge, MA: South End Press, 1990, Peter Matthiessen, *In The Spirit of Crazy Horse*, NY: The Viking Press, 1983 and Gaidi Faraj, *Ourstory: Afrikans from Antiquity to the 21st Century*, Atlanta, GA: Akoben House, 2008 (first published in 2000), pp.120-123.

23. Promos are those who may appear to not (and possibly may not) be homosexualized but who zealously defend the homosexualizing of Afrikans agenda (be that "rights," pedophilia, ourstorical distortion or whatever), often to a greater extent than the homosexualized Afrikans themselves. Promos usually appear under the guise of being the defenders of "defenseless" homosexualized Afrikans.

24. Mwalimu K. Bomani Baruti, "Lies, Lies and More Lies," in Mwalimu K. Bomani Baruti, *Mentacide*, Atlanta, GA: Akoben House, 2005, pp.65-67. It never ceases to amaze me what yurugu's sycophants will do to appease their masters in order to bring warriors down to their miserable mentacidal level so that they, too, can appear revolutionary.

25. In addition to this just being a general problem, the mentality that specifically accompanies the homosexulized and/or

effeminized Afrikan who otherwise would be a warrior is well worth considering (Mwalimu K. Bomani Baruti, *Yurugu's Eunuchs*, Atlanta, GA: Akoben House, 2008). In the wisdom of Hannibal Tirus Afrik, "You can't build warriors with people of questionable gender orientation."

26. Atlanta, GA: Akoben House, 2009, pp.71-73.

27. Ibid, pp.71-72.

28. Afrikan proverb.

29. Medase Cashawn Myers for bringing this commonsensical thought to our attention.

30. In response to the question "Do you hate the white man?," Malcolm X gave us all the response that is needed to justify our stand on this matter.

> We don't even think about him. How can anybody ask us do we hate the man who kidnapped us four hundred years ago, brought us here and stripped us of our history, stripped us of our culture, stripped us of our language, stripped us of everything that you could use today to prove that you were ever part of the human family, brought you down to the level of an animal, sold you from plantation to plantation like a sack of wheat, sold you like a sack of potatoes, sold you like a horse and a cow, and then hung you up from one end of the country to the other, and then you ask me do I hate him? Why, your question is worthless! (*The End of White World Supremacy*, NY: Arcade Publishing, 1971, pp.79-80)

31. Robert A. Hill and Barbara Bair (eds.), *Marcus Garvey: Life and Lessons*, Berkeley, CA: University of California Press, 1987, p.211.

32. Amos N. Wilson, *Blueprint for Black Power*, NY: Afrikan World InfoSystems, 1998, p.849. He goes on, in answering the question of "Why Black Nationalism?," to more specifically detail that:

> Black or Afrikan nationalism is...a nationalism of liberation and self-determination, not of conquest and domination. It is premised on the precept that Blacks as a people should not be the subjects of another people nor should they subject other peoples; that Black peoples and nations should exercise their full rights to develop and utilize their material, human and spiritual resources primarily for their own benefit and well-being and for the benefit and well-being of others as they see fit to do. They view their personhood and humanity, their nationality and ethnicity as equal to that of any and all

other persons or peoples, that they are not the inferiors of others and are not destined by god or man to exist in forced servitude to others. And when, and if, and for however long they may be willfully subjected to the domination of others, they are commissioned by their inalienable right to freedom as human beings to resist such domination and overthrow it as soon as humanly possible. This is the bedrock credo of Black nationalism today as it manifests itself in the United States of America, across the Diaspora and in the world. (p.850. Also see Kwasi Konadu's distinction between nationalism and Black nationalism in *Truth Crushed to the Earth Will Rise Again*, Trenton, NJ: Africa World Press, 2005, p104)

33. Power, used against us, is so defined by Nana Kwaku Berko I-Ifagbemi Sangodare (fka Wade N. Nobles) in this way when he said that "power is the ability to define reality, and to make others accept your definitions as their own."

34. Or, as the Wolof say, "Your friend's enemy is your enemy." This is much more true than the popular saying "The enemy of my enemy is my friend."

35. Adiama, pronounced 'Ah-dee-'ah-mah, is a Twi word meaning reciprocity. Reciprocity is the act or process of receiving what one gives and giving what one receives, of mutual exchanges (even when what is exchanged may be different in form [the value is in the eye of the recipient], or giving and taking, and not immediately forthcoming [it is assumed that what is given or received comes at the time it is needed]). As a story is told among the Akan to illustrate this Ma'atian concept, there was Esie (eh-see-a), a termite mound about ten feet tall, and Kagya (kah-jah), a fairly short plant. Because it was so far away, Kagya wanted to get closer to the sun's warmth and, because Esie felt she was too close, she wanted to be shaded from it. It was agreed upon that Kagya should climb to the top of Esie. And, so it was. Kagya got his wish of being closer to the sun's rays through benefit of Esie's height and Esie of much needed shade under Kagya's leaves. This was an act of adiama or, in the english language, reciprocity.

36. Spiricide is the killing or continuous suppression of the existence, connection and/expression of Spirit in human consciousness.

37. Kobi K.K. Kambon makes a thought worthy point about this

relative to the "theological misorientaiton" of many Afrikans. (*Cultural Misorientation*, Tallahassee, FL: Nubian Nation Publications, 2003, pp.55-57)

38. Asa G. Hilliard, Larry Williams and Nia Damali (eds), *The Teachings of Ptahhotep*, Atlanta: Blackwood Press, 1987, pp.24-25.

39. Phillip Valentine extensively talks about the extent of this defilement in *The Wounded Womb*, Temple of the Healing Spirit / University of Kemetian Sciences, 1994).

40. Mwalimu K. Bomani Baruti, *The Sex Imperative*, Atlanta, GA: Akoben House, 2002.

41. Some worthy thoughts about the systematic use of the media against Afrikans and our surrender to its siren's call can be found in Anthony T. Browder, "Television and its Influence on African American Children" (in Anthony T. Browder, *From The Browder File*, Washington, DC: The Institute of Karmic Guidance, 1989, pp.47-50), Johnson, *Seven Steps Toward Black Reemergence* (pp.27-30) and Amos N. Wilson, *The Developmental Psychology of The Black Child* (NY: Africana Research Publications, 1978, pp.112-114).

42. We live in a world where there is little respect for Asase Yaa. The roots of this hatred championed by european people, brought about by their need to establish their control over nature by subjugating her life forms and abusing and exterminating them at will, lie at the foundations of the westerners' need to elevate themselves above everything outside of their despiritualized minds and, thereby, to "objectively" study and "know" themselves. They felt and still feel that a sterile objectivity, where they imagine themselves separated from everything and, then, theoretically separate what is there into the smallest, most distinct parts, allows them to control everything. This "control" gives them a sense of thereby owning and knowing all, including themselves. On this point, Jedi Shemsu Jehewty (fka Jacob H. Carruthers) showed critical evidence that Europeans believed that "humans are in a deadly contest against nature for survival and prosperity" and, therefore, "any negotiation with nature in the European mind is merely a strategy, a subterfuge to gain an advantage toward nature's unconditional surrender"....treating it "as a defiant slave to be broken" (*Intellectual Warfare*, Chicago:

Third World Press, 1999, p.44). However, I believe his most succinct and damaging indictment of their attitude toward Nature is in his statement that, in the european mind, "the changing of nature's nature is the ultimate object of science." (Ibid) Also see Jacob H. Carruthers, *MDW NTR: A Historiographical Reflection of African Deep Thought From The Time of The Pharaohs to The Present*, London: Karnak House, 1995, p.102. I also briefly pointed out the contradiction of their belated efforts to "save the planet" in the *Eureason* essay "A Godless Reason."

43. In fact, "in some traditions, the same word is used to refer to the land or soil and the human community or family." (Chukwunyere Kamalu, *Person, Divinity & Nature*, London: Karnak House, 1998, p.28)

> All over Africa the Earth is regarded as a spirit, and in Akan society, she ranks after God and is the second deity to be offered a drink at libations. (Kofi Asare Opoku, *West African Traditional Religion*, Jurong, Singapore: FEP International Private Limited, 1978, p.56. The full discussion is on pp.56-60.)

44. Ibid, pp.91-92.

45. Though the reader needs to study his entire tenth chapter, the following is taken from the end of Kimbwandende Kia Bunseki Fu-Kiah's main discussion on Asase Yaa. He says,

> The people of Africa see the earth as a huge parcel. They see it and compare it to the sachets or amulets that they sometimes carry on their body. Comparing the earth to a *futu* ("sachet") that one carries as a charm or otherwise is a very important clue in understanding the monumental value one puts into this *futu*, the earth. It is an analogy by which the African is saying that the earth is as important as any important and close thing in one's life. This planet, in the African's eyes, remains a sachet, something one carries and even hides in spite of being seen, in reality, as a huge container. This container represents, at once, power (*lèndo*), energy (*ngolo*), radiations (*minienie*), medicine (*n'kisi/bilôngo*), food (*madia*), salts (*Miûngwa*), water (*maza*), oil (*mafuta*), waves (*minika*), poison (*yimbwa*), and drinks (*ndwîndu*). To understand this concept about earth as *futu dia n'kisi wakânga Kalûnga* ("a parcel of medicine wrapped up by Kalûnga, the self-complete power"), for "his" creatures, is the greatest key to the understanding of life on earth. Without this key, is is almost impossible to understand all other principles that drive and control our

lives. (*Self-Healing Power and Therapy*, Baltimore, MD: Imprint Editions, 1991, p.116)

46. Sudanese proverb.

47. If we are to get at the heart of Europeans, we have to look at them in their purest historical and contemporary form. We have to observe them in their most traditional mental state. Just as we know to go to the most uncontaminated places in rural Afrika to find what exists of who we most are, we have to look to those deepest parts of Old Europe to see them as they are without the social facades and political compromises their social and individual personalities adopt in order to control others' image of them until they are able to control those others from within and, eventually, change others into them. Their normal state of "emotional depression" is well expressed when looking at the Finns of Old Europe today. They provide a glimpse into this classic sour european personality that is, bluntly stated, frozen in time.

> Finns have the lowest birth rate of any European nation and the highest suicide rate. The people "brood" and even describe themselves as brooders. They seldom speak to other Finns, less known strangers. They stare down as they walk. (July 4, 1999 episode of *60 Minutes*)

But we should not make the mistake of assuming that the Finnish personality is atavistic. It is no throwback to some bygone european personality. It simply sits at the normative center of the cold european personality that is extremely mean-spirited relative to humanity. (Anthony Ephirim-Donkor makes the contrasting point about Afrikans at this, the most basic level of human interaction – contact. Among the Akan, an average Afrikan ethnic group, "greetings are mandatory. Failure to greet or respond when greeted is a sign of disrespect, hostility, and anger towards the other." *African Spirituality: On Becoming Ancestors*, Trenton, NJ: Africa World Press, 1997, p.96.) The european personality in its natural, unmasked state is best preserved in Old Europe. In the heart, in the "soul," hidden behind the image they project to others, there has been no thaw. The european's uniqueness is evident, even as they speak of themselves – "Ice, no feeling, nothing" (from the movie *The Jackal*).

48. Erving Goffman used this term to describe how individuals consciously manipulate their environment, others and themselves,

as if playing a role on a stage, to convince others that they are something they are not for purposes of control and/or manipulation (*The Presentation of Self in Everyday Life*, Garden City: NY: Anchor Books, 1959). As we understand that individuals mirror their people, this concept does have a larger, macro application at the level of people and their society.

49. Namibian proverb. The Dama phrase it, "The snake may change its skin but stays a snake. It has always two tongues." And the Ewe teach that "the stump that stays in a river for a hundred years does not become a crocodile."

50. This blind flight is reminiscent of the calculated herding of the characters by the genetically modified sharks in the movie *Deep Blue Sea.* Like chased animals frantically running to escape the visible corrals, we have been chased away from our traditions, our haven, our freedom. In fearful flight, we have run in every direction left open to us, not knowing that each direction, each escape route, carried us even more deeply and securely into the clutches of the european madness. Each "escape" has been nothing but a delusion, enabling the hunter's noose to pull itself ever more tightly around all memory of who we are as spiritually-grounded Afrikans. Because we thought they were sure escapes, with each misguided flight we became more comfortable with our distance from self and our transmogrification into an inferiorized alien being.

51. Mwalimu K. Bomani Baruti, "Mentacide," in Mwalimu K. Bomani Baruti, *Mentacide*, Atlanta, GA: Akoben House, 2005, pp.5-10.

52. For if truth is the possession of every given people, then the literature and/or oral tradition of our people will give us all of the universal truth we need in any reality. (Mwalimu K. Bomani Baruti, *Asafo: A Warrior's Guide to Manhood*, Atlanta, GA: Akoben House, 2004, p.81)

53. Yoruba proverb.

54. Tshi proverb.

55. Tichaona Chinyelu, "Louder than Oppression," in Tichaona Chinyelu, *In The Whirlwind*, Brookline, MA: Whirlwind Publishing, p.24.

56. Carruthers, *MDW NTR* and A. Hampaté Bâ, "The Living Tradition," in UNESCO General History of Africa (Vol.I), J. Ki-

Zerbo (ed.), Berkeley, CA: University of California Press, 1981, pp.166-203.

57. Janheinz Jahn, *Muntu: African Culture and the Western World*, NY: Grove Weidenfeld, 1990 (first published in 1958), p.27.

58. Marimba Ani, *Let the Circle Be Unbroken*, NY: Nkonimfo Publications, 1997 (first published in 1980), p.40. Also see Jahn, *Muntu*, pp.121-155. Europeans are not oblivious to this power, as evident in the instructions of their greatest motivational speakers to their audiences to think and speak as if you already are and/or have what you want to become and/or possess.

59. Knock on wood is a precautionary ritual actually performed by saying "knock on wood" while knocking on some real wood, as one would knock on a door. It is designed as a plea to Spirit not to make something come true that the person arrogantly, i.e., while having no control over its happening, said would not happen or has not yet happened. For example, someone might say they would never allow themselves to be imprisoned. Then, realizing that the Universe might make this happen just to show them that this is not for them to say/decide, offers these three words and the knock itself as an apology and hope that they will not.

60. It is also done to continue something good that is happening, but to a lesser degree.

61. Yoruba proverb.

62. Mwalimu K. Bomani Baruti, *Centered: Building Afrikan Realities*, Atlanta, GA: Akoben House, 2009, pp.116-119.

63. Guevara, *Guerrilla Warfare*, p.109.

64. negroes are akin to Cerberus, the three-headed guard dog to Hell's doorway. And, even though some may want to argue the technicalities, these modern day, two (or three) faced sycophants have been honored by Europeans with guarding the gateway to another mentacidal hell prized by many Afrikans, the gateway to a privileged subintegration into european-insanity. They, like Cerberus, must ensure that those who enter are true devotees because it is their job to make sure that none who enter leave.

65. Obviously, speaking to the importance of this offense against self and community, we find this same warning issued in the Bible (Proverbs 13:3) which says, "He that keepeth his mouth keepeth his life; but he that openeth wide his lips shall have destruction"

and the Qur'an (Suru 31 Luqman, verse 19) which says, "and pursue the right course in your going about and lower your voice; surely the most hateful of voices is braying of the asses."

66. Not being able to leave a disagreement without having the last word is another habit that follows those unable to control their tongues. In their determination to have the final say in every dispute, they fail to see that the last word is not always spoken. In fact, silence can be one of the greatest indicators of power. Often, people secure in their power (especially over the presence and/or will of their opponent), do not give the last word. There is no need. Their decision or point is understood by most all involved, except, seemingly, their opponent. It is understood that the discussion ends with them, regardless of who remains talking.

67. This should be obvious to those among us who realize why they were brought here and are, therefore, determined to confront and correct what is wrong. "If 'the one who was born to fight' deserves the name, he must earn it on the battle field and not sitting under a tree." (Akan proverb)

68. Hilliard, Williams and Damali (eds.), *The Teachings of Ptahhotep*, pp.20-21.

69. "Those who can do. Those who can't teach."

70. Remember our proverbial wisdom on the value of silence: "A full tin makes no noise, an empty one does" (Tsongan); "An overly loquacious person is someone to flee from" (Yoruban); "Precious beads do not rattle" (Akan); "The one who talks, thinks, but the one who does not talk thinks more" (Bugandan); "The wisest animal is the giraffe. It never speaks" (Tanzanian); "The much-talker does not know much" (Zigulan), "A talkative bird will not build a nest" (Afrikan), "The talker talks and causes death in his family" (Hayan), "A good thing sells itself" (Akan); "It is the silent lion that is stalking you" (Zambian) and "The lion that kills is not the one that roars" (Xhosan).

71. "The Book of Ptahhotep" in Maulana Karenga (ed.), *The Husia*, Los Angeles: The University of Sankore Press, 1984, p.45.

72. Luther Standing Bear.

73. Ayi Kwei Armah, *Two Thousand Seasons*, Popenguine, Senegal: PER ANKH, 2000 (first published in 1973), p.314 (p.204 in the Heineman edition).

74. Akan (proverb). The Akan proverb "If you do not fear the

battle front, you do not fear the front where words are weapons" is equally true.

75. Afrikan proverb.

76. Akan proverb.

77. We have to acknowledge that honoring those most in denial of who they/we are is intensely treasonous. So, whether under the rubric of "family" or "unity," claiming people who hate you because you are Afrikan, people who do not want to be Afrikan, is treason. This is especially true if they are actively participating in the assault against you and mentacidally believe that to be connected to you is to lessen their identity and humanity. The only way we should be willing to claim credit and feel a sense of pride in the presence and/or accomplishments of one of our own is for them to feel/recognize themselves as a part of you. If they in no way consider themselves connected to you, to be in any way a part of your story, lineage, future, claiming them is tantamount to hating self.

78. In other words, "Anything that somebody does that is not good for Black people is wrong; and anything that somebody does that is good for Black people is right" (Hannibal Tirus Afrik).

79. And, even here, we must ask the question of the greater Afrikan good as Queen Nzingha did when her sister was tortured, beheaded and tossed overboard a portuguese ship in an effort to demoralize and derail her war efforts to defend her people against european incursion.

80. Kwame Nkrumah.

81. J.C. deGraft-Johnson, *African Glory: The Story of Vanished Negro Civilizations*, Baltimore, MD: Black Classic Press, 1986 (first published in 1954), p.22.

82. Akan proverb.

83. Kamau Kambon defined subtle suicide for us as the process of doing to ourselves those things that gradually poison our bodies (and minds) to death such as smoking, drinking, eating meat, sugar, salt, kwk. (*The Last Book*, Raleigh, NC: Blacknificient Books, 2005). In the same vein, we can define subtle homicide as the act of assisting in the killing of other Afrikans through the promotion of (subtle) suicidal behavior among each other.

84. New age pesticides offer an interesting analogy to consider as to the way in which treason undermines cohesiveness, stability

and life in the target group. Increasingly, chemical insecticides are designed to appear as food. They are placed near where insects live with the objective of them being carried back home by those venturing out in search of food. Especially in the case of ants and termites, the poisonous "food" is taken back to the colony where it is transferred to other members, eventually killing the entire colony. Using the same method, Yurugu releases genocidal propaganda into the naive and weak-minded among us. Those so infected, in turn, spread these poisons (poisons which they see as benevolent gifts) throughout our community. This technology is not dissimlar to the biological warfare used against the Indigenous people of this land who were given diseases through "gift" blankets and rags inside sealed tins. If anything, the mechanism containing the poison changes form but the content/intent remain constant.

85. It has been said that they follow the letter of the law while we consider the intent, a much more humane, thoughtful and just interpretation.

86. The same can be said of lying which requires prevaricators to, in some way, believe that they are smart enough to trick (outthink) the persons they are trying to fool into believing that what is being said is true, even though it is a lie.

87. Akan proverb.

88. Akan proverb.

89. See the "The Typology of People of Afrikan Ascent" in my *Centered*, pp.47-52.

90. Of these, the most obvious are those who are closest to Europeans in thought, word and deed. Prime examples are the most ardent homosexualized Afrikans and their Afrikan promoters or, rather, "promos."

91. Chicago: Third World Press, 1991 (fist published in 1965).

92. NY: Grove Press, Inc., 1967 (first published in 1952).

93. Boston, MA: Northeastern University Press, 1989 (first published in 1931).

94. Remember that we are dealing with a mind that most seeks pleasure and that most pleasures itself through the corruption of innocence – a mind that sees its own damaged self as the ideal toward which all else must be completely turned.

95. Jacob H. Carruthers, *Essays in Ancient Egyptian Studies*, Los

Angeles, CA: University of Sankore Press, 1984, p.106.
96. In an effort to make "good sportsmanship" and arrogance compatible, what it constitutes has become an aggressively contested arena itself.
97. Given this, if athletics are supposed to be a primary molder of a developing child's character, what does it say about the quality of these young athletes' integrity as human social beings?
98. The Akan say, "If a stranger understands a town's affairs, it is because of a citizen."
99. Baruti, "A Godless Reason," pp.63-109.
100. Ibid, pp.71-75.
101. Ibid, p.72.
102. And we cannot forget their use of the dead for food. From this discussion their sexual perversions relative to the dead make perfect sense and cannot be omitted from any analysis of their asili. That necrophilia (where individuals become sexually stimulated by and engage in sexual intercourse with corpses) is common enough among them historically and contemporaneously to be scientifically classified and studied is statement enough of their depravity (moral corruptness). We are right to wonder what goes on in their mortuaries. And, following this line of thinking, the movies "Solient Green" and "The Road" offer fine examples of the future they rapidly see approaching.
103. Adolf Hitler was only one of the most notorious and visible personalities in the european record who systematically desecrated the dead. He used the precious stones and metals taken off the bodies of his victims, even down to the fillings of their teeth, to help finance his war machine. We have to consider this when looking at our patterns of conspicuous consumption in conjunction with the murder rate of our youth. Our youth are buried with their adornments, attached to their bodies and inside their mouths. Together, collecting in the cemeteries, that which will not return to dust with them accrues daily as repositories of material wealth upon which Yurugu can draw in time of emergency.
104. Ourstorically, Afrikans, wanting to always keep family close, preserved their deceased within their homes (or compounds). They wanted to remain near all family members. Europeans, as evident throughout their "modern" landscape, bury their dead family members far away from where they live. Those

of us who live within the geopolitical boundaries of europeans do the same, out of emulative practice, ignorance and rejection of our traditions and because of of laws that mandate cemetery burials. We do not do this because it is a culturally natural tradition. According to Cheikh Anta Diop and others, Afrikans never cremated their deceased either. We, unlike Europeans, were not a nomadic people. Therefore, we had no need to reduce the size and weight of our ancestors to that of ashes so that they could be carried around with us. Some might argue that this is evidence of a feeling of closeness with their ancestors, and we would be foolish to argue that Europeans shared no affinity with their ancestors. All we have to do is look around at the monuments, city names, personal names, language, kwk., to know that this is not so. But, generally speaking, their practice reflected a fear, or rather dread, of the dead that has no equal anywhere on the Continent. They honor their dead not out of love but out of seeing them as a source of power, the key to their psychological esteem. In addition, for them, this self-serving honor of the dead has no universal application to the rest of us. Look at what they have done to the bodies, possessions and places of burial of those passed in the lands of people of color throughout the world. With them, grave robbing turned into the art of treasure hunting under the auspices of exploration and discovery. Because they are disconnected from spirit, they see this sacrilege as no more than an easy way to amass wealth and an effective tactic of psychological warfare against others. It obviously poses no problem for they lack a conscience.

105. The magnitude of this priority is so beautifully and matter-of-factly framed by Frances Cress Welsing, speaking as only an Afrikan woman can.

> Black children are our most valuable possession and our greatest potential resource. Any meaningful discussion of the survival or the future of Black people must be predicated upon Black people's plan for the maximal development of all Black children. Children are the only future of any people. If the children's lives are squandered, and if the children of a people are not fully developed at whatever cost and sacrifice, the people will have consigned themselves to certain death. They will be destroyed from without or from within — by the attack of their own children against them. And they may be

> destroyed by both. (*The Isis Papers*, Chicago: Third World Press, 1991, p.239)

106. "Every parent teaches as they act" (Kemetic proverb).

107. We must be ourstorically alert enough to distinguish between the mission of a conscious Afrikan's role in the educational setting and that of persons who do not understand the value of our children or the mission of the western educational institution. There is a consequential difference between educators, teachers and programmers.

> Some *teachers* (those who simply give information, although this information is inherently, eurocentrically politicized and who may even present the image of being Afrikan centered) are not *educators* (those who give knowledge and wisdom knowingly within an Afrikan centered context). Others who stand in front of our classrooms do not understand the vocation of teaching at all. They are merely *programmers*, nonthinking individuals who receive income in exchange for spoon feeding us what they have memorized or reviewed overnight without analysis or consideration (or, in most cases, even knowing) of the needs of our students or nation. (Mwalimu K. Bomani Baruti, *Notes Toward Higher Ideals in Afrikan Intellectual Liberation*, Atlanta, GA: Akoben House, 2006, pp.71-72)

108. Ptahhotep.

109. However, they know contradictions when them see them. Intuitively, they know that a fundamental instruction for those who are rearing them should be that you "do not separate your mind from your tongue" (Kemetic proverb).

110. Yoruba proverb.

111. Interesting examples of this parasitic behavior in the insect and nonhuman animal world that reflect the doings of european culture and individuals are found in Carl Zimmer's *Parasite Rex* (NY: Touchstone, 2000).

112. Warriors have to know just what is meant by the term "civilization" in order to understand exactly what we are dealing with in this crude, despiritualized reality. We must remember that civilization is derived from the word "civil," which references the treatment of people toward each other. Any intelligent, feeling human who gives it some serious thought would naturally come to the conclusion that civilization should not be measured by the amount or level of mechanical technology a society produces

or accumulates, the height of its buildings and monuments or the expanse of its empire or breadth of its domination. In agreeement, many take a more human approach. They contend that the most important factor determining whether a society is a civilization or not is the quality of the life of its women. And, though this is a more than reasonable measuring rod, they have not gone far enough. They stopped short of the highest definition, one based on the conditions of the children. We say children because they are the most defenseless of all and are dependent on adults, both women and men, for their well-being. Therefore, as Afrikans conscious of the importance of definitions for perceptions, and as student-practitioners of our Ancestors' family/child-centeredness, we must employ the knowledge of the children's treatment foremost in our assessment of the degree to which a society is civilized. This will lead us to conclude that the state of their lives most reveals the human quality of the character of the society developed by their parents or those who rule their parents' minds. When this more spiritually-grounded definition is used, if significant numbers of a society's children are starving, homeless, mis- and diseducated, sexually violated, drugged or otherwise intoxicated, spoiled, obese, suicidal, incarcerated (and/or are on death row), then that society is not a true civilization. So, obviously, people lost in love with the West are using the wrong indicators for measuring civilization. Directly contributing to this convenient oversight, and central to our discussion here, is the point that civilization, defined in progressive, civil terms, takes quite a long time to develop/evolve. It does not happen overnight. There are no shortcuts, no easy roads leading to civilization. It is a phenomenal occurence in extraordinary, almost geologic, time. In order for it to be all it should be, and is capable of being, it must pass the test of time. Just as individuals have to go through a correctly mastered epigenetic queue of stages in order to correctly develop fully, societies do also. However defined, "A complete article must have gone through various stages in its creation" (Haya proverb). For example, according to one classic eurocentric model of cognitive development, there are four stages that individuals normally pass through in their cognitive development. The first is sensorimotor, which is said to occur between birth and two years of age. Here, the person becomes acquainted with how one's body functions and gains control over these functions. An important lesson learned in the latter part of this stage is that just because something is removed from sight does not mean that it ceases to exist. Afterwards follows the preoperational stage between the ages of two and seven where the child begins to use language/symbols but remains basically egocentric in orientation toward others. The concrete operations stage occurs between seven and eleven years of age. This is where concepts gain importance and we begin to systematically connect this understanding with what exists in the environment in an meaningful (intellectually interactive) way. Many of us never go beyond this stage in our intellectual development. The final stage is the formal operations one. People who reach this point can think conceptually without having to actually see any manifestation of that thought. This is the cognitive domain of hypothesis, theory and abstraction. Even though all individuals are supposed to go through the stages in this order, the speed of their progression differs. And, in fact, some may even have to go back and repeat some incompletely learned process before moving forward. Regardless, this is an epigenetic process where each stage builds on the stage which preceded it and lays the foundation for whatever stage follows it. None can be skipped if an individual is to become fully developed cognitively (Jean Piaget and Barbel Inhelder, *The Psychology of the Child*, NY: Harcourt, 1969). So, too, do different "human" groups go through stages of cognitive development (i.e., the development of their personality/mind in terms of self- and other-perception). If everything is similar in evolution and process, then, though there may be relatively more or fewer stages (and stage durations) marking the development of individuals, societies/nations and the cosmos, there is commonality/similarity in that such stages do indeed exist. They do follow a logical, natural, predetermined order. They are progressive. They have a universal reason for being. And they are all necessary for the full maturation of the being or entity. Therefore, distinct genocultural groups of people uniquely go through a series of epigenetic stages through which their mind is created. Moreover, in terms of the civilization concept, each stage has a primary, humanizing component, a dominant factor which moves a people together to better understand and embrace their spiritual and human (moral and ethical) essence. There are lessons within this component of which they must fully experience and learn from together in order to master their humanity and assimilate it as an essential part of their being. Without this experience and a mastery of its lessons, ways of wisdom which after a certain point can never be fully acquired, their existence lacks a true, dynamic, functional humanity. That traditionally Afrikans have prioritized the development of a person's character, their humanity, versus Yurugu's greatest formative focus on the individual's mechanical thinking, their individual survival self, is a good starting point for those who wish to study this core developmental difference. It is also instructive to note that those who are successful in overtaking others in their material or informational development, who do this by surreptitiously using the long established mechanical base of others while rejecting the significance of their accumlated humanity, are only able to take what they are capable of understanding and which fits their underdeveloped, immature interpretation of reality. (George G.M. James deftly spoke of this discrepancy in his explanation of Socrates' persecution at the hands of his own when he made the grave mistake of trying to bring [as intact as he could] an Afrikan cosmology [way of knowing and purpose in thinking] that gave a human meaning to life into their limited consciousness. (*Stolen Legacy*, NY: Philosophical Library, 1954).) However, over time, their awareness of their human inferiority (especially spiritual, psychological and emotional, in terms of this particular discussion) has grown. But they sleep with deceit. That is the only way they know. So, it is only natural that, in the face of others' humanity, they pretend. Only possessing the capacity to ape the humanity in others is a congenital psychopathic fault. Ignorantly and arrogantly displaying this mimicry as evidence of some existent humanity in them is an insult to our intelligence. It is a facade which well reflects the kind of mind the Tswana speak of in the proverb "He makes a ladder of other people's backs." Human, like mechanical, technology (i.e., ways of doing things, i.e., technique) does not fully develop without extensive trial and error over thousands of generations. Considerate, balanced, lasting human technology, because of the intricacies of psychology, emotion and spirit involved in its realization, comes only through the greatest of meaningful, survivable suffering. The Yoruba proverb questioning, "You have wisdom, but you haven't suffered? Who is your teacher?" speaks to this universal. Yurugu has *never* experienced this humanizing experience. It's "civilization" is nothing more than a collection of simple advancements on the material legacy stolen from others. But it is completely without human substance and depth. It is a feral culture, bereft of emotional content. And, as is made mythologically clear, there is no escape or redemption/correction for what they have become and have always been. Today, after every attempt to humanize themselves in others' eyes has failed, their incompleteness is becoming more and more obvious to the world. Nonetheless, still blindly rushing down the path of their proud tradition of deceitful arrogance, they diligently work to euroversalize their deficient (despiritualized, dehumanized) personality as normal and *the* human norm. At the same time, they continue to try to make up for their deficient humanity by pretending to embrace a forever lost human "side." But, as in Piaget's model, they have reached far beyond the point of no return on the human component of civilization's stages and this flaw in their being is beyond correction (something well pointed out in Marimba Ani's rendering of the Dogon myth of Yurugu where it is stated that "Yurugu, *forever* incomplete, was doomed to perpetually search for the completeness that could *never* be his" (*Yurugu*, "Author's Note, italics mine)). And, of course, we should not be confused by either the initiative to make themselves human or the redefining of humanity along european lines. Their inhumanity is not something they truly want to correct anyway. Any humanizing movement they simulate can be little more than a social facade designed in the tradition of their rhetorical ethics to stave off revealing questions about their humanity until all others are completely brought in line with their callous sterility.

113. Fu-Kiau, *Self-Healing Power and Therapy*, p.54.

114. *Merriam-Webster's Collegiate Dictionary* (10E), Springfield, MA: 1999, p.1365.

115. Akan proverb.

116. Hilliard, Williams and Damali (eds.), *The Teachings of*

Ptahhotep, p.25. The Yoruba proverb "The person who eats large helpings does not care that there is a famine" also speaks to the deep psychological flaws characteristic of the greedy person.

117. Ibid.

119. Louis Gama, Quilombo leader.

120. The Akan of West Afrika call this intuition "tiboa" (pronounced tee-bwah). It speaks to "the part of the person that relates to the spirit or soul (sunsum/Kra) of a person to guide them through life." It is also used in reference to "self-knowledge" and "conscience" (Obadele Bakari Kambon, personal correspondence, October 25, 2005).

121. "Theophobic" is defined as the fear of the Creator. Of this, there is great evidence in their mythology.

122. Though profoundly steeped in the cultural politics and religious nationalism of Europeans, John S. Mbiti is one who does a good job of describing the all pervasiveness of Afrikan people's spiritual connection. He observed that:

> Because traditional religions permeate all the departments of life, there is no formal distinction between the sacred and the secular, between the religious and non-religious, between the spiritual and the material areas of life. Wherever the African is, there is his religion: he carries it to the fields where he is sowing seeds or harvesting a new crop; he takes it with him to the beer party or to attend a funeral ceremony; and if he is educated, he takes religion with him to the examination room at school or in the university; if he is a politician he takes it to the house of parliament. Although many African languages do not have a word for religion as such, it nevertheless accompanies the individual from long before his birth to long after his physical death....Traditional religions are not primarily for the individual, but for his community of which he is part. Chapters of African religions are written everywhere in the life of the community, and in traditional society there are no irreligious people. To be human is to belong to the whole community, and to do so involves participating in the beliefs, ceremonies, rituals and festivals of that community. A person cannot detach himself from the religion of his group, for to do so is to be severed from his roots, his foundation, his context of security, his kinships and the entire group of those who make him aware of his own existence. To be without one of these corporate elements of life is to be out of the whole picture. Therefore, to be without religion amounts to a self-excommunication from the

entire life of society, and African peoples do not know how to exist without religion. (*African Religions and Philosophy* (2E), Oxford, UK: Heineman, 1990 (first published in 1969), p.2)

123. See the essay "A Godless Reason" in Baruti, *Eureason.*

124. "The Book of Khun-Anup," in Karenga (ed.), *The Husia*, p.31.

125. Nana John Henrik Clarke spoke of this identification and training in nationbuilding when he said:

> *Our children should be picked out and trained for leadership from birth. You can watch how that child handles a fork; watch that child's ability to share with the group; watch that child's ability to protect the group and to accept the training that will make that child improve. We should spot leaders early and begin to train them.* We should make a priesthood of this effort. (*Notes for an African World Revolution: Africans at the Crossroads*, Trenton, NJ: Africa World Press, 1991, p.18)

And this is exactly what Wade W. Nobles (Nana Kwaku Berko I-Ifagbemi Sangodare) meant when he spoke about the creation of character through the process of centered education within the intergenerational transmission of character.

> It is important that we focus on an African centered educational process that creates character. One that creates the character that allows us from the beginning of time to face the world and reality, a process to make sure that our images and our interests will be present long after we are gone. That's why we need to begin to look at that. Character is not just some word that needs to be overused and exploited. We as Black people know that whenever a word is heard, someone will pick it up as theirs and use it as a new weapon. Character is something very precise; yet, we struggle with the preliminary definition of the word. I argue that character is the preliminary mark of a people, which signifies their distinctive qualities. All that is still very general because we don't know what distinction means and we don't know what quality means. One's character is the complexity of mental and spiritual traits which mark a people and is a detectable expression as evidence of their ability to transmit their own hereditary information. If we're not passing to the next generation of African children the essence of what it is to be African, we have no character. The fundamental evidence of our having character is that we pass, in very precise ways, what it means to be normal. (*Seeking the Sakhu*, Chicago, IL: Third World Press, 2006, p.289)

126. Baruti, *Yurugu's Eunuchs*, pp.29-31.
127. Ibid, pp.21-23.
128. "Ptahhotep," (in Karenga, *The Husia*), p.47.
129. "When what you have is not good, you don't go and take what belongs to someone else" (Akan proverb).
130. *Stolen Legacy*, Newport News, VA: United Brothers Communications Systems, 1989 (first published in 1954), p.106. Jedi Shemsu Jehewty (fka Jacob H. Carruthers) also goes to great lengths to prove that even though Kemetic (deep Afrikan) thought/philosophy played a very substantial role in the birth and development of greek "philosophy," that influence and impetus was not all that there was to their classical way of thinking (*MDW NTR: A Historiographical Reflection of African Deep Thought From The Time of The Pharaohs to The Present*, London: Karnak House, 1995). Innocent C. Onyewuenyi's work, *The African Origin of Greek Philosophy: An Exercise in Afrocentrism* (Nsukka, Nigeria: University of Nigeria Press, 1993) has also been instrumental in establishing the impossibility of an original greek (european) philosophy because their time in existence and level of academic maturity could not have allowed for it. This truth is also discussed throughout the works of Cheikh Anta Diop and Yosef A.A. ben-Jochannan among so many other Afrikan centered scholars. The european (greek) asili played a major selecting role in deconstructing and rebuilding Afrikan knowledge along european lines. Therefore, we must be careful when we unqualifiedly say that greek philosophy is Afrikan philosophy. The Greeks were not Afrikan in civility or intent.
131. According to James,

> The Egyptian Mystery System, like the modern University, was the centre of organized culture, and candidates entered it as the leading source of ancient culture...the Egyptian Mysteries had three grades of students (1) The Mortals, i.e., probationary students who were being instructed, but who had not yet experienced the inner vision, (2) The Intelligences, i.e., those who had attained the inner vision, and had received mind or *nous* and (3) The Creators or Sons of Light (i.e., true spiritual consciousness)....[otherwise described] as the equivalents of Initiation, Illumination and Perfection." (pp.27-28)

132. As distinct from "hardwired," which indicates innate,

instinctual or fused beyond separate identification (as in a chemical change), "softwired" describes thoughts which have been socialized or implanted from outside. They are separable, i.e., identifiable as being separate from, or added onto, the original. Hardwired thoughts are inextricable/permanent, while softwired ones can be removed.

133. According to Freud, the id is those impulses which are most subconscious. They are those unrecognized (genetic and) social forces which compel the individual to think, speak and act along the lines of certain imperatives and desires operating below the level of consciousness. For Freud, in speaking of Europeans but in the classic european way of euroversalizing this theory to everyone else, the two dominant imperatives were sex and aggression. In assessing the id in Afrikans, thinking warriors would determine its dominant imperatives differently. They would be more in line with what would logically be concluded from Amos N. Wilson's statement about what guides the mentality of Afrikans in yurugu's world.

> Simply because we choose to forget a traumatic event, simply because we choose not to learn of a traumatic history and a history that may make us feel ashamed, does not mean that that history is not controlling our behavior. Simply because we don't know our history, and may have not heard of it, does not mean that the history does not control our behavior. One of the most profound things that we've learned in psychology is that the most powerful forces that shape human behavior are those factors that are consciously *not* remembered by human beings, that are unknown by the person, are those experiences the individual can swear he's never had. That is one of the paradoxes of human behavior, that the very things that shape us and make us behave the way we do, see the world the way we see it and relate to people the way we relate to them, are those things that occurred in our lives at points we cannot remember or recall. (*The Falsification of Afrikan Consciousness*, p.34)

Nonetheless, returning to Freud's eurocentric conclusions, the id is considered to be only one of the three main parts of the individual's psyche. Directly related to the id are the ego and super ego. The super ego is that part of the mind comprised of the rules and morality given the individual by the immediate responsible adults and society. It is the individual's socialized, normative personality. The third division of one's psychology, the ego, serves to mediate between the id and super ego.

134. See the chapter on "Complementarity: The Quality of IWA in Love."

135. Epigenetic is a term we have seen previously to describe progressive relationships, be they of learning, building/construction, coming into consciousness, kwk, where each stage or level builds on the preceding one and lays the foundation for the one following it. In almost every epigenetic formation, though, there is no absolute, or even sometimes clear, demarcation between the stages or levels.

136. Of course, it would be more appropriate to reconceptualize "slave masters" as *evil enslavers*. That it would be a more accurate description of the kind of beings they were/are, making it a more politically correct descriptive for warriors.

137. In his book *KMT*, Ayi Kwei Armah spoke of two types of scholars: the "keepers" and the "sharers." Keepers hoard knowledge in order to use it to control the people or to give it to tyrants so that they can use it to dominate them. Sharers understand that knowledge is not a commodity that is sought in order to elevate one's self above others. Its purpose is not to divide but to unite people in a common elevation of truth through analytically equipping individuals with the means to acquire a working knowledge of self. Warriors need to see themselves as sharers and attempt to act accordingly. It is not a choice per se. It is a natural and necessary outgrowth of our responsibility in our communal ReAfrikanized nationbuilding effort. Nothing in creation gives us the right to hoard the information, knowledge and wisdom that our people need to rebuild and empower ourselves. Having the privilege of extensively studying that which is Afrikan and that which is not, gives us no right to be self-centered, opportunistic "keepers." We have no afreason to apologize for being sharers. It is an honor. In order to make a people whole, we must always be humble, giving "sharers" who speak in whatever language our people understand. (Mwalimu K. Bomani Baruti, *Nyansasem: A Calendar of Revolutionary Daily Thoughts*, Atlanta, GA: Akoben House, 2008, p.Obubuo 3 | November 3)

138. This same profound distinction applies to priests, as we have already noted, relative to today's pastors, ministers and preachers whose "wisdom" is confined to the religious realm and

serves the politicized interests of people other than their own. Such is the contradiction of europeanized Afrikans of the cloth. They are unable to reconcile oppression with war, except that war be in service of their oppressors who oppress Afrikans.

139. Baruti, *Asafo*, pp.88-96.

140. Kemetic proverb.

141. Swahili proverb.

142. Swahili proverb.

143. Both are Afrikan proverbs. Specifically, the Akan say that "If you and a fool have an argument, he succeeds." Malachi Z. York made the same point when saying, "To answer ignorance is ignorance."

144. Amadou Hampaté Bâ demonstrates the significance of this principle through the guiding words of his character Wangrin, a wisdom the character had gained from earlier lessons.

> When one's enemies plot to harm one, one must continue to smile in the face of adversity. In this way one's enemies will miss the opportunity for rejoicing they had so much looked forward to. They will begin to doubt their success, and that will cause them to suffer the pain they had intended to inflict on others. The ability to conduct oneself in such a way as to disappoint one's enemy's expectations enables one to take revenge with dignity and without any outward show of emotion. (*The Fortunes of Wangrin*, Bloomington, Indiana: Indiana University Press, 1999 (first published in 1973), p.66. The second and third chapters are also instructive in this way.)

145. Hausan proverb.

146. Mwalimu K. Bomani Baruti, "Subjective Objectivity" in Baruti, *Eureason*, pp.17-51.

147. Though humility is professed as a virtue in european culture our focus is on those qualities which are actually normatively practiced in society. In european society, humility is not (and cannot be) normatively practiced.

148. Kemetic proverb.

149. NY: Garland Publishing, Inc., 2000, pp.87-158.

150. Of course, sleepwalker is a very fitting descriptive of such individuals. And, as Ralph Ellison so duly noted, "There are few things in the world as dangerous as sleepwalkers."

151. Medase Nana Kofi Sechi for helping us overstand that we are rising out of those who came before us and that, therefore, all

who came into this physical reality through them should be referred to as "ascendants" and not "descendants." Of course, as in contrasting the enslaved with slaves (i.e., the ever rebellious whose identity was clear to them with the vanquished who saw themselves as no more than others' property, respectively), the term descendants does have a use in referring to those who have chosen to fall from the grace of our Ancestors.

152. The following is merely an introduction to Amos N. Wilson's searing critique of the other-directedness of so many Afrikans.

> The other-directedness of the modal Afrikan political-economic personality is compatible with White American and European domination of Afrikans because it permits Afrikan consciousness and behavior to be manipulated by "others than themselves," primarily by White Americans and Europeans. The center of psychological gravity, the source of motivation of the other-directed Afrikan, lies outside himself and in the hands of others than himself. Who this type of Afrikan thinks he is, his self-perception, is the product of the history of his interactions with others than himself, i.e., with aliens. For he has no knowledge of himself prior to his coming into contact with his exploiters and dominators. For him, prior to his captivity and enslavement or his colonization by aliens, especially Europeans and White Americans, he is practically non-existent, unconscious, invisible, or at best, possessed of a savage consciousness and existence he would rather not recall. Consequently, his identity was and is one given him by others; one he infers from how others – aliens – interact with him; one he infers and abstracts from accounts and histories of himself written by his alien exploiters and dominators. Moreover, the world he inhabits is constructed by others, his captors, his past and his future delimited by those who despise him. He is the plaything of the other. Bereft of a knowledge of self, of his own history and culture, subjected to a distorted and twisted sense of his origins and reality, all these conditions perpetuated deliberately by his White handlers, he identifies with the alienated images, history and culture fashioned and imposed on him by alien Whites who are free to re-fashion them, and do when the occasion calls for it. His consciousness, constructed as it is by the other, essentially the reactionary product of his domination by the other, brought into existence by the other, he cannot conceive of a future existence independent of the other, a future wherein the other is no longer in some way

> supreme. For him, there is no world for him without White people in it, without White people defining it, or world where he is the dominant force and is self-creating and responsible for bringing his consciousness into being and visibility through his interactions with himself and his kind. (*Blueprint for Black Power*, pp.123-124)

This stands in stark contrast to the inner-directed Afrikan whose vision and work is empowered and empowering of Afrikan people.

> The reclamation of their Afrikan identity and the construction of an Afrocentric consciousness by Afrikan peoples is crucial to the empowerment of the Afrikan individual and the Pan-Afrikan community. Such a reclamation of identity and transformation of consciousness would permit Afrikans to shed their "other-directed" personality and behavioral dispositions, to greatly diminish their reactionary orientation to the world, particularly their reactionary relationship to European Americans and other ethnic groups. This would greatly reduce the power of these groups to adversely shape the attitudes, interests, motives and behavior, and consciousness of Afrikan peoples and thereby markedly reduce their ability to exploit, manipulate and dominate them as well. The Afrikan-centered personality is primarily pro-active in orientation. It is a self-defined, self-directed personality that is both "inner-directed" and "tradition-directed" as well as responsive to immediate and future reality. *It is an autonomous construction, not one created and motivated by aliens.* Its potentials and resources are developed and utilized primarily for its own perpetuation and enhancement, and for the benefit of humankind. (Ibid, p.135)

153. And this fact applies to any other nonAfrikan religion, regardless of its origins. Our warrior scholars have made the political/controlling nature of all religions abundantly clear.

154. They know that the Divinity of any powerful people reflects their appearance (when anthropomorphized), character, interests, imperatives and vision. Bearing this in mind, they necessarily reject the notion that a people's gods are not political. So, the demand by those who seek to psychologically destroy them that they explain their beliefs and images to them so that they can approve or dismiss them is nonsensical to minds grounded in a knowledge of self. As Nana Yao Opare Dinizulu unequivocally declared, "We do not have to justify our Gods to anyone." (*The Akan Priest in America*, Long Island City, NY: Aims of Modzawe, 1974, p.2)

155. Popenguine, Senegal: PER ANKH, 2000 (first published in 1978), pp.108-113 (pp.92-96 in the Heineman edition).

156. Here, our mentacide (in assisted genocide) is apparent. We will kill each other in service to europeans and self hatred but not touch europeans.

> You are a hypocrite, because your "turn the other cheek" ideology, really only applies to white folks! You only turn your cheek to white folks, but you don't turn your cheek to Blackfolks. (Akil, *From Niggas to Gods, Part One*, Saint Louis, MO: Nia Communications/Press, 1993, p.15)
>
> Blacks kill Blacks because they have never been trained to kill Whites, therefore, it is outside their experience. Historically, the European system has encouraged the killing of Blacks and since Blacks have been led to believe that they are part of the psychopath's system, they simply follow the practice. (Bobby E. Wright, *The Psychopathic Racial Personality and other essays*, Chicago: Third World Press, 1984, p.3)

157. Larry D. Crawford (Mwalimu A. Bomani Baruti) "The Cultural Continuum," in Crawford (Baruti) *negroes and other essays*, pp.63-65.

158. I remember a conversation with students nearly two decades ago over Ice T's song "Cop Killer." They questioned why Europeans would allow such an inflammatory (to the justifiably paranoid European) song to go public. My response was simple. They do this because, in a severely oppressed but vanquished group, it lines their pockets while feeding an anger which is wholly reactive, if not regressively inactive, and, therefore, poses no meaningful threat. Again, it is an anger that lines their pockets. Interestingly, the disactivity and contradictory nature of this "anger" is most evident in the rapper himself who, for all his thug imagery, became most known for his role as a police officer in the *Law and Order* television series. Evidence of his confusion over identity is also clearly brought out in his book *The Ice Opinion* (NY: St. Martin's Press, 1994) and the television show *Ice Loves Coco*.

159. Clarke, *Who Betrayed the African World Revolution?*, p.76.

160. The Healers, p.109 (pp.92-93 in the Heineman edition).

161. Another dialogue to this effect can be found in N. Xavier Arnold's *The Genocide Files* (Marlow Heights, MD: Tana Lake Publishing, 1997, pp.71-72).

162. Yoruba proverb.

163. Martin R. Delany, *The Condition, Elevation, Emigration, and Destiny of the Colored People of the United States*, Salem, NH: Ayer Company, 1988 (first pulbished in 1852), pp.37-38.

164. Also known as Harriet Tubman.

165. "The Book of Khun-Anup" is an example of this instruction to do for self relative to wrongdoers and wrong doing. It says:

> Punish those who deserve punishment and none will equal your righteousness....The balancing of the land lies in Maat – truth, justice and righteousness. Do not speak falsely for you are great; do not act lightly for you have weight; be not untrue for you are the balance and do not swerve for you are the standard. You are on the level with the balance. If it tilts, then, you will lean too. Do not drift, rather steer. Do not rob, rather act against the robber....If you turn your face from violence, who will punish wrongdoing? (in Karenga (ed.), *The Husia*, p.32)

166. Armah, *The Healers*, p.307 (p.269 in the Heineman edition).

167. Armah, *KMT*, p.345.

168. Science fiction is the window to their soul (or, at least, the vacuum wherein that spiritual presence should be found but, instead, we find a machine's blueprint). Science fiction is simply their imaginary vision of where they ideally see themselves as going and being. We have to remember that this media show is their future, their fantasy of conquering what they currently consider the most significant final frontier. These actors are the fulfillers of their imagination. However, we cannot miss the fact that the vast majority of western science fiction fantasies of extraterrestrial encounters feature unprovoked invasions by violently aggressive, relentless, ruthless alien beings bent on destroying the human race. Such stories also reflect their terrifying fear that "others" will come and do to them what they have done, and continue to do, to others. For, in the heart of their heartlessness, they know that nothing they have or know will save them from an overdue reckoning.

169. Kwame Gyekye, *An Essay on African Philosophical Thought: The Akan Conceptual Scheme*, Philadelphia: Temple University Press, 1995, throughout but especially succinctly summarized on p.153.

170. We all classify people, no matter how liberal we claim to be. It is important and necessary for human sanity because it removes the need, and impossible task, of assessing each and every individual we encounter or view in a world of so many. Categories help define individuals into manageable streams of thought and behavior where range may exist but limitations allow for generalizing definitions. We will do this as long as there are different people, families, communities, villages, tribes, clans, sects, nations, worldviews, kwk., no matter how loud we proclaim, behind the veil of white supremacy, to all be members of one human race. (Larry D. Crawford (Mwalimu A. Bomani Baruti), "negroes" in Larry D. Crawford (Mwalimu A. Bomani Baruti), *negroes and other essays*, Atlanta, GA: Akoben House, 2000, pp.145-46)

171. Jacob H. Carruthers well framed this discussion in his essay "Science and Oppression." He argued that,

> First, we must understand more precisely why scientific methodology has such a limited usefulness for oppressed people. The answer, in short, is that it is the Master's science, not only in the sense that he uses it to control his subjects but also in the sense that it was established through and for oppression. That is, the original assumptions *are* oppression, suppression, and repression. Thus, the science or methodology is not neutral or objective; it is the science of control through intervention and/or the unnatural alteration (if possible) of all objects. (In Daudi Ajani ya Azibo (ed.), *African Psychology in Historical Perspective and Related Commentary*, Trenton, NJ: Africa World Press, 1996, p.188)

In yurugu's mind, Afrikans are little more than objects to be manipulated.

173. Baruti, *Centered*, pp.116-119.

174. Kwadwo A. Okrah, *Nyansapo (The Wisdom Knot): Toward an African Philosophy of Education*, NY: Routledge, 2003, pp.38-39.

175. This choice is not without a political basis because, in generalizing what it means to be human as a birthright, it not only allows them to unqualifiedly include those who based on their actions would any where fall outside the margins of being human (e.g., serial killers, cannibals, pedophiles, kwk). It enables them as a group, just based on their presence, to be thusly misdefined.

176. Trenton, NJ: Africa World Press, 1997, pp.54-56.

177. Mwalimu K. Bomani Baruti, "Self-Serving Spirituality" in

Mwalimu K. Bomani Baruti, *Mentacide and other essays*, Atlanta, GA: Akoben House, 2005.

178. I have already spoken about this confusion of consciousness because it is centered in whiteness and the validation of Europeans in *Notes Toward Higher Ideals in Afrikan Intellectual Liberation*, especially the "Validation" essay. In *Nationbuilding*, Kwame Agyei Akoto describes this phenomenon well in relation to these individuals whose core definitions of Afrikan liberation are chained to european definitions of reality. In relation to the "defensive accommodation[ist]" posture that characterizes their politics, Akoto notes the following:

> The limitation of this response is that this new found awareness is fashioned into badges, Kente strips and aggressive demeanors that intensify the expressed determination to achieve the respect as well as the positions and status otherwise denied us because of a presumed ahistoricity and cultural inferiority. However, those positions, the status and the symbols and certificates thereof, the institutional and cultural context in which they occur and from which they are derived are a-priori and unqualifiedly Eurocentric. After exhaustive research and verification of the heroic nature of Afrikanity, we are often satisfied to parade our new found humanity and heroism before the world hoping at least for vicarious if belated validation and certification from the ruling white elite. We hope for a truce on historical distortion, and cultural inferiorization through appeals to reason and morality. No fundamental questions of morality, ethics, or national character are raised or considered, that would challenge that overbearing and hegemonic Eurocentric cultural construct which has distorted and crippled the intellectual potential of our people. But it is nonetheless from this very Eurocentric construct that we seek final validation and acceptance. (pp.191-192)

179. But if the human being is a spiritual being and has an ideal domicile in the ancestral world, then why will it decide to live in a less than ideal milieu? We must understand that ethical existence and generativity is practiced in the mundane and not at Samanadze [ancestral world]. In fact the only way to become a spiritual personality is to be a human being first since one cannot achieve ancestorhood until the person has been born, lived, died, and resurrected as a spiritual personality. The world then is the testing ground for ethical existence and generativity, the sole criterion for judgement in the ancestral world. What will a spirit be without first

> manifesting itself among the living? It will have no name and could not be invoked by the living for any reason or purpose because it does not exist. (Ephirim-Donkor, *African Spirituality*, p.41)

180. Chinua Achebe, *Things Fall Apart*, NY: Anchor Books, 1994 (first published in 1958), p.122.

181. Kimbwandende Kia Dunseki Fu-Kiau explains in detail their significance for Afrikans.

> In debates, in ceremonies, in judgments, in joy as well as in misery, proverbs are frequently used to reprimand, to criticize, to compare, to segregate, to encourage, to punish, and to heal. They are used to teach, to explain and to thoroughly code and decode....For African people, proverbs constitute a special language. Sometimes, for many, proverbs are considered both a secret and a sacred language...[They] are used to prevent the leak of very fundamental principles of the society, i.e., to prevent the outsider from auditing the debate to have access to any basic systematic concepts of the structural organization of the society, especially it's secrecies....Proverbs, as a means of intellectual communication of great ideas within the community, are said and learned within the community, at a public house..., in the market place, during the initiation period, during the work time, anywhere in the bush, on the street, at home as well as while running during a hunting party. Proverbs, in African context, are laws, reflections, theories, customs, social norms and values, principles, and unwritten constitutions. They are used to justify what should be said or what has been said. (*Tying the Spiritual Knot: African Cosmology of the Bântu-Kôngo: Principles of Life & Living*, NY: Athella Henrietta Press, 1980, pp.93-94)

182. As has been said, "To know proverbs is to know one's Ancestors" (Igbo proverb).

183. Contrarily, according to Frantz Fanon, "The business of obscuring language is a mask behind which stands out the much greater business of plunder" (*The Wretched of the Earth*, NY: Grove Press, 1968, p.189).

184. Okot P'Bitek quoted in Okrah, *Nyansapo*, p.88.

185. Information is not knowledge and knowledge is not wisdom. The transformation of information into knowledge and it, in turn, into wisdom is an epigenetic process. Facts and ideas must be experienced in order to become knowledge, and only through the course of time does it become an even more profound

wisdom. (A Brazilian proverb teaches "Knowledge cuts up the world; wisdom makes it whole.") This natural sequence is a major clue as to what is wrong with western philosophy and, in turn, "progressive" culture. They have confused knowledge and information with wisdom. In looking at the irreconcilable Afrikan-european thinking traditions, they replaced the Efik proverb that "Knowledge is better than riches" and the Kikuyu proverb that "Knowledge is power" into their "information is power." We, following in their footsteps, have come to accept that accumulated information or knowledge is wisdom. This is not true, or at least not necessarily so. Such a hierarchy fits a cultural anti-aging bias that evolved from a resource-scarce, desperate survival of the fittest, where the elderly became less desirable as community members because of their inability to provide for self or others (as well as the reactionary politics of european elders at any given time when they were able to gain a decidedly powerful political foothold). They came to be seen as liabilities, as undesirable burdens. And, that is why, in this society, the elderly have been forced to politically organize themselves into a very powerful lobbying group. This unnatural hierarchy also fits a progress oriented society where the most rapid, and often most irresponsible due to a lack of experience, change is in the hands of their youth. This model of intentionally and systematically misinterpreting information for knowledge and knowledge for wisdom remains unchanged throughout european history. It is best exemplified by their incomplete "mastery" of the ancient Kemetic Mystery System, which caused them to think that they were wise but in truth and reality their learning was nothing more than a major misaccumulation of Afrikan wisdom. The ancients referred to such people as the "half wise." Europeans see information as knowledge and wisdom. Afrikan wisdom teaches that children may acquire as many or more clothes as their parents, but they will never have as many rags. In other words, while information can be accessed instantaneously by anyone, only time brings the wisdom necessary to correctly understand and apply information and the knowledge gained from it. Wisdom is a function of time, much time. For Europeans, as a people, it requires much more time than they have claimed to be in the civilized milieu.

186. Kwadwo A. Okrah, *Nyansapo (The Wisdom Knot): Toward an African Philosophy of Education*, NY: Routledge, 2003, pp.47-50 and 70-75 and Ephirim-Donkor, *African Spirituality: On Becoming Ancestors*, p.118.
187. Yoruba proverb.
188. The quality and quantity of a people's proverbs are also reflective of this. In this assessment, it is also important to determine whether their proverbs reflect their true nature or seem to be an unpracticed, stolen legacy.
189. Another wonderful thing about proverbs is their adaptability to situational interpretation. They are subject to multiple interpretations without losing the current of their wisdom. They fit the context within which they are spoken. "A child asked her mother to teach her proverbs, her mother told her that a thing must happen to necessitate a proverb" (Igbo proverb). And their meaning, while carrying that same current, expands and intensifies according to the growth and development of the knowledge base of the listener/thinker. This supports, and is wholly in line with, the Afrikan assumption that a person should continue to learn the entirety of his or her life. The ancestral acceptance of this afrism is reflected in the Afrikan proverb "He who ceases to learn ceases to be wise" as well as the Swahili proverbs "Learning is for life, eating is for today" and "Education has no end" and the Haitian proverb "Education is the work of your entire life."
190. Okrah, *Nyansapo*, p.41. And though he makes an important point (a point eloquently echoed in the Yoruba proverb "A person who knows proverbs has the last word in a dispute"), the ability to speak beautifully must be taken in traditional cultural context and should not be overemphasized in this reality because of its priority of power over others and being able to "destroy" others with unrighteous, deceitful words. In traditional Afrikan society, the importance of verbal eloquence did not surpass or come in conflict with the use of proverbs (both as employed by adults and inculcated in attentive children) as a primary source of character building. The practice of proverbial wisdom leading to mastering the ability to outthink someone in conversation did not play as important a role in the development of a person as its role in strengthening one's mind (thinking processes) and character.
191. Haya proverb.

192. Hausa proverb.
193. Temne proverb.
194. Yoruba proverb.
195. Fulani proverb.
196. Tunisian proverb.
197. I say "made available to Afrikan people," because what we have said has largely been recorded on paper and kept out of our sight by others (even when recorded by us). Those insecure, supremacist others, who can see us as no more than their slaves, want, more than anything else, to keep us blinded to the possibility of our warrior spirit. And, though all the while keeping this information in their libraries for their edification, they have systematically kept as much of what our Ancestors said which would help us know that pacifism and forgiveness is not the norm for our people in the face of threat and assault. As in all other areas, much which would empower us, though it exists, has been kept from us.
198. Kwame Nkrumah succinctly defines imperialism thusly:

> In general, imperialism is the policy which aims at creating, organizing and maintaining an empire. In other words, it is a state, vast in size, composed of various distinct national units, and subject to a single, centralized power or authority. This is the conception of empire: diverse peoples brought together by force under a common power....the annexation of one nation or state by another and the application of a superior technological strength by one nation for the subjugation and the economic exploitation of a people or another nation constitutes outright imperialism. (*Towards Colonial Freedom*, London: Panaf Books, 1979 (first published in 1962; first written in 1945), pp.1-2)

199. According to the self-serving,racist propaganda of Europeans, "happy slaves" were Afrikans who firmly believed that their God-given, proper role in life was to be the unpaid, abused/violated, self-hating chattel of Europeans. Like gleeful children, they are thrilled beyond words and more than little delighted over being chosen to fulfill this, their hightest, ambition.

1. *The Mind of Africa*, Chicago: The University of Chicago Press, 1962, p.115.

2. I would also fundamentally differ with Abraham on his use of some terminology such as "African cultures," in that differences among Afrikan people are ethnic and not cultural.

3. Mwalimu K. Bomani Baruti, "Irreconcilable Differences," in Mwalimu K. Bomani Baruti, *Eureason*, Atlanta, GA: Akoben House, 2006.

4. Amos N. Wilson explains this state of lost consciousness in terms of "other-directedness" (*Blueprint for Black Power: A Moral, Political and Economic Imperative for the Twenty-First Century*, Brooklyn, NY: Afrikan World InfoSystems, 1998, pp.123-125).

5. Namibian proverb.

6. Amos N. Wilson, *The Falsification of Afrikan Consciousness: Eurocentric History, Psychiatry and the Politics of White Supremacy*, Bronx, NY: Afrikan World InfoSystems, 1993, p.23.

7. It is generally believed in "modern" social sciences that there are layers of the human personality. Western social science, with its despiritualized orientation (though now working feverishly to pretend otherwise), includes only the layers of society, group and individual in considering what makes up an individual's personality. As Afrikans, though, we know it is deeper than this. We know we are more than what can be seen and quantified. We know that Spirit must be taken into account in any assessment of the individual. And we recognize that even within Spirit there are layers of greater and lesser, or otherwise differentiated, affect. We recognize that these layers penetrate and surround the physical human capsule.

8. For example, Adolf Hitler spoke German, Mussolini Italian, Napoleon Bonaparte French, King Leopold II Flemish, P.W. Botha Afrikaans, Christopher Columbus Portuguese and Andrew Jackson English.

9. Yoruba proverb.

10. Mwalimu K. Bomani Baruti, *Homosexuality and the Effeminization of Afrikan Males*, Atlanta, GA: Akoben House, 2003.

11. Mwalimu K. Bomani Baruti, "A Godless Reason," in Baruti,

Eureason, pp.63-109.

12. Pleasure is primarily associated with the physical. It is solely in the realm of the mundane plane. Though Europeans do, Afrikans do not interpret pleasure as love itself, only as a limited aspect of it. The emotional letting associated with pleasure is extremely ephemeral and can be reduced to a quantitative accumulation, in that its "lasting" achievement is marked by a necessary repetition of physical acts which are a measure of its efficacy and longevity. Hedonism is it in its most refined quality. Happiness, on the other hand, is mainly felt in the psycho-spiritual realm. It is, if you will, an otherworldly state of being and, often, can exist in an individual over a greatly extended period of time, if not a lifetime. It is a qualitative phenomenon that, once becoming one with it, is not subject to the vagaries of time or ephemeral physical sensations. These experiences, correctly given and received, only serve to enhance its presence and increase the level of one's awareness of self and reciprocal obligation to others. Selfless love and godlikeness are its finest manifestations (Mwalimu K. Bomani Baruti, *Complementarity: Thoughts for Afrikan Warrior Couples* (DVD), 2006).

13.

> Do not be mistaken. Do not let the confusion of eureason take you beyond the truth of where we are and what haunts this place. They say that "the greatest trick the devil ever pulled was convincing the world he didn't exist." We should not be so easily fooled. There is evil here, immeasurable evil. And that evil has come to lay an absolute claim of domination on this world. There is a remarkable record of this. Like good, evil has ancestors, too.Evil is rewarded in evil places. And, as the historical evidence and all around us today continue to demonstrate, european society is an evil social organization. Europeans have worked very hard to carve out a space where they can comfortably be their godforsaken selves. This is most evident in their repeated invasions of others' domains. In these barbaric atrocities, they have murdered or otherwise forced everyone in these places to submit to the white supremacist ideal. From incipient seed to the farthest branches, their evolution reveals an "evil genius" at work. People use all forms of euphemisms to window dress "evil," a most apt term. But there is no more accurate description of yurugu's mind and way of thinking, speaking and doing. No matter what name we call it, what angle we look at, what position or how deeply

we find ourselves entwined within its deadly coil, it all boils down to evil. We only stay confused or experience being repeatedly blind sided and shocked about the immorality and unethicalness of the order in the chaos about us when we forget that evil rewards evil. It promotes and sanctions it. Goodness is not part of the equation, except in service of evil ends. There are no mistakes, no inadvertent acts, no contradictions. This is one of the fundamental truths about which we should never become confused. Within evil, in evil environments, evil triumphs. That is its domain. There it rules, regardless of the delusion of peace and love. In an evil place, evil people thrive. Evil is rewarded. Evil spirits congregate and coalesce. Those who do wrong prosper. The more wrong, the greater the prosperity. In evil places, good people are punished and sacrificed for the good of evil. (Mwalimu K. Bomani Baruti, *Centered: Building Afrikan Realities*, Atlanta, GA: Akoben House, 2009, pp.117-118)

14. Ayi Kwei Armah, *Two Thousand Seasons*, Popenguine, Senegal: PER ANKH: 2000 (first published in 1973), p.60 (p.28 in the Heineman edition).

15. Here, too, we must look at the concept of morality, for the very idea of morality implies the presence of both vices and virtues in human life. Morality implies choice. And choice implies options. In a complementary Universe and human reality, the existence of one vibration necessitates the presence of its "opposite." One cannot be recognized or given value without the other. Light can be neither recognized nor given definition or value without darkness and darkness can only be recognized and given definition and value in the presence of light. The same applies to virtues, those qualities which speak to a person's goodness, and vices, which speak to crucial individual faults. Virtues define vices, and vice versa. One cannot be explained without reference to the other. Morality requires that we be abundantly clear about the importance of cultural context for any social phenomenon, for what is and is not morally correct is socially defined, and, depending on the nature of the asili, that definition ranges from extreme individualism to universal law. We cannot think as Afrikans intelligently operating in this world without knowing that an individual's choices of vices and virtues are socially derived. In their lifetimes, individuals do not devise the cultural matrix or the boundaries within which their choices

are made. Since those boundaries are social phenomena, the preferences of vices and virtues of the individuals in a given society are a social choice, individually agreed upon in the form of a social contract.

16. Baruti, "Irreconcilable Differences."

17. Un-downgradable vices are those tendencies/behaviors which have remained so offensive to nonEuropeans that even the intellectual/scientific machinations of european cultural imperialism have not yet been able to reduce, through the forces of redefinition and subassimilation, their normally recognizable repulsiveness and harmfulness into inevitable, normal human tendencies/behaviors.

18. For all of those caught within the tractor beam of the Western cultural matrix, insanity has been redefined as obsession and obsession as simply individualism. Only those insanities which are obviously odd, that so strikingly stand out as hopelessly unsuitable for the public sphere (at this stage in the euroversalization of humanity), those that cannot be redefined, hidden or made to fit into any reasonable definition of human normalcy, are scientifically classified as insanity. Everything else that would be considered insane by the normal human community becomes either idiosyncratic, harmlessly peculiar or a disease. However, we must understand that insanity covers a range of abnormalities from the completely visible to the invisible. And, because of the general, basic insanity of the European mind, a great deal of that range falls within what we now, as definitionally powerless, quasi-sane participants in another's psychotic mind game, consider to be sane is truly insane. However we want to look at them, though, warriors have to remember that vices are irreducible. They cannot be made into anything other than expressions of wrongness.

19. Dama proverb.

20. Kemetic proverb.

21. Swahili proverb.

22. NY: The New American Library, 1952 (first published 1903).

23. Indivinity means to be without divinity/spirit. It is a companion term for deicide which is defined as the process of killing off/removing the Creator and/or deities or, rather, in the

context of where such a concept could originate, yurugu's supplantation of all divinity.
24. What is called the "zero sum game" is a theory, thesis and set of rules in western economic analyses used to predict human behavior. It has three very important components or, rather, assumptions to it. Everywhere in european culture and society, these three are inextricably, intimately interwoven. The first of these is that people are naturally greedy. "Naturally" is the key word in this western scientific definition because "natural" means innate, inborn, inherent, unchangeable. It means that people have no free will, no choice, no self-control, in this matter. Their genes biochemically carry these unalterable instructions. Second, resources are scarce and limited. They come in fixed amounts and are not replenishable. And, third, people will naturally fight over these scarce and limited resources. Violence *and* aggression are taken as normal human behaviors which must be externally controlled for. These assumptions are supposed to characterize any and every interaction between people. Using them as our universal guide to human behavior, we are supposed to be able to logically reduce the probability of any given outcome to simple, easily predictable, quantifiable probabilities. We should know, however, that these assumptions, these generalizations, apply to them, not us. To use their reasoning to interpret any Afrikan reality (condition, situation, act) would not make sense. We are not they. (Mwalimu K. Bomani Baruti, "Zero Sum" in Baruti, *Eureason*, pp.189-199)
25. Machiavelli, *The Prince*, p.84.
26 . *Merriam Webster's Collegiate Dictionary* (10E), Springfield, MA: 1999, p.697.
27 . *Webster's New Universal Unabridged Dictionary*, NY: Barnes & Noble Books, 1996, p.1151.

28. It is quite interesting how these characteristics so precisely mirror the majority of Bobby E. Wright's descriptives of the basic psychopathic racist personality. Those most related to this immediate discussion include the following: the inability to experience guilt or accept blame for wrongdoing, giving the appearance of honestness but being driven exclusively by selfishness, making promises and commitments with no intention

of fulfilling or keeping them and fiercely dismissing any personal responsibility when confronted with this contradiction, a virtual absence of ethical development and regard for appropriate patterns of behavior, a total ambivalence toward morality (concepts of right and wrong) and an outright rejection of any legally institutionalized authority over him or her. (*The Psychopathic Racial Personality*, Chicago: Third World Press, 1984, pp.5-6)

29. I have addressed this phenomenon of normative lying in several places already. It must be understood as an asilic, cultural imperative if we are to understand the ease and deliberateness with which lies are created and woven into the social fabric of other sustaining lies that make up western society.

> Lying is a Western norm. For instance, in Western society, when is a lie a lie or murder murder? Only when you are caught. Europeans society has been about the business of perfecting the lie and making it a legitimate norm. Morality is political in this cultural context. The politics of morality found it appropriate to pardon the likes of Nixon and Clinton who did nothing wrong in the context of Western thought and behavior. Their behavior follows in the rich tradition of ranking officials in western society before and after them. They were just dumb enough to publicly get caught.
>
> The European is a spoiled child caught up in a lie, a grand lie, built upon a foundation of lies that has required innumerable lies to corroborate. In fact, this brat is entangled in the mother of all lies. His lie is the compilation of generations of impacted lies. There are so many lies, in fact, that it would require a new beginning to clear the original lie. And, even then, the memory would, and should, continue to taint new beginnings until truth tellers prevail. This collection of lies are bound to each other to the point where truth is indistinguishable from lie. And that becomes the purpose for the lies as the child seeks to survive in the world of lies it has created. With so many lies on the table, and more issued daily, it becomes nearly impossible to tell truth even when the child admits it, for that truth is usually a means of sustaining other lies that insure his privilege. The child is also quite aware that, for those who are not deceived by his lies, to admit that even one lie is a lie is to initiate the dreaded process of unraveling all the others. The spoiled child is caught, alone and afraid, trying to garner allies of true believers willing to be friends if he will continue to let them play with his toys. Spoiled children cannot be unspoilt except in what appears to them as the cruelest, most painful

of ways.

Outside of a fundamental moral deficit, Europeans make for the best liars because they begin the practice as soon as they begin to talk. They are socialized in the arts of manipulation and circumvention. They are allowed to disagree with adults as if adults. They, therefore, receive extensive practice in these arts in their efforts to get what they want from the adults who hold the financial and political keys to their temporary happiness. They are forced to learn to lie better in order to insure they win arguments with wiser and more experienced liars. In becoming initiated into the European collective, they become master liars, masters of the what Marimba Ani describes as the "rhetorical ethic," while they are still but children.

This is not accidental. It is an intentional part of their child rearing agenda designed to produce offspring like themselves. Their children are raised to fight with them in preparation for fighting all others. Aggression, in "civilized" society, is bred. (Larry D. Crawford (Mwalimu A. Bomani Baruti), "The Truth of Liars," in, Larry D. Crawford (Mwalimu A. Bomani Baruti) *negroes and other essays*, Atlanta, GA: Ankoben House, 2000 pp.82-83)

Extreme individualism removes the possibility of a moral base, especially in Western culture, because anything that produces a profit or physical pleasure is morally correct. Regardless of the truth of an individual's statement, convincing others of its truth is what is most important. Skill at manipulating others' minds is the ultimate priority. Truth itself is irrelevant. It is set by the winner. So rules are meant to be broken. And because winning is everything, and deception the easiest and surest way to winning in Western society, there can be no moral rules except those arbitrarily given by the winner. It is the master of the lie who wins. For a lie is only a lie when one is caught. (Mwalimu K. Bomani Baruti, *The Sex Imperative*, Atlanta, GA: Akoben House, 2002, p.205)

Lying reaches its most impactful and politically powerful level when those lied to about their natural state of mind accept the definition of self given them by those lying to them.

A major problem making the study of our heritage so difficult yet necessary is this widespread misinterpretation of the history and priorities of the people who have contained and molded us over the last 500 years or so in this Western cultural wasteland. Any credible student of the Afrikan will look at the oppressor rather than the oppressed for the causes of the conditions of the oppressed.

With that in mind, think about this. If European culture is insanity then at the fundamental level that humans define and perceive reality we, as Afrikans and people of color, have a very serious problem. If a cultural minority becomes the power majority and, this minority, through military, media and religious might force the majority cultures to adopt its culture as their own, then insanity becomes the norm and is redefined as sanity. Accepting another's reality as your reality makes their reality yours. If the global majority is right then Europeans are wrong, how dare they stand in judgment? If the vast majority of people on the planet eat insects (high in protein content) as a regular, daily part of their diet (which is true) but Westerners don't, who is the oddball?

> Unfortunately, as is the case with European cultural imperialism, if the insane can convince the sane that insanity is sanity, then the sane majority become insane and insanity becomes universal and comes to be seen as sanity. Those individuals or groups who dare to hold on to their original sanity become universally depicted as the truly insane (backward), and those who are carriers of the original insanity become universally depicted as the truly sane (modern). (Larry D. Crawford (Mwalimu A. Bomani Baruti), "The Cultural Continuum," in Crawford (Baruti), *negroes and other essays*, 37-38)

These peculiar and enduring european cultural philosophies must be contrasted with that of the Afrikan, which is so well summed up by A. Hempaté Bâ.

> In African tradition, speech, deriving its creative and operative power from the sacred, is in direct relation with the maintenance or the rupture of harmony in man and the world about him. That is why most traditional oral societies consider lying as an actual moral leprosy. In traditional Africa the man who breaks his word kills his civil, religious and occult person. He cuts himself off from himself and from society. Better for him to die than to go on living, both for himself and for his family....When a man thinks one thing and says another he cuts himself off from himself. He breaks the sacred unity, the reflection of cosmic unity, creating discord in and around him. ("The Living Tradition," in J. Ki-Zerbo (ed.), *General History of Africa, Vol.1*, Berkeley, CA: University of California Press, 1981, p.172)

30. In order for it to be lasting it must be profound, easily retrievable although deeply embedded in our subconscious memory.

31. There is little difference between this term, "rhetorical ethic," and the Indigenous People's concept of "forked tongue." Both speak to the lying nature of Europeans. Both recognize that Europeans first look to decipher/unravel the humanity in others. They then exploit that humanity by pretending commonality of humane belief and interests. Most humane peoples cannot believe that any human being, no less a population of them, can naturally be that evil. And this confusion of fact with fantasy leads many of us to confuse actual with ideal states. For those able to distinguish between the two, it is obvious that you cannot tell a people who expends so much of it's energy and gets so much satisfaction out of destroying the fabric of other people's lives to "get a life." *This is their life*. The belief that a like mind exists in every being who appears human, a belief held so dearly by victims of their own humanistic delusion, helps facilitate their own inhumane exploitation. They empower it so much so that once they are able to realize the pervasiveness and intensity of this timeless, systematic deceit, they often find themselves beyond recovery. Once the expoiters are solidly in the dominate position, they push aside this farce of common humanity and elevate themselves in a delusional "supremacy," that is, unless they are dealing with a large population wherein it would take a great number of generations to convince them to believe in the lie of our common humanity.

32. Machiavelli, *The Prince*, p.92-93.

33. As John Henrik Clarke reminds us, "...in dealing with the iceman, you must concede that in matters of power, he is more practical than you are, because he deals without sentiment....in the game of power, conscience is absent from the makeup of the European." (*Who Betrayed The African World Revolution?*, Chicago, IL: Third World Press, 1994, pp.72 and 25)

34. Quoted in Robert Greene, *The 48 Laws of Power*, NY: Viking, 1998, p.xx. It is interesting to note that this book, as in other homegrown bibles of interpersonal domination, was written in honor, and in the tradition, of Machiavellian thinking. As stated in the acknowledgements: "It was in the scheming world of Fabrika that Joost and I saw the timelessness of Machiavelli and from our discussion in Venice, Italy, this book was born."

35. *Yurugu: An African-Centered Critique of European Cultural*

Thought and Behavior, Trenton, NJ: Africa World Press, 1994, pp.311-335.

36. Erving Goffman used this term to describe how individuals consciously manipulate their environment, others and themselves, as if playing a role on a stage, to convince others that they are something they are not for purposes of control and/or manipulation (*The Presentation of Self in Everyday Life*, Garden City: NY: Anchor Books, 1959). As we understand that individuals mirror their people, this concept does have a larger, macro application at the level of people and their society.

37 . Mwalimu K. Bomani Baruti, "Bearings," in Baruti, *Eureason*, pp.111-161.

38. Ma'at is the Kemetic goddess of universal harmony and justice. She also represents the principles of truth, righteousness, reciprocity, balance, order and propriety. As a primary force in the Universe, Ma'at is the progressive, generative spirit that constantly moves and organizes all life toward equilibrium within itself and in relation to others. (See Jacob H. Carruthers, *MDW NTR: Divine Speech*, London: Karnak House, 1995 and Maulana Karenga, *Maat: The Moral Ideal in Ancient Egypt*, NY: Routledge, 2004.)

39. That, as his time in this reality came to an end, Tupac embraced a personal philosophy of Machiavellianism is a profound statement of where our children have been led. That he had brazenly and myopically moved so far in this eurocentric direction says volumes, not only of his progressive cultural (particularly political) uprootedness (relative to the culture of his ancestors), but of that of those to whom he spoke and represented as a cultural icon. This brilliant young warrior was not introducing anything new to the mind of his generation. He was only articulating the philosophy most descriptive of what they had already adopted. Of this we must take note with the greatest seriousness possible if we are to return our children home. They have inherited such a barbaric, desensitized, dog-eat-dog, immoral world that, no wonder, they have used their genius to find better defensive ways to cope with their growing insanity. They have lost hope and sight of their origins and see no other option for survival than numbing all their humanity and healing their gaping psychological wounds by filling them with things, drugs, violence

and erotic sensations. If we do not understand why this unnatural ideology of indifferent, selfish predation has come so naturally, so easily, we will surely completely lose them to the deadened chaos of the western desert.

Chapter Five || The Quality of IWA in War

1. NY: International Publishers, 1968, p.112.
2. Ibid, very beginning of book.
3. "Trickle down disrespect" is the term we use to describe the behavior of relatively more favored dispossessed individuals toward those they believe people more powerful than them disrespect *in a society where one's self-esteem is based on degrading others*. They act on the belief that, even while they are less powerful than those they consider powerful, they can still safely act as if they have some power because they have the sanction and protection of the powerful. This sanction and protection comes from knowing who the powerful blatantly disrespect, for these are seen as easy victims for those not as disrespected. We are reminded of this truth in the Akan proverb, "He who has no power depends on he who has it." (The Kemetic proverb "How doth man purchase power but by being a slave to him who giveth it?"equally speaks to this.) In a society where power is most commonly measured by one's ability to disrespect others with impunity, even relatively less powerful persons receive a measurable degree of satisfaction from having someone beneath them to disrespect. This is both an intra- (within/among) and intergroup behavior. Those people who have been earmarked to remain at the lowest rung of the social hierarchy are politico-economically used and abused by newcomers (and those individuals among more powerful groups who through misfortune fall from grace) as easily exploitable doormats and stepping stones for their rise into the more powerful ranks in society. They know that their predacious disrespect of those more dispossessed than they will be subtly authorized and safeguarded. Their approval and protection is given by the more powerful people in society.

The need to disrespect those "beneath" them is assumed as a personal obligation by treasonous, self-hating, mentacidal individuals within the targeted group itself who wishfully seek some form of asylum within the lower ranks of whatever relatively more powerful (i.e., influential) group(s) they serve against their own.

4. Colorism (or what is increasingly being called "shadeism") is a relevantly similar phenomenon. See Larry D. Crawford (Mwalimu A. Bomani Baruti), "Racism, Colorism and Power," in Larry D. Crawford (Mwalimu A. Bomani Baruti), *negroes and other essays*, Atlanta, GA: Akoben House, 2000, pp.115-141.

5. P. xiii.

6. Zaire proverb.

7. Deculturalization, an aspect/outcome of culturacide (to kill a culture), is the process whereby a people:

1. are taken out of their natural cultural environment,
2. are placed in an alien and alienating one that is counter and against their own,
3. are forced to adopt and internalize this alien culture's beliefs, values, technology, imperatives and aspirations,
4. come to accept this decisively foreign personality as their own, and
5. fully reject everything of meaning which they come from and, therefore, their essence and self.

Deculturalization's first three stages are the outcome of external, enemy forces. The last two are orchestrated by effects engendered and generated within the false consciousness created within the victims through a dysfunctional, self-destructive, disempowering socialization. This false consciousness naturally manifests itself in whatever "new" institutions and community these people create for themselves within the bounds of the negative, limiting definitions given them of themselves by their oppressors. In no social transformation are the stages mutually exclusive or without meaningful connection. They, too, are epigenetic. Within the five stages of deculturalization presented here, the stage at which a people is most dramatically and effectively transformed into something other than themselves is the third. It is during this period when they have been separated from their source long enough to begin to confuse an alien space, people and standard with their home, hope and vision. Often, though, there are even more horrific results for the human psyche of the vanquished than simple self-confusion. Often, they find that the torture given by their undeniable mirror images, the hateful force with which they are slammed against themselves by those who work toward their self-negation and the disarming deception of the occupying culture's "universalizing" theories cause them to seek escape into a delusion that will carry them away from any and everything that will lead them into denial of *any* cultural direction. Within our community, these special individuals totally refuse to accept the possibility that they are thinking and acting within the social context of any culture at all. Next to actually committing suicide, this is the worst stage of deculturalization because it allows deeply self-hating Afrikans to believe that there is truly no such thing as culture. For them, culture actually comes to be defined as whimsical, ephemeral and idiosyncratic, without logical, lasting basis or purpose. Worst of all, when noneuropean, it is seen as regressive and harmful to self-expression. Having been caught in the deadly avalanche of the icicled minds formed in the Earth's last massive glacier to their disadvantage, such individuals are rootless. They have rejected the unequivocal significance of culture to their very existence, all the while held captive to horribly anti-Afrikan cultural beliefs and practices.

8. Revolutionary words are some of a warrior's most potent weapons. So, to disrespect a warrior's library is to disrespect his or her weapons, an act considered treasonous on any viable frontline.

9. Nyang proverb.

10. *Message to the People*, Dover, MA: The Majority Press, 1986. Of course, a one possible, practical, planned solution to this, at the community level, is communal libraries maintained by responsible bibliophile archivists which everyone contributes to with rules disallowing the removal of such books from the premises.

11. Zulu proverb.

12. Regarding of abuse, we should quickly tell a woman to leave her physical abuser and never go/look back because, in general, we know that "once an abuser always an abuser." (Somehow this

does not transfer to our relations with Yurugu. With them, we tell ourselves that we should stay and that we can change them into something more manageable.)

13. Akan proverb.

14. Teumari (tay-oo-mah-ree) is the Amharic (Afrikan) term for what we mistakenly call mentees. As with Jegna, it carries a much deeper responsibility and character qualification than the homosexualizing eurocentric term.

15. *The Mis-Education of the Negro*, Hampton, VA: U.B. & U.S. Communications Systems, 1992 (first published in 1933), p.130.

16. *The Black Student's Guide to Positive Education*, Bowie, MD: Nubia Press, 1996, pp.66-97. It's worth mentioning that this list, with its accompanying "Don'ts" list, in many respects, is similar to the contrasting lists Haki Madhubuti supplied in his *Black Men: Obsolete, Single, Dangerous?* (Chicago: Third World Press, 1990, pp.8-10). With respect to Kondo's "Do" list, Madhubuti offers a "MAXIMUM CULTURAL DEVELOPMENT: Revolutionary Mentality" one. And his contrasting "SURVIVAL CULTURAL EXISTENCE: Accommodationist/Riot Mentality" would correspond to Kondo's "Don't" in terms of personal priorities.

17. James Brown, "The Man in the Glass," *Soul on Top*, 1969.

18. Mwalimu K. Bomani Baruti, *Centered: Building Afrikan Realities*, Atlanta, GA: Akoben House, 2009, pp.102-103.

19. See Ra Un Nefer Amen, *An Afrocentric Guide To A Spiritual Union*, Bronx, NY: Khamit Corp, 1992, Mwalimu K. Bomani Baruti, *Complementarity: Thoughts for Afrikan Warrior Couples*, Atlanta, GA: Akoben House, 2004, Nwasha and Montsho Edu, *Akoma Day: A Celebration of Black Love* and Sobonfu Somé, *The Spirit of Intimacy* (excluding Chapter 13 because of its erroneous assertion of homosexuality as an Afrikan tradition), NY: William Morrow and Company, 1997.

20.
> Simply because you are being exposed to ourstory you are very privileged. And privilege carries responsibility. With it, you accept the difficult and humbling task of learning and teaching others so that your generation's liberating mission can be fulfilled and correctly passed on to future generations. It is because of your privilege that you have an undeniable responsibility to your ancestors, those around you, and those yet to come. (Mwalimu K. Bomani Baruti, "Groundings With

My Daughters," in Mwalimu K. Bomani Baruti, *Mentacide*, Atlanta, GA: Akoben House, 2005, pp.115-116)

21. Asa G. Hilliard, Larry Williams and Nia Damali (eds), *The Teachings of Ptahhotep*, Atlanta: Blackwood Press, 1987, p.17.

22. These meaningless debates over which undesirable is least offensive gives the illusion that one must be chosen. It legitimizes the false assumption that the two nonsensical propositions or positions are the only two possible choices. Degree of difference between two wrongs is irrelevant for a people mentacidally manacled to a greater wrong. Either compromised position will continue to advance us along the road straight to physical, mental and spiritual hell. (Mwalimu K. Bomani Baruti, *Yurugu's Eunuchs*, Atlanta, GA: Akoben House, 2008, p.12)

23. Angolan proverb.

24. References to the point and utility of "Black Firsts" have been made elsewhere.

> In our proud celebrations of "Black Firsts," we applaud Afrikans for *finally* repeating, or building on, the accomplishments already done by Europeans. We act as if we began here. While this criticism is not designed to negate any of our accomplishments while we have been dominated in this or any other land, it should force us to place them in the context of the accomplishments of, at the very minimum, 6245 years of advanced Afrikan civilization. (For those who would ask why I am counting today, we are still advanced. That is why they still seek to destroy us.)....Do not misunderstand this critique of "Black Firsts." We must be clear about what, in reality, we are doing to our children. Making our children focus on individually being "first" in an area where none of us has been allowed to go before in the European world is, on the surface, an honorable success-motivating strategy. It motivates them into higher levels of struggle. And it forces Black-into-white subintegration by using our children as battering rams to invade areas, heretofore in this white supremacist reality, inaccessible to us. But, at the same time, and an even more significant issue for Afrikan warrior scholars working toward ReAfrikanization and nationbuilding, our children's misguided infiltration, subintegration and, ultimately, assimilation and amalgamation into whiteness, becomes the ultimate goal of "Black Firsts" themselves. The goal becomes to show Europeans that we are as good as they in whatever they do and, therefore, in proving our equality in all things, they should feel compelled to welcome us into their

hearts and minds with deracialized, open arms. This agenda for the success of our children is no more than the subtle subintegrationist strategy of a vanquished people trying to conceal their sacrificing of their own children's extraordinary talents to their masters, so they too can be accepted as human. No matter how you look at it historically, their goal is still to convince Europeans, to influence them. Most of us still see them as holding all validating power that is socially and culturally derived. So our, and our children's, "Black Firsts," as measured against white progress, are designed to prove something to them, not us. (Mwalimu K. Bomani Baruti, *Asafo: A Warrior's Guide to Manhood*, Atlanta, GA: Akoben House, 2004, pp.85-86)

Of course, most of these anglo/europhiles are merely resting on the laurels of their glorified negro ancestors. They would never think to honor any Afrikan judged by western society as one who fought this racist system or who worked above and beyond the call of duty to move us away from an assimilated possession of european culture. The respect of negro historians is reserved for Europeans and those Afrikans who evinced some form of european validated success....The greatest collection of these historical figures fall into the category of "Black Firsts," epitomized by individuals such as Madame C.J. Walker, our first Black millionaire, who became rich by developing products to make our features look more European; or Crispus Attucks, who holds the distinction of being the first individual (Afrikan or otherwise) to lay down his life for the winning side in a european civil war that ended with the sovereign beginning of yet another racist european terrorist empire. negro scholars have to start and stop at piecemeal Afrikan "contributions" because any serious analysis of the lessons ourstory could bring us with respect to who we are as a unique cultural and traditional people, as well as the forms and outcomes of our interactions with others, might cause them to question the very foundation and reason for their false sense of security in the house of our enemy and be revealed for the intellectually impotent traitors that they are. (Mwalimu K. Bomani Baruti, *Notes Toward Higher Ideals in Afrikan Intellectual Liberation*, Atlanta, GA: Akoben House, 2006, pp.17-18)

25. See the chapter "The Role of Elders" in Baruti, *Centered*, pp.131-138.

26. Baltimore, MD: Imprint Editions, 2000. Also see J.A. Sofola, *African Culture and the African Personality*, Ibadan, Nigeria: African Resources Publishers Company, 1973, pp.90-

91.

27. To paraphrase Kamau R. Kambon, "How is what I am doing and preparing to do going to help with the ReAfrikanization of Afrikan people?"

28. An important publication addressing this is Balogun O. Abeegunde's *Afrikan Martial Arts: Discovering the Warrior Within* (Atlanta, GA: Boss Up Inc. Publications, 2008). The line, "They say karate means empty hands, so then it's perfect for the poor man" by Dead Prez ("Psychology," *Lets Get Free*, 2000) should also give warriors cause to contemplate what we need to know in the martial world. Omowale Malcolm X also brought up a thought worthy point when saying,

> Guerilla action takes heart, it takes nerve and he doesn't have that. He's brave when he has tanks and airplanes, he's brave when he has bombs and a whole lot of company along with him. But you take that little man from Africa or Asia and turn him loose in the woods with a blade -- that's all he needs -- and when the sun goes down, it's even steven.

29. In concerned instruction to his daughter, E. Jerome Johnson reminds us of one of the most critical traditions that our children must be taught if they are to become enduring warriors of Afrikan liberation.

> Our children should be told of the great wars of resistance fought by our ancestors in an effort to prevent domination from others and to maintain our way of life. We have been taught of the defeats, but not the victories. We are told of African self-betrayal, but not of African cooperation and loyalty. When we did win, how did we do it? Success, or memory or success, instills confidence, whether on the sports field, the classroom, or the battlefield. Erase the memory and confidence fades. (*Seven Steps Toward Black Reemergence*, Hawthorne, CA: Southsphere Press, 2006, p.143)

30. Hannibal Tirus Afrik.

31. "Message to the Grassroots."

32. Afrikan proverb.

33. Be mindful of those teachers who insist on referring to themselves and their students as African Americans. They are generally not comfortable with being an African and will defend "African American" vehemently, claiming they are both. Ironically, you seldom see the African side of these individuals. (Yaa Asantewa Nzingha, "Reparations +

Education = The Pass to Freedom," in Raymond A. Winbush (ed.), *Should America Pay?*, NY: HarperCollins, 2003, p.310)

This statement, of course, applies everyone in our community who labels him or herself and other Afrikans in this way.

Chapter Six || Complementarity: The Quality of IWA in Love

1. This is understood to mean two heterosexual Afrikans. It must be recognized that the problem of relationships in western[ized] society is far greater than an issue of personalities or gender roles. And this is why the reactive feminist approach of emasculating or demasculinizing males and/or masculinizing or defeminizing females simply will not work to correct our relationship problems. In addition to it having no place in the Afrikan community, homosexuality is no solution. Generally speaking, it is the nature of the culture (arising out of its asili), not the individual, which is the problem. If, for a moment, we can put aside the genocultural personality (which is also an asilic product) and strictly look at the culture within which individuals operate, we can see that culture dictates the nature of relationships, intimate and otherwise. Individuals may choose within cultural constraints the form (official, informal, serial, monogamous, kwk) and type (heterosexual, homosexual, asexual, kwk) of relationship they involve themselves in, but the nature of the power relations within the relationships are significantly, if not wholly, predetermined by the culture in its most ancient asilic roots. This is critical to understand because, without it, we confuse diversity with difference. (We fall for the intellectual traps that would lead us to believe, based on the propagated, managed depiction of european women, that two homosexual[ized] and/or effeminized males or two homosexual[ized] and/or masculinized females have more peaceful relationships than heterosexual couples when the exact opposite is statistically true. Even if you change the personalities or natural preferences into unnatural ones (for

Afrikans, that is) of the individuals involved in relationships, the nature of these abnormally polarized relationships will not change. Only the relative roles would shift, as in a power shift. But the differential would remain constant. An imbalance in power is the most destructive force in relationships. Yet, this imbalance is built into the very foundation of all western relationships. It is necessary, for, without this imbalance, relationships could not be normal for them. And, not that this is a problem per se because what is normal for them should be expected of them. The problem is that we are assuming that this is normal for us, which it is not. And many of us, intellectual and lay alike, with no basis in fact whatsoever, are working to fabricate interpretations of relationships among our ancestors to fit this abnormal condition, so we can find a home in this lopsided reality. In the face of a world questioning their innate sanity, Europeans are attempting to alter the public image (i.e., make imbalance normal) without changing who they naturally are. Who they are is no more changeable than their culture, which is no more changeable than their asili. This we have to understand. And time, and global cultural domination, have given them no reason to consider their error in being. In fact, it has strengthened the resolve of their cultural arrogance. Like a bully without opposition, european culture has become stronger and more surefooted in the imposition of its insanities with every defeat and oppression of others. In its mind, it has no real reason to even consider a reason to change.

2. These stages are discussed in much greater detail in Mwalimu K. Bomani Baruti, *Complementarity: Thoughts for Afrikan Warrior Couples*, Atlanta, GA: Akoben House, 2004.

3. To dispense with some persistent confusion in terms of an individual's ability to choose a complement for him or herself, we must also note that, unlike what we have been told, Afrikan parents have never unilaterally chosen who their children were to marry. Certainly, because of youth's immaturity, throughout our traditions, such adults retained the right and responsibility of ensuring that their offspring's choices of the family they were to marry into were healthy and wise.

> Africans marry with long deliberation, preparation, and rationality, not just at a glance, sporadically and emotionally. In Africa love is generally directed by the adults who have

> gone through the mills. Parental guidance can hardly be wrong, for parents do not ill-advise their children. The first objective of love, is to secure a well-to-do partner, to marry the wise. (G.K. Osei, *The African Philosophy of Life*, London: The African Publication Society, 1970, p.14)

But we have never held this "right and responsibility" as a despotic power over our children's heads. That disparaging misinformation, i.e., the "hive" thesis of the absence of individuality in traditional Afrikan society (adequately debunked in all its weaknesses by the Akan proverb, "The family is like the forest, if you are outside it is dense, if you are inside you see that each tree has its own position"), has remained a well planted western concoction that still works wonders in influencing and alienating us from our communal traditions by making us believe that the adults did not permit the youth to express or act on (individual) choice.

4. And, because of the traditions they naturally came to respect and honor through observing their practical application among the adults who preceded them, they knew that "if a marriage has no support it spoils" (Akan proverb).

5. Kofi Asare Opoku, *West African Traditional Religion*, Jurong, Singapore: FEP International Private Limited, 1978, pp.125-133.

6. It is interesting that this quality was important enough for the Akan to originate the proverb that "patience makes a marriage succeed." In marriage and elsewhere, these Ancestors tell us, only "the fool regards patience as undesirable."

7. Swahili proverb.

8. Akan proverb.

9. We must make a distinction between "rearing" our children and "raising" them. Rearing them is a political act, full of conscious Afrikan intent and clear in the knowledge of being at war with an enemy who is ever present in the lives of our children. Raising them is simply the perfunctory behavior of Afrikans who see this enemy as their friend, protector and sole reference group. Mari Evans clearly distinguishes the two.

> [R]aising is "providing for," while rearing is "responding to." Raising can be satisfied by providing the essentials: food, shelter, clothing and reasonable care. "Rearing" is a carefully thought out process. Rearing begins with a goal and is supported by a clear view of what are facts and what is

truth (and the two are not necessarily synonymous). Rearing is complex and requires sacrifice and dedication. It is an ongoing process of "preparation"....Obviously, something *different*, some carefully thought out *process*, some long-range *political* view is present when one has a clear sense of one's reality and, therefore, intends to rear presidents, rulers, or *free men* and *women*. ("The Relationship of Childrearing Practices to Chaos and Change in the African American Family," in Carlos Moore, Tanya R. Sanders and Shawna Moore (eds.), *African Presence in the Americas*, Trenton, NJ: Africa World Press, 1995, p.306)

10. Of note in terms of the "correct" sequence of this progression, we have to recognize that we are not in traditional Afrikan society, at least not yet. So, we see quite a few deviations among warriors, especially in the first four stages. The personal chaos disproportionately injected into the lives of Afrikans living in an intensely anti-Afrikan society distorts a warrior's sense of order, understanding of interpersonal respect and exercise of delayed gratification at the subconscious level. As a result of being socialized in an alien and disordered, relative to Afrikan sensibilities, culture and society, we often do not discover our Afrikanity until we have already procreated or the selfishness of individualism or diverging political orientations bring separations that often, for all intents and purposes, leave children being raised/reared by one progenitor parent.

11. We need to make the time to logically consider the probability and possibility of healthy warrior relationships within western culture and society. While we have an Afrikan ideal after which to model our complementary relationships, again, we are not in traditional Afrikan society. We are in a determined anti-Afrikan society. Therefore, it is advantageous for us to question the viability of sound complementary relationships within this cultural context. You cannot have a wholesome relationship in a culture that is not wholesome. As above, so below. And this is what some of us refuse to grasp out of fear or incredulity over the work that would have to be involved. (This is not to say that you cannot be Afrikan in european society– if there are no other options. But it is to say that what you build together can only be an approximation because of the distractions and battles that will crop up if you are true to your Ancestors). I.e., we cannot build

healthy relationships within european culture – "healing" our relationships will ever be a business for them because our relationships will always be in chaos – most of their income comes from creating temporary solutions to permanent problems of their creation. Logically, this leaves only one answer.

12. Mwalimu K. Bomani Baruti, *Centered: Building Afrikan Realities*, Atlanta, GA: Akoben House, 2009, pp.141-142.

13. Abibifahodie ('ah-bee-bee-fah-'hoe-dee-ay) is a Twi word meaning "Afrikan Liberation." It is being used to greet revolutionary Afrikans (as well as acknowledge sneezes, instead of saying "Bless you") in order to affirm regularly and as often as possible our victorious destiny.

14. When understood correctly, this is not a statement against polygamy.

Chapter Seven || The Character of Revolutionary Community

1. Kwasi Konadu, *Truth Crushed to the Earth Will Rise Again*, Trenton, NJ: Africa World Press, 2005, 2005.

2. Maulana Karenga, *Kawaida Theory*, Inglewood, CA: Kawaida Publications, 1980.

3. The Nguzo Saba are the seven principles of Kwanzaa: Umoja (unity), Kujichagulia (self-determination), Ujima (collective work and responsibility), Ujamma (cooperative economics), Nia (purpose), Kuumba (creativity) and Imani (faith).

4. "Mashariki" is here best translated as centered, sacred, protected communal space, to include those who inhabited it.

5. Hannibal Tirus Afrik.

6. To use Ella Baker's words,

> I have always felt it was a handicap for oppressed peoples to depend so largely upon a leader, because unfortunately in our culture, the charismatic leader usually becomes a leader because he has found a spot in the public limelight.

7. This brief statement of the concentric circle model of defense is a modified version of the subchapter "The First Line of

Defense" in my *Asafo: A Warrior's Guide to Manhood*, Atlanta, GA: Akoben House, 2004, pp.157-158.

8. Blacksmiths are fitting examples of this. There are numerous stories of the "loneliness" of the life of ironworkers within larger villages.

9. No doubt, this exterior extended to every environment men, women and children found themselves in and is practically reflected in the physical arrangements of these individuals.

10. Ayi Kwei Armah, *Osiris Rising*, Popenguine, West Africa: Per Ankh, 1995, p.251.

11. Marcel Griaule, *Conversations with Ogotemmêli: An Introduction to Dogon Religious Ideas*, London: Oxford University Press, 1965, pp.84-88.

12. Of course, "we" must be qualified because, even though negroes exist as the majority in the Afrikan population of this country, there is a clear distinction between them and us. negroes are fighting for most favored consumer status, while warriors are working to become empowered, independent, sovereign, self-defining producers.

13. Nepotism naturally "establishes a self-preserving preference for kin" through intergenerationally regulating the quality control and progressive specialization of skills, keeping family members in protected, invigorating spaces, affording a trusted means for the accumulation, preservation and distribution of resources and providing an orderly channel through which culture can be transmitted without compromise.

14. The ongoing, successful reverse racism attack against affirmative reaction should have been expected. It is of little significance because that's not the direction we should have gone in the first place. It should have been expected and the vast majority of those for whom it was designed to benefit have exhibited no loyalty to Afrikan people. W.E.B. Dubois encapsulated this fact well in his revelation that:

> The upper class Negro has almost never been nationalistic. He has never planned or thought of a Negro state or a Negro school. This thought and solution has always been an idea upsurging from the masses, because of the pressure which they could not withstand and which compelled racial institution or chaos. (*Dusk of Dawn*, Millwood, NY: Kraus-Thomson, 1975 (first printed in 1940) p.305)

Perhaps, Marcus Mosiah Garvey worded it better when he said:

> The traitor of other races is generally confined to the mediocre or irresponsible individual, but unfortunately, the traitors among the negro race are generally to be found among the men higher placed in society, the fellows who call themselves leaders. The man who will compromise rights of his race can be classified in no other way than that of a traitor also.

Given this, Amos N. Wilson's critique of assimilationist leadership, as he discussed nationalist leadership, will suffice on this issue.

> While we may look at the assimilationist leadership, as black nationalists who carry on the legacy of Marcus Garvey *we* must also look at ourselves. While we may gloat to a degree in the failures of the assimilationist leadership and show them the squalid outcome of their leadership – how they fought for equal housing and yet now a major problem is homelessness; how they fought for integrated schools and now a major problem is dropout-ism and illiteracy; how they threw their bodies before tractors and threw their bodies before traffic to get us into the colleges and universities, yet we find now our major problem is the decline of black students on the university level, the decline of black teachers on college campuses, the decline of black teachers in the schools, period, and the decline of the education of black people as a whole; how they struggled to get a justice on the Supreme Court and how we face injustice everyday in the courts of the United States and the world-over; how they struggled to get us to have window dressing jobs and now our children and people are unemployed in the streets of our cities, how we are facing the possibility that we may have a 70% or more unemployment rate among black males in the future; how they placed their faith in the so-called law, a law which is only as good as the people who enforce it; how their faith in redeeming the white man from his pathological racism has shown that this faith is hopeless... – we must *also* accept our responsibility in the decline (to a degree) of our ability to carry out the Marcus Garvey legacy. How has this occurred? To a degree, *simultaneous* with the rise of assimilationist leadership, I think we had a rise of pseudo-nationalistic leadership – a nationalist rhetoric without a nationalist substance, a people who talked a good nationalism but who do not behave and actualize what that nationalism means. (*Afrikan-Centered Consciousness versus The New World Order*, Brooklyn, NY: Afrikan World InfoSystems, 1999, pp.65-66)

15. Akan proverb. In other words, "If you owe allegiance to more than one person you get lost" (Akan proverb).
16. Leachim Tufani Semaj, "Towards a Cultural Science," in Daudi Ajani ya Azibo, *African Psychology*, Trenton, NJ: Africa World Press, 1996, p.199.
17. John Henrik Clarke, *Who Betrayed The African World Revolution?*, Chicago, IL: Third World Press, 1995, p.36.
18. Medase Ife Seshet Robinson.
19. The timeless wisdom of learning from those who came before is expressed by J.A. Sofola in his retelling of a proverb.

> ...there is a proverb in our country which says that when three or more people are going along a narrow path in the bush and the man in the front happens to fall into a ditch, it is a lesson to those others coming behind him. (*African Culture and the African Personality*, Ibadan, Nigeria: African Resources Publishers Company, 1973, p.22)

In making the same point, the Akan say, "Someone's scars are what we use to cure our diseases." Such wisdom also inevitably leads conscious parents to a very fundamental principle in the rearing of strong warriors, as conveyed in the Akan proverb, "If a spark from the fire burns you, you shake it off onto your child before you take it off him too."
20. Just as europeans and negroes do before lending support, we need to know the *exact* position of those organizations and individuals we are considering assisting on the issues of interracialism, homosexuality, subintegration and any others infecting and assaulting our community.

Chapter Eight || Character Flaws

1. "The Book of Khakheper-Ra-Soneb," in Maulana Karenga (ed.), *The Husia*, Los Angeles: The University of Sankore Press, 1984, p.78.
2. "The Book of Dialog With the Soul," in Karenga (ed.), *The Husia*, p.80-81.
3. *20 enemy forces within a revolutionary organization that must be combated*, Detroit, MI: Black Workers Congress, 1971. It

would be unfair to warriors intent on finding truth in those whose thought, word and deed is contradictory to not qualify the inclusion of Forman's list in this work, for Foreman was a subintegrationist at heart. On this point, though, he exhibited no contradiction. Given this, it should be understood that my interpretation of the enemy forces of which he speaks may, depending on the issue, dramatically differ from what he intended to convey. Unquestionably, a study of these rules would prove beneficial for warriors contemplating the quality of their character.

5. Jacob H. Carruthers, *The Irritated Genie*, Chicago: The Kemetic Institute, pp.113-114. Sadly, this dismissal of self/race first in our liberation efforts continues. Of course, we know why many outspoken "revolutionaries" cannot espouse Dessalines nationbuilding liberation philosophy. He promoted an unqualified Afrikan priority. They are following political ideologies, although grafted from the original Afrikan order, that have always prioritized others before Afrikans under the guise of creating a socialist/communist world for all humanity. And Afrikans continue to fall for this because of our innate humanism and, in this reality, desperate desire to escape millennia of oppressive, racist pain. Because of their divided (often mentacidally so) loyalties, they are unable to distinguish the original socialism in Dessalines' revolutionary Afrikan mind from that of their dispossessed "comrades" seeking but self-alienated, other-oriented fodder with which to overthrow their empowered brethren so that they can take their turn at ruling a culturally, psychologically defeated world.

6. Mwalimu K. Bomani Baruti, *Notes Toward Higher Ideals in Afrikan Intellectual Liberation*, Atlanta, GA: Akoben House, pp.88-105.

7. Vincent Harding, *There is a River*, NY: Vintage, p. 206.

8. *The Irritated Genie*.

9. Fundi Sanyika Anwisye's *The African Personality: Lubrication for Liberation* is one of the best tools we have for resolving conflict through applying the practice of actually listening available to our community. (Saint Louis, MO: Blessings Not Curses Publications, 2007)

11. Akan proverb.

12. Randall Robinson, *Defending the Spirit*, NY: Dutton, 1998,

pp.265-274.

13. The assumption that everybody must be involved is a backward approach toward a consistent revolutionary progression because it calls for unity before consciousness instead of consciousness before unity, which is an underlying requirement among a group where the idea of a need for revolution is a contested area. There are a number of concrete reasons why unity before consciousness is fundamentally flawed. To begin with, it first assumes a progressive movement toward a unified consciousness (an inevitable mass political consensus). Secondly, it assumes no political agenda of its organizational leadership (independent of that stated for the masses) and, in the case that such an agenda does exist, it is fully in line with what is good for the people, i.e., is honest and ideologically non-arrogant on the part of those giving the movement direction, i.e., does not undermine the people's understood interests. And, thirdly, it assumes that the social, cultural and intellectual framework within which the people in need of revolution have wallowed has not infected their minds to the degree that their capacity to progressively think outside of its matrix has not been irreparably or severely intergenerationally hampered to the point of making "liberation" meaningless in the long run. Given the pervasiveness, depth and tenacity of mentacide in the global Afrikan community, the last assumption about a unification prerequisite for revolution should be considered deeply.

> The need to include everybody in our war, especially those who boast about subsisting in the deepest states of mentacide, who hate the idea that someone might think that somewhere in them there might be anything recognizable as Afrikan, is extremely problematic. If we have to get over anything it is the idea that it is necessary to bring everybody into the fold in order to win. This is the diversity sham working its finest magic on the minds of those Afrikans seeking an easy way to peace. It is the idea that everyone of Afrikan descent must be brought into the decision making fold because we think we are a democratic family. It intentionally forces us to overlook the fact that there are those in our family who hate us. The diversity sham operates on the principle that you cannot make revolutionary progress without everyone included. It is so easy to become completely misdirected when believing that everybody must be together in order to

> return home. (Mwalimu K. Bomani Baruti, *Centered: Building Afrikan Realities*, Atlanta, GA: Akoben House, 2009, pp.78-79)

We have been fighting against divisiveness for so long that we have forgotten that it, too, has benefits.

14. Baruti, *Centered*, pp.89-96.

15. At the same time, we cannot operate on the principle of total peace among all members of our community when there are so many Afrikans who are consciously fighting with all their might against any form of Afrikan community or nationalism. These closet negroes and confused lost souls are absolutely opposed to the idea of "race first." Hindsight tells us that we cannot assume that everyone is on the same page or in the same book, or even in the same library or library system.

16. "Khun-Anup," in Maulana Karenga (ed.), *The Husia*, Los Angeles: The University of Sankore Press, 1984, p.32.

17. The latter part of this explanation of elitism is taken from the first endnote in my *Centered.*

18. The entire opening statement of this point on colorism is as follows:

> Most of us would have little to no problem agreeing that the range of color Afrikan people possess is awesome. Black, in all its splendid hues, is indeed beautiful. It should also go without saying, that this variation is useless as an index for judging individual beauty, intelligence, aspirations and the like. One's complexion is intrinsically irrelevant to any and all of these qualities. Yet we practice the European model of a racial hierarchy, ranking and judging each other based on our level of melanin. And, having adopted it, any value we believe we independently, consciously or not, attach to different complexions in our community is merely a pathetic imitation of its racist beliefs at the societal level. So, in this new age of consciousness raising it must be realized that we cannot embrace a color-based hierarchy among Afrikans without, at some level, accepting as truth a hierarchy of color among humans. There is no denying that the social organization of our community along lines of color precisely mimics the order fabricated by white supremacy. Black America (Afrikans) serves as a classic microcosm in white supremacy's global macrocosm. The only appreciable difference is that we "discriminate" without power. (Larry D. Crawford (Mwalimu A. Bomani Baruti), "Racism, Colorism and Power," in Larry D. Crawford (Mwalimu A. Bomani

> Baruti) *negroes and other essays*, Atlanta, GA: Ankoben House, 2000, pp.115-116)

How demonic – to set a people against the color of their skin.

19. Raymond J. Corsini, *The Dictionary of Psychology*, NY: Brunner-Routledge, 2002, p.318.

20. The Napoleon Complex refers to the psychological condition of persons who have developed a sense of inferiority because they lack average height. In an effort to correct for this "disadvantage," they attempt to overcompensate for this "disadvantage" by trying to aggressively and absolutely control/rule over others. Through mentally and/or physically belittling (ruling over) others, they feel elevated above them. This can also be said of groups who feel themselves lesser than/inferior to other groups for whatever reasons (intellect, melanin, lack of emotional content, kwk), so they put an enormous amount of their energy into subjugating and mercilessly abusing them. We would say these individuals or groups are "power hungry" or on "power trips."

21. As taught by the Akan, "If two elephants have a quarrel in the forest, the trees and leaves there are in trouble."

22. Del Jones, *The Black Holocaust: Global Genocide*, Philadelphia, PA: Hikeka Press, 1992, p.36.

23. "Bendera" is the Kiswahili word for flag. In the conscious community, it is most commonly heard when referring to the red, black and green flag created by Marcus Mosiah Garvey to symbolize, respectively, the blood, skin and land of Afrikan people.

24. Ayi Kwei Armah, *Osiris Rising*, Popenguine, West Africa: Per Ankh, 1995, p.182.

25. Ibid, p.154.

26. John Henrik Clarke's instructed us, "Do your best work."

27. Ayi Kwei Armah, *KMT: in the house of life*, Popenguine, Senegal: PER ANKH, 2002, p.97.

28. This confusion of western issues with Afrikan identity is quite evident in the "black holes" of which I spoke in *Centered*.

> Aspiring warrior scholars also need to be warned about the pseudocenters in our communities whose mission is not to radically empower Afrikan warrior scholars, but to derevolutionize them for Europeans. There are many such organized traps with Afrikan veneers. I prefer to call them

> "black holes." (This is not a derogatory use of the word "black," as we historically find in eurosupremacist thought, but a use that implies a void.) They can theoretically be defined in the same way that all knowing western science defines that abstractly hypothesized enigma in outer space, which they have never seen and do not have the possibility of knowing about. These "black holes" drape themselves in causes the compassionate warrior naturally gravitates toward. They are recognizable through their liberalism in political membership and their vehement defense of european ways found among their membership. This cannot be concealed for long from critical thinkers. The problem is disconnecting from them once we become involved. Even for bright minds, it can be difficult to moderate the intensity of the attachments to individuals who knew what they were about but who concealed it from us until we were in too deep to dismiss those pseudo-centers without the pain of disconnection from those whose ideal/image we had learned to love. (p.37)

29. A more appropriate title for such "men" might be fagimists in that they are working to redefine manhood along feminist lines.
30. This point is well argued than as done by Valethia Watkins in her essay "Womanism and Black Feminism: Issues in the Manipulation of African Historiography" (in Jacob H. Carruthers and Leon C. Harris (eds.), *African World History Project: The Preliminary Challenge*, Los Angeles, CA: Association for the Study of Classical African Civilizations, 2002, pp.245-284).
31. Nowhere is the distinction between feminism and womanism or motherism more clearly evident than when looking at the different political orientations of Afrikan and European women. Afrikan women are womanist while European women are feminist. "Womanism" centers around working toward equality with and respect by men. It also holds motherhood as its most central priority. This must be contrasted with "feminism," which is simply the normal dominative psychology of Europeans, only concentrated in and directed by female politics. It is a european-style matriarchy without any true concern for motherhood or nurturance. Feminists want to supplant european males in their positions of power so they can be the primary dominators. There is no desire for equality here, only the psychotic need to have power over others. Individualism naturally dominates this political orientation. We must recognize that spiritually barren

women (whether married or not) spawn sterile, unemotional (even if loud and active) offspring. This is a battle between european females and males with other females simply serving as political fodder. And this is why it is so strange, and even comical, to hear of adult Afrikan males claiming to be revolutionaries also claiming to be feminists. In the desperate search to make that which is European Afrikan, looking at our "traditions" through jaundiced, nearsighted historical eyes, Afrikans who would be the men defending the honor of Afrikan women have turned to man-hating philosophies to assist in the destruction of Afrikan manhood and traditional Afrikan womanhood in service to another's reverse sexism. These are some of the reasons why I say a Black feminist is as oxymoronic as an African centered European, a Black male claiming to be a feminist even more so.

32. Mwalimu K. Bomani Baruti, *Homosexuality and the Effeminization of Afrikan Males*, Atlanta, GA: Akoben House, 2003, p.42.

33. Baruti, *Centered*, pp.108-110.

34. Beware of irresolution in the intent of thy actions, beware of instability in the execution; so shalt thou triumph over two great failings of thy nature. (Kemetic proverb)

As a rock on the sea shore, stand firm, and let not the dashing of the waves disturb you. Raise you head like a tower on a hill, and the arrows of fortune drop at your feet. In the instant of danger, the courage of your heart will sustain you; and the steadiness of your mind beareth you through. (Kemetic proverb)

Remember that "courage is the fruit of a decision made in the heart" (Afrikan proverb) and that "whatever a courageous man desires to do, he does" (Akan proverb).

35. Akan proverb.

36. Marcus Mosiah Garvey.

37. Kimbwandende Kia Bunseki Fu-Kiau's explanation of Afrikan psychology, in contrast to Yurugu's, is more than adequate for illustrating this difference.

> The African therapist conducts therapy publicly outside or inside the house, but always in the presence of family members and close friends. The Western therapist talks of private sessions. An African therapist will not use the word *private* in any situation related to health, for the individual is not an isolated "thing"; he is like a spoke in the social wheel.

> To heal an individual is to heal the whole wheel, the whole society and vice versa. The African therapist takes time with his patient, become one with him within the social wheel. The Western therapist is in rush; he does not have anything to share with the patient. From time to time he glances at the clock. The African does not worry about time, for his main concern is the patient with whom he shares the pain. *(Self-Healing Power and Therapy*, Baltimore, MD: Imprint Editions, 1991, p.47)

In *The Healing Drum* (Rochester, VT: Destiny Books, 1989), YaYa Diallo makes a similar observation.

38. James Allen, NY: Barnes & Nobles, Inc., 2007 (first published in 1902). The same applies to Rhonda Byrne's rehashing of ancient common sense, but in the fantasy world of western individualism, in *The Secret* (NY: Atria Books, 2010).

39. Warriors should recognize that truth is as old as the Afrikan. And this writing is only another "european" work which was adapted as selectively from the wisdom of our Ancestors as every other thing stolen and claimed as original european thinking. Although speaking more generally, brilliant scholar of Afrikan and european intellectual origins, Cheikh Anta Diop, put it this way:

> It is impossible to stress all that the world, particularly the Hellenistic world, owed to the Egyptians. The Greeks merely continued and developed, sometimes partially, what the Egyptians had invented. By virtue of their materialistic tendencies, the Greeks stripped those inventions of the religious, idealistic shell in which the Egyptians had enveloped them. On the one hand, the rugged life on the Eurasian plains apparently intensified the materialistic instinct of the peoples living there; on the other hand, it forged moral values diametrically opposite to Egyptian moral values....The horizons of the Greek were never to pass beyond material, visible man, the conqueror of hostile Nature. On the earth, everything gravitated around him; the supreme objective of art was to reproduce his exact likeness. In the "heavens," paradoxically, he alone was to be found, with his earthly faults and weaknesses, beneath the shell of gods distinguished from ordinary morals only by physical strength. Thus, when the Greek borrowed the Egyptian god, a real god in the full sense of the word, provided with all the moral perfections that stem from sedentary life, he could understand that deity only by reducing him to the level of man. Consequently, the adoptive pantheon of the Greek was

merely another humanity. This anthropomorphism, in this particular case, was but an acute materialism; it was characteristic of the Greek mind. Strictly speaking, the Greek miracle does not exist, for if we try to analyze the process of adapting Egyptian values to Greece, there is obviously nothing miraculous about it, in the intellectual sense of the term. (*The African Origin of Civilization*, Westport, CT: Lawrence Hill & Company, 1974 (first published in 1955), pp.230-231)

40. Zulu proverb.
41. Akan proverb.
42. *From Niggas to Gods, Part One*, Saint Louis, MO: Nia Communications/Press, 1993, p.15.
43. Clarence J. Munford, *Race and Reparations: A Black Perspective for the 21st Century*, Trenton, NJ: Africa World Press, 1996, p.217.
44. Ewe proverb.
45. Amos N. Wilson, *Afrikan-Centered Consciousness versus The New World Order*, Brooklyn, NY: Afrikan World InfoSystems, 1999, p.62.
46. This includes disarming and subintegrating rationalizations such as "live and let live" and "when in Rome do what the Romans do," which must always be considered in cultural context.
47. Kobi K. K. Kambon, *African/Black Psychology in the American Context: An African-Centered Approach*, Tallahassee, FL: Nubian Nation Publications, 1998, p.45.
48. This does not contradict George Jackson's statement that, "Patience has its limits. Take it too far and it's cowardice." Patience, relative to acting, is not a virtue when you are in the throws of destruction. The virtue of patience, under assault, lies in the warriors ability to unrelentingly operate on the expectation of victory, however long it takes.
49. See the more detailed discussion of this phenomenon in the "Spoilage" subchapter in Baruti, *Homosexuality and the Effeminization of Afrikan Males*, pp.391-398.
50. Spoilage is an intricate part of the west's domination of others subject to its interpretation of reality because it removes future orientation (you only think of/about yourself in the here and now) and the possibility of true, thoughtful leadership because every individual views his or her self as right and individualizes politics

to the point where no one should be in the position of correcting *anyone* else.

51. Programming like the *SuperNanny* offers a glimpse into this evidence.

52. In our Ancestors' words, "A child which is going to turn out to be any good, we do not rear only on a special mat" (Akan proverb).

53. Amos N. Wilson, *The Falsification of Afrikan Consciousness*, Bronx, NY: Afrikan World InfoSystems, 1993, p.34.

54. Amos N. Wilson speaks to this well in his *The Developmental Psychology of The Black Child* (NY: Africana Research Publications, 1978) which is as, if not more, relevant today than when it was first published.

55. Earth, Wind & Fire, *Spirit*, "Burnin' Bush."

56. In addition, we have overly exaggerated in our children's minds their greatness (promise) without any actual accomplishment. We tell them they "are the future" without explaining in concrete terms what that means, without providing the order and discipline that any consciously evolved, humane future would require to be created out of the hateful chaos they have inherited. In an egoistic, me-centered, extremely individualistic, neediness-inculcating reality, children naturally adopt and thoroughly internalize a grandiose sense of self importance that has no basis in what they have done or are planning to do. Their innocence and hyper-inflated arrogance, prompted and applauded by historically and ourstorically ungrounded adults, lead them to dream themselves the creators of a "more" beautiful world who have rightly earned the center of all attention. They are children. Considering what they are told and given, this is to be expected. What should not be expected are adults without the maturity to speak truth to the children and be that truth themselves. One of the songs which has been most employed to emphasize (and, in an world where truth is given through entertainment, even rationalize) this rampant, directionless, irresponsible spoilage is "The Greatest Love of All." In it, we are asked to "teach them well and let them lead the way/show them all the beauty they possess inside/give them a sense of pride to make it easier." The problem in its use as a

theme song is that we are not teaching them anything of worth before placing them in leadership positions, are showing them more external ugliness to imitate than internal beauty to cultivate and are substituting a healthy sense of pride with an excessive, empty, self-centered arrogance. Following the true intent of these lyrics would require the courage in effort that, seemingly, so few of us possess.

57. Marvin Gaye, "Ain't That Peculiar."

58. Fu-Kiau and Lukondo-Wamba, *Kindezi: The Kôngo Art of Babysitting*, Baltimore, MD: Imprint Editions, 2000, p.40.

59. Swahili proverb.

60. Afrikan proverb.

61. If nothing else, this should tell us, as models of what our children aspire, if we want to be the best possible warriors for Afrikan people, we should remove the contradictions.

62. Such youth, reared to think as Afrikans but determined to escape its self-discipline, practice an etiquette without substance. In other words, they are very knowledgeable about how to act in terms of respectful greetings, social arrangements, rituals, kwk, but do perform their roles and responsibilities only superficially in order to keep the adults ignorant of their true desires and intent. They are assisted greatly in their Afrikan pretense because of their a sense of "entitlement" in return for their feigned loyalty and the guilt some of the adults feel, a result of the pressure they receive from children not so oriented, a dysfunctional, reactive guilt that operates in much the same way as that of parents who spoil their children to compensate for an absent parent.

63. An obviously glaring example of this self-centered arrogance are those children who choose not to address adults they encounter in the community. Be not confused. This is an parent/guardian sanctioned choice. Parents/guardians set the standards on protocol and instruct and direct this in their children. This is teaching our children to be selectively Afrikan, especially in distinguishing between those who will spoil them and those who bring discipline into their lives. They are children and must be correctly guided as to proper etiquette regardless of likes or dislikes. We have to remember our truths as a communal people, if we are claiming to be a community. And, in our community, not greeting is a blatant statement of hatred. Along the same lines is the arrogant,

disdainful "correction" of adults by children. Only within the cultural context of western society would a child think it normal to instruct adults as if they are their elders.

64. "The Book of Ankhshesonqi," in Karenga (ed.), *The Husia*, p.65. And, in terms of instruction, as Ptahhotep guides us to think through the timeless wisdom of our Ancestors,

> If you are a wise man, train up a son who will be pleasing to God. If he is straight and takes after you take good care of him. Do everything that is good for him. He is your son, your Ka begot him. Don't withdraw your heart from him. But an offspring can make trouble. If your son strays and neglects your counsel and disobeys all that is said, with his mouth spouting evil speech, then punish him for all his talk. God will hate him who crosses you. His guilt was determined in the womb. He who God makes boatless cannot cross the water. (p.22)

Maulana Karenga's *The Husia* translation of this says,

> If you are parents of worth and wisdom, train your children so that they will be pleasing to God. And if they do what is right, following your example, and handle your affairs as they should, do for them all that is good. For they are begotten of your own heart and soul. Therefore, separate not your heart from them. But if they fail to follow your course, oppose your will, reject all counsel, and set their mouth in motion with vile words, then drive them away. For they are not your children and were not born for you. Those who are guided do not go wrong, but those who willfully lose their way will not find a straight course. (p.42)

65. Accusations of balance based on ability promoting laziness is one of the arguments eurocentric political science used in their attempts to discredit Afrikan communalism. Chancellor Williams does an excellent job of plainly placing this fallacy in the context of the indigenous humanity of sharing based on ability, opportunity and luck, given that everyone involved had put forth their best effort.

> Originally, there were no drones in the community. It appeared to be inconceivable that anyone would sit back and live on the labors of others. Sluggards had no place in the society. Nor did this mean that each person was expected to produce the same as every other person. What was expected was that each should do his best, his best being an honest effort to do all that he is able to do. Returning from the hunt, therefore, if Kodjo has killed three wild boars, Kofi two, Asare one and Mensah nothing at all, while high praises were

> showered on the successful ones, Mensah was not in disgrace, and he was not made to feel ashamed, unless it was reported that the reason for his failure was that he slept in the shade of the trees while the others worked. But as long as his efforts were the same as the others, his share was the same because he had done as much as Kodjo, really. This means that if the labor was equal, then obviously Kodjo himself was not wholly responsible for outcome, no more responsible than he was for his greater height, swifter fee, his handsome appearance, or the mole on his nose – all of which were due to a power outside of and beyond Kodjo and the rest of mankind. Here then the earlier Africans had an insight into life's realities and the basis of justice that clashes head-on with our theories of individualism and individual initiative which rule out assisting forces, make the individual his own god absolutely, and therefore entitled to all the fruits of his labor, physical or intellectual. (*The Re-Birth of African Civilization*, Hampton, VA: U.B. & U.S. Communications Systems, Inc., 1993, p.109)

We see evidence of this in the traditional market where Sisters will send customers to the "stalls" of other Sisters whose business has not been as good as theirs. With an expectant, visionary insight, he continues, saying,

> The African community of brotherly and sisterly relations must be saved, reorganized and modernized. It should be a self-reliant, socio-economic community that provides full scope for individual initiative, individual freedom and individual rewards, while at the same time putting the community's welfare first. For it will be in the successful community that individual members may realize their highest potential and success. (p.110)

66. "Eurationalizers" is but another term we use to identify the psychology of those Afrikans who see and use eureason as an explanation for their anti-Afrikan, i.e., self-hating, thought and behavior.

67. Swahili proverb.

68. In addition to just the fact that interrupting another is the result of thinking that what you have to say is more important than what they are saying, children interrupt adults so that they will not have to experience the pain of correction or be subjected to the discipline of learning from being wrong. And, because they are allowed to do this, they come to feel that this interrupting of others (again, a delusional, arrogant act of individualized supremacy in

itself) is not disrespectful but rather it is their civil and human prerogative.

69. Interestingly, in the "conscious" community, there are individuals (even "elders") who do not speak to those whose politics they disagree with. This is especially the case with those compromised or ideologically other-oriented "revolutionaries" who intend to force centered Afrikans into conformity with their alien agendas. We have to remember that, in our traditions, not speaking to someone is tantamount to saying "I hate you." In our tradition, you do not speak to enemies and you know that when someone does not speak to you, they consider you as foe. This is the understanding that warriors should operate within when dealing with individuals trying to use such child's psychology on us.

70. Amos N. Wilson provides some excellent guidelines for this in his *The Developmental Psychology of The Black Child*, p.67.

71. In this role, we need to be conscious of the fact that we have many "living martyrs" – those who are sacrificing their all for us now but have not been physically killed by our enemies. We know they have been targeted. We should act accordingly.

Chapter Nine || The Primary Qualities of Respectful Warriors

1. "Psychology," *Lets Get Free*, 2000.
2. Efik proverb.
3. "Ptahhotep," Maulana Karenga (ed.), *The Husia*, Los Angeles: The University of Sankore Press, 1984, p.42.
4. Afrikan proverb.
5. Afrikan proverb.
6. "Phebhor," (in Karenga (ed.), *The Husia*, p.68.
7. Mwalimu K. Bomani Baruti, *Centered: Building Afrikan Realities*, Atlanta, GA: Akoben House, 2009, pp.71-76.
8. Ethiopian proverb. The Taoist equivalent is "to be sincere with the insincere is dangerous." John Henrik Clarke reminded us of the kind of people we come from in terms of sincerity and

trust.

> We came out of a society that did not write out agreements. If we said something verbally, our mouth was sweet. That meant we could be trusted, and we didn't have to write it into law. If anybody sees you creating a pattern, they know it's yours. You don't have to copyright the pattern because nobody's going to steal it. Once more we see honor and obligation running through the totality of our society and the totality of ourselves. (*Who Betrayed The African World Revolution?*, Chicago, IL: Third World Press, 1995, p.70)

This is the type of people we must return to within our centers, if we are to nationbuild consciousness.

9. "The Book of Amenomope," in Karenga (ed.), *The Husia*, p.62.

10. Earth, Wind & Fire, *All N' All*, "Be Ever Wonderful," 1977.

11. Swahili proverb.

12. To use Che Guevara's description of the guerrilla soldier,

> Another fundamental characteristic of the guerrilla soldier is his flexibility, his ability to adapt himself to all circumstances, and to convert to his service all of the accidents of the action. Against the rigidity of classical methods of fighting, the guerrilla fighter invents his own tactics at every minute of the fight and constantly surprises the enemy. (NY: Monthly Review Press, 1961, p.25)

13. Azanian proverb. We should also see that, for warriors, blood, sweat and tears are libation.

14. Amos N. Wilson, *Afrikan-Centered Consciousness versus The New World Order*, Brooklyn, NY: Afrikan World InfoSystems, 1999, p.68.

15. Wolof proverb.

16. "The Book of Khakheper-Ra-Soneb," in Karenga (ed.), *The Husia*, p.77.

17. "To Be An Afrikan Woman," in Burnett Kwadwo Gallman, Marimba Ani and Larry Obadele Williams (eds.), *To Be Afrikan*, Atlanta, GA: M.A.A.T., Inc., 2003, pp.37-43.

18. Clenora Hudson-Weems offers an equally respectable listing of admirable qualities in Afrikan women in her *Africana Womanism: Reclaiming Ourselves* (Troy, MI: Bedford Publishers, Inc., 1993, pp.55-73). Her list includes: Self-Namer, Self-Definer, Family-Centered, In Concert with Males in Struggle, Flexible Roles, Genuine Sisterhood, Strength, Male Compatible,

Respected and Recognized, Whole and Authentic, Spirituality, Respectful of Elders, Adaptable, Ambitious and Mothering and Nurturing.

19. A beautiful example of such courage is documented in the video "Praying the Devil back to Hell."

20. Kali Sichen, e-mail correspondence September 10, 2007 (italics mine). Some may question why this is the tradition. The answer is simple. Women are the closest to life and, therefore, are the least likely to arbitrarily or definitely call men to kill each other. So, if the women are calling for war, you know there is preponderant reason.

21. Meda ase to the Kambons for this most appropriate term.

22. From this, he offers a sound path to economic solvency for Afrikan people.

> A radical change for the better in the economic fortunes of the Afrikan community requires a commensurate radical change in the nature of the character of the social relationships and connections its members share with each other. For an economic system and the political power it generates are finally founded on the system of social relationships which inhere in a community of persons. And that foundational system is but itself the concrete behavioral manifestation of the group identity and consciousness shared by that community of persons. (*Blueprint for Black Power: A Moral, Political and Economic Imperative for the Twenty-First Century*, Brooklyn, NY: Afrikan World InfoSystems, 1998, pp.315-316)

23. See this discussion in the essay "Subjective Objectivity" in Mwalimu K. Bomani Baruti, *Eureason: An Afrikan Centered Critique of Eurocentric Social Science*, Atlanta, GA: Akoben House, 2006, pp.17-51.

24. *Sankofa: African Thought and Education*, NY: Peter Lang, 1995, p.114. Kwadwo A. Okrah also speaks to this universally accepted definition of "education" in traditional Afrikan society.

> Intellectual education found expression in History, Geography, Science, Religion, Logic and Oral Arts. Clan and community history was taught. The type of soil suitable for certain types of crops, weather changes that control agricultural regimes were also taught. Fallow system and shifting cultivation including both crop rotation and land rotation were taught [and this was Agricultural Science]. Children were taught Astronomy so that they could know the

> stars and the sky to be able to determine weather conditions on the seas and also the type of fish associated with those conditions. All these were taught to children in an informal structured manner. There were no classrooms where lessons could be changed from a subject to another. Rather, the everyday political, economic and other social activities including children's own observations were the process through which these subjects were learned. Children's belief in and acceptance of morals, lessons and roles drawn from legends, proverbs, and initiation ceremonies were reinforced by practical examples in adult life relative to the norms of society. (Okrah, *Nyansapo*, p.40)

See a fuller discussion of this concept in Mwalimu K. Bomani Baruti, *Asafo: A Warrior's Guide to Manhood*, Atlanta, GA: Akoben House, 2004, pp.104-109.

25. As historically aware Afrikan warriors, we cannot limit our analysis and interpretation of the national european military force to the active, organized, federal army, navy, air force, marines and coast guard. That would be exceedingly naive. Though not equally obvious or glorified, the CIA, FBI, Secret Service, Blackwater, police on the street, SWAT, national guard/reserves, forest rangers, border patrol, personal and corporate security guards/forces, neighborhood watch groups, militias, "camps" (groups of war re-enactors like the Sons of the Confederacy), bodyguards, private detectives, and bouncers, to name a few, are all part of the military force. They all protect its capitalist interests. And they all act above the law in applying armed violence against those who may pose a threat to their employers whom they take great pride in protecting. We must also note that there is no disconnect between the military agencies in any society/country/territory within the european nation. We cannot realistically distinguish between the CIA, Scotland Yard and Mossad. They independently operate as one against all perceived as a threat to global european imperialism.

26. It will become even more so as Yurugu is able to fulfill their dream of turning the world into a boundless battlefield of never-ending war.

27. Martially, yurugu's goal has been to strip our community of everyone who protects it. This is an attrition process, accompanied by instilling a sense of alienation, external orientation and desire to be protected by others, while remaining

completely comfortable in a state of defenselessness.

28. We have to admit, however, that becoming defenseless in the face of a proven, catastrophic threat requires some degree of complicity, a developing weakness which becomes increasingly evident as those doing so come to more apologically rationalize and, therefore, accept their destruction as normal. For one, Hubert Henry Harrison reflected on this phenomenon in terms of a universal perception of it.

> Now, ask all the peoples of all the world what they call a people who smilingly consent to their own degradation and destruction. They call such a people cowards – because they *are* cowards. (*When Africa Awakes*, Baltimore, MD: Black Classic Press, 1997 (first published in 1920), p.26)

29. "If you fight with your tongue only, you lose the battle" (Akan proverb).

30. Mutulu Shakur.

31. If nothing else, there is a logical time frame for concrete revolutionary action. As theorized by Clarence J. Munford revolutions have a shelf life of about "one human generation" (*Race and Reparations*, Trenton, NJ: Africa World Press, 1996, p.155).

32. Hilliard, Williams and Damali (eds.), *The Teachings of Ptahhotep*, p.23.

33. Ibid., p.33.

34. A point needing to be made here is of the unreasonable individualism of so many among those aspiring to leadership positions (really an aspiration which should not exist in that leadership should be based on group selection and not individual decision), a by-product of our socialization into yurugu's world. We have stopped thinking in terms of building armies. Our focus is on individual heroism, on being seen and raised above others as the most worthy savior, as *the* "one." This must stop if we are to succeed as an army. We cannot speak of *nation*building without producing an army which can selflessly do this work, even given that each individual warrior should independently know what to do and be able to build an army by his or herself.

35. Frantz Fanon articulated one question on the test for assessing loyalty in asserting that "you could be sure of a new recruit when he could no longer go back into the colonial system"

(*The Wretched of the Earth*, NY: Grove Press, 1968, p.85).

36. When speaking of Afrikans, by "capacity," I do not mean "ability," as in the physical presence of the brain. I mean that such an individual is not so encumbered by eureason that she or he cannot even consider the possibility of an "alternative" (i.e., in this case, different and better) perspective. I mean that such an individual is intellectually curious and intrepid enough to openly listen to, logically consider, seriously embrace and permanently internalize correct Afrikan thought. Capacity here means mental, not biological, ability.

In any case, warrior scholars must be very careful of using "alternative" as a descriptive of that which is Afrikan because it gives the impression that it is a lesser option and not the main thing we should pursue, a mentality that keeps that which is european as primary and at our center.

37. This same logic applies to the forgiveness and forgetfulness pleas of so many of our vanquished. In a comparative answer to the I sound "angry" reaction of neutered negroes and lost souls, no interned Japanese is trying to make it appear as if the Europeans who held them captive suffered as they did. No european Jew is trying to humanize their brother nazis. No real Irish or Arab is trying to project any of their pain onto the British or European, respectively. It is only we, Afrikans without a sense of our power and in awe of our destroyers, who are willing to buy any logic, even that which somehow turns us into culprits, to forgive the unforgivable and convince disease to allow us to wallow in it. Only those who cannot visualize a reality without Europeans would stoop this low against our Ancestors. Equally ignorant is the myth that oppressors are as hurt by their physical and psychological violence as those they oppress.

38. Ayi Kwei Armah, *KMT: in the house of life*, Popenguine, Senegal: PER ANKH, 2002, p.278. This is quite evident in the contemporary *criminal* justice system (see Mwalimu K. Bomani Baruti, "The Hunt is On," in Mwalimu K. Bomani Baruti, *Mentacide*, Atlanta, GA: Akoben House, 2005, p.18) where those responsible for arresting, fabricating evidence, and knowingly prosecuting and sentencing us are left untouched by the *criminal* justice system even after they are revealed for the lying, maliciously deceitful criminals that they are. With respect to the

few cases where Afrikans are given a court ordered monetary compensation for their loss, the Afrikan community is still victimized. We continue to "finance our own destruction." When we get so excited over these "victories," we forget that the money used to pay this compensation comes out of our own pockets. When we jump around celebrating some individual Afrikan winning this or that very minor monetary award (considering the magnitude of the damage to our families and community, not to mention the considerable profits going to lawyers from [or politically and consumptively loyal to] other communities), we forget that the money for the awards almost exclusively comes from our local tax dollars. They do not come from the pay of those who committed the acts. They come from the tax dollars of the residents who live in the community of those whom the acts were committed against. We are the ones who live in and provide the majority of the tax base in those metropolitan areas in which we are disproportionately violated. Therefore, the millions of dollars paid out in more than justified lawsuits for violations others commit against us is paid by us. Like those who seek to turn the other cheek in order to model a suffering they believe will teach chronic racists to love them, we are paying the penalty for being violated. We are being charged for the damages of those who legally abuse us. The individuals who commit these acts do not live in our community; they do not pay taxes in our community. Therefore, they do not suffer for their crimes. They commit these crimes against us and are rewarded for doing so. Here, crime truly does pay. The victim pays the criminal. When Afrikans are awarded money by the court for our losses, it in no way financially impacts the european community or those individuals who committed these acts of brutality. In fact, there is no evidence that these individuals are in any way negatively impacted. There is no evidence that they suffered from communal ostracization or by being unable to find jobs with similar or even greater economic rewards. A family rewards its members when they do well, when they serve and protect them from others they perceive as threats to their safety and sanity. So these criminals are applauded by their community with employment and income for their efforts to beat, torture, murder or otherwise keep us at bay. They continue to be honored as the hardworking, sincere, dedicated agents of white aggression that they are.

39. Especially today, with the general acceptance of the illogic that Europeans today are innocent because they were not physically present to physically perform and directly reap the capital from this damage, we have to understand that they are their ancestors as we are ours (a Kiswahili proverb reminds us that "The child of a snake is a snake"), they are in terms of lying and refusing to accept blame for anything they have done wrong and, continuing to benefit from the ongoing exploitation and interest of what accrued from their original profits. Is not receipt of stolen property a crime equal to the original theft? Ignorance of the stolen nature of the property is irrelevant in western courts (at least for us), so why should the current generations of Yurugu be exempt from this legal precept? And, assuming ignorance, once aware, if what was stolen is not immediately returned in full, what does this say about their innocence?

40. Queen Mother Audley Moore. A theoretical elaboration of the accuracy of this point is given in Daudi Ajani ya Azibo's "The Psycho-cultural Case for Reparations for Descendents of Enslaved Africans in the United States," *Race, Gender and Class*, 18 (2011) 1-2.

41. Munford, *Race and Reparations*, pp.428-429.

42. Bobby E. Wright, "Mentacide: The Ultimate Threat to the Black Race" p.67. This we also find expressed through the Akan proverb, "If you spill blood, blood alone can straighten it." Repayment in kind, or reciprocity, is a universal principle. So is the timeless understanding that for every action there is an *equal* and opposite reaction. There are inevitabilities from which Europeans are running (as Thomas Jefferson said, "I tremble for my country when I reflect that God is just."). They know what they have done but hope to escape the natural, necessary consequences. As they have arrogantly turned this world upside down to fit their abnormality, they are also insolent enough to hope to do this to the Universe. As in their god-vying mythology, they believe themselves smart and powerful enough to change those laws to their ill-gotten advantage also. They believe that the Universe is as gullible as we, as a people, and others they have encountered, have proven ourselves to be. And, because of their spiritual immaturity and need to avoid just correction, they expect

that the lies, misinformation, "apologies" and transference of cause and blame to others (if not a more advantageous spreading about of it) will also fool universal law. In their steady, insistent, murderous work against our consciousness, their desperate assumption is tha,t if they can manipulate mankind into forgiving them, then the Universe will read that sympathetic energy and follow suit. They not only want to be above human law, but they also want to be above universal law. They want to be able to do wrong and not be reciprocated to the magnitude of what they have done and whatever, in addition, is required for correction.

43. Quoted from the AnkBbea National Shrine of Afrikans in America in Kwame Agyei and Akua Nson Akoto, *The Sankofa Movement*, Washington, DC:)yoko InfoCom, Inc., 1999, p.26. How could the priest not go to war? Just understood in the context of every family having its own priest, if the community, village, society and/or nation went to war, the priests went to war.

44. "A fool does not see danger even when warned" (Ovambo proverb).

45. The game of chess is instructive here. When attempting to mate the king of an opponent, who is without any other moveable pieces, you always give him a free space to move into before the final mating move in order to avoid stalemate.

46. Portions of this subchapter were taken from my *Centered*, pp.126-129.

47. We must also be cognizant of this fact when we consider survival preparedness in the wooded, or otherwise "wild," spaces in this land. A multitude of factors to consider include the following: they have been in practice, quantitatively and qualitatively longer than most of us; they thoroughly know these areas (living and frequenting them for hunting, camping, touring); they expect us to come there; they are heavily armed and prepared; they respect no boundaries and they will be on the lookout to kill.

48. This is critical for Afrikan warriors to understand. It might be different if this threat were new or unknown to us. But we are well versed in the way of Europeans. Nothing coming from them should surprise us, nothing. So, the idea of discussions about the nature or magnitude of the threat makes no sense, whether we are able to visibly perceive it at this particular moment or not.

49. A consciousness of selective memory is not conscious. "A

warrior has to be a warrior wherever they are" (Hannibal Tirus Afrik).

50. Http://www.youtube/watch?v=LU8DDyz68kM.

51. In the words of don Juan Matus of the Yaqui Native American tribe,

> When a man decides to do something he must go all the way, but he must take responsibility for what he does. No matter what he does, he must know first why he is doing it, and then he must proceed with his actions without having doubts or remorse about them.

52. *African Spirituality: On Becoming Ancestors*, Trenton, NJ: Africa World Press, 1997, p.45.

53. He also reminded me of those elders in ourstory who understood that there are no civilians in war (that everyone has a role and place on the frontline) and who risked their lives by placing themselves high up in the trees or at the top of man-constructed towers as snipers, if you will, to assist the younger warriors fighting the enemy on the ground (Walter Hawthorne, "Strategies of the Decentralized: Defending Communities from Slave Raiders in Coastal Guinea-Bissau, 1450-1815," in Sylviane A. Diouf (ed.), *Fighting the Slave Trade*, Athens, OH: Ohio University Press, 2003, p.159).

54. Clarke, *African World Revolution*, p.7.

55. "Battle Fatigue" is a collection of the subchapters "Still Waters" (Baruti, *Asafo*, pp.177-182), "Morale" (Baruti, *Centered*, pp.108-110) and "Progress" (Baruti, *Centered*, pp.96-99) with a few minor modifications.

56. Although "Blood does not dry on the warrior's spears" (Afrikan proverb) time should be made to clean, sharpen and rest them.

57. Azanian proverb.

58. Our frustration in battle is greatly exacerbated because consciousness is a rude awakening to the dangers of yurugu's fearful, violent reaction against others because of their own inferiority. We are everywhere and from every angle under constant bombardment with manifestations of the insidious european intent toward others. As Francis Cress Welsing defined it,

> *[T]his system [of white supremacy] consists of patterns of perception, logic, symbol formation, thought, speech, action*

and emotional response, as conducted simultaneously in all areas of people activity (economics, education, entertainment, labor, law, politics, religion, sex and war). (*The Isis Papers*, Chicago, IL: Third World Press, 1991, p.ii)

And, as Richard King summarized,

> Seldom has this planet witnessed a confrontation, a war of such dimension. It is a true example of total war, that is at times subtle or overt, mental or physical. It is a warfare raging through every form of human expression from art to politics and religion. No safe ground exists, no neutral territory, no fence to straddle, all of us are involved. The confrontation between black and white is a total war for survival. (*African Origin of Biological Psychiatry*, Hampton, VA: U.B.&U.S. Communications Systems, Inc., 1994, p.113)

Consciousness does not sleep. Day and night we become more aware of their moves to destroy us. We see their psychopathic, genocidal insanity. We see our reactive, suicidal deathwish. It outrages and anguishes us to see our family blindly, willingly rush toward a white death. For awakening Afrikans, consciousness does not bring peace. It brings the war to your doorsteps. On the other hand, for mentacidal Afrikans, "ignorance is bliss."

59. Ayi Kwei Armah places this negro voice in the context of those Afrikans whose weakness and fear lead them to traitorously dissent against warring against the European invasion.

> Now [Europeans] want to control everything that goes on. From the coast to the forests, to the grasslands, even to the desert. And they will. If we help the whites get this control, we stand to profit from the changes. Those foolish enough to go against them will of course be wiped out. I'm among those who'd rather profit than be wiped out....Nothing will ever make me stand against those guns....in this world there are those who thrive, and there are those who don't. Those who thrive, thrive because they respect power. They see where it comes from, and they take care to place themselves beside it, never against it. (*The Healers*, London: Heinemann, 1978, pp.31-32)

60. Akan proverb.

61. Akan proverb.

62. When looking at the lowest levels of everyday survival of my people, I feel despair tug at my heart every time Brothers or Sisters on the street ask me for a dime, a piece of a meal, a hand to shake in recognition that they are not invisible. Every Afrikan who is Afrikan at heart should feel compelled to do something concrete

about whole human beings recast in the image of lone creatures, scavenging for food, drugs and whatever else to which their vision has been reduced.

63. The Zanzibar Revolution masterminded by John Okello (*Revolution in Zanzibar*, Nairobi, Kenya: East African Publishing House, 1967), Robert Charles' stand against a frenzied mob of 20,000 lynchers (Munford, *Race and Reparations*, p.217) and the Haitian Revolution which permanently scarred yurugu's ego (Jacob H. Carruthers, *The Irritated Genie*, Chicago, IL: The Kemetic Institute, 1985) are but a few of the examples of us rising and winning against all odds.

64. Commodores, "Heroes." It should go without saying that "he who stands in the battle-front does not fear death" (Akan proverb).

65. True, lasting frontline complementarity is more easily achieved than most imagine.

> One other definite conclusion can be drawn from the collective revolutionary experience about the initial meetings that take place between two potential complements that lead to the development of lasting warrior relationships. They both tend to be doing their work when they first meet. This does not mean that they are oblivious to the need for companionship. It only means that finding a mate is not their sole priority or an overriding focus. Therefore, using this pattern as a guide, if you are doing your work, your study, your communal involvement, your communicating, attending to the needs of our people as a nation, your complement will be there also. You will find each other. Let your example be your attraction. (Mwalimu K. Bomani Baruti, *Complementarity: Thoughts for Afrikan Warrior Couples*, Atlanta, GA: Akoben House, 2004, p.14)

66. That an addict (drugs, alcohol, sugar, salt, kwk) is "always" an addict and, therefore, must be on constant guard against contact with such substances, less they relapse, is an acknowledged fact within psychological circles.

67. Here, density would be a measurement of the degree to which we remain able (capable) or willing to digest/listen to and learn from the logic of our Ancestors, knowing it will nullify our european addictions. It is a measure of our fortitude in resisting genocultural oppression. The greater the density, the less the alien access. The less the density, the more likely eureason can

find fertile ground within which to plant itself. The range of the latter state is a measure of fluidity. It tells us of the degree of our lack of commitment to move in the Way of our Ancestors.

68. This statement about just what should be meant by Afrikan progress in the face of this anti-Afrikan european reality is a modified version of the concluding chapter in my *Sesh: An Afrikan Centered Guide to Writing and Self-Publishing*, Atlanta, GA: Akoben House, 2007, pp.154-156. It bears repeating.

69. Even being still is movement. We are always moving in some direction.

70. Mwalimu K. Bomani Baruti, "Irreconcilable Differences," in Mwalimu K. Bomani Baruti, *Eureason*, Atlanta, GA: Akoben House, 2006, pp.201-241.

71. Ayi Kwei Armah, *Two Thousand Seasons*, Popenguine, Senegal: PER ANKH, 2000 (first published in 1973), p.303.

72. *The Healers*, p.204.

73. Ibid, p.100.

74. As worded by Akomfo Shango, each oath should end with the words:

> I take this Oath in honor of my Ancestors To fight for OUR Spiritual, Mental And Physical Restoration and Liberation worldwide, against the whites, their offspring and collaborators. If I fail to devote each day of my life to OUR victory May this Oath kill me and be a curse on my entire family.

75. Kwame Agyei Akoto, *Nationbuilding: Theory & Practice in Afrikan Centered Education*, Washington, DC: Pan Afrikan World Institute, 1992, pp.61-62.

76. In studying conflict in Nature, it is interesting to note that "The ram withdraws before it attacks" (Akan proverb).

77. "Bravery is exhibited at the battlefront but not at home," as well as "Bravery in the house is no bravery" (Akan proverbs).

78. Guevara, *Guerrilla Warfare*, p.87.

79. Akua Njeri (complement of honored Ancestor Fred Hampton and mother of Fred Hampton, Jr.).

80. J.A. Sofola, *African Culture and the African Personality*, Ibadan, Nigeria: African Resources Publishers Company, 1973, pp.103-118.

81. Afrikans do not look at death as something to fear. It is simply another rite and state in the transformative cycle of a

constant spirit. "Death" is simply the movement into another interrelated realm. Ancestors, because of their connection as family, the model of righteousness they have given the community and their ability to channel more spiritual power into the community, were placed in a position of great honor. An ancestor's power was connected to her or his name. So it is only spiritually logical that you are present in the physically living community for as long as your name is called.

82. There is a difference in focus and accomplishment between those able to very early in their lives decide what they want to do/become (identify their calling) and those who are unable to make this decision until later, if ever.

83. Taken from the "Passing on the Legacy: From Generation to Generation," The 6th Annual Abakosem Sunsum program (held in Atlanta, GA), May 3, 2009, pp.9-11. Meda ase Marimba Ani.

Chapter Ten || Returning to Our Way

1. And this must be qualified when speaking of some Afrikans claiming this honor. Too many in the "conscious" community do not want to be held up to an Afrikan standard. They advocate the least common denominator, and such a "standard" is the most superficial and indefinite possible, so they can contradict our traditions and still be considered conscious.

2. "He who lies by the fire knows how it burns." "One who stays in the water does not fear cold" (Akan proverbs).

3. People without good character cannot build institutions with good character. Even though bad character can provide a foil by which to measure good character, only good character can provide an adequate model of good character for the warrior to follow. Like builds like. This relationship between leadership and "the masses," between the character of those who lead and that of those who dutifully follow, is the whole point of the argument Jacob H. Carruthers (whom we should call Jedi Shemsu Jehewty) put forth in his discussion of "The Farmer Whose Speech is Good" (*MDW NTR: Divine Speech*, London: Karnak House, 1995, pp.143-

170). Those who establish the standard need to be that standard as an example of its essentiality and worth, not consider themselves above it. This is the optimal Way of our Ancestors.

4. As said by so many of our ancestral and living jenoch,

> Africans must throw away the religion imposed on them by the Europeans. We must go back to the God of Africa. The African must go back and discover his real soul if he is to attain salvation for himself. Every race ascribes to its deity its own physical, mental and peculiarities carried to the higher power of perfection. The time has come for the Blackman to forget and cast behind him his hero worship and adoration of other races, and to start our immediately to create and emulate heroes of his own. We must canonize our own martyrs and elevate to positions of fame and honour Blackmen and women who have made their distinct contributions to our racial history. (G.K. Osei, *The African Philosophy of Life*, London: The African Publication Society, 1970, p.28)

5. The saying that "what the fool does in the end, the wise man does in the beginning" is an appropriate thought here.

6. *Matigari*, Trenton, NJ: African World Press, 1998, p.70.

7. Or, given available time, learn as much of its practical vocabulary as possible.

8. The contradiction in speaking another's language, like in eating their food, wearing their clothes and worshiping their gods, is well pointed out by Amos N. Wilson:

> What language do you speak? When did you learn that language? Was that the language Afrikan people were speaking when taken into slavery in the Caribbean and the Americas? In other words, the language we speak at this moment *is* the slave language, the language that our slave ancestors were forced to learn....That language, with its words defined by history and by an experience, is the language we use to guide our behavior. It's the language we use today to talk to ourselves. It's the language we use today to learn about ourselves and to learn about the world. It's the language we use today to understand ourselves. Is there any wonder then that we are still confused?...we have not escaped slavery. We are still using a slave language and we speak the language of slaves. *(Afrikan-Centered Consciousness versus The New World Order*, Brooklyn, NY: Afrikan World InfoSystems, 1999, pp.95-96)

Another of our esteemed Ancestors, Cheikh Anta Diop, made this same point in an essay originally published in 1948 titled "Can We

Talk of an African Resistance?" (London: Karnak House, 1996, pp.33-45). Likewise, our Ancestors cannot effectively communicate with us if we see through the lens of a foreign mind.

9. "It is the fool whose own tomatoes are sold to him" (Akan proverb).

10. You must be careful of what you read and listen to because everything you take in affects the way you think and feel. The proverbs that instruct individuals to avoid people who are verbose and contentious are an indication of the power negative thoughts can have on what we visualize and, in turn, realize. This is no different from telling someone to be careful where they drive, work, live, play or walk. Everything that enters your mind affects your spirit. Overlooking the relevance of this to our deepest and innermost thinking is why so many of our scholars can deftly explain our situation as a people but have subintegration-focused solutions which will pull us even further into another's morass. These misguided savants see their reading and weighing of any and all literature equally as the key to intellectual liberation and, most importantly, they believe doing so has no meaningful effect on their psyches and spirits beyond that which they control.
Afrikan warriors must maintain their Afrikan center first. There is far too much literature that speaks to the Afrikan Way for one individual to read and study in her or his lifetime. Furthermore, if truth is manifest in all human groups and, therefore, can be found among any human group, why are we going to others to find the truth that is self-evident in our own words. Know to read us first. But also know that Afrikans are deeply embedded spiritual beings. So to access the knowledge beyond the books, you must be willing to be still and quiet for quality periods of time daily.

11. We cannot, and should not want to, do anything to allay their fears. With what they have done, and continue to do, they are reasonable and to be expected.

12. An example of this was given in *Centered: Building Afrikan Realities*.

> An elder in our community here has given us a shining example of what our response to them should be whenever and wherever we have gathered in solemn communion with our Ancestors. While pouring libation for us, he also takes a moment to pour for them. But, instead of pouring their libation in the ground of our sacred space as he does for us,

> he goes outside to spit that portion of the liquid reserved for them on the dead concrete to welcome them away. They must be dismissed and distanced as we do any other contagion. (Atlanta, GA: Akoben House, 2009, p.46)

This request for ancestral assistance in the removal of these threats should not be limited to those in the community who are treasonous. It needs to be earnestly applied to all anti-Afrikan beings.

13. Baruti, *Centered*, pp.141-142.

14. More to the point, if we understand the inextricable and all encompassing connection between mind and spirit, we know that our thoughts are our prayers. Therefore, the question becomes, "What are you thinking?"

15. If done correctly, socialization is guided by experience.

> Teaching by elders and learning by children is the only method for preserving the culture and for passing on the wisdom. If the children are to achieve greatness, the elders must teach them, for, "wisemen are not born." Men become wise when they obediently listen to the wisdom passed on by the elders. (Jacob H. Carruthers, *Essays in Ancient Egyptian Studies*, Los Angeles, CA: University of Sankore Press, 1984, pp.102-103)

16. Kwame Nkrumah.

17. Mwalimu K. Bomani and Yaa Mawusi Baruti, "Celebrating Holidays," *Abibifahodie with Mwalimu & Yaa Baruti*, War on the Horizon Internet Radio, July 1, 2011.

18. Harold Melvin & The Blue Notes, "Wake Up Everybody."

19. Mwalimu K. Bomani Baruti, "The Game," in Mwalimu K. Bomani Baruti, *Mentacide*, Atlanta, GA: Akoben House, 2005, pp.121-131.

20. Akan proverb.

21. In his discussion of "the psychology of self-hatred and self-defeat," Amos N. Wilson appropriately critiques the contradictory thought of subintegration-oriented negroes on this issue.

> We have a leadership that has sought to get us to accept the status quo: the control of the world by the European. You errantly hear some of us conceding that it's the white man's world so we may as well learn how to live in it or just get along. The assimilationist often accepts, consciously or unconsciously, the idea that the white man will continue to rule the world. He bases his ideology and political action on the concept that somehow our destiny is not to overthrow the

> white man, that our destiny is not to remove this pathological person; that our destiny is not to suppress and bring these sick people under control to heal them in some sort of way, to convert them, to even become a part of them. Our destiny becomes not one that sees the very system and very ideology upon which these oppressors move as one of sickness and insanity and therefore in need of replacement by an Afrikan-centered and healthy ideology that comes out of our own self-knowing. This leadership wants us to accept this sickness as normality and to follow these pathological beings into self-destruction....our destiny is *not* one of trying to become a member of this gang of thieves, but to end its existence here on earth, to inhibit its rapacious ways and to bring this group of people to heel! Yet we have a leadership that makes us think that our only crime has been that we've been left out on the looting of these thieves. We get a leadership that cries about how we're only getting a certain percentage of their robbery and thievery. We must recognize...that it is not about getting a piece of the stolen gains of these people, but to stop their thievery and rape of the world, period! So it is not about being left out of the mainstream; it is about bringing into being a new world order. (*Afrikan-Centered Consciousness Versus The New World Order*, pp. 61-62)

We should note, though, that although Wilson's critique is specifically directed toward the negro misleadership, his analysis applies to lay and leader alike among the vanquished.

22. *The Last Book*, Raleigh, NC: Blacknificent Books, 2005 and *The Declaration of Dr. Kambon*, Raleigh, NC: Blacknificent Books, 2006.

23. Akan proverb.

Akoben House Order Form

Please send

_____	copies of ***Sovereignty*** ($19.95 each)	$ _____
_____	copies of ***Clarity*** ($21.95 each)	$ _____
_____	copies of ***A Warrior's Love*** ($16.95 each)	$ _____
_____	copies of ***Message to The Warriors*** ($19.95 each)	$ _____
_____	copies of ***IWA: A Warrior's Character*** ($24.95 each)	$ _____
_____	copies of ***Centered*** ($16.95 each)	$ _____
_____	copies of ***Yurugu's Eunuchs*** ($18.95 each)	$ _____
_____	copies of ***Nyansasem: Revolutionary Daily Thoughts*** ($19.95 each)	$ _____
_____	copies of ***Sesh*** ($16.95 each)	$ _____
_____	copies of ***Eureason*** ($19.95 each)	$ _____
_____	copies of ***Notes Toward Higher Ideals in Afrikan Intellectual Liberation*** ($16.95 each)	$ _____
_____	copies of ***Battle Plan*** ($14.95 each)	$ _____
_____	copies of ***Kebuka!*** ($18.95 each)	$ _____
_____	copies of ***Mentacide and other essays*** ($16.95 each)	$ _____
_____	copies of ***Asafo*** ($19.95 each)	$ _____
_____	copies of ***Complementarity*** ($18.95 each)	$ _____
_____	copies of ***Homosexuality and the Effeminization of Afrikan Males*** ($29.95 each)	$ _____
_____	copies of ***The Sex Imperative*** ($19.00 each)	$ _____
_____	copies of ***Excuses, Excuses*** ($17.00 each)	$ _____
_____	copies of ***negroes and other essays*** ($17.00 each)	$ _____
_____	copies of ***Chess Primer*** ($12.95 each)	$ _____

Shipping & Handling: $ _____

($6 for 1 book and $4 for each additional book.)

TOTAL ENCLOSED: $ _____

NAME: ________________________________

ADDRESS: ____

Send this order form, along with your check or money order (made payable to Akoben Village), to:

Akoben House, P.O. Box 10786, Atlanta, GA 30310 OR order by credit card at

www.AkobenHouse.com

Made in the USA
Coppell, TX
22 May 2020

26300086R00272